THE ROUTLEDGE COMPANION TO MEDIA EDUCATION, COPYRIGHT, AND FAIR USE

Media literacy educators rely on the ability to make use of copyrighted materials from mass media, digital media, and popular culture for both analysis and production activities. Whether they work in higher education, in elementary and secondary schools, or in informal learning settings in libraries, communities, and non-profit organizations, educators know that the practice of media literacy depends on a robust interpretation of copyright and fair use. With chapters written by leading scholars and practitioners from the fields of media studies, education, writing and rhetoric, law and society, library and information studies, and the digital humanities, this companion provides a scholarly and professional context for understanding the ways in which new conceptualizations of copyright and fair use are shaping the pedagogical practices of media literacy.

Contributors: Malin Abrahamsson, Timothy R. Amidon, Patricia Aufderheide, Jonathan Band, Catherine Burwell, Brandon Butler, Dànielle Nicole DeVoss, Bill D. Herman, Renee Hobbs, Smita Kheria, John Landis, Dan Lawler, Thomas C. Leonard, Nadine Levin, Ed Madison, Stephanie Margolin, Ewa McGrail, J. Patrick McGrail, David Cooper Moore, Caile Morris, Chris Morrison, John S. O'Connor, David Ramírez Plascencia, Clancy Ratliff, Cyndy Scheibe, Aaron Schwabach, Jane Secker, Chareen Snelson, Chris Sperry, Scott Spicer, Kyle Stedman, Jeremy Stoddard, Rebecca Tushnet, Charlotte Waelde, Esther Wojcicki

Renee Hobbs is Professor at the Harrington School of Communication and Media at the University of Rhode Island, where she directs the Media Education Lab, which advances media literacy education through scholarship and community service. She is author of *Copyright Clarity: How Fair Use Supports Digital Learning* and six other books that examine media literacy and learning.

THE ROUTLEDGE COMPANION TO MEDIA EDUCATION, COPYRIGHT, AND FAIR USE

Edited by
Renee Hobbs

Routledge
Taylor & Francis Group
New York London

First published 2018
by Routledge
605 Third Avenue, New York, NY 10017

and by Routledge
2 Park Square, Milton Park, Abingdon, Oxon OX14 4RN

First issued in paperback 2021

Routledge is an imprint of the Taylor & Francis Group, an informa business

Publisher's Note
The publisher has gone to great lengths to ensure the quality of this reprint but points out that some imperfections in the original copies may be apparent.

Library of Congress Cataloging-in-Publication Data
A catalog record for this title has been requested

ISBN 13: 978-1-03-209572-1 (pbk)
ISBN 13: 978-1-138-63889-1 (hbk)

Typeset in Bembo
by Apex CoVantage, LLC

Dedicated to the memory of Elizabeth Thoman

CONTENTS

Part I

FOUNDATIONAL ISSUES

1

MEDIA EDUCATION, COPYRIGHT, AND FAIR USE

Renee Hobbs

When my longtime colleague and friend Elizabeth Thoman, founder and director of the Center for Media Literacy in Los Angeles was developing a curriculum to help educators explore the pervasiveness of violence in the media, she did not worry about whether teachers and communities would engage with the topic. From the volume of phone calls and letters she was receiving back in the early 1990s, she knew that parents, educators, and community leaders were clamoring for resources to help them teach about media violence as a social issue. Thoman had designed the comprehensive Beyond Blame: Challenging Violence in the Media curriculum to promote dialogue, discussion, and critical thinking among children, young people, and adults of all ages who were being bombarded with violent images from the media and popular culture.

For example, for middle school students, lessons include activities that invite students to become more aware of what they are watching on television and to consider why television violence attracts attention. Students analyze TV and film narratives to study how aggressive behavior is presented as a "solution" to social problems and how heroes engage in violence that is often depicted as justified and noble. They explore how media violence may affect behaviors, increase fear, and contribute to desensitization. They consider the various responsibilities of the media industry, government, and viewers in relation to media violence.

Of course, Thoman wanted to reduce children's exposure to media violence, knowing that exposure to too much media violence can be harmful. She also wanted to change the impact of violent images by enabling youth to deconstruct different genres, including news, cartoons, drama, sports, and music. She also wanted people to consider the complex parameters of media violence as a social and political issue, including First Amendment concerns, the consequences of Reagan-era deregulation of the media industry, and the role of violence as part of the American mythology of independence. All in all, Thoman believed that media literacy education could be a necessary component of violence prevention.

Although the Center for Media Literacy was located in Los Angeles, only minutes away from major television and film companies, Thoman was certainly not worried about the topic of media violence being "too controversial." But she did worry about the legality of her intention to use copyrighted materials as part of the curriculum. She intended to package the lesson plans and curriculum materials along with a VHS tape with clips from a variety of movies and television shows that featured violence in all its many forms. She did not want her small non-profit organization to face a lawsuit.

Ever since the early 1980s, educators had been using home videotape recording to capture television programs, advertising, and news using short clips for educational purposes in the classroom. Media educators make active use of copyrighted works in the practice of teaching and learning, using artifacts of popular culture, mass media, digital media, or other artifacts that are not traditionally defined as educational media. But the question of whether curriculum materials could be created and sold with clips from commercial copyrighted media content, including materials produced by major television networks, was an open one and a source of concern.

After consultation with a copyright lawyer, Elizabeth Thoman decided to move forward using a clip compilation reel as part of the curriculum. She placed a label on the packaging, asserting her fair use rights to use copyrighted content without payment or permission, citing Section 107 of the 1976 Copyright Act, which states:

> Notwithstanding the provisions of sections 106 and 106A, the fair use of a copyrighted work, including such use by reproduction in copies or phonorecords or by any other means specified by that section, for purposes such as criticism, comment, news reporting, teaching (including multiple copies for classroom use), scholarship, or research, is not an infringement of copyright. In determining whether the use made of a work in any particular case is a fair use the factors to be considered shall include: (1) the purpose and character of the use, including whether such use is of a commercial nature or is for non-profit educational purposes; (2) the nature of the copyrighted work; (3) the amount and substantiality of the portion used in relation to the copyrighted work as a whole; and (4) the effect of the use upon the potential market for or value of the copyrighted work. The fact that a work is unpublished shall not itself bar a finding of fair use if such finding is made upon consideration of all the above factors.

The Beyond Blame curriculum became one of the best-selling curriculum products at the Center for Media Literacy, reaching thousands and thousands of students, teachers, and community members. When Thoman (2003: 609) reflected on her work in an article published in the *Federal Communications Law Journal*, she noted that the conceptualization of the public interest was becoming a "vast wasteland." The problem? In part, she acknowledged:

> [the] morass of contradictions in the intellectual property, copyright, and Fair Use regulations (and their interpretations) which threaten to stifle and even shut down the process of critical inquiry—of comment and criticism that is so fundamental for an educated citizenry in a democratic society in this or any century.
>
> (Thoman (2003: 609)

In the article, Thoman described the typical questions that she had experienced in teaching teachers:

- "Can I show that movie clip in the classroom?"
- "Can I make thirty copies of this ad so every student can read the fine print?"
- "Can my students bring in taped examples from TV that demonstrate different persuasion techniques?"

She recognized that the climate of fear was impacting teachers' confidence in using media literacy pedagogies, noting that teachers felt their jobs could be at risk if they or their students bring unauthorized material into their classrooms. She described how librarians had been forced into the role of copyright police and how school district lawyers, lacking expertise in copyright law, often too strictly interpreted the doctrine of fair use. Even more troubling, she noted, was the position of educational producers and textbook publishers, who were quite often a division of some larger media conglomerate. Their reluctance to incorporate contemporary media as "texts" for analysis into curriculum materials was strangling the development of media literacy education in the United States.

In many senses, the volume you are holding in your hands is the product of Thoman's own legacy because she was among the first to urge media literacy educators to address the problem of copyright confusion. Aware that this volume will be read by those from across a wide disciplinary spectrum, in this chapter, I orient the reader to this complex and multifaceted field. First, I provide some definitions of media education that reflect its diverse interdisciplinary formulations in relation to the dialectic of protection and empowerment, which helps to explain why there are so many different perspectives on issues of copyright and fair use in the context of education initiatives. Then I preview the contributions of the authors in this volume, whose chapters collectively provide a state-of-the-art examination of the intersections between media education, copyright, and fair use.

Matters of Definition

Of course, the terms "media education" and "media literacy" are just some of many now in circulation to describe the competencies people need to thrive in relation to mass media, popular culture, digital media, and contemporary culture. Scholars and academics have been debating "what to call it" for more than fifty years as they aim to describe the dynamic and multifaceted competencies needed for thriving in a world full of media. In the 1970s, the term "critical viewing skills" became popular (Brown 1991). During the 1980s, academic conferences in communication featured raging debates about the use of terms like "media literacy" and "media education," as scholars sought to distinguish between teaching with and teaching about media. Tyner (1998) considered media education to be a transitional concept in recognition of the sensitivity around definitions and terms associated with expanding the concept of literacy. In the 1990s, the need to distinguish between focusing on educational processes and learning outcomes emerged. For example, the term "youth media" emerged as the preferred term to describe a particular set of pedagogical practices whereby students analyze and create media outside of educational institutions (Goodman 2003). More recently, definitions and terminology have emerged that acknowledge the differences between teaching in higher education settings and working with younger learners, both in and out of school (Aspen Institute Task Force on Learning and the Internet 2014).

Among the international community of media literacy scholars, the term "media literacy" can be a source of continuing debate because some languages lack a term that equates to literacy. The emergence of terms like "media competence," "media fluency," and "transliteracy" reflects the global growth of the field (Grafe & Breitner 2014). With the support of the European Union, media literacy education researchers have developed, implemented, and assessed how media literacy may help address the challenges of discrimination in contemporary societies (Ranieri 2016), and scholars have even begun to examine youth media programs in developing nations (Asthana 2012). Approaches to media literacy education in urban schools assume distinct forms that connect to students' lived experience and identification with popular culture (Morrell et al. 2013). Overall, the field is replete with diverse theoretical and methodological frames and practical initiatives designed to influence support the work of parents, teachers, and children and young people in particular community contexts.

Definitional issues continue to be a challenge partially because of the exceedingly rapid changes in technology and the rise of digital authorship. A constantly changing media ecosystem has encouraged a forward-looking orientation toward the practice of learning how to create and compose with media formats, genres, and tools. Digital media technologies have changed dramatically over a relatively short period of time. Thinking back to my own authorship experiences with making media, I made my first film on Super 8 film while an undergraduate in the late 1970s; about then I also got to make my first video using a Sony Portapak video camera, with videotape reel-to-reel recording. I typed my dissertation on a DEC Pro 350 computer in the 1980s, with a very primitive word processor; I started using CompuServe in 1989 to use a new technology called e-mail. Through this, I was also able to host lively discussion board dialogues between my college students at Babson College and students enrolled at Ohio State University. In the 1990s, I made my first documentary film using a high-end video camera, working with a professional editor using a nonlinear editing system. I worked with a team of web developers and programmers to create an interactive digital learning game for girls ages 9–14. By the time I created the Media Education Lab website using Drupal and created my own WordPress blog, web technologies had already become relatively simple for nonspecialists to use.

Today, I assign my students the job of creating podcasts, infographics, vlogs, screencasts, and even memes. So it's no wonder that the definitions are in flux. As a variety of disciplines and subdisciplines have contributed to the field, they all engage learners in analyzing and creating media. The dynamic quality of the terms used reflects the changing nature of media systems and enrolls a wide variety of stakeholders well beyond those in the scholarly and academic community.

Today, activists, librarians, business leaders, government officials, and creative media professionals are part of the media education community, even if they use terms like "new literacies," "critical literacy," "connected learning," "digital media and learning," "digital citizenship," or other terms. As we will see in this chapter, media education is aligned in relation to a dialectic of empowerment and protection, reflecting the public's complex love–hate relationship with mass media, popular culture, and digital media. Each of these perspectives offers insight on how copyright and fair use are conceptualized as a dimension of learning and teaching.

Dialectic of Empowerment and Protection

Paradigms of empowerment and protection affect how media literacy educators conceptualize their goals and shape their pedagogical strategies, which is why digital and media literacy education may differ from place to place, depending on the particular values and motivations of educators (Hobbs & Tuzel 2017). Protectionist perspectives have been part of U.S. cultural discourses about media since the introduction of film at the turn of the 20th century (Polan 2007). Concerns about media violence increased during the 1960s and 1970s as Marshall McLuhan's engaging thesis about the interplay between form and content ("the medium is the message") and the return of tribalism ("the global village") influenced a generation of educators, who were observing shifts in the attention spans, interests, and values of students who were growing up with commercial television.

Research on media effects has examined the differential processes by which media may have influence on attitudes and behaviors (Valkenberg & Peter 2013). George Gerbner first helped to explore the relationship between media usage and children's aggressive behavior and built alliances with those concerned about advertising, materialism and exposure to gender, racial, and ethnic stereotypes, with the goal of "trying to awaken television viewers from their stupefaction" (Stossel 1997: 1). When the birth of cable television brought into American living rooms a 500-channel universe, one that was largely free from the regulatory demands placed on broadcasting, medical professionals and child development specialists grew concerned about the impact of media on children's attention span (Villani, Olson, & Jellinek 2005). Reflecting the perspective that media literacy education could counter the negative effects of media, Elizabeth Thoman developed *Media&Values*, a magazine that ran for fifty-nine issues from 1977 to 1999, growing to a distribution of over 10,000 copies, with media literacy lesson plan kits to encourage educators to bring lessons to life in the classroom (Robb Grieco 2014).

Media literacy educators and scholars have been battling to secure their legal rights to use popular culture for critical analysis and learning for nearly thirty years. That's because, in order to critique media and popular culture, it is necessary to make use of examples from Hollywood, Madison Avenue, and Silicon Valley. In the early 1990s, in his efforts to advance media literacy among university students, Sut Jhally at the University of Massachusetts–Amherst developed educational videos demonstrating the deconstruction and analysis of commercial mass media. Jhally made a video for his class using 165 clips from music videos he had taped at home using a VHS video recorder. In the video titled *Dreamworlds: Desire/Sex/Power in Rock Video*, Jhally's narration replaces the music "as clips of scantily clad women, some chained and bound, appear on the screen" (Professor's Class Video 1991). After MTV sent Jhally a cease and desist letter, he took his case to *The New York Times* to defend his right to make fair use of the clips under the Copyright Act of 1976. Today, Jhally's nonprofit organization, the Media Education Foundation, employs a staff of ten and makes a variety of films about the commercialization of childhood, pornography, pop-cultural misogyny and sexism, consumer culture, and the environment. The organization's aim is to inspire students to think critically and in new ways about the hypermediated world around them (Media Education Foundation 2017).

Interest in these issues transcends disciplinary boundaries. Psychologists and education specialists, as they came to recognize that reading and writing were literacy practices bound up with particularities of culture and society (Vygotsky & Cole 1978), also began to need to use copyrighted content in their scholarly and educational work. These scholars used the term "literacy" in a very broad way: to refer to communicative and cultural practices for making sense of the world. The term "critical literacy" (or "critical pedagogy") was used to emphasize the idea that literacy practices were inherently inflected with ideologies of power, as both media messages and pedagogical practices might evoke forms of racism, classism, sexism, and homophobia perpetuating inequality (Shor 1980). Perhaps the most famous of the critical literacy scholars is Henry Giroux, who has identified how free market ideology and privatization may weaken the practice of democracy. Giroux recognizes that if "education has a political role to play," it must imagine itself as a mechanism for changing the world by encouraging both resistance and hope "in order to challenge unquestioned modes of authority" (Giroux 2004: 79).

Teaching people to critically analyze media and explore power relationships in culture is aided by the use of images, films, television shows, news stories, video games, and advertising. Most typical is the practice of learning to identify stereotypes of race, class, and gender. Working in underfunded poor and urban public schools, teachers unveil how media reproduce inequality and justice, thus reducing power differentials between students and teachers. Instructional strategies include reading or viewing media and popular culture from a resistant perspective, producing counter-texts, researching topics of personal interest, and challenging students to take social action (Behrman 2006). In Australia, critical media literacy moved from the margins to the mainstream because it became part of a semiotic "toolkit" in a statewide curriculum (Luke 2000). Critical media literacy is "an educational project that engages with critique of the worlds of work, community life, media and popular and traditional cultures" (Luke 2000: 459). As a result, the products of mainstream popular culture, often produced by Time Warner Disney and News Corporation are used as objects of critical inquiry. Media literacy educators who are oriented to protectionist perspectives make active and regular use of copyrighted content as a means to examine and critique the power relationships and other potential harms and risks of life in a mediatized society.

Empowerment Perspectives

Media literacy educators and students may also use copyrighted content when involved in learning experiences designed for other goals. Empowerment perspectives generally have their theoretical roots in alignment with the work of John Dewey, who first conceptualized the complex and dynamic relationship between communication and education (Dyehouse 2016).

Media literacy educators make an important distinction between teaching with and teaching about media, and yet, in reality, these distinctions are continually blurred. Both strategies require the use of copyrighted content. In the 1930s, high school courses in film appreciation were proposed, implemented, and assessed by Ohio State University professor Edgar Dale as a strategy for engaging adolescents in the discussion of film as a way to build communication and critical thinking skills (Nichols 2006). In the 1960s, the term "visual literacy" emerged in the literature of communication and education (Snelson & Perkins 2009), referring to the perceptual, cognitive, and interpretive competencies associated with understanding and using many new types of images and symbols beginning to flood the cultural environment with the rise of mass market magazines and broadcast television. Developed by a group of educators and artists in Rochester, New York (home of the Eastman Kodak Company), the term was first coined by John Debes and included an emphasis on students as active readers of visual materials, applying concepts like framing, scale, dimension, tone, perspective, and juxtaposition. At the school district level, educators in the 1960s created curricula to teach high school students strategies for using, analyzing, and creating film, sound media, and other media (Friesem, Quaglia, & Crane 2014). Distinguished scholars fueled the visibility of the field by advocating for a multidisciplinary approach that included the disciplines of art history, psychology, education, and the humanities (Arnheim 1969; Kress & van Leeuwen 1996). Arts educators aiming to empower student creativity and learning use copyrighted materials as objects of study and as inspiration for visual learners.

Librarians have long offered instruction on copyright as part of their work to advance information literacy. In the 1970s, they first began providing patrons with information literacy skills (like learning to use Boolean search strategies) for accessing information using new electronic database systems (Behrens 1994). Today, librarians and teacher librarians also provide and receive copyright education through MOOCs (massive open online courses) and online learning platforms. For example, Kevin Smith, Lisa Macklin, and Anne Gilliland are university librarians who offer an online course titled Copyright for Educators and Librarians. The course helps learners understand the history, purpose, and structure of U.S. copyright law and its relevance for educators and librarians. Learners gain knowledge about the scope of copyright's protections and grasp the role of limitations and exceptions to copyright, understanding how fair use fits within an overall framework for copyright analysis. They practice analyzing specific cases and situations to consider how the law may apply to the uses of copyrighted material in educational contexts. In a fully-online learning experience, librarians and teachers watch videos, read, participate in threaded discussions, and complete quizzes to demonstrate their learning (Smith, Macklin, & Gilliland 2017).

Writing teachers are also important stakeholders in educating learners about copyright and fair use. Writing teachers have adapted their pedagogies to meet the changing needs of students by engaging them in both analyzing and producing multimedia texts such as slide multimedia shows and collages. When the field of writing and composition broke away from its parent field of English in the 1970s, scholars and teachers built on the sociocultural theories of literacy circulating in the field and began using the term "multimodal composition" to refer to the practice of helping students compose digital videos, audio essays, animations and websites for both expressive and activist purposes (Palmieri 2012). One pioneer, William Costanzo, used creative instructional practices that helped students investigate the interconnections between viewing, reading, writing, and filmmaking (Costanzo 2008 [1986]). Costanzo described to me how he faced a number of challenges in the development of his writing and composition textbook, *The Writer's Eye: Composition in the Multimedia Age* as his publisher struggled to accommodate his need to make extensive use of examples from advertising, film, and popular media content in his textbook.

The rise of educational technology in the 1980s also depended on a robust interpretation of copyright and fair use for learning. During this time, the term "computer literacy" referred to the new knowledge and skills needed to use hardware and software that was small enough to sit on our desktops. Technology corporations had raced to supply new educational technologies with the promise of revolutionizing classrooms by bringing computers into schools (Hoffman & Blake 2003). But there was some confusion about whether the focus of computer literacy should emphasize teaching *with* or teaching *about* the technology (Moursund 1983). A new paradigm emerged when Seymour Papert published *Mindstorms* (1983), showing how learning to program computers could jump-start children's intellectual curiosity and promote learning. As a student of the developmental psychologist Jean Piaget, Papert advocated for student-centered discovery learning in which students use, apply, and test ideas through participation in project-based learning with media and technology (Kafai & Resnick 1996; Papert & Harel 1991). Today, educational technology and media literacy specialists may emphasize the value of learners being able to "create to learn" by creating infographics, podcasts, animation, and other types of media as a means to develop competencies (Hobbs 2017).

Reflecting a focus on exploring interest-driven learning in out-of-school contexts, Mimi Ito and her colleagues (2013) use the term "connected learning" to refer to learning that uses peer-to-peer networks to demonstrate learning through creative production. When students create media using connected learning, they may explore remix practices as part of their work. Of course, Silicon Valley also sees considerable economic potential for the future of digital learning, and edtech venture capitalists invested $3.1 billion in more than 450 start-up initiatives in 2015, reflecting widespread recognition of the importance of digital media for the future of learning and education (CB Insights 2016). Clearly, for a wide range of stakeholders, concerns about copyright are an important part of the landscape for digital learning, media education, and digital literacy.

Continuing Concerns About Copyright

Like my colleague Elizabeth Thoman, I distinctly remember a time when teachers started to raise concerns about copyright in professional development programs with teachers. Most of the teachers I have worked with in my career as a teacher educator have been unaware that the purpose of copyright law is to promote knowledge, creativity, and the spread of innovation. They generally see copyright as a dimension of private property and lack a broader understanding of the social goals that copyright is designed to enable. I feel lucky to have been able to help bring some measure of copyright clarity as a result of my involvement in the creation of the Code of Best Practices in Fair Use for Media Literacy Education (Hobbs 2010). I am also grateful to Peter Jaszi for supporting my efforts in petitioning the Library of Congress for an exemption that enables K–12 educators to legally "rip" DVDs for media literacy education (Hobbs 2016).

Of course, with 3 million teachers and 50 million students in American public schools, there is still much work to be done. In part because of several well publicized cases in which severe penalties have been directed at individuals involved in file sharing and because of the rise of licensed online multimedia products marketed directly to schools, a climate of fear about potential liability concerning the unlicensed use of copyrighted materials in education continues to be prevalent among educators in higher education and K–12 schools. Undoubtedly, media literacy and media education has been hampered by the perceived restrictions of copyright. Palfrey and colleagues (2009) demonstrated how provisions of copyright law concerning the educational use of copyrighted material interfere with realizing the full potential of digital technology in education. Educators aim to embrace a culture where digital resources are plentiful, building new skills of accessing, curating, evaluating, analyzing, and creating with digital resources. But educational structures, as well as business and institutional structures shaped by copyright law, may limit innovation.

I have taught thousands of teachers about copyright and fair use for media literacy education over the past ten years. Three common areas of concern among American teachers remain as persistent and longstanding issues. First, some teachers hesitate to curate or compose educational materials with copyrighted content, especially when they distribute it to other teachers for use in their classrooms and particularly when they sell their creative work using peer-to-peer educator networks. Second, among librarians and educational technology specialists, there are also concerns about how digital rights management technologies may lock up content and create practical difficulties obtaining rights to use content when licenses are necessary. There is significant copyright confusion and hyper-compliance by gatekeepers such as educational administrators, IT administrators, and librarians, which may interfere with movement toward legal reform. Technological improvements in the rights clearance process, educator agreement on best practices, and increased use of open access distribution are beginning to address this problem, however. Finally, teachers and school leaders are still generally uncertain about the conditions under which student creative work can make use of copyrighted music, images, and other elements, especially when their work is distributed outside the school network or when exhibited at festivals. Too many student media festivals still restrict students from using any copyrighted content in their work, even when many such uses fall squarely under the doctrine of fair use.

Fortunately, broad public interest and scholarship on the topic of copyright and fair use are rising, and this trend has helped build educators' awareness of their rights under the law. Since the publication of Lawrence Lessig's books *Free Culture* (2004) and *Remix* (2008), we are seeing an increase in public awareness about the scope of people's rights under the law. Documentary films, including Ben Lewis's *Google and the World Brain*, Brett Gaylor's *Rip! A Remix Manifesto*, and Kembrew McLeod's *Freedom of Expression: Resistance and Repression in the Age of Intellectual Property* have also helped to build a larger constituency of librarians, educators, and activists who value copyright education.

Media literacy educators themselves have developed innovative digital technology tools that address media literacy, copyright, and fair use issues. For example, D. C. Vito, executive director of the New York City–based nonprofit organization, The LAMP, has developed Media Breaker, which enables learners to comment on advertising using existing examples of copyrighted ad content. Jonathan McIntosh's Gender Remixer is a digital play-and-learning tool that enables users to compare television ads for girls and boys to see how gender is constructed through both visual and audio content. Finally, Common Sense Media has developed online lesson plans and videos for teaching copyright and fair use as part of their digital citizenship curriculum.

Thanks to the rise of YouTube, the use of copyrighted materials is becoming normative in the K–12 classroom, and educators are developing a more sophisticated understanding of how, why, and when they and their students can use media texts for learning. As you will see in the chapters that follow, the concept of transformative use is being acknowledged not just as a legal concept but as a pedagogical one. When educators use digital media not just for content transmission but as an object of inquiry or as a means of sharing meaning, they may deepen their flexibility in analyzing message purpose, target audience, point of view, issues of representation, and other key concepts.

The Routledge Companion on Media Education, Copyright, and Fair Use is designed to advance scholarship in the field by offering an overview of issues as conceptualized by both scholars and practitioners working in a wide range of disciplinary perspectives and educational contexts, including communication and media studies, library and information studies, law and society, education, and the humanities. In the next section, I overview some of the insights from this volume's contributors to suggest how their work advances new knowledge and helps frame new research questions for the future of the field.

Foundational Issues

Part I, "Foundational Issues," includes chapters from contributors who explore broad issues about the nature of copying as part of self-expression and learning; learning about copyright as a form of civic liberal arts learning; how law changes in response to society, technology, corporate, and political interests; how pedagogies empower students to acquire competencies for self-expression in a remix culture; and the shifting legal status of new forms of youth expression and creativity.

We begin by thinking critically about copying and its value to the practice of learning and expression. Throughout history, copying has been understood as a fundamental practice of learning. Access to copies is needed in order for learners to acquire information, of course, but educators themselves have not traditionally defined copying as a transformative use of copyrighted material. Rebecca Tushnet, a distinguished legal scholar at Harvard Law School, offers a chapter entitled "Mix and Match: Transformative Purpose in the Classroom," where she explores some of the many ways in which copying is a practice of both self-expression and learning. Copying is a literacy practice: people copy the work of others as they engage in many forms of creative expression. In a cut-and-paste culture, where concerns about plagiarism are rampant, we may overlook the idea that sometimes the best way to express yourself is to use other people's words. Tushnet argues that as students compose media by using popular culture to represent their own experiences, they are "forming the self" through the selection of meaningful music, pictures, gifs, texts, and even dialogue from movies and TV shows. She demonstrates how courts have found transformative use in forms of expression and communication that do not necessarily conform to the "comment and criticism" language embedded in the doctrine of fair use. She shows that authors may have a transformative purpose when their goals are distinct from that of the original author and when they use copying in the service of another context or purpose.

Many readers of this volume will be interested in learning about creative approaches to teaching about copyright and fair use outside the law school. Communication professors have traditionally taught about copyright in ways that align with professional norms in the fields of music, film, or journalism. But in Chapter 3, Bill Herman offers insight on his experience teaching about copyright as a form of liberal arts education, where he eschews a narrow professional framing and instead offers a broad orientation to critical reading, the practice of legal reasoning and use of evidence, and the role of law in society. He describes his approach to teaching a class entitled Digital Copyright and shows how a close look at copyright connects to a broader array of social, political, and economic issues. In particular, we learn how conflicts over copyright are what make it fun to teach about copyright today. He helps students see how copyright shapes and is shaped by various media business models that help to illustrate the relationship among politics, technology, and social and political values. In a sense, Herman's approach to teaching copyright is designed to help students understand their position as stakeholders in a system where creating and consuming copyrighted content is central to leisure, work, and citizenship.

When nonlegal specialists think about the law, they often see it as fixed and static. Nothing can be further from the truth. For better or worse, the law is continually changing—just as digital technology continues to change. While at one time teachers could easily use their home video recording devices to capture excerpts of copyrighted movies, TV shows, and advertising, today the practice of creating clip compilations has been completely transformed. DVDs and streaming media have replaced VHS tapes and for nearly twenty years now, the law has made it difficult for teachers to make a clip compilation for classroom use, thanks to the Digital Millennium Copyright Act (DMCA). To use excerpts from a film, for example, teachers must first find the specific scenes they want to use and then "rip" the content by bypassing the digital encryption on a DVD or Blu-ray disc. In 2006, this practice was illegal. But as a result of advocacy by college professors and educators, some exemptions have been carved out to protect the use of film clip compilations for education. In Chapter 4, "Circumventing Barriers to Education: Educational Exemptions in the Triennial Rulemaking of the Digital Millennium Copyright Act," Jonathan Band and his colleagues Brandon Butler and Caile Morris unpack the nuances of the law. Band, Butler, and Morris show how these exemptions have become very complicated, noting that, although educators rely on the ability to bring excerpts from movies and digital content into the classroom, unfortunately the law has evolved in ways that dangerously compromise this practice.

Teachers of writing and composition have been leaders in advancing public understanding of copyright and fair use at the college level. In Chapter 5, "Remix and Unchill: Remaking Pedagogies to Support Ethical Fair Use," Tim Amidon, Kyle Stedman, and Dànielle Nicole DeVoss reflect on the centrality of remix culture in a digitally networked world. They have found that students want to use images, sounds, and multimedia from the digital worlds they inhabit, but they struggle with fear, uncertainty, and doubt. Teachers often close down student creativity as a result of their misunderstanding of the law. To give learners access, confidence, and know-how as a form of "rhetorical prowess," the authors recommend a set of empowering learning activities in composition classrooms that include composing musical parodies, engaging in critical photography, and using films from the past to understand the present. They also acknowledge that the process of composing does involve risks associated with the inclusion of multimedia content. Instead of teaching students what they cannot do, by focusing on plagiarism and takedown notices, these composition scholars want to open up opportunities for new types of multimedia composing that are responsive to an expanding conceptualization of fair use.

Human creativity is boundless and continually responsive to both our lived experience and the complex media environment in which we live. Growing up with thousands of characters encountered through movies, video games, and TV shows, today our own lives are intertwined with the narratives we have encountered through media. Significant pleasures are involved in creating fan fiction, which uses old and new characters and stories based on the culture that we experience in mass media. Unfortunately, because the copyright status of fan works is poorly understood, well-meaning educators may trivialize or dismiss such creative efforts. Some fan fiction is likely to violate copyright, while other fan fiction is likely to be lawful fair use. In Chapter 6, Aaron Schwabach, a legal scholar, offers insight and advice to people who are participating, as both readers and writers, in a fan fiction community. Clearly, as a result of common cultural practices for expression and communication, the concept of derivative use is changing within the copyright system. The opportunity for readers and writers to interact through peer-to-peer discussion and review is likely to improve students' awareness of audience. This stands in stark contrast to writing instruction in the typical classroom, where writers are often composing texts for teachers who may not share their knowledge of or interest in a topic.

Researchers and educators may be inspired by the chapters in Part I to explore these questions:

- How do teachers and students themselves understand the expressive value of copying?
- When students begin to see themselves as stakeholders in the copyright system, how may this affect their actual use of copyrighted content?
- Does educator participation in the DMCA rulemaking process really matter now that video streaming, YouTube downloading, and screencasting are replacing the need to "rip" DVDs?
- When writing and composition students learn to use copyrighted content as part of the writing process, how does this affect the development of critical analysis skills?
- In what ways might the online communities of fan fiction authors offer pedagogical insights for writing and composition teachers?

Stakeholders in Copyright Education

In Part II, "Stakeholders in Copyright Education," we look at the perspectives of a wide variety of stakeholders who bring copyright education into the context of their work, including academic librarians, activists, writing and journalism educators, and researchers. We first examine the experiences of librarians, who for a number of different reasons may experience copyright as a source of anxiety. In "Copyright Literacy in the UK: Understanding Library and Information Professionals' Experiences of Copyright," Jane Secker and Chris Morrison interrogate the "copyright literacy" of librarians in the UK. While acknowledging the very real gaps in knowledge and complex perceptions of librarians' previous training experiences in library and information science (LIS) education, the authors recognize that copyright might be the lever upon which a wider approach to digital and information literacy might be advanced.

Pat Aufderheide who helped me to truly understand and use fair use for media literacy education. As I grew in confidence, this knowledge also helped me develop a new set of innovative practices for learning and teaching centered around students as creative media makers (Hobbs 2017). As Aufderheide notes in Chapter 8 in this volume, educating young people on the rights they have to create new culture using elements from the copyrighted world is a gift—one that needs to be passed on to the world. For me, Pat's generosity in enrolling me in this work was the starting place for my own learning on this topic, and in "Codes of Best Practices in Fair Use: Game Changers in Copyright Education," Aufderheide unpacks the deep values that underlie this advocacy. She is aware of how ignorance about copyright leads to self-censorship, when, as she puts it, "people decide not to risk teaching, learning or creating." At a time when copyright protections are "long and strong," as she puts it, a deep understanding of fair use is essential to free expression. Media literacy educators benefited enormously from the opportunity to express their collective judgment about the appropriate interpretation of fair use, given their cultural and creative practices. Communication and film professors, open courseware designers, librarians, archivists, visual artists, and journalists have also benefitted from the application of the "code of best practices" model of copyright education, and each community of practice helps scholars and teachers appreciate the power of context and situation in interpreting the flexible application of the law. When people understand the law, they unleash imagination and freedom to create new content without violating the rights of copyright holders.

Another approach to copyright education comes in the form of innovative journalism education being pioneered by educators working at both the high school and university levels. In Chapter 9, "Creative Commons in Journalism Education," Ed Madison and Esther Wojcicki introduce the Creative Commons licensing model, which frees media creators to choose varying levels of restrictions for their works. Such approaches provide support for new business models for journalism, which is happening as a result of changes in the way people receive and attend to news and information. Of course, student journalists who license their work through Creative Commons also get to reflect on their interests in participating in a knowledge economy.

Future teachers and media professionals are also a prime target for copyright education, and their needs are addressed in Chapter 10, "Blurred Lines and Shifting Boundaries: Copyright and Transformation in the Multimodal Compositions of Teachers, Teacher Educators, and Future Media Professionals," by J. P. McGrail and Ewa McGrail. The authors demonstrate how digital tools may erode former distinctions between amateur and professional. Takedowns that are made lawful by the 1998 Digital Millennium Copyright Act erode confidence in the law and can shape perceptions of copyright by both future teachers and future media professionals. They offer insight on how learners can acquire a solid understanding of fair use and transformative use as provided in the Copyright Act.

Copyright education can occur in a variety of contexts, and, especially in the context of writing and composition, the use of plagiarism detection and automatic essay scoring tools provide a ripe opportunity for teaching and learning about copyright and fair use. In Chapter 11, "Automated Plagiarism Detection as Opportunity for Education on Copyright and Media," Clancy Ratliff notes that educators may appreciate plagiarism detection platforms because they function as a "digital sheriff," offering the promise of deterrence to administrators and faculty who may believe that plagiarism is rampant. Administrators may value how automated essay scoring permits efficient placement into remedial, regular, or advanced writing courses. Ratliff considers the similarities between these digital tools, noting how they both rely on databases of student writing without compensation for students, making money on student writing and compromising student privacy, and work against pedagogical practices of writing as the process of making meaning. Her insights may help educators develop ways of unpacking the values lying behind the algorithms that shape the software tools we use in education.

Next, we consider the point of view of young media creators themselves, as they learn about copyright. Catherine Burwell explores their perspectives in Chapter 12, "Youth, Bytes, Copyright: Talking to Young Canadian Creators About Digital Copyright." Burwell shares what she learned from talking to twenty-five creators across five Canadian provinces, discovering that young creators have strong ethical impulses to respect the creative work of others. In particular, they value attribution as an ethical practice. For some, this was simply about respect, or, as more than one participant phrased it, "giving credit where credit is due." But Burwell's study shows that these understandings are nuanced by the medium in which young creators work. Filmmakers have different perspectives from musicians, for example. Some young artists view attribution as an "alternative form of payment" in an attention economy. For YouTube creators, in particular, attribution in the form of a link or "shout-out" can increase traffic to their own channel and thus potentially raise revenues from advertising.

It's likely that the mere practice of talking about copyright serves to help young people turn tacit knowledge into explicit knowledge. Burwell suggests that talking openly about copyright and about the kinds of artistic practices that musicians use to create new works can be a powerful learning experience. Teachers may not need to be experts on the law in order to facilitate these conversations, which might have the added valued of supporting a balanced view of the law, which includes copyright's support for "the creative activities the law is designed to enable" (Palfrey et al. 2009: 91). Even young people who do not see themselves as digital authors may benefit from these conversations.

Academic librarians who take on the challenge of embedding copyright education in their outreach and education programs can inspire others. At the Hunter College Libraries (CUNY), Malin Abrahamsson and Stephanie Margolin are trying to reach both students and faculty to inform them about the scope of their legal rights under fair use. Unlike college faculty who see a group of students weekly over the course of a semester, many academic librarians must offer one-offs, where instruction is expected to support student coursework in a single sixty- or ninety-minute session. But even short sessions like this, when designed skillfully and targeted with precision, can be powerful learning experiences. When an art teacher at Hunter explained that every semester he is asked by students to explain when it's OK (or not OK) to use found or appropriated materials, the Hunter College librarians got the chance to work with art students to examine work by a group of artists who are using other people's photography in their work. In Chapter 13 in this volume, "Fair Use as Creative Muse: An Ongoing Case Study," you will learn how they demonstrated how to conduct a fair use analysis using four factors. They used a role-playing activity to demonstrate the strong critical thinking that is at the heart of legal reasoning, inviting students to consider the arguments of each side in the fair use analysis of two separate artworks. They then asked students to describe how they wanted to use copyrighted material in their own creative work, letting students' ideas and questions guide the discussion. These librarians value transformative use and appreciate how its application is highly contextualized. Instead of thinking of copyright education as a one-size-fits-all ensemble, they design customized sessions relevant to the needs of the faculty, the discipline, and the learners.

Copyright law affects how researchers design, implement, and assess their work, and in Chapter 14, "Digital Transformations in the Arts and Humanities: Negotiating the Copyright Landscape in the United Kingdom," Smita Kheria and her colleagues Charlotte Waelde and Nadine Levin offer a case study of researchers exploring the digital humanities in the United Kingdom. There, the law permits fair dealing with any kind of work for the purposes of criticism, review, or noncommercial research. But this has posed problems for researchers in the humanities and social sciences due to the narrow interpretation of these exceptions by rights owners and publishers. Although some recent reforms have emerged to support researchers' needs for text and data mining activities, the effect of these reforms in practice has not kept pace.

Music researchers and music educators face particular challenges when it comes to copyright and fair use. The chapter's case study on the use of computational tools to explore musicology, for example, raises important questions about publicly funded projects. Copyright law's strict framing of "noncommercial" use challenges academic projects when the creative work produced may have commercial value. As you will see in this chapter, in their digital musicology project, researchers were able to share metadata about musical scores and recordings but not digital audio files. How valuable is their project, a web-based resource for public users, when human beings cannot test or validate the relevance or "correctness" of particular searches and results? Could the researchers link to existing commercial content on websites like Spotify and Amazon? Were the software tools and annotated musical libraries subject to commercialization, and, if so, how would this affect the public value of the project? Due to the considerable ambiguity around the scope of copyright exceptions and the risks involved, researchers struggled over the scope and overall direction of their work. How ironic that researchers who want to use copyright-protected materials for transformative research may not be even able to share their own work to the public whose tax dollars helped to pay for it.

Clearly, restrictive interpretations of copyright exceptions create real difficulties for researchers who are working at the intersection between academe and industry. Researchers may be inspired by the chapters in Part II to explore some issues that build upon their work, including these questions:

- What kinds of professional development learning experiences support the diverse needs of librarians as they learn about copyright?
- How might we measure students' knowledge about Creative Commons licensing, copyright, and fair use as part of formal and informal learning?
- What kinds of experiences help teachers and students discover the values that underlie algorithms for plagiarism detection and automated essay scoring?
- Regarding issues of copyright and fair use, how are the views of young YouTube creators different from students who have not created media?
- What reward systems could support the increased collaboration of academic librarians, researchers, and university faculty as they develop creative approaches to understanding copyright and fair use?

Pedagogy of Media Education, Copyright, and Fair Use

In Part III of this volume, we focus on particular pedagogical strategies for teaching about copyright and fair use and for the educational use of copyrighted content, especially film and video. We explore how teachers perceive the educational value of film and how copyright shapes the way educators use YouTube. The chapters in this section examine the copyright implications of film digitization and streaming video, provide insight on how children learn about copyright and fair use, and examine how copyright issues are affecting the development of online and digital learning.

There's no doubt that for 21st-century teachers, YouTube has replaced the VHS clip compilation reel of olden days. But many schools still block YouTube, and copyright issues may surface when downloading videos to use in schools or when uploading content containing copyrighted materials. In Chapter 15, "The Benefits and Challenges of YouTube as an Educational Resource," Chareen Snelson describes how educators have used YouTube for both its content and video-sharing capacities. Access to free video content, the ease of curating video playlists, and even basic video editing and online captioning tools make it attractive for both teachers and students. As a teacher educator, Snelson describes some ways that she helps future teachers learn to make effective use of YouTube by sharing assignments from her course entitled YouTube for Educators. In this course, students review media licenses, develop media literacy competencies associated with creating video, and learn the technical skills of video editing. As they produce a mini-documentary, they are invited to actively pay attention to the legal and ethical uses of media for educational video projects. Insights from this course could be valuable for developing innovative approaches to teaching future teachers.

As digital data moves to the cloud, streaming video is becoming normative within the home, school, and library. Blended, hybrid, and fully online courses are also creating new digital environments that necessitate streaming the delivery of video content. From his vantage point in the academic library, in Chapter 17, Scott Spicer provides a comprehensive look at video in higher education, considering the history, the evolving pedagogy, as well as copyright challenges and support models as new approaches to teaching and learning emerge in the digital realm. Recent surveys show that many academic libraries provide access to video streaming but that often these titles are not discoverable via the university library's catalog (Farrelly 2015). Changes to video formats and changes to copyright law have intersected with normative practices of educational use, giving academic librarians the chance to support faculty who are exploring innovative approaches to teaching and learning. Streaming video does help expand campus access to instructional video, but it poses some interesting complications in regard to copyright. Spicer explains some recent court cases that addressed the digitization and streaming of instructional video materials under fair use and also considers copyright issues in making instructional videos accessible to students with disabilities. How should universities handle lawsuits for failing to caption their public massive open online courses (MOOC) and other online video content?

What should be done about the many university VHS/DVD video collections and licensed streaming content in library instructional video collections that are not captioned? It's not easy for academic libraries to maintain local technical infrastructure for the digitization and management of local streaming collections at a time when the costs for licensing streaming video are significant. Today, many feature films and television programs are often available for DVD purchase or at a reasonable rental cost via Netflix, Hulu, Amazon, and other consumer streaming services. How do collection development and technical services librarians interact with information literacy librarians to help faculty and students make effective use of video streaming services? Clearly, the work of the academic media librarian will continue to rapidly evolve as a result of changes in law and technology.

Still, as much as things change, some media education practices are timeless, it seems. In Chapter 16, "Teaching History with Film: Teaching About Film as History," Jeremy Stoddard digs into the use of film in and out of history classrooms, reflecting on the rapid expansion of access to history-related media. Film can be used to engage students in historical thinking, as part of media literacy, or as a way to engage in difficult or controversial history topics. As such, media education in the history classroom has direct implications for critical citizenship (Hoechsman and Poyntz 2012).

When is the right age to begin introducing children to concepts of copyright and fair use? It turns out that children might not need a comprehensive understanding of the American system of intellectual property law in order to understand the fundamental concepts of copyright and fair use. In "'I Got It from Google': Recontextualizing Authorship to Strengthen Fair Use Reasoning in the Elementary Grades," David Cooper Moore and John Landis show how to build children's fair use reasoning skills by emphasizing the development of critical thinking competencies that require students to understand the authorial message, purpose, and context of online images. As children develop skills of image searching, they can use language to identify authorship and purpose. They can describe their own new purposes for using that media and consider some ethical guidelines of "what's OK" and "what's not OK" when using the copyrighted work of others. Although the rise of social media makes it harder to identify the author of much of the digital content that circulates in culture today, a good understanding of the search process enables young children to use flexible, spontaneous search strategies, along with more deliberate and reflective approaches.

When Chris Sperry and Cyndy Scheibe first started created media literacy curriculum materials for social studies education, they were challenged to figure out how to use *Newsweek* covers as part of the curriculum materials. They got advice from two different attorneys: one who said that they could not publish without *Newsweek*'s permission and another who said that the fair use doctrine clearly protected their right to publish these materials, even if they were selling the kits. In Chapter 19, "Resolving Copyright Concerns in the Development of Diverse Curriculum Materials for Media Analysis Activities," they describe their experience with *Newsweek* and explain the multiperspectival nature of media literacy, copyright, and fair use. As they came to recognize that educators have the legal right to critique *Newsweek* content in the classroom without paying for permission to use excerpts of *Newsweek* content, they also point out how a lack of copyright clarity may work to the benefit of media companies. Sensitivity to power dynamics, especially in countries without a strong First Amendment tradition or without intellectual property rights as robust as ones available in the United States, deepens the appreciation of the role of fair use in supporting global media literacy education.

Teaching film to high school students opens up enormous opportunities for creative pedagogy and in Chapter 20, "Approaches to Active Reading and Visual Literacy in the High School Classroom," John S. O'Connor and Dan Lawler offer insights from their work as experienced educators. They describe the process of helping students engage in the close analysis of visual media, supporting students to read actively: to make discoveries, find patterns, and generate new ideas through analysis. Students learn to ask questions of the text with each reading. By generating questions, students wonder about why a filmmaker, graphic novelist, or broadcast journalist composed the work and made certain choices. In doing so, they come to appreciate how media construct reality through representation.

Another set of creative pedagogical opportunities arises in online higher education, which has, over a period of ten years, shifted from a Wild West mentality to one more controlled by institutional politics and bureaucratic processes. In Chapter 21, "Copyright and Fair Use Dilemmas in a Virtual Educational Institution in Mexico," David Ramírez Plascencia describes some experiences related to the use of copyrighted material at a virtual education center at the University of Guadalajara, Mexico. Rapid technological shifts led the university to modify its academic policies concerning the use of copyrighted materials, with a profound impact on the teaching and learning process. Today, at this university, the content of online learning is strictly reviewed, forcing professors to use exclusively free resources and, even in some cases, to create their own materials. Although some see such policies as restricting academic freedom, Plascencia notes that faculty also took the initiative to develop more creative assignments, to use digital collaboration tools, and to rely on open access resources. More and more, assignments include making a video and sharing it on YouTube or Vimeo or creating and displaying an online slide show or text. This chapter reminds us that copyright is constructed within a political and economic context with inherent North–South inequalities and that student learning and faculty intellectual freedoms are shaped by these inequalities. Of course, the future of online learning is still ahead of us, and it's not clear how copyright and fair use will evolve as this pedagogy becomes more and more a part of higher education.

Researchers may be inspired by the chapters in Part III to explore some issues that build upon their work, including these questions:

- How may increased knowledge of YouTube copyright policies impact teachers' use of video in the classroom?
- How do academic librarians support teachers and students in the discovery and effective use of video streaming resources?
- How might children developing their understanding of copyright and fair use affect the development of their critical thinking and communication skills?
- Given the global inequalities of access to information, what global "best practices" are emerging in the use of copyrighted materials for online learning?

Past Is Prologue

In Part IV, we bring the volume to a close by providing a historical perspective that invites us to consider the significance of copyright and fair use in its historical context and its relevance to the future of education and scholarship. In Chapter 22, media historian and librarian Thomas Leonard offers an examination of both the history and the future of copyright. Examining the book trade of the 18th century, Leonard shows how copyright has resembled a 300-year-old game of Monopoly, where American booksellers, once the pirates of the publishing world, have repeatedly adapted and revised the rules to meet their own changing needs. Today, search engines like Google have continued in the pirating tradition, as spiders crawl copyrighted content of the world and the Google Books project has digitized more than 25 million book titles, transforming old volumes into online treasures. When the Supreme Court allowed the Second Circuit Court of Appeals to stand in favor of Google in *Author's Guild v. Google* (2015), the concept of fair use was at the center of the action, and many of the authors of this volume expect it will continue to play a central role in supporting the continuing innovation of media education far into the future. As you will see in the pages that follow, it is clear that educators, learners, authors, and users all benefit from a deeper understanding of copyright and fair use as a fundamental dimension of media literacy and media education.

References

Arnheim, R. (1969). *Visual Thinking.* Berkeley: University of California Press.

Aspen Institute Task Force on Learning and the Internet. (2014). "Learner at the Center of a Networked World." Retrieved from http://csreports.aspeninstitute.org/Task-Force-on-Learning-and-the-Internet/2014/report/details/0054/Task-Force-Download-PDF

Asthana, S. (2012). *Youth Media Imaginaries From Around the World.* New York: Peter Lang.

Behrens, S. J. (1994). "A Conceptual Analysis and Historical Overview of Information Literacy." *College and Research Libraries*, 55(4), 309–322.

Behrman, E. (2006). "Teaching About Language, Power, and Text: A Review of Classroom Practices That Support Critical Literacy." *Journal of Adolescent & Adult Literacy*, 49(6), 490–498.

Brown, J. A. (1991). *Television "Critical Viewing Skills" Education: Major Media Literacy Projects in the United States and Selected Countries.* Mahwah, NJ: Lawrence Erlbaum Associates.

CB Insights. (2016, April 18). "Ed Tech Chill: Ed Tech Startups See Funding Slump and Deals Flatline." *CB Insights.* Retrieved from www.cbinsights.com/blog/ed-tech-2016-funding-drop/#head1

Costanzo, W. (2008). *The Writer's Eye: Composition in the Multimedia Age.* New York: McGraw-Hill.

Dyehouse, J. (2016). "Jeremiah Dyehouse on John Dewey." In R. Hobbs (Ed.), *Exploring the Roots of Digital and Media Literacy Through Personal Narrative* (pp. 170–179). Philadelphia: Temple University Press.

Farrelly, D. (2015). "Pricing and Other Issues in Streaming Video." American Library Association. Association for Library Collections and Technical Services. Retrieved from www.ala.org/alcts/confevents/upcoming/webinar/111115

Freedom of Expression™: Resistance and Repression in the Age of Intellectual Property. Film. Director: Kembrew McLeod.

Friesem, J., Quaglia, D., & Crane, Ed. (2014). "Media Now: A Historical Review of a Media Literacy Curriculum." *Journal of Media Literacy Education*, 6(2), 35–55.

Giroux, H. (2004). "Cultural Studies, Public Pedagogy and the Responsibilities of Intellectuals." *Communication and Critical/Cultural Studies*, 1(1), 59–79.

Goodman, S. (2003). *Teaching Youth Media.* New York: Teachers College Press.

Grafe, S., & Breiter, A. (2014). "Modeling and Measuring Pedagogical Media Competencies of Pre-Service Teachers (M³K)." KoKoHs Working Papers No. 6, 76. Retrieved from www.kompetenzen-im-hochschulsektor.de/Dateien/WP_No._6_Current_International_State_and_Future_Perspectives_on_Competence_Assessment_in_Higher_Education.pdf#page=80

Hobbs, R. (2010). *Copyright Clarity: How Fair Use Supports Digital Learning.* Beverly Hills, CA: Corwin/Sage.

Hobbs, R. (2016). "Lessons in Copyright Activism: K–12 Education and the DMCA 1201 Exemption Rulemaking Process." *International Journal of Information and Communication Technology Education*, 12(1), 50–63. doi:10.4018/IJICTE.2016010105

Hobbs, R. (2017). *Create to Learn: Introduction to Digital Literacy.* New York: Wiley-Blackwell.

Hobbs, R., & Tuzel, S. (2017). "Teacher Motivations for Digital and Media Literacy: An Examination of Turkish Educators." *British Journal of Educational Technology*, 48(1), 7–22. doi:10.1111/bjet.1232

Hoechsmann, M. & Poyntz. S. (2012). *Media Literacies: A Critical Introduction.* New York: Wiley Blackwell.

Hoffman, M., & Blake, J. (2003). "Computer Literacy: Today and Tomorrow." *Journal of Computing Sciences in Colleges*, 18(5), 221–233.

Ito, M., et al. (2013). *Hanging Out, Messing Around, and Geeking Out: Kids Living and Learning With New Media.* Cambridge, MA: MIT Press.

Kafai, Y., & Resnick, M. (1996). *Constructionism in Practice: Designing, Thinking, and Learning in a Digital World.* Mahwah, NJ: Lawrence Erlbaum Associates.

Kress, G., & van Leeuwen, T. (1996). *Reading Images: The Grammar of Visual Design.* New York: Routledge.

Lessig, L. (2004). *Free Culture: The Nature and Future of Creativity.* New York: Penguin Press.

Lessig, L. (2008). *Remix.* New York: Penguin Press.

Luke, A. (2000). "Critical literacy in Australia: A Matter of Context and Standpoint." *Journal of Adolescent & Adult Literacy*, 43(5), 448–461.

Media Education Foundation. (2017). "Mission." Retrieved from www.mediaed.org/about-mef/what-we-believe/

Minsky, M. (1986). "Introduction." In C. Solomon, M. Minsky, and B. Harvey (Eds.), *LogoWorks: Challenging Programs in Logo*. New York: McGraw-Hill.

Morrell, E., Duenas, R., Garcia, V., & Lopez, J. (2013). *Critical Media Pedagogies: Teaching for Achievement in City Schools*. New York: Teachers College Press.

Moursund, D. (1983). "Precollege Computer Literacy: A Personal Computing Approach." International Council for Computers in Education, University of Oregon, Eugene, Oregon. Retrieved from http://pages.uoregon.edu/moursund/Books/PCL/PCL-1983.pdf

Nichols, J. (2006). "Countering Censorship: Edgar Dale and the Film Appreciation Movement." *Cinema Journal*, 46(1), 3–22.

Palfrey, J., Gasser, U., Simun, M., & Barnes, R. (2009). "Youth, Creativity, and Copyright in the Digital Age." *International Journal of Learning and Media*, 1(2), 79–97.

Palmieri, J. (2012). *Remixing Composition: A History of Multimodal Writing Pedagogy*. Carbondale: Southern Illinois University Press.

Papert, S. (1983). *Mindstorms*. Cambridge, MA: MIT Press.

Papert, S., & Harel, I. (1991). *Constructionism*. New York: Ablex Publishing Corporation.

Polan, D. (2007). *Scenes of Instruction: The Beginnings of the U.S. Study of Film*. Berkeley: University of California. Press.

"A Professor's Class Video Runs into an MTV Protest." (1991, May 18). *New York Times*. Retrieved from www.nytimes.com/1991/05/18/arts/a-professor-s-class-video-runs-into-an-mtv-protest.html

Ranieri, M. (2016). *Populism, Media and Education: Challenging Discrimination in Contemporary Digital Societies*. New York: Routledge.

Rip! A Remix Manifesto. (2009). Director: Brett Gaylor. [Film.]

Robb Grieco, M. (2014). "Media for Media Literacy: Discourses of the Media Literacy Education Movement in Media & Values Magazine, 1977–1993." Doctoral dissertation, Temple University School of Communications and Theater.

Shor, I. (1980). *Critical Teaching and Everyday Life*. Chicago: University of Chicago Press.

Smith, K., Macklin, L., & Gilliland, A. (2017). "Copyright for Teachers and Librarians." *Coursera*. Retrieved from www.coursera.org/learn/copyright-for-education

Snelson, C., & Perkins, R. (2009). "From Silent Film to YouTube™: Tracing the Historical Roots of Motion Picture Technologies in Education." *Journal of Visual Literacy*, 28, 1–27.

Stossel, S. (1997, May). "The Man Who Counts the Killings." *The Atlantic*. Retrieved from www.theatlantic.com/magazine/archive/1997/05/the-man-who-counts-the-killings/376850/

Thoman, E. (2003). "Screen-Agers . . . and the Decline of the 'Wasteland.'" *Federal Communications Law Journal*, 55(3), 601–609.

Tyner, K. (1998). *Literacy in a Digital World*. Mahwah, NJ: Lawrence Erlbaum Associates.

Valkenberg, P., & Peter, J. (2013). "The Differential Susceptibility to Media Effects Model." *Journal of Communication*, 63(2), 221–243.

Villani, V. S., Olson, C., & Jellinek, M. (2005). "Media Literacy for Clinicians and Parents." *Child and Adolescent Psychiatric Clinics of North America*, 14, 523–553.

Vygotsky, L., & Cole, M. (1978). *Mind in Society*. Cambridge, MA: Harvard University Press.

Further Reading

Aufderheide, P., & Jaszi, P. (2011). *Reclaiming Fair Use*. Chicago: University of Chicago Press.

2

MIX AND MATCH

Transformative Purpose in the Classroom

Rebecca Tushnet

A 2012 article in *Time* magazine began, "From the day kids pick up their first No. 2 pencils, they're taught that copying is wrong" (Steinmetz 2012). But that's backward. From the day kids pick up their pencils with a teacher, they are taught to copy: tracing the shapes of letters and numbers, then copying them on the dotted lines below the exemplars. Teaching about the creation of other media, including art and music, proceeds similarly, providing students with models that they can use to learn techniques or compare to their own work. But because of modern concepts of intellectual property, this practice—learning by copying, which is to say learning as it's always been done—can be rendered invisible even as it's completely foundational.

There are kinds and contexts of copying of which teachers disapprove, and rightly so. But if we get the starting rule backward, we will mistake the necessary components of successful teaching and learning, as well as the important distinction between plagiarism and copying. And while much acceptable copying sticks to "building blocks," not all of it does or should need to.

Noncommercial remixers have very little to fear from copyright law, which now strongly protects transformative uses. But what about other noncommercial uses? Increasingly, courts have recognized transformative *purposes* as sufficient to justify fair use copying: where the fair user copies a work, even an entire work, in order to give it a different meaning and message, fair use can readily be found. This chapter examines the continuing fair use claims of copying for teaching and other educational purposes, and arguing that they can further important free speech values. There is a link between the importance of copying to its status as fair use, and it helps to explain why fair use doesn't require transformation in the *content* of a work. Content transformation is not the key indicator of whether a person's use furthers free speech interests. Particularly in an educational context, copying itself can be a vital part of freedom of expression.

Copying for Access

The benefits of access are often the most visible. If the television series *Game of Thrones* is having a significant cultural impact or sparking a conversation about rape and the depiction of rape in popular culture, then access to the show improves a person's "ability to participate in making and interpreting that culture" (Tushnet 2004). But if some people can't afford access (and a teacher's Netflix subscription is unlikely to provide her a license to show the work in a classroom setting, even if *Game of Thrones* comes to Netflix), then their ability to participate—whether by creating transformative responses or otherwise—is cut off from the beginning. Educational exemptions for libraries and for classroom teaching are therefore vital to promote democratic values, especially in an era where funds for materials are constantly being cut (17 U.S.C. §§ 108, 110; Balkin 2004: 50–54).

The expressive value to the reader of her copy of *To Kill a Mockingbird* does not depend on whether that copy was made with the copyright owner's authorization, nor does the expressive value of whatever flows from her exposure to the book. Speech's value to its audience "isn't just in its existing somewhere in a bookstore—the value lies in consumers actually hearing or reading it. . . . [R]epublished work is materially more valuable to readers than the original that they can't get, that costs too much, or that they don't know about" (Volokh 2003: 726). Uses in schools and libraries therefore "advance copyright's general aim of promoting cultural and political discourse" (Goldstein 2003: 208). This vitally important access to works can sometimes be had only if the copyright owner's price need not be paid.

Empirical studies have shown that access to works increases their value and assists in the production of new works. Works whose copyrights have expired are cheaper, more readily available, and more likely to be used as part of new works (Heald 2008: 1031–1063; Buccafusco & Heald 2013: 1). Likewise, Barbara Biasi and Petra Moser (2016) have shown that free access to German science books during World War II, when German copyrights in such works were suspended, encouraged more scientific work, particularly in disciplines such as mathematics in which knowledge production was less dependent on physical capital. In schools, where novelty is not necessarily as important as the student's ability to produce a work of appropriate quality—a good research paper about World War II, for example—this benefit of access is particularly important.

Without fair use, copyright can distort the "marketplace of ideas," especially in schools. For an especially telling example, consider the case of these instructional multimedia producers:

> *Who Built America?* is an award-winning historical CD-ROM series for high school and college students that uses numerous primary sources. Owners of the sources' copyrights often wanted large payments for use of historically significant works, payments the authors couldn't afford. They substituted federal government and public domain works, altering the way students will understand the past; the materials now overemphasize the federal government's role in Depression-era society and culture.
>
> (Tushnet 2004: 565–566)

In an age of cash-strapped school systems, groups with very specific agendas, including anti–fair use copyright owners, are taking advantage of this dynamic to provide schools with free teaching resources that, subtly or not so subtly, promote a specific political position, complete with carefully selected facts or opinions couched as facts (Gillespie 2009: 274–318). Fair use of other materials is one way to fight back against such distortions.

Students' interests in obtaining access to speech may thus apply even if we don't think that copying is a valuable activity. But that's not all. Copying regularly has profound free speech value for the copiers themselves. People regularly copy in order to speak, to connect with existing works, to affirm their allegiance, or to say other things. (I use the term "copying" to encompass both physically reproducing a work in concrete form—copyright's reproduction right—and singing, playing, and otherwise communicating—copyright's performance and distribution rights.)

Copying as Argument

Copying can serve important persuasive goals: it can connect the speaker with the audience, appeal to relevant authority, and signal affiliation and membership in a coherent group. There is a reason that schools historically had children recite the Pledge of Allegiance together, rather than having each come up with some patriotic statement. The fact that children have the constitutional right to refuse to say the Pledge is another indication of its power: recitation, which is to say copying, can be extremely meaningful, and no one should be forced to endorse the Pledge if it conflicts with his or her fundamental commitments. And the Pledge is only the start of the day; copying continues to have similar meaning and utility throughout educational practices.

Popular culture, including political culture, is rampant with argumentative copying. When House Republicans are attempting to explain GOP immigration policy in .gif form, using clips taken from popular movies and television shows, and President Barack Obama's official Tumblr reblogs numerous memes to connect with young citizens, it's hard to deny that copying is an important means of communicating (Tushnet 2015). Apparently, these politicians, who have good reason to know what works as persuasion, think that connecting their messages to existing cultural productions makes their political messages more likely to be accepted.

Copying may also be important as an appeal to authority: words from one source are more credible and persuasive than the same words from another source. A *Consumer Reports* review of a product, quoted in an ad, makes the ad better—and also sends the message that *Consumer Reports* is worth listening to (*Consumers Union of the United States v. Gen. Signal Corp.* (2d Cir. 1983)). As Ralph Waldo Emerson said, "a writer appears to more advantage in the pages of another book than in his own. In his own, he waits as a candidate for your approbation; in another's, he is a lawgiver" (Garber 2003: 19–20). (Alert readers may notice the author's own use of this tactic.)

Martin Luther King, Jr.'s "I Have a Dream" speech contained vivid expression that was unique neither to King nor to that particular speech. Keith Miller argues that King's copying helped promote his agenda of racial justice by drawing on familiar words that reassured white listeners: "King skillfully inserted his arguments against segregation into a web of ideas and phrases that moderate and liberal white Protestants had already approved. . . . Using words his listeners had already heard, he reinforced what they already believed" (Miller 1992: 195–196). The speech twice quoted the Bible and borrowed other biblical language; it also quoted the Declaration of Independence, the song "America," the spiritual "Free at Last," and several other sources (Hansen 2003: 53, 58, 61–62, 101–103, 108–109, 115, 119–120). "King's listeners retained his ideas and phrases more easily because the familiar strains of his sermons made them more memorable. . . . Had he instead supplied sermons with profoundly original content, he would never have legitimized his radical tactic of civil disobedience and his radical goals of ending racism, poverty, and war" (Miller 1992: 192). King apparently thought his practices were perfectly acceptable, making no attempt to hide his borrowing and copying from well-known sources (Miller 1992: 135–136). Although his use of unattributed copying in academic pursuits violated scholarly norms, it's hard to disagree with King about the rhetorical power of the quotations he chose for "I Have a Dream." (Indeed, when the filmmakers of the King biographical picture *Selma* reworked King's speeches for fear of a copyright lawsuit from the King estate, they removed rhetorical as well as veridical power from the film.)

The subsequent appropriation of "I Have a Dream" also illustrates the way that quotation in a new context makes new meanings. King's line about wanting his children to be judged not by the color of their skin but by the content of their character was appropriated by affirmative action opponents: they relied both on King's powerful rhetoric and King's powerful aura as a civil rights hero in order to persuade (Lesher 1996). This use of authority—and, it is to be hoped, its further deconstruction in class as students discuss whether such a use was fair in an ideological rather than copyright-related sense—is exactly what students often need to learn to do in order to navigate the world around them.

Copying as Transformative Repurposing for Analysis and Self-Expression

We might categorize some kinds of copying as "remix," discussed extensively in other chapters in this volume, because of the way that copying can recontextualize images and sounds by situating them among other images and sounds.

For example, images of women in popular culture can be repurposed not necessarily in healthy ways. Media studies teachers analyze images in class for the larger messages that they are sending. But so do other people, including the makers of "thinspiration" videos, which can be read as both pro- and anti-anorexia. Thinspiration videos involve a lot of copying and repurposing of existing popular images in ways that the originals did not intend and might violently reject, and yet one might argue that they also expose truths about mainstream culture and its demands to regulate female bodies. They are transformative even without explicit commentary explaining their relationship to the original; they use copying in order to speak in the videomaker's own voice, however disturbing that voice sounds. Virginia Heffernan (2008: 16) describes the films:

> Filmmakers are reticent with commentary. If they explain their images in any way, it's with oddly peppy title cards ("Enjoy!" "Thanks for watching!") or a series of unsigned quotations, compiled as if for a commonplace book. A thinspiration auteur makes her voice heard almost exclusively through these cards. . . .
>
> Shooting photos just for a video is also rare. Instead, thinspiration consists of personal, archival and file photos (some taken from Photobucket and other photo-sharing sites) that have been inventively sequenced and edited, often using the so-called Ken Burns effect of pressing in on significant details.

Heffernan (2008) explains that the films recontextualize the images they use, allowing pure copying to be profoundly transformative: "Film of runway shows, as it appears on fashion Web sites, presents the models as confident, beautiful, 'fierce,' where the same roll, in the hands of a thinspo filmmaker, can make them look disfigured and diseased."

At the same time, copying can help provide a voice for people who feel literally wordless. As one thinspiration filmmaker said, "The songs I use . . . say exactly what I need to but can't figure out how" (Heffernan 2008). People who make playlists of songs to express themselves use almost the same words: copying and arranging allows them to communicate their own inner lives (Parnell 2006). That's a small intervention into culture but a meaningful one both for playlist creators and for those around them. Another investigation found that men use song lyrics to speak about their own experiences with abortion. The songs provide words and perhaps permission to express emotions that they didn't have without copying. This repurposing of song lyrics is another instance of copying as a means of self-expression and of political speech, and it illustrates the ways in which pop culture is itself political, providing means of understanding and articulating the self in society ("Are You Changed?" 2008).

Poetry—lyrics without music, one might say—has long served similar functions, even before the rise of today's popular music. As many young women have done throughout the years, Anne Frank copied a poem to celebrate a friend's birthday, combining it with stickers (possibly copyrighted by someone else) to create a personal tribute (Lange 2003: 463, 482). Chief Justice Rehnquist, dissenting in *Texas v. Johnson* (1989), could think of no more eloquent way to argue for the value of the American flag than by quoting John Greenleaf Whittier's poem "Barbara Frietchie," among other sources whose reproduction added power to his argument. Likewise, reprints of W. H. Auden's poem "September 1, 1939" filled a deep need in many people to explain their feelings about September 11, 2001 (Burt 2003: 533, 534–535; Volokh 2003: 726–727). We recite poetry because it seems to us to express profound truths that could not be better expressed—could not even be expressed at all—with other words. After all, to dissect a poem is in some ways to destroy it. One has to study the poem itself, not some other words used to describe the poem, in order to understand it.

Students can do the same thing across many media, connecting popular culture to their own experiences. Selection of meaningful music, or pictures, or texts—as in the classic commonplace book—is a standard means of forming the self and explaining that self to other people. Protesters use quotes from the blockbuster musicals *Hamilton* ("Tomorrow there'll be more of us") or *Les Misérables* ("Do you hear the people sing/Singing the songs of angry (wo)men"); they use images of the late Carrie Fisher as General Leia Organa to claim that "a woman's place is in the Resistance"; in many other ways, they express their commitments by copying to show their cultural competencies.

In education, copying serves the same purposes, as when students make collages of pictures and words in order to explain some concept or event in their own lives. Selection of what to copy is, in fact, an editorial, interpretive task, as the contents of a newspaper's letters to the editor testify. Such picking and choosing, sorting and arranging involve creative authorship that, in other contexts, is recognized by copyright law as creating a new work (17 U.S.C. § 101 (2000)).

Transformation in Purpose in Fair Use Law

In recent years, courts have readily found transformation in the purpose for which a second comer uses a work to be a strong indicator of fair use. Even without transformation in content (such as a parody) and without targeted criticism or commentary, a purpose separate from that of the original author supports fair use (Reese 2008: 494). While educators have traditionally not made claims that their uses are transformative, this growing case law provides an opportunity for them to explain the educational power of copying in ways that fit squarely into the narrative of transformative purpose.

In litigated cases, courts have held that copying to put works in a larger context or to use works as evidence in an argument is transformative. Examples include copying scientific works to support a patent application by showing the state of the prior art (*American Institute of Physics v. Winstead PC* (N.D. Tex. 2013)); copying a blog post as part of a disciplinary proceeding to show that the writer had violated professional norms (*Denison v. Larkin* (N.D. Ill. 2014)); copying instructional videos as part of an argument that the instructor was lying (*Carter v. Autry* (W.D. Va. 2014); *Savage v. Council on American–Islamic Relations* (N.D. Cal. 2008)); and even copying a headshot of a person as part of an article attacking that person (*Katz v. Google Inc.* (11th Cir. 2015); *Dhillon v. Does* (N.D. Cal. 2014)). As Brandon Butler (2015: 495) has argued, the added value that comes from selecting, organizing, and enabling research, which has been recognized as transformative in the creation of databases (*White v. West Publishing Corporation* (S.D.N.Y. 2014)), can also be found in many teaching contexts.

Even unpublished works, traditionally given the most protection against fair use, can be fairly used when the context involves sufficient analysis and interpretation surrounding the copied work. In *Sundeman v. Seajay Society* (1998), the Fourth Circuit found that a scholar's use of portions of an unpublished manuscript in a lecture presentation was transformative in that it used the work "to shed light on" the author's development as an author, review the quality of the work, and comment on the author's biographical history, giving the scholar's use a "further purpose" and "different character."

Historical contextualization can also be fair use: the influential Second Circuit held that posters designed to promote concerts by the Grateful Dead had their purpose transformatively changed by a book chronicling the history of the band. Therefore, the book's copying of the posters in smaller form as part of a visual timeline of the band's history was fair despite the existence of a licensing market for the posters. The copyright owner might have wanted to get paid for the use, but it had no right to control or monetize a transformative, historical use (*Bill Graham Archives v. Dorling Kindersley Ltd.* [2d Cir. 2006]). Similar historicization and contextualization permitted copying artwork for a book about the artist (*Warren Publishing Company v. Spurlock* (E.D. Pa. 2009)). Professor Matthew Sag (2012) has labeled such uses as examples of a "creativity shift," which occurs when an informational work is used for a creative purpose or when a creative work is used for an informational purpose—both common activities in teaching. Sag's empirical analysis shows that a creativity shift is a very strong predictor of a fair use finding in litigated cases.

But what about the fact that no communication is univocal, given the variety of interpretive positions held by audiences? Isn't it readily possible to redefine the original author's purpose to include possible educational uses, even if that wasn't the main goal, refuting any transformativeness claim? In some cases, it is clear that no new purpose is involved. If the material being copied is a practice test, then copying for the purpose of letting students take the practice test won't be transformative (Butler 2015: 497)—though copying the same test for the purpose of analyzing how educational testing has changed over time, or for comparing how one company's textbooks match up to the tests it sells separately, would be.

For materials not created specifically for the educational market, however, it is simpler for educators to show a separate purpose. Courts have proven willing to find transformative purpose based on objective characteristics of a particular defendant's use, such as the copied work's place within a broader context. For example, the Second Circuit also found that a news organization's posting of a recording of a company's earnings call was transformative because the news organization sought to report on the content of the call, not to convince people of the company's soundness and likely profitability (*Swatch Group Management Services v. Bloomberg L.P.* (2d Cir. 2014)). Evidentiary use, that is, was inherently different in purpose from the original purpose: "[the copier's] message, 'this is what they said'—is a very different message from [the original speaker's]—'this is what you should [know or] believe'" (*Fox News Network, LLC v. TVEyes, Inc.* (S.D.N.Y. 2014)). This type of transformativeness also allows educators to bring in the value of access, previously discussed, by arguing that teaching with primary materials, including "newspaper and magazine articles, advertisements, manifestoes, and even popular entertainment" has a different purpose than the original function of such documents (Butler 2015: 518).

More generally, copying that is part of an interpretive project often has a transformative purpose. Copying an image merely in order to express outrage about it can be highly transformative, as when Jerry Falwell used a *Hustler* caricature of him in fund-raising to show exactly what was at stake in the culture war between conservative evangelicals and pornography-supporting liberals (*Hustler Magazine, Inc. v. Moral Majority, Inc.* (9th Cir. 1986)). Teaching need not be so ideological as Falwell's use, nor so explicit, to productively integrate copyrighted materials into discussions of history, current events, interpretive theories, or other subjects of instruction.

Sometimes, people believe that fair uses are required to criticize the original, in the sense of saying negative things about it or at least in the sense of analyzing its elements. Criticism is certainly a favored form of fair use. However, copying that doesn't directly criticize the original, such as the use of images in memes, also fits within this model of transformative purpose. *Cariou v. Prince* (2d Cir. 2013), a case about appropriation art, held that fair use need not involve criticism or interpretation of the original, as long as the purpose and possibly the target audience were sufficiently different. The broader lesson of *Cariou* and similar cases suggests that if a particular community, whether that's the "art world" or the teenagers generating new memes, perceives a work as having a new meaning or message compared to the original, fair use doctrine will find transformativeness even if judges themselves aren't quite sure what's going on (Francis 2014: 693; Tushnet 2013).

Copying that speaks about the copier—the self-constituting copying previously discussed—can likewise be transformative. The copier's message may be "This is how to understand me" or "This is how I feel and think, which can't otherwise be put into words"; this is a different message than the original. Likewise, the copying with which this chapter began—copying used to educate students about proper techniques—also has a different instructional purpose than whatever the communicative purpose of the original work was. As Butler explains, "One effective way to teach a craft or skill is to use an existing work as an example of good or bad practice, or as raw material for critical assessment of the work's relative strengths and weaknesses" (2015: 519).

Conclusion: Embracing Transformative Purpose to Defend Education

Although some have criticized the expansive application of the concept of transformativeness, arguing that it's been used in so many ways that it both swallows up fair use and threatens the stability of the overall copyright regime (Ginsburg 2014: 3), I think that transformation in purpose is a valuable and useful concept. Transformation in purpose *or* in content generally involves the addition of labor to create value, whether that labor is in building an interpretive scaffold around a work, changing the content or context of the work in order to send a different message, or putting the work together with numerous other works in order to create a larger meaning out of the juxtaposition. Transformation in purposes allows fair use doctrine to recognize some of the ways in which pure copying can be important to freedom of expression, just as parody and satire are important to freedom of expression.

Recent Georgia State litigation offers a cautionary tale about fair use claims: there, the university conceded that its uses of excerpts in electronic course reserves were not transformative, which weighed heavily against the university's fair use defense (*Cambridge University Press v. Patton* (11th Cir. 2014); Butler 2015: 511). Even though the trial court ultimately found that only a few of the university's unauthorized uses were infringing because the market for licensing many of the copied works didn't exist, the university's case would have been far stronger if the educators involved had spoken of their copying as transformative and free speech supporting, in the way that courts in other situations have now begun to do (Butler 2015: 473). Butler appropriately concludes that the door is still open for "a kind of fair use argument that could afford educators far greater flexibility, predictability, and scope in exercising their fair use rights"—the argument founded in the need to copy to achieve a transformative educational purpose. The court of appeals in the Georgia State case explicitly refused to decide what would happen if educators made a transformativeness argument (Butler 2015: 514). It is time for educators to do so.

References

Balkin, J. (2004). "Digital Speech and Democratic Culture: A Theory of Freedom of Expression for the Information Society." *New York University Law Review*, 79, 1–58.

Biasi, B., & Moser, P. (2016). "Effects of Copyrights on Science: Evidence From the WWII Book Republication Program." Retrieved from http://papers.ssrn.com/sol3/papers.cfm?abstract_id=2542879

Buccafusco, C., & Heald, P. J. (2013). "Do Bad Things Happen When Works Enter the Public Domain? Empirical Tests of Copyright Term Extension." *Berkeley Technology Law Journal*, 28, 1.

Burt, S. (2003). "'September 1, 1939' Revisited: Or, Poetry, Politics, and the Idea of the Public." *American Literary History*, 15(3), 534–535.

Butler, B. (2015). "Transformative Teaching and Educational Fair Use After Georgia State." *Connecticut Law Review*, 48, 473–530.

Emerson, R. W. (1803–1882). *The Complete Works*. 1904. Vol. VIII. Letters and Social Aims. Retrieved from http://www.bartleby.com/90/0806.html

Francis, J. (2014). "On Appropriation: *Cariou v. Prince* and Measuring Contextual Transformation in Fair Use." *Berkeley Tech. Law Journal*, 29, 693.

Garber, M. (2003). *Quotation Marks*. New York: Routledge.

Gillespie, T. L. (2009). "Characterizing Copyright in the Classroom: The Cultural Work of Anti-Piracy Campaigns." *Communication, Culture, and Critique*, 2, 274–318.

Ginsburg, J. C. (2014). "Letter From the US: Exclusive Rights, Exceptions, and Uncertain Compliance With International Norms—Part II (Fair Use)." Columbia Center for Law & Economic Studies, Working Paper No. 503: 3. Retrieved from http://ssrn.com/abstract=2539178

Goldstein, P. (2003). *Copyright's Highway: From Gutenberg to the Celestial Jukebox*. Stanford, CA: Stanford University Press.

Hansen, D. D. (2003). *The Dream: Martin Luther King, Jr., and the Speech That Inspired a Nation*. New York: HarperCollins.

Heald, P. J. (2008). "Property Rights and the Efficient Exploitation of Copyrighted Works: An Empirical Analysis of Public Domain and Copyrighted Fiction Bestsellers." *Minnesota Law Review*, 92(4), 1031–1063.

Heffernan, V. (2008, May 25). "Narrow Minded." *New York Times*. Retrieved from www.nytimes.com/2008/05/25/magazine/25wwln-medium-t.html.

Lange, D. (2003). "Reimagining the Public Domain." *Law & Contemporary Problems*, 66, 463–482.

Lesher, D. (1996, October 25). "GOP Pulls King Segment From TV Ad for Prop. 209." *Los Angeles Times*, A26.

Miller, K. D. (1992). *Voice of Deliverance: The Language of Martin Luther King, Jr. and Its Sources*. Athens: University of Georgia Press.

National Review. (2008, June 11). "Are You Changed?" *National Review*. Retrieved from www.nationalreview.com/article/224740/are-you-changed-interview

Parnell, H. (2006, March 1). "Downloading Empathy to Your iPod." *Washington Post*. Retrieved from www.washingtonpost.com/wp-dyn/content/article/2006/03/01/AR2006030100635_pf.html

Reese, R. A. (2008). "Transformativeness and the Derivative Work Right." *Columbia Journal of Law & Arts*, 31, 494.

Sag, M. (2012). "Predicting Fair Use." *Ohio State Law Journal*, 73, 58.

Steinmetz, K. (2012, September 10). "The Knockoff Economy: How Copying Hurts—and Helps—Fashion." *Time*. Retrieved from http://style.time.com/2012/09/10/the-knockoff-economy-how-copying-hurts-and-helps-fashion/

Tushnet, R. (2004). "Copy This Essay: How Fair Use Doctrine Harms Free Speech and How Copying Serves It." *Yale Law Journal*, 114, 535–546.

Tushnet, R. (2013). "Judges as Bad Reviewers: Fair Use and Epistemological Humility." *Law & Literature*, 25, 20.

Tushnet, R. (2015, March 19). "I'm Not a Regular Republican, I'm a Cool Republican." [Web log comment]. Retrieved from http://tushnet.blogspot.com/2015/03/im-not-regular-republican-im-cool.html

Volokh, E. (2003). "Freedom of Speech and Intellectual Property: Some Thoughts After *Eldred, 44 Liquormart*, and *Bartnicki*." *Houston Law Review*, 40(3), 698–748.

Further Reading

Butler, B. (2015). "Transformative Teaching and Educational Fair Use After Georgia State." *Connecticut Law Review*, 48, 473.

Center for Social Media. (2008). "Code of Best Practices in Fair Use for Media Literacy Education." Retrieved from http://cmsimpact.org/code/code-best-practices-fair-use-media-literacy-education/

Reese, R. A. (2008). "Transformativeness and the Derivative Work Right." *Columbia Journal of Law & Arts*, 31, 494.

Tushnet, R. (2004). "Copy This Essay: How Fair Use Doctrine Harms Free Speech and How Copying Serves It." *Yale Law Journal*, 114, 535–546.

3

TEACHING COPYRIGHT AND LEGAL METHODS OUTSIDE THE LAW SCHOOL

Bill D. Herman

Before the mass adoption of the Internet, few undergraduates learned much if anything about copyright. A professor teaching communication law might spend a week or two on intellectual property, including copyright but probably also subjects like trademark and the right of publicity. Library and information science programs have long taught copyright to master's students, but undergraduate degrees in the field were (and still are) rare.[1] Even in graduate schools of law or library and information science, courses generally covered copyright as a technical, isolated subject of interest to specialists. Few courses covered the political context or broader cultural impact of copyright.

Narrow interest on campus mirrored the broader world's unconcern. Congress passed bills extending copyright terms (Copyright Term Extension Act 1998) and creating whole new sets of rules for digital media (Digital Millennium Copyright Act 1998), and few even noticed. Yet the dawn of the new century saw an explosion of news coverage, academic writing, and activism around copyright (Vaidhyanathan 2004). Much of this work advanced the claim that old media interests had hijacked the copyright system to protect outdated business models at the expense of innovation in the digital era. These critics eventually mounted enough political power to put a halt to further expansions of copyright—a remarkable feat (Herman 2012, 2013b).

By 2008, when I joined the Department of Film and Media Studies at Hunter College, City University of New York (CUNY), I was part of a wave of copyright scholars who had either entered the academy or had already been there and found their way to the subject. I knew of courses taught by communication studies faculty who were trailblazers in this area—in particular, Kembrew McLeod and Siva Vaidhyanathan. Still, I was pleasantly surprised when the department encouraged me to create and teach my own version of a class focused on copyright. Thus, I created Media 365: Digital Copyright, teaching it most semesters from Fall 2009 to Spring 2015.

I looked forward to fusing legal principles and cultural interrogation with a new generation of learners. This kind of course fits into a niche that is increasingly important in communication departments of all kinds—one that connects law and policy, political process (and its failures), media business models, and the evolution of media technology.

As I developed and taught the course, though, I found myself focusing a great deal on legal process, the role of the courts in government, and the tools of the legal trade. I have long found the law to be fascinating, and its central role in society is hard to argue. Thus, I sought to infect my students with my enthusiasm for knowing the law, as well as giving them enough understanding of the system of laws, policies, and regulations that they would develop a better understanding of legal issues and systems much more broadly. This model is even portable to other areas of law—and therefore a potential curricular model that could be applied in many academic departments.

In this chapter, I explore some of the goals, contents, and strategies of teaching copyright, especially for undergraduates who are not in pre-law. Several other faculty, especially in communication and media studies, have also taught such a course. I thus sought out the syllabi and a selection of other teaching materials such as essay prompts. Of the faculty whom I could identify as having taught such a class, each generously agreed to share the latest syllabus. They are Peter Decherney (University of Pennsylvania, Departments of Cinema Studies and English), Tarleton Gillespie (Microsoft Research, New England; Cornell University, Departments of Communication and Information Science), Kembrew McLeod (University of Iowa, Department of Communication Studies), John Simson (American University, Department of Management), Aram Sinnreich (then at Rutgers University, School of Communication and Information; now at American University, School of Communication), Siva Vaidhyanathan (University of Virginia, Department of Media Studies), and Shawn VanCour (New York University, Department of Media, Culture, and Communication). Renee Hobbs (University of Rhode Island, Department of Communication Studies) also shared an example of a massive open online course (MOOC) she has co-taught with Kristin Hokanson. Casey Rae (SiriusXM; Georgetown University, Communication, Culture, and Technology program) was also good enough to share the syllabus from a graduate course that deals substantially but not so exclusively with copyright. Virginia Kuhn (University of Southern California, School of Cinematic Arts) also wrote back to confirm that copyright is a major part (about 30%, she estimates) of all of her courses but not any single course.

In this chapter, I attempt to provide reflective transparency about how and why I teach copyright outside the law school. While I know and speak the most about my own goals and strategies, I also discuss the other courses, especially other undergraduate courses in communication departments. My course is relatively unique in its special emphasis on legal methods; I warn students that, over the semester, I try to cram an abbreviated version of the first year of law school into the margins of the class. In part, this is a reflection of my interest in the law and legal methods. It is also, though, a reflection of the value of such legal education as part of the undergraduate experience. Additionally, faculty make curricular choices in light of the needs of the students they serve. My academic peers who are teaching copyright outside the law school teach student populations that are substantially different from Hunter's student body, which may contribute to the differences between my class and the other courses. I also have my own points of view about and areas of research into copyright; these also shaped my pedagogical choices. These add up to fairly different courses, with mine including a relatively larger emphasis on the fundamentals of legal methods and the law per se—and thereby less on the interdisciplinary questions raised by the copyright debate.

In the following pages, I begin by explaining the context in terms of the student population and available resources. Next, I discuss the course's target learning outcomes, and I identify the similarities and differences versus other instructors' goals. Then, I give an overview of the subjects covered in the course and the assigned readings. After that, I discuss the course's major writing assignment and the exams. I conclude with a brief argument that more schools should offer a course like this—whether a course on copyright specifically or a course that adopts this deep focus on legal methods but attached to another area of law.

Context: Student Population and Campus Resources

My strategies for teaching the course reflect the context at Hunter, including a diverse student population and limited support resources for students. Understanding this context may prove helpful to other faculty who teach or hope to teach undergraduate versions of a similar course, though this section may prove somewhat less helpful to other readers—for instance, those who hope to create an online general education class.

As one of the selective four-year colleges in CUNY, Hunter features one of the most diverse—and dogged—student bodies in the country. "CUNY sees itself as one of the only affordable pathways to opportunity for the city's underprivileged. Last fall, minority students made up around 75 percent of the student body. Over half were Pell Grant recipients, and about a third came from households making less than $20,000" (Wexler 2016). Students are also especially likely to have immigrated to the United States—a quarter of incoming students were born abroad in 2014—or to be the children of immigrants. This comes with incredible linguistic diversity. In 2014, 33% of incoming freshmen had a native language other than English, and 67% spoke a language other than English at home ("Factbook 2014" n.d.: Table 10).[2] Among the entire student body in 2014, students spoke 107 languages and came from 155 different countries ("Factbook 2014" n.d.: Table 14).

The financial situation in many students' households is a source of particular concern and distraction. At Hunter, 78% of students receive need-based financial aid ("CUNY—Hunter College: Best College" 2015). This share is substantially higher than that at all of the other campuses where the other courses discussed here have been taught: American (54%), Cornell (47%), Georgetown (38%), Iowa (46%), New York University (53%), Penn (48%), Rutgers (55%), Southern California (39%), and Virginia (33%) ("National University Rankings" n.d.). Many college students, even at private schools, work to help pay for their own education or living expenses. Informal observation suggests that not only do nearly all Hunter students work, many do so in order to make meaningful contributions to family budgets—with some even being the primary breadwinners.

I loved my time teaching Hunter students, perhaps especially because I was also a first-generation college student and Pell Grant recipient. They are extremely intelligent, have tremendous grit (Stoltz 2015), and are impressively self-directed. Most of the students continue to study and succeed despite one or more major obstacles that most college students at selective colleges do not face. When it comes time to do something as difficult as researching and writing about complex legal questions, however, most have not been ideally prepared. Many are also short on sleep and mental bandwidth as they struggle to stay afloat.

Hunter itself also faces a very challenging funding environment. Across the country, states have de-invested in higher education, contributing to inequality via the very institutions that are supposed to ameliorate it (Mettler 2014; Mortenson 2012). Not only is CUNY part of this trend, political support for the school is so thin in Albany, the state capitol, that Governor Andrew Cuomo's latest budget initially proposed a $485 million cut in state funding for the school (Yee 2016). This was eventually defeated, but not having their budget slashed is a thin victory for a university system that is already struggling with subpar infrastructure, salaries (Skelding 2016), and student services.

The college also provides thin support for students seeking writing help. Students have received widely varying amounts of training in how to conduct high-level research and write a sophisticated research paper. They also have little time to get writing help outside the classroom. Yet those who pursue such help are regularly disappointed. The writing center is staffed by upper-class undergraduates, and yet it is still apparently understaffed; several of my students reported having trouble getting substantial help that is of the duration and regularity required to make real progress. This is not to impugn the tutors or the center but to identify that the school simply does not seem to have the capacity to give the quality or quantity of writing support that would be ideal for this specific student population. In sharp contrast, at Fordham, tutors are graduate students or degree-holding professionals (the latter having graduate degrees and/or substantial relevant experience), with a majority of those on the main campus being PhD students in the humanities ("Rose Hill Tutors" n.d.). Further, students can use up to 90 minutes of the service, per week, during the semester ("Writing Center: About Us" n.d.). Compared to Hunter, Fordham has much more help available, even as a much smaller share of the Fordham student body desperately needs it.

Thankfully for Hunter and its students, the deficit in resources is not nearly as true for research assistance. The library is reasonably well staffed, even compared to the library staff at some better funded schools.[3] Yet this was of less use for teaching the course than writing support would have been, as the research requirements were so unique to the course that I devoted substantial class time to teaching these techniques and working with students directly when they had questions.

Target Learning Outcomes for My Copyright Course

My target learning outcomes are substantially different from other versions of the course, especially those taught by other communication faculty in the undergraduate curriculum. My version of the class focuses relatively more on black letter law (legal questions and methods that determine the outcomes of cases), whereas the other undergraduate communication courses tend to spend more time on other topics that are more of a piece with the rest of a liberal arts curriculum. This is partly a reflection of my students' more substantial need for foundational instruction on the nature of the legal system—few of them have lawyers in the family, for instance—but it also reflects my desire to use the course as a vehicle for introducing the fundamentals of the legal system more broadly.

First I discuss my teaching goals; then I describe the other courses' learning outcomes. Finally, I say a bit about why I chose my outcomes, including why I focused more on strictly legal questions and less on the broader array of topics that are common in other courses.

As I taught it, Digital Copyright advances a very ambitious set of target learning outcomes. In particular, by the end of the semester, students are expected to be able to:

1. Define copyright, including how copyright differs from other areas of law such as trademark, patent, and publicity rights.
2. Identify the exclusive rights of copyright holders and the most important categorical exceptions to and limitations on those rights.
3. Describe the four factors of fair use,[4] as well as how the courts interpret those factors.

4. Explain the major tenets of copyright that are specific to digital media, including especially Title I and Title II of the Digital Millennium Copyright Act and related case law.
5. Apply the major tenets of copyright and its exceptions/limitations to a variety of potential scenarios.
6. Describe the policy conflicts over copyright in the contemporary era and how these affect various people and policy goals.
7. Explain the key tenets of the U.S. legal system and how it fits into the broader system of government.
8. Conduct basic legal research.
9. Use legal research and legal reasoning to write about copyright law.

This is an exceptionally ambitious set of objectives for a one-semester course. Objectives one through six, the topic-specific subject matter objectives, would themselves present plenty to cover in one semester. These outcomes are professionally relevant to the majority of the course's students who intend to work in the media industry. As media professionals, they will likely help create works that are worth protecting and also take part in decisions about if, when, and how other creators' content can be used. Students typically enter the course expecting to focus largely on such subject matter mastery. Along the way, though, they also receive a sliver of a legal education, providing benefits I describe further later in the chapter.

Objective seven is also a subject matter objective, but it is a foundational understanding that makes it possible to learn and understand topics of the course per se—something akin to a refresher on trigonometry at the beginning of Calculus I. As I taught the class in successive semesters, I began to see how a refresher on civics needed to be included not only toward the beginning of the course, but also stitched into other discussions over the first half of the semester. Students generally had a limited understanding of the role and workings of the courts, let alone in relation to the other branches of government—such as the difference between legal decisions (which courts make) and policy decisions (which, in principle at least, they leave to the other branches).

Objectives eight and nine are listed last for reasons of logic (they build on the earlier steps), not diminished emphasis. Throughout the semester but especially after the midterm, the class is in large part a streamlined version of a course on legal research and writing. Students must learn how to conduct basic case law research, grounded (via objective seven) in an understanding of the basics of the legal system. They then have to apply this research in constructing a coherent and well evidenced legal argument in the form of an eight- to ten-page term paper, which identifies a copyright dispute and argues for one side (later in the chapter). Students also have to be able to apply their subject knowledge to write cogent arguments about copyright law during examinations.

Students thus gain much more from the class than an understanding of the basics of copyright and its role in the digital political economy. Rather, it forces students to learn a new way of thinking, researching, and writing, all built on vocabulary and rules that are mostly foreign to them. Some understanding of legal research and the legal system is broadly helpful in work and in life, even for those who will never practice law. (Understanding the differences between civil and criminal law, for instance, is quite valuable and yet in surprisingly short supply. This is true for virtually all of the legal foundations required to properly understand a copyright case.) More importantly, though, it builds students' skills and confidence in a world where work is increasingly specialized and technical, and where new and longtime employees alike are expected to learn new universes of concepts, vocabulary, and systems, with rapid turnaround times and minimal supervision. Thus, the most important learning outcomes for the class are probably not students' knowledge of the intricacies of copyright but an expanded ability to come in with no real knowledge of a specialized area and rapidly get up to their elbows in the relevant jargon and research techniques.

The class also connects a broader array of social, political, and economic issues that copyright impacts or helps illustrate. This is best exemplified by learning outcome number six, covering "the policy conflicts over copyright in the contemporary era and how these affect various people and policy goals." This is the area that makes copyright interesting today, where it was boring in 1980. These include why people create and what ratio of content is created for the types of incentives that copyright rewards; the politics of copyright in historical and forward-looking terms, including the various communication strategies of various policy actors; and how copyright shapes and is shaped by various media business models. Such topics help students to see the relationships between politics and political interests, technological developments, industry trends and strategies, and political communication. This helps a graduate to be better prepared to start a new business or organization, contribute vision and leadership to an existing one, and even be a better citizen.

On the syllabus as actually delivered, I never defined my learning outcomes explicitly, even though I was reasonably clear if implicit about these goals in class. Thankfully, Hunter and other colleges have begun nudging faculty toward such clarity, even if it has also contributed to syllabi becoming ever longer. Doing so helps students—and even instructors—to better understand how everything fits together and why each part of the class belongs, from each lecture or reading to each graded component. Faculty should thus take these seriously and include them in their syllabi. The outcomes described here represent what I would include in future versions of the class.

Learning Outcomes in Other Copyright Courses

In reviewing syllabi and course materials for other courses, I noticed that no other courses have the legal methods goals that are present in my course, even though I am sure these are implicitly covered. The other undergraduate courses offered in communication departments (as well as Decherney's graduate course) focus more on critical, political, or historical coverage, whereas my course is closer to (if not entirely) an undergraduate version of a copyright class one might find in a law school. For instance, in Aram Sinnreich's (2014: 1) syllabus for Copyright, Media and Culture, taught at Rutgers University's School of Communication and Information, he states:

> By the end of the course, students will be able:
>
> - To understand the origins and function of intellectual property law
> - To recognize the role of copyright in regulating culture and commerce
> - To participate in the growing public debate over the "copyfight" and the appropriate limits of intellectual property law
> - To strategically use existing copyright law for business and creative purposes

Similarly, Kembrew McLeod's (2014: 1) course Copyright Controversies, taught at the University of Iowa's Department of Communication Studies, promises to teach students:

> How digital technologies have dramatically changed media and popular culture landscapes; the advent of relatively cheap editing programs that allow anyone to collage media

> on their home computers and enable people to become cultural producers; technologies that allow more people to break the law in the eyes of copyright industries; historical look at collage practices, from pre-digital era to present; ethical and legal questions surrounding the use and re-use of copyrighted materials; the notion of free speech in a media age.

This emphasis on broader social, economic, technical, and political forces runs across all of the other for-credit communication studies classes as well. Gillespie (2009: 1) promises to teach about "recent legal battles in the context of the historical and ideological relationships between authorship, technology, commerce, law, and culture." Vaidhyanathan (2016) similarly covers topics including but not limited to "[t]he social and cultural roles that copyright plays in American and global culture. The role that copyright plays within the larger field of intellectual property. The ethical dimensions of copyright infringement and copyright enforcement. The global political economy of copyright, and how it affects global flows of music, images, video, and software." VanCour (2013: 1) has a similar array of learning outcomes, and in particular he seems to zoom in on "the history and goals of copyright and intellectual property regulations in the U.S. and their impact on the creation, distribution, and consumption of media and related cultural products at home and abroad."

These courses all fulfill very valuable and important roles in the communication curriculum. As with the similar (if diminished) portion of this focus my class, they help students prepare to be visionary leaders in the media industry of the future, as well as to be more informed citizens and consumers of media. These are of a piece with the broader liberal arts mission of these departments. Yet these courses all, to at least some extent, also help students to understand the actual legal machinations that shape copyright case law. It is simply that they emphasize the former, and their learning outcomes illustrate this.

The courses outside the undergraduate communication curriculum are, unsurprisingly, somewhat different in their focus, goals, and pedagogy. In Peter Decherney's (2015) graduate course at the University of Pennylvania's Department of English, the assigned readings imply an especially strong emphasis on history, as well as substantial coverage of political contest over copyright, the effects on industry, the intersection with technology, and the fundamentals of fair use. This reflects Decherney's own research interests in cinema history and his own copyright advocacy—notably, his regular efforts before the U.S. Copyright Office that have led to the exemptions to the Digital Millennium Copyright Act's anticircumvention provisions that allow film professors and educators broader rights to use film excerpts for learning purposes (Sender & Decherney 2007).

Casey Rae's (2015) course, part of Georgetown's Master of Arts Program in Communication, Culture, and Technology, is much more future-focused. While it is largely about copyright, it also tackles questions such as:

> What's the future for media access and discovery in an era of seemingly infinite access? How will the current copyright regime handle an influx of new creators, and what business models can support this brave new world of always-on connectivity and media saturation? How might practitioners navigate a shifting landscape for creativity and commerce while pushing forward with new innovations and modes of expression? Who gets to put a price point on access to culture in the 21st century and beyond?

Covering all of what Decherney and Rae cover and doing it well would be all but impossible in an undergraduate course, but in this case, each has the luxury of working with top graduate students. Moreover, the purpose of such graduate courses is much less the mere transmission of knowledge and more a dialectic conversation, facilitated by an expert. Decherney and Rae will readily admit that they are not sure how copyright will evolve, how this will affect existing and future industries, and so on. By showing students how the sausage is made, though, they prepare students to have those conversations and generate new insights.

Some faculty offer an even more specialized focus on copyright. In Music Publishing and Copyright, taught in the Department of Management at American University's Kogod School of Business, John Simson (2016) offers a strategic and laser-focused approach to the subject. It is the most intensely specialized of any of the credit-bearing courses discussed here, mostly zooming in on copyright as applied in music publishing. For instance, the course covers topics such as the business side of the craft of songwriting and coauthorship (wk. 2, p. 2), when and how a songwriter might transmit their rights (wk. 3, p. 2), licensing for TV and movies (wks. 10–11, p. 4), and "special publishing issues related to compositions written by recording artists" (wk. 5, p. 3). It is still somewhat interdisciplinary, though; along the way, students "explore several major changes that have occurred as the 'traditional music industry' has been transformed by digital technology and changing business models" as well as "who the major players are in the music publishing industry" (p. 1). The course also examines "the tension created by technologies that have blurred distinctions that have long existed in music publishing and how those conflicts are likely to be resolved" (p. 1). Simson thus promises to teach historical, political, strategic, and forward-looking perspectives on changes in the industry. Still, the course is most obviously useful for either aspiring musicians or for those who seek to work in management roles in the music industry. This is exceptionally specialized, but it surely makes it a real gem for the targeted audience. I am also unsurprised that there is sufficient demand for it. My own class regularly includes at least a half dozen musicians per thirty-two-student section, and many of the rest were at least considering working in the music industry—this despite the course not being advertised as (or being) music specific and despite no outreach to the Music Department.

The other class, an online open course taught by Professor Renee Hobbs and Technology Integration Coach Kristin Hokanson of the University of Rhode Island, is "Copyright Clarity." The class is designed for educators:

> In this course, you will learn about the most common myths and misinformation related to copyright and fair use. You'll learn how copyright law protects both the rights of authors and audiences and about three prevailing views of copyright in relation to digital media and digital learning. You will gain practice in conducting a situational analysis to determine when you need to ask permission, buy a license, claim fair use, or use alternative licensing schemes like Creative Commons. By gaining copyright clarity, you will become an advocate to help others appreciate how fair use supports digital learning and understand the scope of our rights and responsibilities under the law.
>
> (Hobbs & Hokanson 2014: para. 1)

Compared to even Simson's class and my own, this is exceptionally functional, targeted squarely at helping educators make decisions about the appropriate uses of copyrighted material. (The curriculum is almost as functional, though they do save the sixth and final module for discussing "The Future of Copyright.") For those teaching such a course—a useful overview of copyright, especially one intended for users of copyrighted works who may underestimate their rights under the law—these learning outcomes present a very useful starting point.

Explaining Differences in Learning Outcomes

Each of these courses contains a blend of straightforward coverage of the law on one hand and of a broader array of topics on the other, with sharply varying ratios between the two. These other topics especially include historical developments, policy debates over the direction of copyright, effects on industry and various industries' agendas, and the intersection between copyright law and media technologies. I started researching copyright law because I find all of these topics, and the relationships among them, utterly fascinating—a view surely shared, to at least some degree,[5,6] by all of the professors named here. That this animates these courses, then, should be unsurprising. It also presents a fantastic teaching strategy: use these controversies as a way to get student engagement and explain the law along the way. By seeing where and how the law applies, students start from a position of more substantial interest.

My course deviates substantially from the other communication classes, with learning goals that nearly turn the class into a law course per se. Part of this decision was driven by an effort to balance out the department curriculum. The department has a bountiful set of production courses, but a majority of students take more traditional—that is, nonproduction—courses. The vast majority of these are focused on studying, analyzing, and even critically interrogating media content of various kinds. There should be room for several of these classes in any communication major, but realizing that this content rules the major quickly pushed me toward introducing more "hard" skills (Andrews & Higson 2008) and more social science into my courses, across the board.

There are legitimate reasons for pushing back against the expanding professional or even occupational emphasis in higher education overall. Yet going back to at least the founding of land grant institutions in the late 19th century, there has long been an emphasis on colleges teaching both "the liberal and the practical" (Grubb & Lazerson 2005: 3). In a department where the curriculum is more balanced, this course can and perhaps should be more balanced between those two poles. In a department that is almost entirely practical and/or social scientific in focus, a more critical or historical focus may be warranted. In Film and Media Studies at Hunter, however, students who do not choose production tracks leave with limited direct training for work in the media business—and, because of their economic backgrounds in particular, are unlikely to have the personal connections that can help one secure entry-level work in desirable industries with promising career tracks. By focusing more on developing an understanding of an area of the law of substantial use to media professionals, the class seeks to give them at least one more bit of preparation for media careers. Further, the demand that they quickly learn and competently use a highly specialized language, which is mostly new to them, also teaches what is considered a valuable skill in most professions.

The focus on legal methods more generally, though, is also an example of the type of educational outcome that is commendable even under the paradigm that guides a more classical education. First, many of the students come with a limited understanding of even the basics of the policymaking and legal process. (One especially bright and seemingly well prepared student missed an exam question because he believed U.S. senators are appointed.) Thus, Digital Copyright students become more informed citizens and more capable future leaders. Second, legal research and writing is just plain hard, and this makes such a focus a good tool for stretching students' capacity to do difficult intellectual work of any kind. For example, despite my undergraduate degree in philosophy, I cannot remember any of Heidegger, but I remember that it was really difficult; studying the works of such thinkers definitely expanded my ability to read, think, write, and speak coherently about difficult topics. Similarly, years after graduating, few of my students will be able to recite the reasoning of the so-called Betamax decision

(*Sony Corp. of America v. Universal City Studios, Inc.* 1984), but the ideal is that they walk away as better thinkers, readers, and writers.

Introducing Fundamentals of Copyright Law

I explore the content arc of the course in this section and the one that follows. Ideally, this chapter persuades those readers who are college faculty to try teaching a copyright-focused course or to advocate for one in their own or in other relevant departments. Alternately, it may convince some readers to offer a class on another legal topic that adopts a similar focus on legal methods. This roadmap will prove especially helpful for them. Yet it is also for anybody interested in integrating copyright or other legal education into any part of any curriculum for adults (or even high school students) outside the law school. It also may help spark further discussion among those already teaching such courses.

The class cleaves neatly in two, and this section discusses the first half, which introduces the fundamentals of copyright and some basics on the legal system overall. While there are meaningful differences between subjects covered here and those covered by the other faculty who have taught similar courses, these are examined only briefly here due to space limitations.

What follows implies that the class proceeds in an exactingly logical order. While this is the course's blueprint, I count on and even encourage students to ask a panoply of questions. Many of these come at the "wrong" time in the semester; my students typically ask about peer-to-peer trading before we have even finished covering what copyright protects. Yet I find this crucial to maintaining engagement in the lectures, and I even reward such behavior by giving quick answers when possible—even if it is just a very short version of a longer explanation that is coming later. On campuses where there is not a culture of students freely asking questions or for instructors who have not had luck fostering such outrageous curiosity, it may be best to structure group discussions or other activities to break up the logical progression of the subject matter. There is a lot to master in a short time, so showing some mercy on the student brain is in order. Also, I believe there are still substantial improvements I could have made in structuring the course and delivering the materials; some of these are hinted at in the "Further Reading" section at the end of the chapter.

The one required text that I used across all semesters is Mary LaFrance's *Copyright Law in a Nutshell* (2011). While it is intended more as a supplementary text to a copyright casebook, nearly every chapter makes sense if read on its own (or at least in sequence), and students consistently report that it is quite accessible. When I started teaching the course, I also assigned a second text that includes more critical coverage of the topic. Over successive semesters, I tried several, such as books by Jessica Litman (2000), Tarleton Gillespie (2007), and William Patry (2011). Students generally appreciated these books but, surprisingly, responded that they wanted to focus more solidly on the more properly legal materials. This led to paring down the other readings to a chapter here and there, focusing more on LaFrance and relevant cases.

The class starts with an overview of copyright (Crews 2012: 1–8) and a discussion of why we have copyright (Yen & Liu 2008: 510–515). Next is an introduction to the legal system (Bureau of International Information Programs 2004), how to read case citations ("Case citation" 2016: § 10, "United States"),[7] and an introduction to the art of reading cases as written by one of the department's adjuncts.[8] These civics and legal readings start what I call the "first year of law school, shoved in along the margins" part of the class. These are the only readings on the subject, but I say more in lectures, spread throughout the semester. Other topics include the difference between criminal and civil cases; the structure of the federal court system and the appeals process; the difference between constitutional, statutory, case, and administrative law; the nature of legal precedent; and the difference between legal and policy decisions. The other communication syllabi mostly lack dedicated space to include these topics; in part, this surely reflects those student populations typically coming to college with more of this knowledge than Hunter students do. Yet even the few Hunter students with parents who are lawyers appreciated this coverage, so other instructors may wish to consider adding a bit more.

Coverage of copyright law per se begins with the question of what can be copyrighted (*Feist Publications, Inc., v. Rural Telephone Service Co.* 1991),[9] ownership and formalities such as registration ("Registering a Copyright with the U.S. Copyright Office" 2016),[10] and the duration of copyright protection (*Eldred v. Ashcroft* 2003). Next I cover the exclusive rights of copyright holders, some of the more salient limitations on those rights, the basic elements of infringement (*Bright Tunes Music v. Harrisongs Music* 1976; Herman 2013a), and civil remedies against infringers (*Sony BMG Music Entm't v. Tenenbaum* 2013). The *Bright Tunes* case presents an especially good opportunity to make light of oneself in class; I like to sing (badly but happily) the original song over top of George Harrison's song to highlight the melodic similarity. One can use audio mixing or sometimes find examples online,[11] but that is far less memorable for the students.

After all of that and a lot of building impatience among the students, I finally get to fair use (*Campbell v. Acuff-Rose Music* 1994; *Harper & Row v. Nation Enterprises* 1985). Parts of this discussion can be very fun. In discussing *Campbell*, I seek six volunteers, then pass out three copies each of the lyrics to Roy Orbison's "Oh, Pretty Woman"[12] and of the parody version by 2 Live Crew, "Pretty Woman." Students then read the song—about one-third per volunteer—to the whole class. After each song, I foster a discussion about the meaning of the lyrics. One of the random lessons students leave with is that the Orbison version's lyrics are creepier than most people realize; in most semesters, a student makes this observation with little or no prompting. This sets up students to recognize the saccharine, overly romantic spin on what is ultimately a rather misogynistic view of gender roles and sexuality. Within that context, the 2 Live Crew version's removal of the sugar coating, combined with the racialized discussion of Black women, presents a substantial contrast. At its best, the class discussion includes students both recognizing the racialized misogyny of the 2 Live Crew version and the racial privilege of the Orbison version's mainstream acceptance. In all discussions, though, students readily see the basis for the court's "parody" conclusion, allowing them to make their own decisions about whether this is warranted in the context of what they already know about fair use. Most semesters, at least some students have concluded that this is not a fair use, making some of the same arguments as the dissent—whether or not this was part of the assigned reading.

It is broadly understood among copyright scholars that, where *Campbell* presents a foundational finding of fair use (Jackson 1995), *Harper & Row* is the model for a case that finds infringement despite at least a colorable fair use claim. To understand *Harper & Row*, students really have to grasp Gerald Ford's place not only in history but also in the pantheon of U.S. presidents. In particular, they need to grasp that Ford's most important action was pardoning Richard Nixon and that Ford is otherwise not a significant figure in U.S. history. (This is less riotous than students reading profane filth out loud, but it can also be pretty funny.) After all, the case centers on the leftist news magazine *The Nation* gaining access to Gerald Ford's as-yet-unpublished autobiography, then scooping the authorized publication with their own detailed recounting of Ford's inner emotional state as he pardoned Nixon—the heart that gave the work its commercial value. Much of the other fun, though, comes from students asking many detailed questions about related hypothetical scenarios. A good discussion or examination question, for instance, asks whether and how the court might have differed if *The Nation*'s article had come out after Ford's book was published.

Next, I include a discussion of the statements of best practices in fair use (Aufderheide & Jaszi 2011), with two examples that are especially relevant to media studies undergraduates ("Documentary Filmmakers' Statement" 2005; Jaszi et al. 2008). This framework presents a fantastic opportunity for group work in which students apply fair use to hypothetical situations and explain their reasoning. For instance, one might create a class handout with three hypothetical examples of using material as part of a documentary—perhaps one each that is clearly fair use, one clearly infringing (e.g., *Elvis Presley Enterprises, Inc., v. Passport Video* 2003), and one in more of a gray area. Groups could then decide their answers for each, designate a member to defend each position (ideally a different member for each case), and present their brief analysis before the whole class.

By this point, students can put it all together to see how a court might rule for a plaintiff or defendant. To illustrate, I developed something I call the "copyright case flowchart." This encourages students to consider copyright cases in a logical order. At each step, there's a specific answer required for the plaintiff's case to proceed, and any answer that takes one off the path means that the defendant wins. (I use a series of PowerPoint Smart Art process charts to illustrate this.) Before giving the copyright flow chart, though, I give an analogy: a lawsuit over getting injured in a car accident. For that, the questions are:

1. Did the cars collide? (Proceed if yes.)
2. Was the plaintiff operating the car? (Proceed if yes.)
3. Was the car crash the plaintiff's fault? (Proceed if yes.)
4. Is there a categorical exemption (e.g., some cities will impose a snowstorm exemption)? (Proceed if no.)
5. Is there substantial injury due to the crash (versus, e.g., a possible nick that cannot be identified in a large set of obviously preexisting dents and scratches)? (Proceed if yes.)
6. Does the defendant have a defense that negates his or her own legal liability (e.g., manufacturer-created mechanical failure)? (Proceed if no.)

This analogy leverages the lived experience of the students; even young adult New Yorkers, many of whom do not drive, understand this much of how civil liability works on the roads. This sets up the copyright case flowchart, which I describe in lecture. It goes as follows:

1. Is the original work copyrighted? (Proceed if yes.)
2. Is the plaintiff the registered copyright holder? (Proceed if yes.)
3. Is the use one of the six exclusive rights in Section 106? (Proceed if yes.)
4. Is the use covered by a statutory exemption (e.g., classroom performance)? (Proceed if no.)
5. Is the use substantial? (Proceed if yes.)
6. Is the use protected by an affirmative defense such as fair use? (Proceed if no.)

In addition to understanding copyright more generally, this helps students understand how the law works more generally—that a plaintiff has the burden of proof and that this means they have to prove several different things in a specific, logical order.

Creativity, Digital Copyright, and Copyfights

This is the point where the class begins to deviate more from black letter law, not only in the interest of helping students contextualize the law but also to encourage them to think about the broader purpose and the conflicting policy goals of copyright. It is also where the "digital" part of Digital Copyright comes in. The first class after the midterm, though, I meet students in a computer lab and show them how to conduct basic case law research on LexisNexis Academic. Since I am a Mac user, it is very straightforward to use QuickTime to record a class presentation, and I record this class and post it online, at Vimeo or YouTube. This allows students to rewatch the lecture at their leisure if they run into any difficulties applying the research techniques as they research their papers. A few students specifically thanked me for this, and surely more watched at least select portions. Most students are seemingly comfortable using these research tools by the end of the lecture, but others apparently follow up by watching the video and filling in the gaps. (View counts jumped quickly, and one semester's lecture (Herman 2013c) is now at fifty-five views, suggesting it has even helped folks outside the course.) Even for the students who are not using the video after class, though, it demonstrates a commitment to guiding students through a new and difficult research domain. It thus provides an example of the kind of extra instructional push that demonstrates a broader "investment in the lives, careers, and development of [one's] students" (Bain 2004: 148) that is such a foundational element of successful college teaching. In the classes from this point until the paper is due, I also regularly check in at the start of class to see where students are on their papers, what else needs an explanation, and what if anything needs to be revisited; if one student is brave enough to ask such a question, several more are also confused and thus appreciate the answer.

I then discuss why people create the kinds of works that are subject to copyright protection. While my assigned reading is a very accessible section from James Boyle's (2008: 42–82) *The Public Domain*, this is decidedly inspired by Yochai Benkler's (2006) work on different information production strategies (pp. 41–48). Virtually all the students are themselves creators of substantial creative work, even if we only include their photography; most of this is for nonmonetary rewards such as fun and social bonding, though a few are doing work that they hope will someday be marketable. I ask them to talk about their incentives and then use this to illustrate the limitations—and possible disadvantages—of incentives targeted at protecting works for sale.

Next, I explore secondary liability. I start this with the broader sense of the concept in the context of noncopyright examples—a parent's liability when a child breaks a figurine in a store, an employer's responsibility when a rogue employee defrauds customers, and so on. I then discuss the standards for contributory infringement and vicarious liability, though largely as a setup to discussing secondary liability as applied to the providers of potentially infringing technologies (*MGM Studios, Inc. v. Grokster, Ltd.* 2005; *Sony Corp. of America v. Universal City Studios, Inc.* 1984). I then provide a somewhat detailed explanation of Title II of the Digital Millennium Copyright Act (17 U.S.C. § 512), focusing on the notice-and-takedown process with YouTube as an illustration rather than a reading of the statute (which I do not recommend for any human) or related case law. While not the subject of assigned readings, I include an explanation of the political history of this part of the law (Herman 2013b: 47–52) to help students understand the policy goals of the statute.

I then cover digital rights management (DRM) technology and its regulation under Title I of the DMCA (17 U.S.C. §§ 1201–1205). This topic can be difficult to explain, but I include it because I believe it to be one of the core parts of the copyright debate—in addition to the debates over the length and extension of copyright terms, the line between infringement and fair use, and the notice-and-takedown regime for allegedly infringing content online. The statute bans the circumvention of most DRM without the permission of the copyright holder, even when the use would otherwise be permitted—such as a fair use. This is a substantial threat to communities of users who rely on exemptions and limitations for their work (Herman & Gandy 2006; Sender & Decherney 2007). This subject also happens to be a major part of my research to date, letting me bring in a more extensive discussion of the politics behind copyright law. In addition to the relevant sections of LaFrance (2011 §§ 12.3–12.5), I assign a bit more from Boyle (2008: 83–89), as well as bits by Gillespie (2007: 50–64), Patry (2011: 231–244), and Yen and Liu (2008: 510–515). Each of these is a particularly eloquent and insightful contribution to the discussion over whether and how DRM technologies should be protected by copyright. In class, so that students can understand the technical limitations of encryption-based DRM and the motivation for such regulation, I perform[13] the introduction and first section of Cory Doctorow's (2004) anti-DRM presentation given to Microsoft, in which he describes cryptography, why the application of encryption to DRM creates inherent vulnerabilities, and why this perpetually fails to stop circumvention. We also discuss what I consider the two most significant cases in this area (*Chamberlain Group v. Skylink Technologies* 2004; *Universal City Studios v. Reimerdes* 2000), trying to identify the slim space between lawful and unlawful circumvention of encryption.

I conclude with a discussion of the debate over the Stop Online Piracy Act (Stop Online Piracy Act 2011), as well as the political mobilization around the bill (Herman 2013b: 180–205). While the class has touched upon politics lightly at first and more substantially after the midterm, this is the first part of the class that is primarily about the politics of copyright. This is the culmination of the shift that happens in the second half of the semester, when the course moves decidedly out of the focus on canonic case law and into the territory covered more thoroughly by the other communication faculty previously discussed—the intersection of law, politics, technology, and industries.

I assign students to reading a good bit of case law, focusing primarily on the more canonic cases. Other faculty tend to assign fewer case readings, and those that are assigned tend to be more controversial and current rulings. In my review of syllabi, I found that other than my course, Sinnreich (2014) seems to be the other instructor who assigns a lot of cases. (That class actually covers more cases, but these are explicitly described as "debates," and the selection is focused more on contests of ideas about what copyright is for, such as the case between Princeton professor Ed Felten and the recording industry (*Felten v. Recording Industry* 2001)). Nobody else seems to assign a detailed reading of *Campbell v. Acuff-Rose* (1994), let alone something as foundational but boring as *Feist v. Rural* (1991). The other communication courses are much heavier on secondary readings, including many of the professors included in this chapter assigning one another's writings. All of these courses look extremely interesting, but I believe my strategy also has merit, and I believe it is a particularly good fit for the students and the curricular context at Hunter. Reading case law advances all of the learning goals set out here: challenging students to absorb this new and difficult language in its raw form, reinforcing the importance of broader legal principles to understanding specific outcomes, and even showing them especially good models of careful research and well written arguments.

Assignments and Exams

The keystone of the course is the term paper, which is basically a short (about ten-page) legal brief. The overview states:

> Choose a potential or actual (in-progress) legal dispute in which the core question is whether the use of a copyrighted work is a fair use. You may not choose a case that has already been decided in court, unless you are opposing the published opinion. You are

also not to choose a case that is "too easy," such that any sensible application of copyright law would make the outcome a foregone conclusion. Once you have chosen a topic and had it approved by Professor Herman, write a legal analysis in which you choose a side—either infringement or fair use—and argue for your position. If you don't have any specific topics in mind, consider picking a "reuse artifact," or an online work that makes creative use of a major media property.

I illustrate what such an artifact might look like by giving an example in class, such as my favorite episode of Bad Lip Reading (2013), which is a web series that creates humor by adding deliberately mistaken audio dubbing to change the words being "spoken" by people on screen. This is intended to be and is embraced as a paper that is a fun and interesting application of materials that could otherwise be rather dull. In addition to Bad Lip Reading, students have imagined a broad range of hypothetical copyright cases. One student wrote about a hypothetical suit resulting from the web series "Honest Trailers," which uses film footage to make humorous criticism of movies. Another argued for an outcome should the creators of the podcast "Serial" sue over a parody version. Other students wrote about actual cases that settled out of court. One involved a graphic designer suing Target over a dog-themed design on a T-shirt. Another was between a photographer and a painter who took obvious inspiration from these photos. Almost every paper has involved a fun, interesting set of events around which to build a paper, thus better holding the interest of both students and their professor as grader. One paper was even prophetic; the student[14] wrote a model paper arguing against the district court decision in *Cariou v. Prince* (2011), and the decision was actually overturned by the Second Circuit the following year (*Cariou v. Prince* 2013).

In developing their work, students must apply any relevant cases assigned during the semester and find at least five additional relevant cases to cite. They also need to use at least five print news sources in their work. I suggest that, after a brief introduction of the facts, they simply organize the rest of their paper (save for a conclusion) around the four fair use factors, citing relevant cases for each and then applying the case law to the subject of their paper. In the weeks before the final paper is due, I require a preliminary bibliography and then a detailed outline. This forces them to think about this big project as proceeding in steps, and it forces them to do the steps with a reasonable amount of time budgeted for each. It also gives me at least some capacity to intervene when a student is really struggling but does not proactively seek help.

In the weeks that students are researching and writing, I start every class with a discussion of how the paper is proceeding. I let students ask questions, and as soon as anyone gives me even the slightest direction for explaining what they are struggling with, I load up LexisNexis Academic or a new Word document or an example paper, and I show the students what comes next or how to solve their problems. If nobody gives me a specific question, I will start asking whether anybody wants me to re-explain something specific, such as (the week before the bibliography is due) how to look up cases. The emphasis is on reassuring students that they can do this, that I'm excitedly insistent on helping them get there, and that each of the steps that leads to a good term paper can be learned, repeated, and mastered.

I tell students, at the start of the semester, that this will probably be one of the very hardest assignments they complete at Hunter but that they can definitely do it. (Both parts of this are important.) At the beginning of the semester they doubt the difficulty, by midproject some doubt its possibility, but by the time the papers are turned in, they almost all agree on both counts. Anonymous written comments included, for instance, "I was pleasantly surprised at how much fun I had writing the term paper" (Spring 2015) and that the class "improved my writing" (Fall 2014).

In my review of course syllabi, I found few faculty who ask students to engage in this kind of legal research and writing. Different types of writing assignments are often assigned to students that require them to defend a claim or position. For instance, Vaidhyanathan assigns five 1,000-word essays, asking students to agree or disagree with statements or to answer questions such as:

- In the digital age we no longer need copyright. Copyright is merely an instrument of censorship. We should just do away with the whole system and let everything flow freely.
- Does GoldieBlox have a fair use right to use a version of the Beastie Boys' song "Girls" in a video advertisement for its toy systems?
- What is the biggest problem with music copyright, and what should we do to correct it?

The GoldieBlox question is very similar to a midterm question I used, but the other two are far more sweeping than my paper or anything I ask in exam questions. I believe Hunter students could also answer these questions, but my course focuses more on the law and less on the broader policy questions. Simson's class has weekly written assignments, each of which is more like a "think piece" than a full paper, but he invites students "who are particularly interested in a special topic and wish to write a paper of 10–12 pages in length" to do so as a substitute for the final exam.

Exams in my class are also quite challenging. This is even though they are open book, open note, and open computer/phone/tablet/e-reader; I want students to be able to find and apply relevant legal information, not just ask them about the (much more limited) amount I could expect them to memorize. I tell them not to use the Internet during exams, on the honor system, but I warn them (and honestly believe) that, if they are looking up information on the Internet during the exam, they are wasting their time. The best sources for information are the assigned readings, especially if they start with LaFrance (2011).

The exams are so demanding because they depend on students getting quickly up to speed on the basics of legal reasoning, plus the basics of copyright law, then being able to apply it all in context. For instance, I usually have an essay question asking students to choose a side in an actual or hypothetical fair use case I have not taught; they must develop a complete argument applying each of the four factors. One such example shows the images from a photographer's complaint against a painter whose works are clearly at least inspired by the photos (*Greenfield v. Pankey*, 2013).

Multiple-choice questions also require students to apply rather than merely to regurgitate the course knowledge. For example:

> Imagine that *The New York Times* finds out that a small news website has been taking the facts (and just the facts) out of their stories, writing news stories based on these facts, and publishing those stories that do not copy the *Times'* writing. Which case would be most relevant in deciding if this is infringing?
>
> A. *Campbell v. Acuff-Rose*
> B. *Feist v. Rural*
> C. *Harper & Row v. The Nation*
> D. *Eldred v. Ashcroft*

To get this right, students need to be able to see that the question is about whether copyright protects facts—and to know enough about each of the four cases (or at least the correct answer—*Feist*) to know which one to use here. Even the format of the question highlights what is often the first problem of legal research and writing: of the potentially relevant cases, which is the most applicable and thus the best starting point?

As with the term paper, the goal is to challenge students to learn more material and more difficult material than they thought possible. The midterm is usually not a very happy experience for the students. But after I promise to curve as needed at semester's end, I take a whole 75-minute class (or half of a once-a-week meeting) to go over the answers and review the fundamentals and admonish them to work extra hard on the term paper, most students lean into the challenge and redouble their efforts for the rest of the semester. The final exam is usually much easier for them, in part because it again asks them to show their (now rather solid) mastery of fair use and a few other first-half topics. It is also easier for them, though, because it gives them more opportunities to share opinions on the controversies covered in the second half of the class. This is the same learning mode they've mostly mastered, and it shows in their answers.

Student satisfaction with the exams and the course overall really shows in the course evaluations, with commenters generally identifying exams as tough but fair, such as "The midterm was hard but justified" (Fall 2014). Whatever role the exams play in motivating them to keep up with the materials, students clearly believe they have learned a great deal. One writes, "I found myself learning much more than I expected" (Spring 2015). Another says, "I learned a lot about a subject that was more complicated than I thought" (Fall 2014). A third writes, "At first it was overwhelming and I was worried about the exam and the content. But by midterm I was relieved and then, as soon as we started fair use and reading the cases, it got SUPERB [*sic*] AMAZING" (Spring 2015). For the two most recent semesters (Fall 2014 and Spring 2015), the overall course instructor evaluation was 6.7 out of 7. Clearly, this course design works well for the student population.

Why Undergraduate Copyright Classes—and Other Law Classes—Belong on More Campuses

A class devoted to the detailed examination of a single area of law can be an incredibly valuable part of the upper-division curriculum at any four-year college campus. Setting aside the topic of the course, the class represents an important contribution for the broader mission that colleges serve. It teaches students a much more nuanced understanding of the legal system, including an in-depth understanding of the interplay among the different branches of government. Especially if the class includes a legal research paper, this forces students to conduct sophisticated research. For most college populations—those at the vast majority of the nation's 5,300 colleges—such work is a lot to ask for, presenting quite the "stretch" goal (Duhigg 2016: 124–132). Few of them will become lawyers, and most will not have much use for detailed application of legal methods, but virtually all will need the skill of learning and applying arcane systems of knowledge at a high level in a short period of time.

More faculty and students should have such an experience. Even instructors whose expertise has not already led them into legal research can succeed with such a class, as demonstrated at NYU by Shaun VanCour—though in that case, a focus more on secondary materials and less on case law may be both necessary and appropriate.

Among legal topics to consider for adding to a curriculum, copyright is both a highly practical subject and one that is especially interesting to students. It is also a great subject for an introduction to the law. Relative to most other legal topics, its principles are easier to grasp[15] and more fun to argue about. It is also one of the few areas of law that has an identifiable impact on ordinary people's lives and that is also the subject of federal but not state or local law, making the research materials easy to find and much more straightforward to assemble. Copyright thus provides a fantastic candidate for conveying both the subject matter and the related legal methods, providing the right level of difficulty to stretch students and force them to learn a new and different mode of thought. I urge faculty and administrators at a wide range of schools to consider adopting it.

Notes

1 The searchable database of ALA-accredited programs (American Library Association 2017) lists just sixteen undergraduate programs today, after decades of overall expansion in major offerings.

2 All percentages for student populations are recalculated relative to the number of students from whom data were successfully collected, since (for all items) the data is missing for a third or more of students.

3 Tony Doyle, now a tenured associate professor, proved especially helpful. There was also the fortuitous coincidence that he is also interested in copyright law.

4 These are set out in 17 U.S.C. § 107, which reads in part:

> In determining whether the use made of a work in any particular case is a fair use the factors to be considered shall include—
> (1) the purpose and character of the use, including whether such use is of a commercial nature or is for nonprofit educational purposes;
> (2) the nature of the copyrighted work;
> (3) the amount and substantiality of the portion used in relation to the copyrighted work as a whole; and
> (4) the effect of the use upon the potential market for or value of the copyrighted work.

5 The editor of this volume may actually be less intrinsically interested in copyright than most or even all of the other contributors. Most of the rest of us got into copyright for its inherent interest, or because it plays a central role in certain industries. However, in both conversations and her published work, Professor Hobbs gives every impression of being primarily concerned with keeping copyright in its place and reducing its hindering effects on those who have other things to do—such as media literacy education. The reader is holding proof that this, too, can be powerful motivation to study the topic.

6 Robert Alpert, an IP attorney with decades of practice.

7 This is an excellent example of where Wikipedia has real value. The section on U.S. citations is the best short introduction to the subject that I have seen.

8 While earning my PhD at the Annenberg School for the University of Pennsylvania, I was fortunate enough to take a fantastically useful version of just such a course from Paul M. George, Associate Dean and Director of the Biddle Law Library.

9 In addition to readings noted here, I assign the appropriate sections of LaFrance throughout the semester.

10 Works are, in theory, protected even when not registered. Under 17 U.S.C. § 411, however, "registration continues to be a prerequisite to filing a civil action for copyright infringement of a United States work" (LaFrance 2011: § 4.2).

11 These are often subject to DMCA takedowns, so instructors may want to use browser plug-ins to save the audio files to their hard drives.

12 One of the random lessons students leave with is that the original version's lyrics are creepier than most people realize.

13 I have also tried showing video of the original talk, but the quality is unbearably bad. This also makes it much easier to pause and unpack a lot of the technical terms so that students will be able to continue following along.

14 The student, Nora Egloff, has since earned an MLIS and found success as a media archivist. She is just one of the many fantastic Macaulay Honors students I have had the pleasure of teaching.

15 In fairness, my view of copyright's simplicity is partially shaped by my second strongest area of legal research, telecommunications law—a labyrinth, inside a vortex, wrapped in obfuscation.

References

American Library Association. (2017). "Searchable DB of ALA Accredited Programs." Retrieved from www.ala.org/CFApps/lisdir/index.cfm

Andrews, J., & Higson, H. (2008). "Graduate Employability, 'Soft Skills' Versus 'Hard' Business Knowledge: A European Study." *Higher Education in Europe*, 33(4), 411–422. Retrieved from http://doi.org/10.1080/03797720802522627

Aufderheide, P., & Jaszi, P. (2011). *Reclaiming Fair Use: How to Put Balance Back in Copyright*. Chicago: University of Chicago Press.

Bad Lip Reading. (2013). "'Medieval Land Fun-Time World' Extended Trailer: A Bad Lip Reading of Game of Thrones." Retrieved from www.youtube.com/watch?v=5Krz-dyD-UQ

Bain, K. (2004). *What the Best College Teachers Do*. Cambridge, MA: Harvard University Press.

Benkler, Y. (2006). *The Wealth of Networks: How Social Production Transforms Markets and Freedom*. New Haven, CT: Yale University Press.

Boyle, J. (2008). *The Public Domain: Enclosing the Commons of the Mind*. New Haven, CT: Yale University Press.

Bright Tunes Music v. Harrisongs Music, 420F. Supp. 177 (S.D.N.Y. 1976).

Bureau of International Information Programs. (2004). "Outline of the U.S. Legal System." Washington, DC. Retrieved from http://usa.usembassy.de/etexts/gov/outlinelegalsystem.pdf

Campbell v. Acuff-Rose Music, 510U.S. 569 (1994).

Cariou v. Prince, 784F.Supp.2d 337 (S.D.N.Y. 2011).

Cariou v. Prince, 714F.3d 694 (2nd Cir. 2013).

Case citation. (2016, April 24). "Wikipedia, the Free Encyclopedia." Retrieved from https://en.wikipedia.org/w/index.php?title=Case_citation&oldid=716927113

Chamberlain Group v. Skylink Technologies, 381F.3d 1178 (Fed. Cir. 2004).

Copyright Term Extension Act, Pub. L. No. 105–298 (1998).

Crews, K. D. (2012). *Copyright Law for Librarians and Educators: Creative Strategies and Practical Solutions*. Chicago: American Library Association.

"CUNY—Hunter College: Best College." (2015). Retrieved from http://colleges.usnews.rankingsandreviews.com/best-colleges/hunter-college-2689

Decherney, P. (2015). "ENGL 595/SM 595: Copyright and Culture." Philadelphia: Cinema Studies/English, University of Pennsylvania. Retrieved from http://decherney.nfshost.com/ccx2/home.html

Digital Millennium Copyright Act, Pub. L. No. 105–304 (1998).

Doctorow, C. (2004). "Microsoft Research DRM Talk." Retrieved from www.craphound.com/msft-drm.txt

Documentary Filmmakers' Statement of Best Practices in Fair Use. (2005). Retrieved from http://cmsimpact.org/code/documentary-filmmakers-statement-of-best-practices-in-fair-use/

Duhigg, C. (2016). *Smarter Faster Better*. New York: Random House.

Eldred v. Ashcroft, 537U.S. 186 (2003).

Elvis Presley Enterprises, Inc., v. Passport Video, 349 F.3d 622 (9th Cir. 2003). Retrieved from http://caselaw.findlaw.com/us-9th-circuit/1173854.html

Factbook 2014—Hunter College. (n.d.). Retrieved from www.hunter.cuny.edu/institutional-research/factbook-2014

Feist Publications, Inc., v. Rural Telephone Service Co., 499 U.S. U.S. 340 (1991).

Felten v. Recording Industry, No. 01 CV 2669 (D.N.J. 2001). Retrieved from www.eff.org/node/68101

Gillespie, T. (2007). *Wired Shut: Copyright and the Shape of Digital Culture*. Cambridge, MA: MIT Press.

Gillespie, T. (2009). *Communication/Information Science 4290: Copyright in a Digital Age*. Ithaca, NY: Cornell University Press, Communication/Information Science.

Greenfield v. Pankey [Plaintiff Complaint], No. 13 Civ. 9025 (S.D.N.Y. December 31, 2013). Retrieved from http://lquilter.net/library/Greenfield-v-Pankey-SDNY-20131231-2dAmendedComplaint.pdf

Grubb, W. N., & Lazerson, M. (2005). "Vocationalism in Higher Education: The Triumph of the Education Gospel." *The Journal of Higher Education*, 76(1), 1–25.

Harper & Row v. Nation Enterprises, 471U.S. 539 (1985).

Herman, B. D. (2012). "A Political History of DRM and Related Copyright Debates, 1987–2012." *Yale Journal of Law & Technology*, 14(1). http://digitalcommons.law.yale.edu/yjolt/vol14/iss1/2/

Herman, B. D. (2013a, August 28). "Blurred Lines: Offensive, But Probably Not Copyright Infringement." Retrieved from www.shoutingloudly.com/2013/08/28/blurred-lines-offensive-but-probably-not-copyright-infringement/

Herman, B. D. (2013b). *The Fight Over Digital Rights: The Politics of Copyright and Technology*. New York: Cambridge University Press.

Herman, B. D. (2013c, April 17). "More on Using LexisNexis to Find Print News Sources & Related Cases." Retrieved from www.youtube.com/watch?v=E9LpRln-uzQ

Herman, B. D., & Gandy, O. H. (2006). "Catch 1201: A Legislative History and Content Analysis of the DMCA Exemption Proceedings." *Cardozo Arts & Entertainment Law Journal*, 24, 121–190.

Hobbs, R., & Hokanson, K. (2014). *Copyright Clarity*. Kingston: University of Rhode Island (Online). Retrieved from www.canvas.net/courses/copyright-clarity

Jackson, M. (1995). "Commerce Versus Art: The Transformation of Fair Use." *Journal of Broadcasting and Electronic Media*, 39, 190–199.

Jaszi, P., Aufderheide, P., Donaldson, M. C., Falzone, A., Hyde, L., Ito, M., . . . Urban, J. *Code of Best Practices in Fair Use for Online Video*. (2008). Retrieved from http://cmsimpact.org/code/code-best-practices-fair-use-online-video/

LaFrance, M. (2011). *Copyright Law in a Nutshell* (2nd ed.). Eagan, MN: West.

Litman, J. (2000). *Digital Copyright: Protecting Intellectual Property on the Internet*. Amherst, NY: Prometheus Books.

McLeod, K. (2014). *COMM2087: Copyright Controversies*. Communication Studies. Iowa City: University of Iowa Press.

Mettler, S. (2014). *Degrees of Inequality: How the Politics of Higher Education Sabotaged the American Dream*. New York: Basic Books.

MGM Studios, Inc. v. Grokster, Ltd., 545 U.S. U.S. 913 (June 27, 2005).

Mortenson, T. G. (2012, Winter). "State Funding: A Race to the Bottom." Retrieved from www.acenet.edu/the-presidency/columns-and-features/Pages/state-funding-a-race-to-the-bottom.aspx

National University Rankings. (n.d.). Retrieved from http://colleges.usnews.rankingsandreviews.com/best-colleges/rankings/national-universities

Patry, W. F. (2011). *How to Fix Copyright*. New York: Oxford University Press.

Rae, C. (2015). *Creative Industries: Reinvention Amidst Disruption*. Washington, DC: Communication, Culture, and Technology, Georgetown University. Retrieved from https://blogs.commons.georgetown.edu/cct-636-fall2015/syllabus-2015/

Registering a Copyright With the U.S. Copyright Office. (2016). Retrieved from www.copyright.gov/fls/sl35.pdf

Rose Hill Tutors. (n.d.). Retrieved from www.fordham.edu/info/20133/our_tutors/245/rose_hill_tutors

Sender, K., & Decherney, P. (2007). "Defending Fair Use in the Age of the Digital Millennium Copyright Act." *International Journal of Communication*, 1, 136–142.

Simson, J. L. (2016). *MGMT 305: Music Publishing and Copyright*. Washington, DC: Kogod Management Department, American University.

Sinnreich, A. (2014). *04:567:425: Copyright, Media and Culture*. New Brunswick, NJ: School of Communication and Information, Rutgers University.

Skelding, C. (2016, April 1). "CUNY Union Plans to Hold Cuomo to Contract Payment Promise." Retrieved from www.capitalnewyork.com/article/city-hall/2016/04/8595512/cuny-union-plans-hold-cuomo-contract-payment-promise

Sony BMG Music Entm't v. Tenenbaum, 719F.3d 67 (1st Cir. 2013). Retrieved from https://law.justia.com/cases/federal/appellate-courts/ca1/12-2146/12-2146-2013-06-25.html

Sony Corp. of America v. Universal City Studios, Inc., 464U.S. 417 (1984).

Stoltz, P. G. (2015). *Grit: The New Science of What It Takes to Persevere, Flourish, Succeed.* San Luis Obispo, CA: PEAK Learning.

Stop Online Piracy Act, Pub. L. No. H.R. 3261 (2011).

Universal City Studios v. Reimerdes, 111 F. Supp. 2d F. Supp. 2d 294 (S.D.N.Y. 2000).

Vaidhyanathan, S. (2004). "The State of Copyright Activism." *First Monday*, 9(4). Retrieved from www.firstmonday.org/ojs/index.php/fm/article/view/1133/1053

Vaidhyanathan, S. (2016). *MDST 3102: Copyright, Culture, and Commerce.* Charlottesville: Media Studies, University of Virginia. Retrieved from https://collab.itc.virginia.edu/syllabi/public/88e19dd9-058a-4ca7-b0b1-ec5bdda6bc45

VanCour, S. (2013). *MCC-UE 1405: Copyright, Commerce, and Culture.* New York: Media, Culture, and Communication, New York University. Retrieved from http://steinhardt.nyu.edu/scmsAdmin/media/users/rlb18/MCC_UE_1405_SampleSyllabus.pdf

Wexler, E. (2016, March 11). As a New Fiscal Year Approaches, Who Will Fund CUNY's Senior Colleges?" Retrieved from www.insidehighered.com/news/2016/03/11/new-fiscal-year-approaches-who-will-fund-cunys-senior-colleges

"Writing Center: About Us." (n.d.). Retrieved from www.fordham.edu/info/20131/about_us

Yee, V. (2016, March 24). "Cuomo Faces Loud Backlash Over Push to Cut State's CUNY Funding." *New York Times*. Retrieved from www.nytimes.com/2016/03/25/nyregion/after-moving-to-cut-cuny-funding-cuomo-faces-loud-backlash.html

Yen, A. C., & Liu, J. P. (2008). *Copyright Law: Essential Cases and Materials.* St. Paul, MN: Thomson/West.

Further Reading

Allen, V. (2007). "A Critical Reflection on the Methodology of Teaching Law to Non-Law Students." *Web Journal of Current Legal Issues*, 4. Retrieved from http://letr.org.uk/references/storage/CG6VHZ5Q/allen4.html

Levy, J. B. (2006). "As a Last Resort, Ask the Students: What They Say Makes Someone an Effective Law Teacher." *Maine Law Review*, 58, 50–99.

Monseau, S. C. (2005). Multi-Layered Assignments for Teaching the Complexity of Law to Business Students." *International Journal of Case Method Research & Application*, 17(4), 531–540.

Rahim, M. M. (2015). "Lecturing for Non-Law Background Students: Assessing the Cognitive Load of Case and Legislation-Based Lecturing Approaches." Presented at the Corporate Law Teachers Association Conference 2015, Melbourne, VIC. Retrieved from http://eprints.qut.edu.au/83063/

4

CIRCUMVENTING BARRIERS TO EDUCATION

Educational Exemptions in the Triennial Rulemaking of the Digital Millennium Copyright Act

Jonathan Band, Brandon Butler, and Caile Morris

Imagine that you are a film studies professor at a university. You plan your course syllabus, picking readings from an introductory textbook, as well as excerpts from authorities in the field. You plan for several days where you hope to show clips from films in order to illustrate your overall points about style, content, and storytelling strategies so that the students may perform close critical analysis. On a day when you need multiple clips from several different films, you think to yourself that it would be easier to make a clip disc compiling all of the clips rather than having to change out each film, taking time to switch discs or tapes out and set up the specific scene and wasting precious teaching moments. Making such a disc sounds simple in theory and should be simple in execution.

What you may not take into account in this scenario is that making a clip disc could violate Title 17 of the U.S. Code depending on the method you use to isolate, or "rip," the clip and on what form of technology the full film is on (e.g., VHS, DVD, Blu-ray disc, or streaming). Many forms of technology used to deliver films to consumers, including DVDs and Blu-ray discs, contain "digital locks," called technological protection measures (TPMs), designed to prevent the average consumer from copying the movie. In addition to the digital protection included within the DVD or Blu-ray disc, there is a law designed to prevent the unlawful circumvention or workaround of TPMs.

This law, called the Digital Millennium Copyright Act (DMCA), has complex provisions that determine what circumvention is lawful and what is unlawful through what is written in the statute itself and through a rulemaking that occurs every three years to create temporary exemptions. This law and the triennial rulemaking can create a significant variance in how educators at different levels and across different subjects can utilize copyrighted works with their students while staying within legal limits under copyright law.

The first part of the chapter explains what the DMCA is and how it came to be, the next part explains the general triennial rulemaking process, and the third part explains how the exemptions that deal specifically with education have evolved from the first rulemaking process to the most recent iteration. Take note that this is meant to be a general guide and not specific legal advice.

What Is the DMCA?

In October 1998, President Bill Clinton signed the DMCA into law. Congress passed Title I of the DMCA to implement two treaties adopted by the World Intellectual Property Organization (WIPO) in 1996: the WIPO Copyright Treaty and the WIPO Performances and Phonograms Treaty (Band 2001). The treaties required each signing party "to provide adequate legal protection and effective legal remedies against the circumvention of effective technological measures." Although some believed that U.S. law already complied with this requirement, the Administration believed that implementing legislation was necessary, and Congress ultimately agreed.

Section 1201 of the DMCA is the specific provision that includes the anticircumvention language that brought the United States into compliance with the two WIPO treaties (Band 2001). Put simply, section 1201(a) of the DMCA prohibits people from breaking a technological lock that controls access to a copyrighted work. Section 1201(a) also prohibits the sale or distribution of a product or service designed to break TPMs. Violators of section 1201 are subject to civil and criminal penalties and may also face liability for copyright infringement under other sections of the Copyright Act (Copyright Office 2000).

The rights, remedies, limitations, and defenses to copyright infringement are separate and apart from the DMCA (Copyright Office 2011). This means that defenses and exceptions to copyright infringement, like fair use, do not apply to the DMCA. Think of the DMCA as a separate law that is related to the Copyright Act but that does not necessarily play by the specific rules of the Copyright Act.

Despite being separate from the exceptions and limitations of the Copyright Act, Congress recognized that there were legitimate reasons for engaging in circumvention or creating tools to engage in circumvention. Thus, Congress created exceptions within the DMCA to reflect these legitimate reasons, some of which are explicitly written into the statute (Band 2001). These include exceptions for reverse engineering (which allows software developers to identify elements necessary for interoperability of a computer program with other programs), law enforcement and intelligence activities, encryption research (to advance the state of knowledge in the field of encryption technology and to assist in development of encryption products), security testing, and nonprofit libraries, archives, and educational institutions (allowing these institutions to determine whether to acquire a copyrighted work) (Band 2001).

The DMCA also authorizes the Librarian of Congress to conduct a rulemaking every three years to determine other legitimate reasons for engaging in circumvention that are not already explicitly exempted in the statute (Copyright Office 2015: 1). This rulemaking authority theoretically allows the DMCA to evolve with changing technology as time passes to honor other legitimate reasons for engaging in circumvention that were unforeseen at the passage of the Act.

Another part of the DMCA provides safe harbors for Internet service providers against liability from the infringing activities of their users. This part of the DMCA, codified at section 512 of the Copyright Act, also is controversial. When criticizing the DMCA, it is important to determine whether the criticism is of section 1201 or section 512. This chapter focuses on section 1201.

The DMCA Rulemaking Process

When President Clinton signed the DMCA into law in 1998, the part of section 1201 prohibiting the manufacture and distribution of circumvention devices and services went into effect immediately. However, the part prohibiting circumvention of a technological protection measure to gain unauthorized access to a copyrighted work would not take effect until 2000 (Band 2001). The two-year gap was provided so that the Librarian of Congress could conduct the first triennial rulemaking process in order to determine appropriate temporary exemptions to this prohibition. These exemptions apply to users of different "classes of works," such as literary works or motion pictures, when these users would be adversely affected by the prohibition to make lawful, or "noninfringing," use of those works.

This rulemaking is the result of a partnership between the U.S. Copyright Office, the U.S. Department of Commerce as represented by the National Telecommunications and Information Administration (NTIA), the Library of Congress, and the greater public. Every three years, the Copyright Office facilitates the rulemaking, which consists of public hearings and written comments from interested members of the public (Copyright Office 2015: 1–3). Interested members of the public include a range of parties, from individuals to large companies, and trade associations to nonprofit organizations.

The written submissions identify classes of works that members of the public would like to access for lawful purposes but are prevented from doing so by the circumvention prohibition contained in section 1201. Classes regularly identified include electronic literary works where text-to-speech functions have been disabled, thereby making the works inaccessible to the blind; motion pictures with technological protections that prevent teachers from creating clip compilations; and software with technological protections that prevent security research and testing.

Once written submissions and hearings are complete, the Copyright Office consults with NTIA. This consultation results in recommendations from both NTIA and the Register of the Copyright Office regarding the proposed exemptions for the Librarian of Congress to consider. After the Librarian has consulted with the record from the public hearings, the written submissions, and the formal recommendations from NTIA and the Register, the Librarian issues a final rule setting out the classes of works that will be exempted from the prohibition on circumvention until the next rulemaking. However, it is important to keep in mind that the Librarian is not required to follow either of the formal recommendations submitted by NTIA or the Register (Band 2015: 3).

Something significant to note is that exemptions granted during a rulemaking process will be effective only during the three-year period until the next triennial rulemaking occurs. The exemptions automatically sunset after three years, requiring the benefiting entity to seek renewal of the exemption and prove again that the prohibition on circumvention would adversely affect the entity's ability to make a lawful, noninfringing use of that class of works

(Band 2015: 3). In the 2018 rulemaking cycle, the Copyright Office adopted a more streamlined renewal process.

With each passing rulemaking since 2000, the process and the exemptions that result have grown more complex and convoluted. This is due mostly to the conflicting pressures that various stakeholders place on the Copyright Office. Consumers, libraries, and educators, in addition to the law clinics and nonprofit groups that represent them, request renewal and expansion of existing exemptions and also request new ones as technologies evolve. The copyright owners and creators usually oppose the exemptions vigorously, arguing that lawful alternatives to circumvention exist, thereby eliminating the need for exemptions (Band 2015: 3–5).

As a result, each passing rulemaking process becomes more complicated to participate in. The rulemaking has become more like a court proceeding, including burdens of proof on those submitting classes of works for exemptions, several rounds of written submissions, and formal hearings. The resulting final rules issued by the Librarian have also become more complicated. In the 2000 rulemaking, the Librarian granted two exemptions and used thirty-five words in total to describe both classes of works. This has grown to twenty-seven classes of works in the 2015 rulemaking with a final rule that spanned over eighty pages, including the language of the exemptions and full discussions of the Librarian's decision making.

From its inception, there has been praise as well as criticism of section 1201 in general and of the triennial rulemaking process in particular. Copyright owners have lauded the protections within section 1201. In a study of section 1201 and the rulemaking process by the Copyright Office, the American Association of Publishers, the Motion Picture Association of America, and the Recording Industry Association of America filed comments expressing how important the current protections in section 1201 are to their members. The associations jointly explained that the "protections continue to enable the exciting new business models that the publishing, motion picture, and music industries are currently using to disseminate their creative works," which are necessary to protect against the "technological changes [that] have made massive copyright infringement even more ubiquitous and profitable in markets worldwide" (Comments 2016: 1–2). These copyright owners feel that the triennial rulemaking has provided an effective safety valve permitting circumvention when necessary for lawful purposes.

Other groups, from the enactment of section 1201 to the present day, have argued that a prohibition on circumvention and the tools required to circumvent have the effect of preventing copying for lawful purposes. That this has in fact occurred is evident from the large number of entities and individuals that participate in the rulemakings every three years to seek exceptions covering lawful uses.

Regardless of viewpoint, any person who follows the rulemaking can see the growing complexity of the process over the past fifteen years. Exemptions for those in the field of education provide a startling example of how convoluted the rulemaking process has become.

Educational 1201 Exemptions in 2000 and 2003

The first rulemaking resulted in two classes of works that were exempt from the prohibition on circumvention of TPMs, neither of which was directly related to education. They were "[c]ompilations consisting of lists of websites blocked by filtering software applications" and "[l]iterary works, including computer programs and databases, protected by access control mechanisms that fail to permit access because of malfunction, damage, or obsoleteness" (Librarian of Congress 2000).

The second rulemaking concluded in October 2003, and the final rule from the Librarian included four exemptions for classes of works. Some of these four exemptions built off the language from the 2000 rulemaking, becoming wordier than in 2000.

One new exemption applies, at least indirectly, to educational uses. It allows blind users to circumvent the controls that disabled the read-aloud function on e-books so that they could access and use the technologies that make reading the books possible. This exemption covers literary works distributed in e-book format when all existing e-book editions of the work (including digital text editions made available by authorized entities) contain access controls that prevent the enabling of the e-book's read-aloud function and of screen readers that render the text into a specialized format.

This exemption was targeted at the average blind or print-disabled user of an e-reader, like a Kindle. However, this exemption allowed schools that use e-readers with their students to comply with the Americans With Disabilities Act (ADA) and provide e-readers that are functional for all users, including those with disabilities.

DMCA 1201 2006 Rulemaking

In October 2006, the Librarian's final rule had expanded to six classes of works, again building off of the 2003 rulemaking, while adding some more language and new exemptions. In addition to renewing the exemption for the blind and print-disabled with e-books, the Librarian for the first time adopted an exemption for educational uses of films. The exemption was for "audiovisual works included in the educational library of a college or university's film or media studies department, when circumvention is accomplished for the purpose of making compilations of portions of those works for educational use in the classroom by media studies or film professors" (Librarian of Congress 2006). In other words, if you go back to imagining yourself as a film studies professor, the 2006 rulemaking provided you an exemption for circumventing any TPMs that existed on motion pictures so that you could compile multiple clips onto one disc for your class.

In the past, educators could use unprotected formats of films, such as VHS videotapes, from which they could easily assemble clip compilations. However, by 2006, distributors of films and television shows were increasingly distributing their content solely on DVDs using a form of encryption known as a content scrambling system (CSS). In order to get the decryption key that allowed the unscrambled viewing of content, the manufacturer of a device such as a DVD player or a computer had to agree to design the device in a way that did not allow the unscrambled copying of the DVD. The net effect was that an educator could not easily copy clips for use in class.

Moreover, DVD technology prevented educators from quickly loading a DVD of the complete film into a DVD player and playing only the clip they wanted. Instead, it could take over a minute to get to the right location because DVDs often contained content that could not be skipped, such as the FBI warnings. Accordingly, film professors made a compelling case that the prohibition on circumvention adversely effected their ability to make fair uses of the films, that is, assemble clip compilations for classroom use. Thus, an exemption was necessary for instructors to continue using film clips in class.

This exemption was short—only forty-four words long—and easy to understand. At the same time, it was narrow. It applied only to audiovisual works in the library of a college film or media studies department—not the film collection in the college's main library. And only instructors of film and media studies courses could use it. In subsequent rulemakings, the exemption broadened but also became more complex.

DMCA 1201 Rulemaking in 2010

This fourth triennial rulemaking kept the same number of classes of works as the 2006 rulemaking. While there was still only one dedicated educational exemption, the number of words used grew substantially, and the exemption was broader in general scope while simultaneously made subject to additional conditions. The exemption applied to:

> Motion pictures on DVDs that are lawfully made and acquired and that are protected by the Content Scrambling System when circumvention is accomplished solely in order to accomplish the incorporation of short portions of motion pictures into new works for the purpose of criticism or comment, and where the person engaging in circumvention believes and has reasonable grounds for believing that circumvention is necessary to fulfill the purpose of the use in... [e]ducational uses by college and university professors and by college and university film and media studies students.
>
> (Librarian of Congress 2010: 43839)

The educational use exemption was broadened in four important ways. First, the source of the copy to be circumvented was no longer restricted to the film and media studies department library. Instead, it applied to any lawfully made and acquired copy, regardless of its source.

Second, the clips could be used by college and university professors in any field rather than just professors of film and media studies. The Register of Copyrights and the Librarian of Congress recognized that the high quality of clips from DVDs could be useful in the classroom in many fields. They could help language students understand dialectical differences through better sound quality; they could reflect the correct musical tone for music and theater students; they could clearly show facial expressions and hand gestures in theater, psychology, sociology, or literature classes.

Third, the 2010 exemption applied to the creation of new work, such as a presentation including a clip, while the 2006 applied only to the creation of a compilation of clips.

Fourth, the exemption was expanded to include film and media studies students. Film and media studies students were often required to show what they have learned by creating presentations including different styles of filming or reporting. These students had a compelling need to include high-quality clips in their presentations.

Significantly, the exemption also was narrower than the 2006 exemption. It covered only "motion pictures" rather than the broader class of works of "audiovisual works" as in 2006. This meant that only motion pictures (which include movies, television shows, commercials, news, and DVD extras) could be included and not the larger class that included video games and other audiovisual works under the Copyright Act. Further, the exemption applied only to DVDs and not other storage media such as Blu-ray. The Register argued that the quality of DVDs was adequate to meet educational needs.

Additionally, the 2006 exemption allowed the use of "portions," while the 2010 exemption allowed only the use of "short portions." Because fair use is not necessarily limited to short portions of a work, this limitation could be more restrictive than what fair use would allow.

Finally, the 2010 exemption added the requirement that "the person engaging in circumvention believes and has reasonable grounds for believing that circumvention is necessary to fulfill" the educational purpose of the use. This language concerning the necessity of the circumvention led to more detailed obligations in subsequent rulemakings.

DMCA 1201 Rulemaking in 2012

The final rule that came out of this rulemaking was far more detailed compared to the previous rules. The document containing the final rule had grown to almost seventy pages, containing in-depth exemptions, the history of the rulemaking process generally and for this particular rulemaking, and explanations why certain language was adopted for each exemption. The educational exemption also grew exponentially. It now had four parts to it, all relating to motion picture excerpts for the purposes of commentary, criticism, and educational uses. The first part of the exemption covered:

> Motion pictures, as defined in 17 U.S.C. 101, on DVDs that are lawfully made and acquired and that are protected by the Content Scrambling System, where the person engaging in circumvention believes and has reasonable grounds for believing that the circumvention is necessary because reasonably available alternatives, such as noncircumventing methods or using screen capture software as provided for in alternative exemptions, are not able to produce the level of high-quality content required to achieve the desired criticism or comment on such motion pictures, and where circumvention is undertaken solely in order to make use of short portions of the motion pictures for the purpose of criticism or comment . . . for educational purposes in film studies or other courses requiring close analysis of film and media excerpts, by college and university faculty, college and university students, and kindergarten through twelfth grade educators.
>
> (Librarian of Congress 2012: 65266)

The second part of the exemption uses this exact language, but instead of "DVDs that are lawfully made and acquired and that are protected by the Content Scrambling System," it is instead applied to "motion pictures, as defined in 17 U.S.C. 101, that are lawfully made and acquired via online distribution services and that are protected by various technological protection measures" (Librarian of Congress 2012: 65266).

The third part of the exemption pertained to:

> Motion pictures, as defined in 17 U.S.C. 101, on DVDs that are lawfully made and acquired and that are protected by the Content Scrambling System, where the circumvention, if any, is undertaken using screen capture technology that is reasonably represented and offered to the public as enabling the reproduction of motion picture content after such content has been lawfully decrypted, when such representations have been reasonably relied upon by the user of such technology, when the person engaging in the circumvention believes and has reasonable grounds for believing that the circumvention is necessary to achieve the desired criticism or comment, and where the circumvention is undertaken solely in order to make use of short portions of the motion pictures for the purpose of criticism or comment . . . for educational purposes by college and university faculty, college and university students, and kindergarten through twelfth grade educators.
>
> (Librarian of Congress 2012: 65266)

The fourth part of the exemption uses exactly the same language as the third part, but instead of applying to films on DVDs, it applies to films on online distribution services.

This exemption was broader than the 2010 exemption in that it covered not only motion pictures on DVDs but also motion pictures on online distribution services. It also expanded the users that were covered to include all college and university students, not just those who majored in film or media studies. It was further expanded to apply to K–12 educators (but not K–12 students).

At the same time, the exemption was narrowed in significant ways. A higher burden was placed on users of the exemption to demonstrate the need for gaining access to high-quality formats. First, circumvention was permitted only for use in "courses requiring close analysis of film and media excerpts."

Second, circumvention was permitted only when other alternatives, such as screen capture software, would not provide sufficiently high-quality clips to meet the educational need. Screen capture software permits the copying of audiovisual content after it has been decrypted. It was unclear whether the use of screen capture software constitutes circumvention within the meaning of section 1201. Thus, it was unclear whether one could use screen capture software without an exemption. Further, proponents of exemptions argued that screen capture software provided copies whose quality was inadequate to meet pedagogical needs.

The Librarian resolved the screen capture issue by providing an exemption for screen capture software and by permitting the circumvention of CSS and the technological protections on streamed content only if screen capture did not produce clips of sufficient quality.

2015 Rulemaking

The Librarian of Congress issued the final rule in the sixth triennial rulemaking in October 2015. The final rule spanned over eighty pages and considered twenty-seven classes of works, four of which related to educational uses of short portions of motion pictures. The exemptions were expanded to apply outside the traditional educational context to massive open online courses (MOOCS) and courses offered by libraries and museums.

College and University Faculty and Students

Like the 2012 exemption, this exemption draws a distinction between screen capture software and other forms of circumvention. The exemption states that circumvention may be undertaken (see Table 4.1):

> By college and university faculty and students, for educational purposes,
>
> (A) Where the circumvention is undertaken using screen-capture technology that appears to be offered to the public as enabling reproduction of motion pictures after the content has been lawfully acquired and decrypted, or
>
> (B) In film studies or other courses requiring close analysis of film and media excerpts where the motion picture is lawfully made and acquired on a DVD protected by the Content Scramble System, on a Blu-ray disc protected by the Advanced Access Control system, or via a digital transmission protected by a technological measure, and where the person engaging in circumvention reasonably believes that screen-capture software or other non-circumventing alternatives are unable to produce the required level of high-quality content.
>
> (Librarian of Congress 2015: 65949)

As in the 2012 exemption, college and university faculty and students may use screen capture technology for educational purposes. The exemption for the circumvention of DVDs

Table 4.1 Circumvention for Educational Purposes—2015 Rule

		Full Circumvention	*Screen Capture*
Colleges and universities	**Faculty**	DVD, Blu-ray, or streamed content for film studies or other courses requiring close analysis and screen capture is inadequate.	All courses
	Students	DVD, Blu-ray, or streamed content for film studies or other courses requiring close analysis and screen capture is inadequate.	All courses
K–12	**Faculty**	DVD or streamed content for film studies or other courses requiring close analysis and screen capture is inadequate.	All courses
	Students	No	All courses
MOOCs	**Faculty**	DVD, Blu-ray, or streamed content for film studies or other courses requiring close analysis and screen capture is inadequate.	All courses
	Students	No	No
Libraries etc.	**Faculty**	No	All courses
	Students	No	All courses

protected by CSS and digital transmissions protected by technological measures was expanded to include, for the first time, Blu-ray discs protected by the Advanced Access Control System. As in the 2012 exemption, faculty and students can rely on this exemption only for film studies and other courses requiring close analysis of film and media excerpts and only if screen capture software and other alternatives cannot produce the required level of high-quality content.

As with the 2012 exemption, the "close analysis" standard could pose a challenge for some faculty and students. Moreover, faculty and students may have difficulty understanding the distinction between screen capture software and software that circumvents CSS.

Primary and Secondary Educators and Students

While university and college faculty and students may be confused about how to apply the exemptions to the prohibition on circumvention, primary and secondary educators and students are likely to be even more so. The exemption that relates to this latter group states that circumvention may be undertaken:

> By kindergarten through twelfth-grade educators, including of accredited general educational development (GED) programs, for educational purposes,
>
> (A) Where the circumvention is undertaken using screen-capture technology that appears to be offered to the public as enabling the reproduction of motion pictures after content has been lawfully acquired and decrypted, or
>
> (B) In film studies or other courses requiring close analysis of film and media excerpts where the motion picture is lawfully made and acquired on a DVD protected by the Content Scramble System, or via a digital transmission protected by a technological measure, and where the person engaging in circumvention reasonably believes that screen-capture software or other non-circumventing alternatives are unable to produce the required level of high-quality content;

> By kindergarten through twelfth-grade students, including those in accredited general educational development (GED) programs, for educational purposes, where the circumvention is undertaken using screen-capture technology that appears to be offered to the public as enabling the reproduction of motion pictures and has been lawfully acquired and decrypted.
>
> (Librarian of Congress 2015: 65950)

The 2015 exemption for educators is broader than the 2012 version in that it now more specifically includes accredited GED programs. As with the college and university exemption, a distinction is drawn between "film studies and other course requiring close analysis of film and media excerpts" and other courses. The K–12 educator exemption is narrower than the college and university faculty exemption, however, in that the K–12 educator exemption does not apply to Blu-ray discs.

The 2015 exemption is broader than the 2012 exemption in that K–12 students are now permitted to use screen capture software. This means that students in high school film studies classes may be taught with high-quality clips from motion pictures but may not utilize the same quality clips in presentations.

MOOC Educators

The exemption that relates to MOOCs states that circumvention may be undertaken:

> By faculty of massive open online courses (MOOCs) offered by accredited nonprofit educational institutions to officially enrolled students through online platforms (which platforms themselves may be operated for profit or for educational purposes), where the MOOC provider through the online platform limits transmissions to the extent technologically feasible to such officially enrolled students, institutes copyright policies and provides copyright informational materials to faculty, students and relevant staff members, and applies technological measures that reasonably prevent unauthorized further dissemination of a work in accessible form to others or retention of the work for longer than the course session by recipients of a transmission through the platform, as contemplated by 17 U.S.C. 110(2),
>
> (A) Where the circumvention is undertaken using screen-capture technology that appears to be offered to the public as enabling the reproduction of motion pictures after the content has been lawfully acquired and decrypted, or
>
> (B) In film studies or other courses requiring close analysis of film and media excerpts where the motion picture is lawfully made and acquired on a DVD protected by the Content Scramble System, on a Blu-ray disc protected by the Advanced Access Control System, or via a digital transmission protected by a technological measure, and where the person engaging in circumvention reasonably believes that the screen-capture software or other non-circumventing alternatives are unable to produce the required level of high-quality content.
>
> (Librarian of Congress 2015: 24)

MOOCs are a relatively recent educational phenomenon, defined by their "massive" size (often thousands of students participate at once—tens of thousands for the most popular courses), by their "open" enrollment policies (anyone who wants to take a course may do so, for free), and by their "online" delivery mechanism (making courses taught by elite U.S. faculty available to anyone in the world with an Internet connection).

The 2015 ruling creates a DMCA exemption for MOOC faculty from accredited nonprofit educational institutions who create short clips for use in their courses, allowing them to copy clips from protected DVDs, Blu-ray discs, and streaming videos so long as the course or lecture requires "close analysis" of the clip. As with college and university faculty, the use of screen capture software does not include a "close analysis" limitation.

The MOOC, however, must be offered by a nonprofit organization, and access to the clips must be restricted to enrolled students. The MOOC must further prevent dissemination of the clips outside the course. The organization that creates the course must be an accredited nonprofit educational institution, but the provider of the software platform may be a for-profit. So a university course offered through for-profit platforms like Coursera (the largest MOOC platform) or Udacity may take advantage of the exemption.

A key limitation and a tricky one for "open" courses is that access to the material must be limited to students enrolled in the course. This requirement is borrowed from section 110(2) of the Copyright Act, also known as the TEACH Act. The use of passwords provided only to enrolled students should sufficiently limit access to the course content to students or learners. The rule also incorporates the TEACH Act's requirement that institutions prevent unauthorized redistribution. Offering streaming rather than downloadable versions of the course content should reasonably limit unauthorized redistribution of the work. Unfortunately, this disadvantages learners with slower Internet access, such as students in developing countries with poor broadband infrastructure or students limited to mobile broadband subject to usage caps.

An interesting aspect of the rule for MOOCs is that it mentions "relevant staff" as needing copyright education in connection with use of the exemption. A long-running question in the section 1201 process has been whether "third parties" can engage in the permitted circumvention on behalf of beneficiaries. In this context, the rule seems to contemplate that staff will be involved in the creation of MOOC clips. This may give MOOC faculty (and staff) additional comfort.

This is the first time an exception has been granted to benefit MOOCs, and there is room for the exemption to grow in ways analogous to the expansion seen in other educational use exemptions. Most importantly, a future exemption might grow to include protection for students, as it does for students in other learning environments (as previously discussed). Another expansion might be to move beyond accredited educational institutions to cover the many nonprofits (National Geographic, the World Bank) and even for-profit companies offering courses relevant to their interests.

Museum, Library, and Other Nonprofit Educational Programs

This last educational category is also new to the rulemaking process and targets more unconventional learning environments. The exemption states that circumvention may be undertaken:

> By educators and participants in nonprofit digital and media literacy programs offered by libraries, museums, and other nonprofit entities with an educational mission, in the course of face-to-face instructional activities for educational purposes, where the circumvention is undertaken using screen-capture technology that appears to be offered to the public as enabling the reproduction of motion pictures after content has been lawfully acquired and decrypted.
>
> (Librarian of Congress 2015: 65950)

These programs, such as adult media or digital literacy programs, help Americans of all ages to develop critical thinking skills to sort through the flood of information they receive each day and to not just consume the information but also to create and share new information with others.

Unlike the other educational exceptions, the Librarian did not think such courses needed access to high-quality excerpts and concluded that screen capture would be adequate for the educators and the participants in these kinds of programs. This exemption has less room for confusion relative to the other educational exemptions, but it also is less useful in that it permits only the use of screen capture software.

Conclusion

The overall lesson from the evolution of the educational exemptions throughout the rulemaking processes is that, with each passing rulemaking, the resulting exemptions have grown slightly more inclusive and dramatically more complex. For the film studies professors discussed earlier, who frequently utilize the educational exemptions to further the education of their students, this complexity means they may not know whether they are violating the law just by preparing for and executing fairly typical lesson plans.

In certain respects, the educational exemptions have broadened, but in other respects they have narrowed. This is due primarily to the conflicting pressures placed on the Copyright Office and the Library of Congress. Professors, teachers, and librarians request the renewal and expansion of the educational exemption. The copyright owners oppose expansion by arguing that alternatives to circumvention exist. During each cycle, the government agencies involved try to strike a balance between these opposing views: they grant exemptions in recognition of the obvious legitimacy of educational uses, then saddle educators with increasingly Byzantine rules to allay content industries' baseless claims about piracy.

As they stand at the writing of this chapter, different rules apply for accessing film excerpts depending on the educational context. Educators across all levels and disciplines must be vigilant and aware of which rules apply to them in order to continue to educate their students both legally and with the best resources available.

References

Association of American Publishers, Motion Picture Association of America, Recording Industry of America (Comments) (2016). "Comments on Section 1201 Study." United States Copyright Office, Docket No. 2015-8. Retrieved from www.regulations.gov/#!documentDetail;D=COLC-2015-0012-0045

Band, J. (2001). "The Digital Millennium Copyright Act." Association of Research Libraries. Retrieved from www.arl.org/storage/documents/publications/band-dmca-memo-16aug01.pdf

Band, J. (2015). "The Complexity Dialectic: A Case Study From Copyright Law." Infojustice.org. Retrieved from http://infojustice.org/wp-content/uploads/2015/03/band03102015.pdf

Copyright Office. (2000). "The Digital Millennium Copyright Act, United States Code Title 17 Chapter 12." Retrieved from www.copyright.gov/title17/92chap12.html#1201

Copyright Office. (2011). "Copyright Infringement and Remedies, United States Code Title 17 Chapter 5." Retrieved from www.copyright.gov/title17/92chap5.html#501

Copyright Office. (2015). "Understanding the Section 1201 Rulemaking: Frequently Asked Questions." Retrieved from www.copyright.gov/1201/2015/2015_1201_FAQ_final.pdf

Librarian of Congress. (2000). "First Triennial Section 1201 Proceeding." Washington, DC. Retrieved from www.copyright.gov/1201/anticirc.html

Librarian of Congress. (2003). "Second Triennial Section 1201 Proceeding." Washington, DC. Retrieved from www.copyright.gov/1201/2003/index.html

Librarian of Congress. (2006). "Third Triennial Section 1201 Proceeding." Washington, DC. Retrieved from www.copyright.gov/1201/2006/

Librarian of Congress. (2010). "Fourth Triennial Section 1201 Proceeding." Federal Register, 37 CFR Part 201. Washington, DC. Retrieved from www.gpo.gov/fdsys/pkg/FR-2010-07-27/pdf/2010-18339.pdf

Librarian of Congress. (2012). "Fifth Triennial Section 1201 Proceeding." *Federal Register*, 37 CFR Part 201. Washington, DC. Retrieved from www.copyright.gov/fedreg/2012/77fr65260.pdf

Librarian of Congress. (2015). "Sixth Triennial Section 1201 Proceeding." *Federal Register*, 37 CFR Part 201. Washington, DC. Retrieved from www.copyright.gov/fedreg/2015/80fr65944.pdf

Further Reading

Digital Media Law Project. (2008). "Circumventing Copyright Controls." Retrieved from www.dmlp.org/legal-guide/circumventing-copyright-controls

Electronic Frontier Foundation. (2010). "The Internet Law Treatise. Copyright: Digital Millennium Copyright Act." Retrieved from https://ilt.eff.org/index.php/Copyright:_Digital_Millennium_Copyright_Act#Anti-Circumvention_and_Anti-Trafficking_Provisions

Electronic Frontier Foundation. (2014). "Unintended Consequences—16 Years Under the DMCA." Retrieved from www.eff.org/wp/unintended-consequences-16-years-under-dmca

Electronic Frontier Foundation. (2016). "List of 1201 Threats." Retrieved from www.eff.org/document/list-1201-threats

5

REMIX AND UNCHILL

Remaking Pedagogies to Support Ethical Fair Use

Timothy R. Amidon, Kyle Stedman, and Dànielle Nicole DeVoss

> Many teachers and producers of media literacy materials now worry that they will misinterpret fair use or are simply unaware of its expansive nature.
>
> (Hobbs, Jaszi, & Aufderheide 2007: 5)

Recently, we delivered a presentation called Classrooms and Copyright: Our Rights and Responsibilities at the 2015 National Council of Teachers of English (NCTE) gathering in Minneapolis, Minnesota. The conference is large; about 4,500 elementary, high school, and college-level educators attend it annually. We opened our presentation by asking attendees why they chose to dedicate their valuable professional development time to a session on copyright. With no hesitation, they told us story after story fueled by fear and anxiety. As we've seen and experienced in past workshops and presentations, teachers have long been concerned about what they can share with students: what they are allowed to photocopy, what they can show in class, what they can stream on their institution's servers. That is, their focus tended to emphasize how choices regarding *consumption* are impacted by copyright and how fair use protected their abilities to share and disseminate content. But, in the 2015 session, as we listened to the teachers' responses, we began to hear a more recently emerging anxiety about what teachers could ask students to *produce*. They wanted to know what sources students could use when creating videos, if it was okay for students to use popular music in a slide show, what sorts of images they could use, how students could share and submit the work that they create, and how they might avoid legal consequences for making a copyright blunder.

These teachers—and we suspect many instructional designers, librarians, and educational administrators—are distracted from doing the rigorous, exciting, contemporary work of media literacy, that is, helping students navigate, analyze, read, and consume digital media *and* supporting students to create, compose, make, and share digital media. Our presentation attendees' understanding of copyright was having a chilling effect on what these experienced educators believed they and their students could do with "protected content" in their classrooms. Given the rhetorical, technical, and legal complexities that surround composing in a digitally networked multimedia culture, we found their responses to copyright understandable—and not necessarily new. Scholars like Larry Lessig (1999, 2004, 2008) and Siva Vaidhyanathan (2001) have been calling attention to these chilling effects for some time. Indeed, writing scholars have been arguing that these sorts of questions and their resulting anxiety and fear are a central component of the ways that intellectual property laws can have chilling effects in our classrooms (Rife 2010; Rife & Hart-Davidson 2006; Hobbs, Jaszi & Aufderheide 2007; Westbrook 2006). In a worst-case scenario, teachers' fears about "breaking the law" or students "getting into big trouble" chill the rhetorical, technical, and cultural meaning-making in which students might engage.

Yet, as we chatted after the session and reflected on our own stances and pedagogies, we wondered what had led us to respond so differently to copyright. We pondered why the three of us tend to view copyright favorably—as a tool that empowers composers, as a cultural/historical framework for understanding composing contexts and distribution. What was it that encourages us to apply U.S. copyright law and its provisions for fair use so liberally, trusting that we won't receive takedown notices or cease and desist orders as instructors or that the compositions that our students create wouldn't become subject to lawsuits?

In this chapter, we describe the flexible, nimble approach we have adopted, which orients broadly toward educators, students, librarians, and instructional designers to *remix and unchill* the chilling effects so many of our colleagues have felt. We see this approach as embracing what Lessig (2008) has called the "read–write culture"—a culture that encourages both the consumption and the production of texts by both professionals and amateurs.

We begin by briefly sharing scenarios where we've encountered copyright's chilling effect on the possibilities within our own classrooms. We share these stories specifically to contribute to the ongoing conversations surrounding copyright, as a way to put into circulation more stories from the classroom, as our experiences (that is, within educational settings) are very different from popular culture cases. We then move to tracing previous scholarship that has explored the chilling effects of copyright law. This sets the stage for three facets that, we argue, can be combined to help us use copyright law to our own and to students' advantage: access, confidence, and know-how. We situate these three facets as a strategic heuristic that can enhance rhetorical prowess and offer the potential to disrupt cultures of fear and the chilling of teacherly practices. We illustrate the heuristic by describing three specific but flexible and adaptable activities that teachers, librarians, and instructional designers might leverage (i.e., composing musical parodies, engaging in critical photography, using past films to understand the present) to engage students in what Lessig (2008) has called read–write composing and consuming practices.

Feeling the Chill: Stories From Our Classrooms

In Tim's upper-division digital composing course, Principles of Digital Rhetoric and Design, students learn about fair use and then create a multimodal remix of another composer's content. Before making their remixes, students explore recompositions commonly found in digital spaces, including literal videos, mashups, overdubs, and remixes. However, when it comes time to share and submit their own remixes, he has observed that students make markedly different decisions regarding whom they grant access to their remixes than those composers whose work they have analyzed. Whereas some students avoid posting their remixes online, choosing instead to save their projects on thumb drives or submit them through the school's learning management system, others post directly to YouTube and/or SoundCloud, thus sharing their work publicly and inviting consumption and critique. In most instances, the different choices students make about how they share their remixes don't have a significant impact as to how Tim can access and assess their remix work, but choosing to share privately or publicly does impact the distribution of the remixes. Distribution choices can also result in remixes being flagged as infringing, in students receiving takedown notices, and/or in students having their remixes blocked until the potential infringement is resolved.

Dànielle integrates some discussion of intellectual property into all of the courses she teaches (which include courses focused on document design, nonprofit communications, writing research methods, and more), and other instructors in the Professional Writing program in which she teaches also do so, drawing upon materials that she created and that live as crowdsourced, organic resources in the program. Several semesters ago, an instructor teaching one of the four core courses required of all undergraduate students in the major—an introduction to web authoring course—asked to speak with her. The instructor was distraught because she found out that after she spoke with her students about intellectual property, one student was so chilled and anxious that she chose to use a stock photography website and purchase all of the graphics and images for her portfolio website. This was brought to the instructor's attention when the student approached her for help navigating the complex terms of use and distribution policies that the stock images were regulated by.

In a creative nonfiction course, Kyle's students recorded audio versions of their personal essays, layering sound effects and music with their words, which had been rewritten to sound better aloud. He gave them a brief overview of their audio options: they could record their own sound effects and music, or they could find files online that were in the public domain or licensed by Creative Commons, or they could use copyright-protected works if they were confident they were following fair use guidelines. His students seemed skeptical about the legality of this latter option; after all, they were sharing these audio files on SoundCloud, a public audio-sharing site, and it seemed illegal to redistribute copyright-protected works without releases or permissions. Their skepticism led Kyle to expect that most would opt for music licensed by Creative Commons, but when the projects came in, he saw he was wrong. Most students *had* used copyrighted music from their personal libraries, and, further, they did so in ways that didn't seem particularly transformative. (The first factor when determining fair use is the "purpose and character of the use"; uses that are more transformative are often seen as more likely to be fair. Leval (1990: 1111) describes transformative uses as those that are "productive" and "employ the quoted matter in a different manner or for a different purpose from the original," as opposed to a use that "merely repackages or republishes the original.") As he reflected, Kyle realized that, for many of the projects, he didn't want to ask students to change their music; it often matched well in ways that enhanced the meanings of the pieces, even if that meaning wasn't "transformative" in nature. The next time he taught this class, he encouraged students to use any music that felt rhetorically right and asked students to post their work behind the password-protected wall of the school's course management system.

A Network of Chills

At times, however, composers and producers aren't asked—the decision is made for us, when we teach, learn, and compose within chilled spaces where institutions find it safer to hyper regulate intellectual property and establish rigorous guidelines and rules rather than allow composers agency and defend fair use approaches (DeVoss & Webb 2008: 92).

Two Supreme Court cases show how chilling effects can affect creators in complex, networked ways. Interestingly, the first documented legal use of the term "chilling" in the context of chilling effects appeared in a Supreme Court case that directly involved teachers. In 1951, Oklahoma instituted a statute that required state employees—including teachers—to commit to a loyalty oath, which included a promise that the employee was not affiliated with the Communist Party, nor would the employee ever join or affiliate with a group that advocated overthrowing the U.S. government. The Supreme Court ruled in *Wieman v. Updegraff* (1952) that the act could not be upheld because it could potentially exclude people from employment due to an organizational membership. One of the justices wrote in his opinion that the right of association is a fundamental right of free speech and free inquiry. He specifically pointed out that teachers in particular require free speech and free inquiry, further stating that "an unmistakable tendency to chill that free play of the spirit which all teachers ought especially to cultivate and practice; it makes for caution and timidity in their associations by potential teachers." In our context here, we see the court recognizing that laws in one context—requiring state employees to make a simple oath—have far-reaching effects into the future actions of others, all the way down to what teachers feel free to say and to teach. The court chose to open that space instead of tamping it down, to make a space for future creativity that wasn't hampered by fear.

Much later, in 2005, another Supreme Court case leaned in the other direction. In the *Grokster* case (*MGM Studios, Inc. v. Grokster, Ltd.* 2005), the court held the peer-to-peer filesharing company Grokster liable for creating software that *could* be used for noninfringing purposes but that more often was used to distribute copyrighted content illegally. Many involved who supported Grokster were concerned that the case could set precedent regarding technology innovation and chill potential future innovation. A concern was that if the judges decided in favor of the content industry, including MGM Studios and its supporters, tech companies might shy away from inventing new products that could potentially violate copyright laws if they could be held liable for users illegally distributing copyright-protected material with the products. That is, it is likely this ruling has had a chilling effect on innovation, as designers have since had to worry about whether their platforms could potentially be used to break the law.

How Chilling Happens

These two cases only scratch the surface of how fear affects composing practices in ways that go far beyond fears of copyright infringement. Chilling is ecological and cross-contextual, not something that is ever as simple as emerging from a single practice or law. Situating accounts of how chilling occurs in media literacy education contexts, then, allows us to look beyond the few cases that go to trial in order to construct a more fine-grained sense of the diverse ways and many means by which chilling occurs across contextual levels.

Common examples of technological and procedural practices that rub up against multimodal composing and that lead to chilling effects include:

- Cease and desist and/or take-down warnings;
- Aggressive digital rights management (DRM) fixed to media;
- Blurring or exploiting ambiguities regarding how the law actually works;
- Interfaces that automatically flag content; and
- Interfaces that crawl, block/prohibit, and automatically remove content.

Chilling, however, doesn't result only from technologies and procedures designed to detect and prevent alleged appropriation of others' intellectual property. For instance, the chilling that resulted from Stephanie Lenz's YouTube video take-down (*Lenz v. Universal Music Corp.* 2015; Fortunato 2009) differs considerably from the ways that Twitter's lack of filtering controls support bullying, doxxing, death threats, and "mob harassment." These issues prompted Suey Park to delete her account (Dixon 2014; Park & Leonard 2014) and Randi Lee Harper to create a Twitter add-on tool (ggautoblocker) that prevents large-scale Twitter harassment and to found the Online Abuse Prevention Initiative (OAPI). Whereas YouTube's interface chills through procedural dynamics (e.g., users are threatened with take-down notices and/or legal action after an algorithm finds the presence of copyrighted material, regardless of whether the use was fair), Twitter's interface chills through the lack of effective technological controls for preventing, eliminating, and responding to misogynistic, sexist, and violent harassment. Digital composers are thus creating in a complex web of influences, some of which serve to chill the creation and distribution of new work, and some of which are directly linked to copyright.

Contexts of Chilling

Of course, there is overlap as sociocultural, technological, and procedural dimensions of interfaces intersect. Consider how social media sites require users to accept or decline terms of use through click-wrap agreements as a condition of access. Whereas some users click—agreeing to terms of use without reading them—others simply give up because the dense legal and technical language found in Facebook's, YouTube's, and Twitter's terms of use statements is time-consuming and difficult to understand. Tim Amidon and Jessica Reyman (2014) argued that terms of use obfuscate how sites collect various forms of user-generated content, for example including language that makes it difficult for users to discern specifically how sites might repurpose and aggregate various types of content (often archived under the sites as data). Ultimately, while some users opt in and others opt out because of the various factors that influence such decisions, each group encounters some degree of chilling as they idiosyncratically self-censor what types of content they'll create and with whom they'll share it, unsure of exactly what they're allowed to do and often relying on various stories they've heard or lore that is circulating to guide what they share and how they rely on previously existing material.

These examples, then, illustrate how chilling effects emerge from what Bryan Pfaffenberger (1992) called *technological regularization strategies*, which overtly and tacitly limit—or, in some cases, deny—access to "people who fit into certain, race, class, gender, or achievement categories" (as cited in Selber 2004: 102). Such strategies create barriers that result in disproportionate access to the tools, knowledge, means, materials, and identities necessary for consuming and producing multimedia. Following Stuart Selber (2004), we believe that paying greater attention to such strategies might allow us to better understand how "use contexts" and "design cultures" work to empower some composers while disempowering others, including students who are too often positioned as consumers of media. One arena in which these strategies are produced and enforced is that of intellectual property.

Chilling in the Context of Media Literacy Education

Media literacy education offers students opportunities to become critical readers of 21st-century texts and can also provide students with access to the tools, knowledge, and experience necessary for producing multimedia texts—which means pushing against chilling in all of its forms. When educators focus on *use contexts*, they attune to how laws, policies, interfaces, politics, and pedagogies can coalesce to limit the opportunities that students have to compose, recompose, and produce the types of multimedia that they might readily consume both inside and outside of the classroom. Within the use contexts of schools and university, students and educators encounter multiple forms of chilling: we are prevented from accessing particular websites. We encounter bandwidth caps, limiting the types of files we might work with while uploading, downloading, and streaming. We discover that administrators have banned the use of tools that enable anonymous browsing because the tools have been misunderstood as politically dangerous. Or we are viewed skeptically or even as subversive when our pedagogies make legal use of the Digital Millennium Copyright Act's anticircumvention exemptions, perhaps by defeating a DVD's technological protection measures/digital rights management for educational purposes (TPM/DRM; USC 17 section 1201). Much of this chilling is fueled by fear, and, just as Jim Porter (2005) and Steve Westbrook (2006) observed, we too see fear functioning as a powerful motivating variable that colors the decisions that administrators, educators, and students make regarding the types of production and consumption activities media literacy learners might engage in.

The implications of fear press on agency. For instance, in a survey of college-level educators' command of fair use knowledge, Martine Courant Rife and Bill Hart Davidson (2006: 14) discovered that educators' certainty regarding their interpretations about fair use—both positive and negative certainties—correlated with the degree of agency that they had: "the tipping point in gaining agency when composing may be knowledge of how fair use/copyright works along with knowledge of the risks of digital writing." It's clear, then, that beyond opening the doors of access to our students, we also need to open the doors of confidence in using copyrighted works in ways protected by fair use law, even when those actions go against prevailing understandings in given educational cultures.

Yet beyond the importance of confidence-building knowledge are policies that aren't built on a robust understanding of fair use law; knowledge alone might not be enough to unchill composing. Many institutions, for example, promulgate conservative and restrictive interpretations of laws within policies that students and educators internalize, limiting the production choices these composers might make. While institutional policies and terms of use policies like those found on YouTube are not law, students and educators unfamiliar with the force of such policies might nevertheless read the policies *as law*. Previously, Tim described the difficulty of licensing a master's thesis under a Creative Commons license due to local policies that seemed to offer—at best—ambiguous insight into whether he had the agency to do so (Amidon, 2011). Ultimately, he was successful, but if he hadn't had access to copyright experts, extensive time to research work-for-hire policies, and the confidence to build his knowledge and that of his committee, he might not have succeeded. Similarly, Rife and Hart-Davidson (2006: 12) pointed to a participant who had used an image with permission of the copyright owner but discontinued use of the image because he "didn't want to fight." Henry Jenkins (2006) told the story of Heather Lawver, a Harry Potter fan who created the organization Defense Against the Dark Arts specifically to help fans respond to the onslaught of cease-and-desist letters they were receiving—a common experience in online fan communities. These examples certainly suggest that knowledge matters, but material resources, time, and access impact the degree of agency that students and educators have. Knowledge is an important first step because it equips students and educators with a media literacy that privileges the discovery of opportunities where multimedia composing might be opened up rather than shut down, but our pedagogies can't assume that students or educators can *make fair uses* just because they *understand fair use*.

A Heuristic for Unchilling: Access, Confidence, and Know-How

Given the complex network of chilling effects and given our culture of cease and desist orders, take-down warnings, and interfaces that automatically identify and block content, how should we proceed as educators? Some educators respond with protectionist pedagogies that result in teachers asking students to compose alphabetic texts with only traditional citations because as teachers we are most aware of and comfortable with our conventions and how they apply to alphabetic texts. Other educators try to keep students from leveraging fair use—for instance, when teachers attempt to remove legal consequences from composing and demand that students use only public domain or Creative Commons materials. This is a gesture that requires students to pay attention to issues of copyright, but it also stifles students from using copyright-protected materials in ways protected by fair use and creates artificially contrived classroom composing activities; today's composers often find themselves producing much more than solely alphabetic texts, where they need to rely on more than public domain or Creative Commons materials. Our students need experience making the difficult legal, cultural, and rhetorical choices about intellectual property that they will encounter in personal, civic, and professional contexts. Instead, pedagogies that reflect our democratic aims:

- Integrate student reading, interpreting, and the application of legal guidelines;
- Encourage students to work with tools and interfaces required for making fair, legal use of copyrighted content when appropriate; and
- Richly connect students with the cultural ideas, texts, and performances through which they make meaning in the world.

Here we offer a pedagogical framework that responds to the complex network of chills with a framework of rhetorical prowess that revolves around access, confidence, and know-how.

This framework is based on the roots of and complexity related to the different types of chilling effects previously explored. We can't unchill until we know where the chill is coming from. Chilling know-how happens through, for instance, inaccurate information (e.g., misrepresenting the DMCA or telling people they can use only 10 seconds of a 3-minute song). Chilling access happens when individuals and institutions ignore the variety of tools available for composing, including open-source and free software options, and when institutional policies govern network bandwidth without any attention to what people are sharing using the networks. Chilling confidence happens when take-down notices are given the power of the final word, when fear of litigation keeps composers from any remixing at all, or when students are asked to submit papers through a plagiarism-detection service where they are always already situated as "criminals."

As Figure 5.1 illustrates, access relates to one's access to tools, means, and materials. Confidence relates to the comfort one feels understanding and navigating copyright considerations. Know-how relates to one's ability to best make use of tools, means, and materials. Take any of those individual elements away, and composers start to feel the chill; they halt their creating, and we potentially lose new, enriching cultural expressions. Access and confidence without know-how results in ability but does not result in actual products—compositions that meaningfully draw upon circulating materials and remix them, mash them, and integrate them in a rhetorically savvy way. Access and know-how without confidence can often result in a significant chilling effect—where writers have the means to produce multimodal texts that draw upon circulating and copyright-protected products, but they're afraid they'll get sued. Confidence and know-how without access results in ideas, but ideas that can't be actually produced or enacted because of a lack of access to the tools of production.

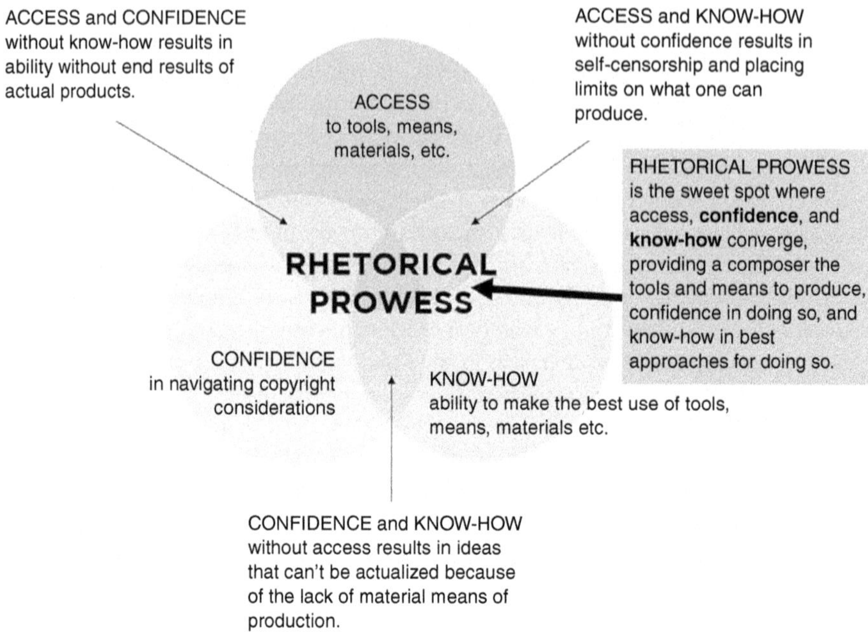

Figure 5.1 Confidence, Access, and Know-How

The sweet spot, which we've labeled *rhetorical prowess*, is the center space where access, confidence, and know-how converge and where a composer has the tools, the confidence, and the know-how required to draw upon circulating materials and create robust remix, mashup, and multimodal texts and, ideally, to share and distribute these texts.

Applying the Heuristic

To illuminate the heuristic, let's return to the stories we shared earlier. Tim's students chose to limit the distribution and rhetorical velocity (Ridolfo & DeVoss 2009) of their work; they are chilled about how to share their compositions and thus limit them to life on a thumb drive. In this case, students have technological access but don't have the know-how about responding effectively to take-down notices or the confidence required to seek public distribution of their work and/or to be ready to argue for their work with a fair use defense. The student in Dànielle's undergrad program purchased images to use on her professional portfolio website, which to us reads as a case of a student having access (to the tools to produce a portfolio and, to some extent, navigate stock photography sites) and know-how (knowledge of copyright protection) but not the confidence to best draw upon circulating materials and put them to use on her website. Kyle's students chose music for their audio essays based not just on what they had access to—after all, they had been introduced to Creative Commons materials but had chosen not to use them—but based on what seemed most rhetorically potent, which, in this case, was copyrighted material that they confidently layered with their recorded voices, a skill showcasing their technical know-how. In his class, however, Kyle asked future students to share their work in a password-protected, limited, private space; he approached the production of class work with a lack of confidence.

What, then, might unchilled student approaches look like, and how might we, as educators, facilitate an unchilling? In the case of Tim's students, Tim might share examples of take-down notices early on so that students can develop a familiarity with the ways in which these notices work, as well as a recognition of the types of compositions that receive such notices. Tim might also ask students to identify places and spaces where they can push back against a take-down notice, specifically to assert a fair use claim. Tim might facilitate peer review workshops dedicated to fair use, in which a peer makes a fair use evaluation. He might also ask students to, in addition to writing and creating their multimodal compositions, author fair use statements prior to saving and sharing their work in a public space. Approaches like these increase student confidence, expand their access to resources and materials, and equip them with the know-how to produce and distribute remix work.

In the case of the student in Dànielle's program, unchilling might happen through Dànielle's sharing examples of professional portfolios and having students, as well as the instructors who advise students on their portfolio production, deconstruct the content—identifying where the design elements came from, including the photos and graphics. Students and faculty might then be able to better identify common approaches and typical strategies for crafting professional portfolios. Dànielle might also address more deliberately the rhetorical choices involved in creating content, talking with students about when to create one's own photographic content versus when to lean on public domain or Creative Commons images. She might also share contexts (for instance, professional) in which students will be using stock photography resources and differentiate these contexts from that of a professional portfolio.

In the case of Kyle's creative nonfiction class, he could have massaged an understanding of fair use more fully into his lesson on how students could revise their original, alphabetic essays. That is, instead of simply asking students to revise their written words to sound more natural out loud for their recording, he could have led them through a discussion about whether any particular copyrighted musical tracks were so central to their stories that they should be mentioned or discussed in the written essays themselves—say, by discussing how much a song mattered to them at the time of their life they're writing about or by adding a section reflecting on the connections between a favorite song and the events recounted. Kyle could have discussed with his class how their subsequent use of this copyrighted music in their audio essays would now be more likely to be fair, since it had been transformed from simply background music into a central, crucial part of experiencing and understanding this text. Armed with that kind of know-how, students could be confident about posting their work on public distribution sites, instead of hidden in the world of locked course management systems.

Implications: The Ethical Responsibilities of Educators

More than a few teachers on our campuses have demonstrated an inaccurate understanding of copyright law and fair use guidelines. But it is nearly impossible to change the viewpoints of people who have internalized a conservative university stance as the absolute truth (Selber 2009: 15).

What our pedagogical framework offers is one way through which we might unparcel fear from production and pedagogies that open up students and educators to risks that might not be encountered if we were to write in abstract contexts void of risk. We believe that risk and fear are not commensurate and can be productively untangled through media literacy education. As media literacy educators, we think that it's important not only to acknowledge that no-risk composing contexts do not exist but also to engage in open discussions—with students, colleagues, administrators, and others—that there *are* risks associated with teaching multimedia composing.

Is it realistic to teach students that composing contexts exist where there are no risks? Is it productive to teach students that composing is so fraught with pitfalls that, unless they do exactly what is legally and institutionally required of them, they will be beset upon by take-down notices and cease and desist demands? Would doing so teach students that being hyper tentative and fearful composers are ideals worth striving for? Is it ethical to forward pedagogies that emphasize what students cannot do with texts and media (e.g., discussing only plagiarism or discussing only take-down notices) but *not* cover in equal measure the ways that fair use might be leveraged to open up opportunities for types of composing that might otherwise be chilled?

While media literacy educators have a responsibility to teach students that courts truly are the only spaces where legal determinations regarding fair use can be made with certainty, students are well served by educators who (1) emphasize that copyright has been mobilized by content owners to chill creators making legitimate use of copyrighted content, (2) draw richer distinctions between the severity and consequences associated with using copyrighted content in multimedia compositions, and (3) offer insight on and practice with tools such as fair use statements that can be used to argue for the legitimacy of their compositional choices.

Offering students opportunities to craft fair use statements or asking students to explore the policies of different media-sharing interfaces are productive learning activities that students might engage in to learn how fair use can and must be argued for. Unless educators take the time to prepare students to respond to infringement claims, potentially fair uses fall by the wayside or are adjudicated in private contexts; the stories of how composers' work is chilled are locked down and unheard. This is particularly problematic because fair use requires public display and discussion.

Lessig (2008: 107) suggested that the central barrier facing composers today is not access to tools but rather "assuring the freedom [composing] requires"; the bulleted list of chilling approaches we have offered are restrictions on compositional freedom. By freedom, Lessig means the legal agency to make use of existing cultural materials. Siva Vaidhyanathan (2001: 186) has made similar arguments and situates access to resources historically and culturally by arguing that this is:

> how creativity happens. Artists collaborate over space and time, even if they lived centuries and continents apart. Profound creativity requires maximum exposure to others' works and liberal freedoms to reuse and reshape others' material.

According to Lessig (2008), our current digital moment and our contemporary applications of copyright law give rise to two distinct economies of cultural production: read-only (RO) and read–write (RW). Read-only (RO) models leverage a "permission culture" in an attempt to monopolize control of both the products and processes through which culture is created. Read-only culture situates consumers as consumers and only as consumers: for instance, students can buy music, consume movies, and play games but not edit, mash, mix, or create these sorts of texts. In contrast, RW models value a remix culture and prosumer practices (Anderson 2003) and situate individuals both as consumers/users and as creators. To engage students in the robust bandwidth of media literacy—that is, from analysis to production, from critique to creation—we require read–write access to media. To enact the rhetorical prowess through which students can best make use of and defend their read–write uses of media, a combination of access, know-how, and confidence is necessary.

Outside of our three stories and contexts, what can media educators more broadly do in their classrooms to enact the heuristic we have offered and, specifically, to help students compose rhetorically powerful texts, taking full advantage of confidence, access, and know-how?

To answer that, in the next section, we sketch out what we hope are flexible, nimble ideas for constructing units or assignments; we offer these as starting points for teachers to adapt, adopt, and use in their own contexts. Note that these units demonstrate the interconnected nature of our threefold scheme for unchilling; that is, it's hard or impossible to unchill know-how and access without addressing issues of confidence at the same time. Our recommendation, then, is for instructors to consider ways to wrap complex approaches to build confidence, access, and know-how into any multimedia composing assignments.

Unit 1: Composing Musical Parodies

In this unit, students write and record parodies of popular songs. The objectives are for students to:

- Practice active transformation of common, circulating, contemporary texts;
- Understand how fair use applies to parody;
- Write in a particular genre (lyrics) and with a particular rhetorical approach (parody); and
- Strengthen their technical abilities in working with digital audio.

Confidence: Study cases about parody and fair use to build confidence that creating and distributing parodies is legal and protected. A good start would be with 2 Live Crew's successful fair use parody defense of their cover of "Pretty Woman" in *Campbell v. Acuff-Rose Music Inc.* (Summaries of this case are available online, but actual court cases are often easier for students to follow than we may expect.) Share the story of the group's album *As Nasty as They Wanna Be* and how the subsequent "clean" version of the album included the cover of the Roy Orbison classic. The work of Weird Al is also excellent to bring into a discussion of parody and the ethics of composing: Weird Al has, when possible, always asked for the permission of the original composer to create a parody. This isn't a legal process (in part because the composer isn't always the one who holds the copyright) but rather an ethical one.

Access: Teach students how to find and use the tools they'll need to create a successful parody of their own. This might include an introduction to open-source recording software like Audacity and apps that make recording audio using a phone or tablet easy. If students want to record themselves singing over the original background music, help students find instrumental versions of songs, perhaps by searching YouTube for instrumental or karaoke tracks and then using one of many YouTube rippers to save copies of the online files or by teaching them how to record audio through the computer speakers as an editable digital audio file.

Know-how: Once students have confidently accessed musical assets and the tools a remixer needs, develop their know-how through lessons that build rhetorical prowess. Study a number of parodies to identify the musical and textual moves that make them successful. Help students write lyrics that parody their original song in ways that suggest the new meaning they want audiences to experience and invite them to revise those lyrics after testing them on the rest of the class. On the technical side, practice recording voices and other audio pieces, building an artist's sensitivity to the different affordances of various kinds of microphones (e.g., on a phone, on a laptop, on a set of earbuds) and the effect of adjusting microphone distance and recording levels. Practice copying, moving, and layering clips of music and sound effects so that the audience hears the message the students intend.

Unit 2: Engaging in Critical Photography

In this unit, students explore and critique aspects of U.S. life by taking photographs of iconic American objects as a way of voicing a critical reaction. The objectives of this unit are for students to:

- Practice using nonlinguistic texts for rhetorical aims;
- Explore the ways in which the meaning of generally copyright-protected materials can be remixed;
- Study the affordances of photography; and
- Develop skills shooting and editing effective photos.

Confidence: Study successful fair use cases that focus on parody and photography. (Of course, parody isn't the only way to defend a work as a legal fair use, but it's a good entryway into conversations about transformative purposes and the four fair use factors as a whole.) Consider starting with the case of *Mattel Inc. v. Walking Mountain Prods.* (2003), in which the court determined that it was fair use for a photographer to sell fine art photographs of Barbie dolls that had been chopped up and cooked into various foods. Another example might be the case of *Leibovitz v. Paramount Pictures Corp.* (1996), where the court decided that it was fair use for the movie poster for *Naked Gun 33⅓* to parody Annie Leibovitz's famous nude photo of a pregnant Demi Moore. An additional starting point might be the recent decision in *Galvin v. Ill. Republican Party* (2015) that it was fair use for a political poster to be digitally altered to make it look like the politician being praised in the original poster was in fact making an escape with stolen money. Look at the original and new photos together with students and explore how, even when certain aspects of fair use were against the photographer (such as when the parodic photograph earned money for the photographer), these cases still showed fair use prevailing.

Access: Teach students how to take, find, and adapt digital photographs for new ends and different meaning. Introduce them to apps that will ease the difficulty of getting their own photographs from phones and tablets onto laptop and desktop computers. Introduce them to search tools that offer more robust options than they might find through a simple Google Image search, including the historic, iconic images available through government and library databases. Show them how to use screenshots to capture photos that interfaces won't allow them to download—a skill that is defensible when being used to practice fair use rights. Introduce them to free alternatives to expensive industry-standard applications like Adobe Photoshop, such as the browser-based Pixlr Editor, which provides cropping tools, background-removal functions, and the capacity to layer multiple image files.

Know-how: Study overtly rhetorical photographs that draw on copyright-protected material to make their arguments or that, through manipulation, present an altered reality, discussing aspects such as the ways the photographer's framing and editing affect the meaning that audiences receive. Practice making small changes to the coloring and cropping of famous, iconic photographs to discuss how these changes affect meanings. Give students time to practice cropping, layering, and editing their own digital photographs of copyrighted, iconic images.

Engage students in peer review by holding class critique sessions, where students are asked to explain what they see in and what meaning they take from an image and then by inviting the composer to explain his or her rhetorical intent.

Unit 3: Using Films of the Past to Understand the Present

In this unit, students build an argument that uses copyrighted film clips as support. Their final product is a short documentary film that makes a focused claim about one way that TV and film has changed in the way it represents particular kinds of bodies, places, or ideas. The objectives of this unit are for students to:

- Critically analyze the role of audiovisual representation in shaping public opinion;
- Work directly to find, edit, and put to use copyright-protected materials;
- Understand the power of the right kind of evidence when supporting a claim; and
- Practice using filmmaking and film-editing tools.

Confidence: Consider launching the unit by introducing and studying cases where defendants successfully used a fair use defense of film clips, such as that of a documentary about Jewish history that fairly used clips from four films owned by the National Center for Jewish Films (*Nat'l Ctr. for Jewish Film v. Riverside Films, L.L.C.* 2012) and when a documentary about early horror and science fiction films fairly used clips from films like *Invasion of the Saucerman* (*Hofheinz v. Discovery Commc'ns, Inc.* 2001). Build student confidence that, with fair use, they can use clips of copyrighted work to support their claims without needing to ask permission or pay licensing fees. Study the four fair use factors to build an understanding of what makes a use more likely to be fair (for instance, using only as much of a clip as is necessary to support a given claim). Draw upon resources like the Center for Media & Social Impact's 2005 *Documentary Filmmakers' Statement of Best Practices in Fair Use.*

Access: Help students access the media clips they need to support their arguments about the changing face of media representation. Teach them to use software that breaks the digital rights management (DRM) on DVDs; direct them to websites that let them download clips they find on YouTube, Vimeo, and other online video sources; show them how screencasting software can capture video and audio from any streaming or saved source on a computer. Introduce them to various free and paid software options for editing video, perhaps starting with the simple tools that are part of default Windows and Macintosh operating systems. Teach them how to collect their own footage, using simple video recording devices like phones and tablets.

Know-how: Help students develop an understanding of how documentary makers utilize video, music, voice, and image strategically within their films to support claims or arguments by watching samples of films, especially those with an overt, easily understandable rhetorical purpose. Ask students to choose brief scenes from these documentaries and then reverse-engineer scripts for those scenes, including written descriptions of the various video, audio, voice, and image components that comprise the frames of those scenes. These activities not only help students to develop critical reading practices by learning how to identify the different rhetorical work that video, music, voice, and images perform within films as critical readers but also provide students with opportunities to strategize and practice critical making by parsing how arrangement and layering of these multimodal elements contribute to the design of multimedia arguments. To take the activity further, ask students to compare these scripts to other writing about films (including books of history and criticism), noting the various ways that authors use sources. On the technical end, help students layer their own narrations and their own footage with the filmic assets they collected. Discuss issues of arrangement, pacing, volume, and voice-overs to help them make the most rhetorically satisfying product for their audience.

Epilogue

Consider these possible futures:

A group of six students in Tim's class study examples of video parodies and build confidence with video editing, sound design, and video production tools. The team decides to construct a parody of a music video rife with misogynistic and patriarchal cultural narratives. The team shoots original video that subverts the ending of the original video with recomposed lyrics that offer a story privileging the woman's power and agency. Nearly all is original, except the background musical track and components of the choreography. The students create a fair use argument before uploading the video to YouTube and post the argument outlining both the transformative changes they have made to the original and the ways that the video offers parodic criticism of the original.

In Dànielle's program, a student builds the visual content for her professional portfolio by seeking out Creative Commons work for graphical content and taking her own photographs to integrate. In her portfolio, she includes work that she's produced in a classroom context, including a movie trailer remix she created to present a retelling of the American classic *Psycho* from Mother's perspective, using clips from other existing films, using a fair use parody defense to support and protect her work and her sharing of it. She had access to the means of production, confidence that her work was protected by fair use, and know-how in terms of how to use original *and* copyright-protected materials to best shape and share her arguments.

In Kyle's creative nonfiction class, all the conversations about copyright have led a student to reconsider the ways music has impacted his life. His writing touches on this theme throughout the semester: He journals creative riffs on the four factors of fair use, playfully considering how he has "transformed" and has been transformed by music; he workshops a personal essay about the changing nature of music "ownership," in which he supplements his own stories with legal cases he has read about while researching the piece. He also records an audio essay that playfully enacts some of the struggles he has had learning new technologies, throughout his life and in this piece, which he records and edits using the open-source software Audacity. His audio essay layers public domain music, Creative Commons music, and copyrighted work that is a fundamental, important part of his creative explorations. He proceeds with confidence about how to use these different types of audio assets, access to the tools he needed to record and edit his piece, and know-how about how to manipulate those assets and tools to the greatest effect. The piece is the keystone of his final portfolio, demonstrating his creative and rhetorical prowess.

References

Amidon, T. R. (2011). "Authoring Academic Agency: Charting the Tensions Between Work-for-Hire University Policies." In M. Courant Rife, S. Slattery, and D. Nicole DeVoss (Eds.), *Copy(Write): Intellectual Property in the Writing Classroom* (pp. 49–78). Anderson, SC: Parlor Press.

Amidon, T. R., & Reyman, J. (2014). "Authorship and Ownership of User Contributions on the Social Web." In D. N. DeVoss and M. Courant Rife (Eds.), *Cultures of Copyright* (pp. 108–124). New York: Peter Lang.
Anderson, D. (2003). "Prosumer Approaches to New Media Composition: Consumption and Production in Continuum." *Kairos: A Journal of Rhetoric, Technology, and Pedagogy*, 8(1). Retrieved from http://kairos.technorhetoric.net/8.1/binder2.html?coverweb/anderson/index.html
Campbell v. Acuff-Rose Music, 510 U.S. 569 (1994).
Center for Media & Social Impact. (2005). "Documentary Filmmakers' Statement of Best Practices in Fair Use." Retrieved from www.cmsimpact.org/sites/default/files/fair_use_final.pdf
DeVoss, D. N., & Webb, S. (2008). "Media Convergence: Grand Theft Audio: Negotiating Copyright as Composers." *Computers and Composition*, 25, 79–103.
Dixon, K. (2014). "Feminism Online Identity: Analyzing the Presence of Hashtag Feminism." *Journal of Arts and Humanities*, 3(7), 34–40.
Fortunato, M. M. (2009). "Let's Not Go Crazy: Why *Lenz v. Universal Music Corp.* Undermines the Notice and Takedown Process of the Digital Millennium Copyright Act." *Journal of Intellectual Property Law*, 17, 147–172.
Galvin v. Ill. Republican Party. District Court for the Northern District of Illinois. WL 5304625 (2015).
Hobbs, R., Jaszi, P., & Aufderheide, P. (2007). "The Cost of Copyright Confusion for Media Literacy." Retrieved from http://files.eric.ed.gov/fulltext/ED499465.pdf
Hofheinz v. Discovery Commc'ns, Inc., No. 00 CIV. 3802 (HB) (S.D.N.Y., 2001).
Jenkins, H. (2006). *Convergence Culture: Where Old and New Media Collide*. New York: New York University Press.
Leibovitz v. Paramount Pictures Corp., 948 F. Supp. 1214 (S.D.N.Y., 1996).
Lenz v. Universal Music Corp., 801 F.3d 1126 (2015).
Lessig, L. (1999). *Code: And Other Laws of Cyberspace*. New York: Basic Books.
Lessig, L. (2004). *Free Culture: The Nature and Future of Creativity*. New York: Penguin Books.
Lessig, L. (2008). *Remix: Making Art and Commerce Thrive in the Hybrid Economy*. New York: Penguin Press.
Leval, P. N. (1990). "Toward a Fair Use Standard." *Harvard Law Review*, 103(5), 1105–1136.
Mattel Inc. v. Walking Mountain Prods., 353 F.3d 792 (9th Cir. 2003).
MGM Studios, Inc. v. Grokster, Ltd., 545 U.S. 913 (2005).
Nat'l Ctr. for Jewish Film v. Riverside Films, L.L.C., No. 5:12-cv-00044-ODW (DTB) (C.D. Cal., 2012).Park, S., & Leonard, D. J. (2014, February 3). "In Defense of Twitter Feminism." Retrieved from https://modelviewculture.com/pieces/in-defense-of-twitter-feminism
Pfaffenberger, B. (1992). "Technological Dramas." *Science, Technology, and Human Values*, 17(3), 282–312.
Porter, J. E. (2005). "The Chilling of Digital Information: Technical Communicators as Public Advocates." In M. Day and C. Lipson (Eds.), *Tech/Web: Technical Communications and the World Wide Web in the New Millennium* (pp. 243–259). Mahwah, NJ: Lawrence Erlbaum Associates.
Ridolfo, J., & DeVoss, D. N. (2009). "Composing for Recomposition: Rhetorical Velocity and Delivery." *Kairos: A Journal of Rhetoric, Technology, and Pedagogy*, 13(2). Retrievedhttp://kairos.technorhetoric.net/13.2/topoi/ridolfo_devoss/intro.html
Rife, M. C. (2010). "Copyright Law as Mediational Means: Report on a Mixed Methods Study of Professional Writers." *Technical Communication*, 57(1), 44–67.
Rife, M. C., & Hart-Davidson, W. (2006). "Is There a Chilling of Digital Communication? Exploring How Knowledge and Understanding of the Fair Use Doctrine May Influence Web Composing." Pilot Study report. SSRN Working Papers Series.
Selber, S. (2004). *Multiliteracies for a Digital Age*. Carbondale: Southern Illinois University Press.
Selber, S. (2009). "Institutional Dimensions of Academic Computing." *College Composition and Communication*, 61(1), 10–34.
Vaidhyanathan, S. (2001). *Copyrights and Copywrongs: The Rise of Intellectual Property and How It Threatens Creativity*. New York: New York University Press.
Westbrook, S. (2006). "Visual Rhetoric in a Culture of Fear: Impediments to Multimedia Production." *College English*, 68(5), 457–480.
Wieman v. Updegraff, 344 U.S. 183 (1952).

Further Reading

Aoki, K., Boyle, J., & Jenkins, J. (2005). "Tales From the Public Domain: Bound by Law?" Retrieved from www.law.duke.edu/cspd/comics/

Aufderheide, P., & Jaszi, P. (2011). *Reclaiming Fair Use*. Chicago: University of Chicago Press.

Center for Social Media, American University School of Communication. "Code of Best Practices in Fair Use for Media Literacy Education." Retrieved from http://mediaeducationlab.com/sites/mediaeducationlab.com/files/CodeofBestPracticesinFairUse.pdf

Hobbs, R. (2010). *Copyright Clarity: How Fair Use Supports Digital Learning*. Thousand Oaks, CA: Corwin.

Rife, M., Slattery, S., & DeVoss, D. N. (Eds.) (2011). *Copy(Write): Intellectual Property in the Writing Classroom*. Anderson, SC: Parlor Press.

6

LEGAL ISSUES IN ONLINE FAN FICTION

Aaron Schwabach

A work of fiction creates a world. Sometimes the world is almost like our world, different only because of the characters that inhabit it or the events that occur in it. Sometimes it is a world entirely unlike our own, with characters that are not even human (Wile E. Coyote, say) inhabiting universes functioning according to entirely different physical and biological laws. Sometimes it is a world like ours but in the past or the future. All of these worlds, strange or familiar, acquire a certain reality in the minds of those who experience them through print, film, video, sound recording, or other forms of expression. And once we have experienced these worlds and gotten to know the characters that inhabit them, we in the audience often want to know more. Sometimes we want new stories faster than the authors can produce them. Other times we are not satisfied with the story we've been given and want to reinterpret it. Still other times we may want characters from one world or story to meet those from another. All of these desires can lead to the creation of fan works.

A fan work is a creative work made by a fan, in any medium, using elements from another work not merely in passing but as a central theme or purpose. A short story about the imagined romance between Tony Stark and Bruce Banner is a fan work, as is a puppet show about Harry Potter and his friends and enemies, or a song about the crew of the *Enterprise*, or a music video of clips from the *Lord of the Rings* films, or a painting of Jasmine from *Aladdin* dressed as Anastasia from the movie of that name.

Many creators of works create or license their own reinterpretations of their existing works, and many works are best known from reinterpretations. Disney's *Snow White*, for example, is probably the best known version of the Snow White tale and characters—better known than the Brothers Grimm version of the story, which in turn is better known than the many versions of the tale the Brothers Grimm collected and distilled into their published version. In turn, Disney has created numerous reinterpretations of elements of the story in books, in video games, and as theme park characters. In the live-action television show *Once Upon a Time*, Snow White becomes an action hero bandit-turned-queen-turned-schoolteacher. Yet none of these versions of Snow White are, strictly speaking, fan works; an essential aspect of fan works is that they are created not by the content creators or owners but by fans: members of the audience for the work. (Most of *Once Upon a Time* is Disney creating fan works based on its own previous work; this sort of internal fandom is a fascinating cultural phenomenon but one unlikely to raise legal consequences, as Disney owns the intellectual property rights in most of the underlying works, and the remainder are in the public domain.)

And that brings us to the central legal concern with fan works: intellectual property law and, in particular, copyright law. Stories are copyrighted; characters can be copyrighted; story elements and settings may, in some cases, be copyrighted as well. A fan work based on an original work that is out of copyright avoids copyright concerns; fans can and do create fan works based on the plays of William Shakespeare, the novels of Jane Austen, the music of Jacques Offenbach, and the paintings of Edouard Manet (and, more infamously, Joseph Ducreux's *Portrait de l'artiste sous les traits d'un moqueur*).

Most fan works, however, are based on more recent works, and these works are still in copyright. Fan works based on the stories, characters, and worlds of *Doctor Who*, *Star Trek*, the Harry Potter series, Superman, Spiderman, Korra, *Twilight*, or any of thousands of other popular works are potentially copyright infringing. The good news for fans who want to create such works is that there is a certain amount of leeway given to them in the U.S. copyright regime; many works are noninfringing at the outset, while others that might initially appear infringing are in fact fair use of the copyrighted elements.

The Threshold Question: Are the Underlying Works or Characters Protected?

Determining whether a fan work violates the copyright in the underlying work on which it is based requires a two-step inquiry: first, whether the underlying work or element (such as a character) is protected by copyright and second, if so, whether the fanfic or other fan work violates that copyright.

The copyright law of the United States protects "original works of authorship fixed in any tangible medium of expression" (17 U.S.C. § 102(a)) including the literary, dramatic, graphic, and audiovisual works upon which fan works are based. Elements of the work that are not original, however, are not protected, nor is "any idea, procedure, process, system, method of operation, concept, principle, or discovery" incorporated therein (17 U.S.C. § 102(b)). Almost all works of fiction will fall into one or more of these categories of copyrightable material, although some story elements (including, perhaps, minor characters) may not and ideas from a work (that young wizards would go to school to learn magic or that a starship exploring the universe would be under orders not to interfere with the development of the new civilizations it discovered) will not. In addition, there is no copyright in any work of the U.S. government (17 U.S.C. §105; generally defined as works prepared by a U.S. government employee as part of that person's official duties), although this rule excludes some works (such as postage stamps created after 1978). Some works created by state and local governments are excluded from copyright registration and thus from some copyright protection, as well, either by that state's own decision or by U.S. Copyright Office policy.

For most works of fiction, however, the main reason a work is in the public domain is the passage of time. In accordance with the Patent & Copyright Clause of the U.S. Constitution (Art. I, § 8., cl. 8), copyright is granted for only a limited time; the clause authorizes Congress "[t]o promote the Progress of Science and useful Arts, by securing for limited Times to Authors and Inventors the exclusive Right to their respective Writings and Discoveries." The first U.S. copyright law enacted after the adoption of the Constitution and its copyright clause was based on the British Statute of Anne (the first modern copyright law), in force in the colonies before independence. This first copyright law set the term of copyright at fourteen years, renewable once; this term has been repeatedly extended since. Many still popular works can be used in fan works without raising copyright concerns because the copyrights have expired. But some of the extensions of the copyright term have been recent, and not all works currently in copyright are subject to the same copyright term; determining whether the copyright on a particular work or character has expired is not always simple.

The fourteen-year term of the Copyright Act of 1790 has been extended many times. The Copyright Act of 1909 set a term of twenty-eight years, renewable once. The Copyright Act of 1976 extended the term for works created after January 1, 1978, yet further, to the lifetime of the author plus fifty years for most individually authored or coauthored works and seventy-five years for most other works. The most recent modification, the Sonny Bono Copyright Term Extension Act of 1998 (CTEA), extended these terms to the lifetime of the author plus seventy years and to ninety-five years, respectively. This extension was challenged as effectively undermining the "limited time" requirement of the Patent & Copyright Clause; however, it was upheld as constitutional by the U.S. Supreme Court in *Eldred v. Ashcroft*, 537 U.S. 186 (2003). The copyright term is now longer than the average human lifetime; most people will never see the copyright expire on any work published during their lifetimes.

The Copyright Amendment Act of 1992 retroactively granted an automatic copyright renewal for works published between 1964 and 1977 so long as those works were otherwise eligible for copyright renewal. The length of this renewal term was extended by the CTEA to sixty-seven years, so that works protected by the Act are still in copyright. The sixty-seven-year extension also applies to works created in or before 1950 only if the copyright on those works was renewed or otherwise extended in some way after 1950; in other words, it does not apply to works created before 1923. International law adds another layer of complexity: under the Uruguay Round Agreements Act of 1994, copyright is automatically extended for works originating in countries other than the United States that are parties to the World Trade Organization (WTO) or the Berne Convention, even if copyright renewal formalities were not complied with.

The result of all this complexity is that all works first published in the United States and published before 1923, all works by authors who died before 1946 (or whose date of death is not known to be later), all works first published in the United States and published between 1923 and 1963 for which copyright was not renewed, and all works first published in the United States before 1977 and published without a copyright notice are in the public domain. All works published after 1989 can be presumed to be copyrighted (other than, as previously noted, U.S. government works), as can most works published between 1978 and 1989, although some exceptions apply.

Many fictional worlds include works straddling the copyright cutoff line. The worlds of Sherlock Holmes and of Bertie Wooster, for example, include works by their original authors that are now in the public domain, as well as works that are still protected by copyright. In other cases, later authors have written new works set in these out-of-copyright universes; thus Gregory Maguire's dystopian Oz novels (which may properly be regarded as Oz fanfic) create no new copyright in the universe created by L. Frank Baum but are themselves copyrighted insofar as they are original works of authorship. A fan work incorporating only material, settings, and characters from the public domain portions of such a universe raises no legal issue; to the extent, though, that the fan work incorporates material from the still copyrighted works, it is subject to the same concerns as are fan works based on more recently created universes. Anyone who wishes may write new Oz stories set in L. Frank Baum's Oz, and those stories may include an alternate character interpretation for the Wicked Witch of the West, as Mr. Maguire did in creating his version of the Witch, Elphaba. Anyone wishing to write stories about Maguire's Elphaba will have to take copyright concerns into account, although that does not mean those concerns cannot be overcome.

Copyright in Characters

Copyright in an entire work is fairly straightforward; everyone can recognize a copy as a copy. Copyright in characters has a more tangled legal history and presents more conceptual difficulties as well. The audience for a work develops familiarity with the fictional characters, just as with real persons; the audience knows the characters not only by name but by personality and perhaps by appearance. A work that takes a single character and places that character in an entirely different setting may nonetheless raise copyright concerns because the character is an original creation of its author. A story that transposes Billy Batson to Brazil, even if he uses none of his Captain Marvel superpowers and never utters the word "Shazam," is nonetheless a Captain Marvel story. Another story may place Brazilian Jewish centaur Guedali Tartakovsky in the United States to equal effect. Guedali is protected by copyright regardless of the approach one takes; he is both sufficiently delineated as a character, and his story is the story being told in the work in which he appears.

These approaches to copyright in characters merit closer examination. Content owners and fans alike often assume that fictional characters are protected; in fact, that is true only some of the time. Characters created as works of visual art—Mickey Mouse, Avatar Aang, Ponyo, Snoopy—present the easiest question: the visual depictions of these characters are protected as works of visual art. (See *Walt Disney Prod. v. Air Pirates*, 345 F. Supp. 108 [N.D. Cal. 1972].)

For characters created through text, the test is less clear. By far the most widely applied test is the "sufficiently delineated" test. This test recognizes that some characters are "sufficiently delineated" to be protected independently of the works in which they appear, and it was first set forth by the federal Court of Appeals for the Second Circuit in 1930 in *Nichols v. Universal Pictures Corporation*, 45 F.2d 119 (2d Cir. 1930). The *Nichols* court recognized that certain characters are stock; in considering the copyrightability of "the characters, quite independently of the 'plot' proper," the Second Circuit pointed out:

> If Twelfth Night were copyrighted it is quite possible that a second comer might so closely imitate Sir Toby Belch or Malvolio as to infringe, but it would not be enough that for one of his characters he cast a riotous knight who kept wassail to the discomfort of the household, or a vain and foppish steward who became amorous of his mistress. These would be no more than Shakespeare's 'ideas' in the play, as little capable of monopoly as Einstein's doctrine of Relativity or Darwin's theory of the Origin of the Species. It follows that the less developed the characters, the less they can be copyrighted; that is the penalty an author must bear for making them too indistinct.
>
> (*Nichols v. Universal Pictures Corporation*, 45 F.2d at 120)

An example readily accessible to almost everyone is set forth in a 1982 case from the Second Circuit discussing the copyrightability of the character Tarzan. Tarzan is a character known to all of us, even those who have never read a Tarzan novel or watched a Tarzan movie. Edgar Rice Burroughs' ape-man is an archetypal character, like Dracula or Merlin. His roots lie as far back as Enkidu in the Epic of Gilgamesh; yet his personality is unique and instantly recognizable. The original work in which Tarzan appeared, *Tarzan of the Apes*, introduced the character fully delineated, as we know him today. ("[T]he delineation was complete upon the 1912 appearance of the first Tarzan title *Tarzan of the Apes*." *Burroughs v. Metro-Goldwyn-Mayer,*

Inc., 683 F.2d 610, 631 (2d Cir. 1982) (Newman, J., concurring)). Tarzan is the feral, orphaned Lord Greystoke, raised in the jungle by apes, who learned French as his first human language yet feels more at home in the trees, away from the humans who so often disappoint him; he enters human society as an adult only to find it far more brutal than the "savagery" of the jungle, and at the end of the first book renounces his claim to humanity, claiming kinship only with the apes.

Tarzan presents a fairly easy case for sufficient delineation, yet even with Tarzan the judiciary struggled to explain clearly what made "sufficiently delineated" to be protected by copyright. At the trial court level, Judge Henry Frederick Werker of the Southern District of New York declared rather confusingly:

> It is beyond cavil that the character "Tarzan" is delineated in a sufficiently distinctive fashion to be copyrightable. . . . Tarzan is the ape-man. He is an individual closely in tune with his jungle environment, able to communicate with animals yet able to experience human emotions. He is athletic, innocent, youthful, gentle and strong. He is Tarzan.
>
> (*Burroughs v. Metro-Goldwyn-Mayer, Inc.*, 1982: 519 F. Supp. 388, 391)

On one level, we all know what Judge Werker meant. Everyone in the United States knows Tarzan, as do many beyond its borders; at some level, he is present in all of our memories. But on another level, Judge Werker's description tells us nothing about the character. Athleticism, innocence, youth, gentleness, and strength are fairly common characteristics for fictional characters on the side of the protagonists in action-oriented stories; everyone from Sokka of the Southern Water Tribe to Barry Allen to Disney's Hercules (although definitely not the original Hercules of myth) possesses these characteristics. Doctor Doolittle can communicate with animals and experience human emotions. A great many characters are in tune with their environments; unless the story is one of adaptation or alienation, for a character to be out of tune with his or her environment would be a distraction. The distinguishing characteristic, perhaps, is that "Tarzan is the ape-man"; however, fiction is filled with feral children, from the aforementioned Enkidu through Romulus and Remus to Tarzan's literary nearly contemporary Mowgli, and beyond them to Lazaro of *Where the River Runs Black*. In his own time, Tarzan was preceded by over three decades by fellow Francophone Saturnin Farandoul. In the end, all that makes Tarzan unique is Judge Werker's circle-closing conclusion: "He is Tarzan." Perhaps that is all that makes anyone, real or fictional, unique: a bare assertion of identity. And perhaps the essence of the "sufficiently delineated" test is something we could never succeed in intelligibly explaining. But we know a sufficiently delineated character when we see one.

The copyright protection of fictional characters is more narrow than the protection of the works in which they appear, though. Tarzan is protected by copyright, but the many other feral child stories on the market do not infringe on that copyright, even when, as in the case of Marvel Comics' Ka-Zar, the feral protagonists are also lost heirs of British nobility. (It is worth noting, though, that the holders of the Harry Potter copyrights have been able to block the publication in the Netherlands of Dmitri Yemets' Tanya Grotter novels, starring—as the name suggests—a gender-flipped Russian Harry Potter clone. It may be that the similarities in the stories extend beyond the lead character: Tanya attends Tibidokhs School for Behaviorally-Challenged Young Witches and Wizards. She sleeps in the loggia of her foster family's apartment. She fights Chuma-del-tort. While these are not perfect stand-ins for Hogwarts, the cupboard under the stairs at Number Four Privet Drive, and Voldemort, the overall pattern of similarities is pretty strong.

The "sufficiently delineated" test is applied throughout the United States. However, one federal appellate court—the Court of Appeals for the Ninth Circuit—has also applied a second test (and once appeared to apply this test exclusively): the "story being told" test. Archetypal *film noir* detective Sam Spade is, apparently, too much of an archetype and not enough of an individual. The court stated, in apparent dicta, that "[i]t is conceivable that the character really constitutes the story being told, but if the character is only the chessman in the game of telling the story he is not within the area of the protection afforded by the copyright." Sam Spade, it turned out, was just such a chessman: "We conclude that even if the Owners assigned their complete rights in the copyright to the Falcon, such assignment did not prevent the author from using the characters used therein, in other stories. The characters were vehicles for the story told, and the vehicles did not go with the sale of the story" (*Warner Bros. Pictures v. Columbia Broadcasting Sys.*, 216 F.2d 945, 950 (9th Cir. 1954)). There is a certain logic to this, perhaps, as Spade's author, Dashiel Hammett, had previously acknowledged: "Spade has no original. He is . . . what most of the private detectives I worked with would like to have been and in their cockier moments thought they approached" (Hammett 1934: intro). The Spade of the original novel is memorable more as an attitude than as a character; the Spade of the movie is memorable for Humphrey Bogart's portrayal of him (in the 1941 version), which in turn is very much of a kind with many other world-weary Bogart characters, up to and including Rick Blaine (who is not only sufficiently delineated to be worthy of protection under the less stringent, more widespread test but whose journey of redemption also constitutes the story being told in *Casablanca*).

The "story being told" test sets the bar for copyrightability of characters much higher but can safely be regarded as of limited effect. Indeed, the outcomes for Tarzan and Sam Spade might have been the same under either test. *The Maltese Falcon* is a story driven by plot, atmosphere, and setting; in contrast, Tarzan's stories are about Tarzan, with widely varied settings, from urban centers to the Earth's core, albeit with a jungle Eden always present, if not in the story then in the protagonist's heart. *Tarzan of the Apes* tells the story of Tarzan; *The Maltese Falcon* is a reflection on the moral frailty of humanity, more bitter and less optimistic than Bogie's turn as Rick Blaine.

This leaves open the copyrightability of characters less memorable than Tarzan. Sherlock Holmes, Batman, and Harry Potter are surely sufficiently delineated; John Watson, Robin, and Hermione Granger probably make the cut as well. But what of Mrs. Hudson, Alfred, and Argus Filch? And while their chief antagonists Moriarty, the Joker, and Voldemort may rank, what of minor villains like Holy Peter, Deacon Blackfire, and Professor Quirrell? The "story being told" test seems especially likely to discriminate against secondary characters, however well delineated; the "sufficiently delineated" test, however, quite probably extends protection even to well realized tertiary characters such as Inspector Lestrade, Ra's al Ghul, and Neville Longbottom.

Copyright in Story Elements

What of 221B Baker Street, the Batmobile, and Platform 9¾? All are identifiable story elements, and all are original creations of the authors of the works in which they appear. The first is, perhaps, the least original; it is merely a London street address that did not, at the time, exist. Platform 9¾ is perhaps slightly more original, as it is not only the number of a platform at King's Cross that did not exist but one that could not exist under the numbering system in use then and now. Neither name, perhaps, is original enough to be worthy of copyright protection in its own right (and names and addresses are ordinarily not copyrightable), but both have been imbued with characteristics and atmosphere that may make them sufficiently delineated. Both are well-known to fans of their respective works, many of whom could draw the locations described from memory. Oddly enough, both have now acquired a sort of reality as well: 221B Baker Street now exists, more or less (the right to receive mail at the address belongs to the Holmes Museum, located nearby) and a baggage cart is half-embedded in a wall at King's Cross below a sign reading "Platform 9¾."

The Batmobile is far more clearly delineated than either of these, and the Ninth Circuit has upheld its copyrightability. In terms very similar to *Nichols* and the other "sufficiently delineated" tests, the Ninth Circuit declared that "copyright protection extends not only to an original work as a whole, but also to 'sufficiently distinctive' elements . . . contained within the work" (*DC Comics v. Towle*, 802 F.3d 1012, 1019 (9th Cir. 2015)).

Some story elements may not only pass the sufficiently distinctive test but may also constitute the story being told. The story being told in *Star Trek*, through multiple films and televisions series, is the story of the *Enterprise* more than the story of any of the characters. The story of Harry Potter is also the story of Hogwarts. And items closely associated with a character may be copyrighted as a "component part of the character which significantly aids in identifying the character" (*New Line Cinema Corp. v. Easter Unlimited Inc.*, 17 U.S.P.Q. 2d 1631, 1633 (E.D.N.Y. 1989)).

Duration: Characters Partially In and Partially Out of Copyright

The problem of works straddling a copyright cutoff date is inevitable for characters in a series. When the copyright on the oldest work in the series expires, other works featuring the character will still be in copyright. The earliest works featuring Mickey Mouse will soon enter the public domain. Common sense should dictate that later stories about the same character cannot extend the copyright in the original; otherwise, copyright in characters could be maintained perpetually by publishing a new authorized story every century or so. Copyright scholar David Nimmer explains that:

> anyone may copy such elements as have entered the public domain, and no one may copy such elements as remain protected by copyright. The more difficult question is this: may the character depicted in all of the works be appropriated for use in a new story created by the copier? . . . [O]nce the copyright in the first work that contained the character enters the public domain, then it is not copyright infringement for others to copy the character in works that are otherwise original with the copier, even though later works in the original series remain protected by copyright.
>
> (1 *Nimmer on Copyright* § 2–12)

This, Nimmer explains, is a consequence of the derivative nature of sequels:

> Subsequent works in a series (or sequels) are in a sense derivative works while the characters which appear throughout the series are a part of the underlying work upon which the later works are based. Just as the copyright in a derivative work will not protect public domain portions of an underlying work as incorporated in the derivative work, so copyright in a particular work in a series will not protect the character as contained in such series if the work in the series in which the character first appeared has entered the public domain.
>
> (1 *Nimmer on Copyright*: § 2–12)

In other words, the copyright term on a character generally begins to run when the character first appears in a form sufficiently delineated to merit copyright protection. Some characters, however, may undergo radical evolution over the course of a series; Mickey Mouse is among this number. The Batman played by Christian Bale is not the Batman played by Adam West. The Taran of *The Book of Three* is not the Taran of *The High King*. Such characters might conceivably enter the public domain piecemeal, so that, for a few years, Taran the naïve and at times somewhat selfish Assistant Pig-Keeper would be in the public domain, while Taran the caring and competent leader would not.

Nimmer adds, "The same rule obviously applies to a character born in one medium who subsequently appears in derivative works in other media" (1 *Nimmer on Copyright Characters*: § 2–12). Once the literary Tarzan has entered the public domain (as has now happened), there is no copyright barrier to making Tarzan movies, cartoons, or games. Commercial uses would still be prevented by trademark (and perhaps unfair competition, contract, and tort law); fan works, however, are rarely commercial.

What Rights, If Any, of the Copyright Holder Are Potentially Being Infringed Upon?

Copyright protects the text—that is, the expression—of a work of fiction and under certain conditions may protect characters within the work. U.S. copyright law grants five rights to the copyright holder: the rights of reproduction, distribution, performance, and display, as well as the right to make derivative works based upon the copyrighted work (17 U.S.C. § 106). It is the last of these that is of greatest concern to the creators of fan works. Fan works are rarely exact imitations of the original work; that would defeat the fannish purpose. While some fan works may involve performance or display or part or all of an original work, even this performance and display are not likely to be in unaltered form. It is inherent in the nature of fan works to take familiar story elements and combine them in unfamiliar ways. While this necessarily involves originality, it may nonetheless infringe upon the copyright in the original work if the new work is a derivative work within the meaning of the Copyright Act.

In a critical sense, fan works are necessarily derivative; they cannot function otherwise. Tolkien pointed out that this was true of all fantasy and perhaps of all fiction: "the Cauldron of Story . . . has always been boiling, and to it have continually been added new bits" (Tolkien 1966: 26). In a legal sense, though, a work is not derivative simply because it is inspired by or contains elements of another work. It is derivative if it is insufficiently transformative.

Every derivative work necessarily involves transformation; at a certain point, the transformative nature of the work surpasses the derivative nature, and the work is a transformative work rather than a derivative one.

Works that are transformative are not derivative within the meaning of section 106(2), even though their source is clear. Retelling a story from another perspective may be transformative, even though the characters, settings, and many of the events described are the same. The shift in viewpoint, the different perception of the relationships among the characters, and the impact of the events described make the retelling an original work, commenting on and critiquing the original (*Suntrust Bank v. Houghton Mifflin Co.*, 268 F.3d 1257 [11th Cir. 2001]). In determining a work's transformative nature or lack thereof, courts are unavoidably analyzing the text and images presented in a critical sense; however, the quality of the work is unimportant. It is unfortunate but unsurprising that many fan works are, regrettably, of rather poor quality; this does not mean that those works are not transformative. For example, parodies—a special category of transformative work, beloved by fan work creators, in which the transformation is intended to be at least in part humorous—can succeed in being transformative even when they fail at being funny:

> The threshold question when fair use is raised in defense of parody is whether a parodic character may reasonably be perceived. Whether, going beyond that, parody is in good taste or bad does not and should not matter to fair use. As Justice Holmes explained, "[i]t would be a dangerous undertaking for persons trained only to the law to constitute themselves final judges of the worth of [a work], outside of the narrowest and most obvious limits. At the one extreme some works of genius would be sure to miss appreciation. Their very novelty would make them repulsive until the public had learned the new language in which their author spoke" (*Bleistein v. Donaldson Lithographing Co.*) (circus posters have copyright protection); *cf. Yankee Publishing Inc. v. News America Publishing, Inc.*, 809 F.Supp. 267, 280 (S.D.N.Y. 1992) (Leval, J.) ("First Amendment protections do not apply only to those who speak clearly, whose jokes are funny, and whose parodies succeed").
> (*Campbell v. Acuff-Rose Music, Inc.*, 510 U.S. 569, 582–583 (1994))

This excerpt from *Campbell* also highlights the close relationship between transformativeness and fair use. U.S. copyright law permits certain uses that might otherwise be infringing, if four statutory factors weigh in favor of a finding that the use is "fair":

> Notwithstanding the provisions of sections 106 and 106A, the fair use of a copyrighted work, including such use by reproduction in copies or phonorecords or by any other means specified by that section, for purposes such as criticism, comment, news reporting, teaching (including multiple copies for classroom use), scholarship, or research, is not an infringement of copyright. In determining whether the use made of a work in any particular case is a fair use the factors to be considered shall include—
>
> 1. the purpose and character of the use, including whether such use is of a commercial nature or is for nonprofit educational purposes;
> 2. the nature of the copyrighted work;
> 3. the amount and substantiality of the portion used in relation to the copyrighted work as a whole; and
> 4. the effect of the use upon the potential market for or value of the copyrighted work. (17 U.S.C. § 107)

Fan works are rarely of a commercial nature, although they are rarely for nonprofit educational purposes either. For most fan works, the first factor will probably weigh somewhat on the fair use side of neutral. The second factor—the nature of the copyrighted work—will usually weigh against fair use: most fan works are based on novels, movies, plays, television shows, and recordings of popular music, all things that are traditionally at the core of the rationale for copyright protection. The third factor will usually weigh in favor of a finding of fair use but may vary enormously from one work to the next. Especially problematic are fanvids in which scenes from a familiar work are set to a popular song or other copyrighted music. Often the entire song is used. While the TV or film clips used to make the video portion of the fanvid are only a small part of the copyrighted work as a whole, the musical portion uses all of the original copyrighted phonorecording; in such a case, this factor weighs against a finding of fair use with regard to the copyright in the phonorecording, although not with regard to the copyright in the film or television series. Most fan works, though, are likely to use only a small portion of the original. The fourth factor—market impact—is viewed by many courts and commentators as the most important of the four. This factor, too, is likely to weigh in favor of most fan works; very rarely does a fan work compete with the underlying work in the marketplace or otherwise harm the market. In fact, fan works tend to have a positive effect on demand by building a stronger community of dedicated fans who will gladly spend money on new works in the series.

There are thus multiple barriers to the finding that any fan work infringes on the copyright in the original. First, the original—whether character or complete work—must be protected by copyright. Next, the use made by the fan work must be derivative and not transformative. And even a use that is not otherwise transformative may nonetheless be protected as fan use.

The Way Forward: What Should Fans and Authors Do?

The copyright status of fan works and copyright infringement is poorly understood both by content owners and by fans. Some content owners publish "fanfic bans," in the apparent misconception that this makes any fan work based on their works infringing. Similarly, some fans include disclaimers ("I do not own *Pirates of the Caribbean* or Captain Barbossa"), in the apparent misconception that these disclaimers make their works noninfringing. In fact, both are irrelevant, although a content owner's express permission of fan works might be construed as a license.

Both parties are not only uncertain of their legal rights but also hesitant to assert them. Most authors of fan works are individuals without the resources for a court battle against an individual author, let alone against Warner Brothers or Disney. Many are minors, creating the additional specter of parental or school liability; even if the minor author is on firm ground and would prevail in a copyright suit, parents or school authorities—especially the latter—may be unwilling to take that risk.

On receipt of a cease and desist letter, most fan work authors (or their parents or school administrators) will typically crumple, removing the content in question even though it might not, in fact, have been infringing. On the other side of the copyright divide, content owners tread warily around their fans because suing one's consumer base (and especially suing children) rarely ends well, as the music industry's travails have shown. Thus some fan works that actually are infringing may remain online.

While a detailed examination of the copyright status of any fan work would require the assistance of an experienced copyright attorney and is thus impractical in most cases, each fan work creator or anyone responsible for their work might take a few simple steps. First, assume that all works created in the 21st century and most created in the 20th century are still in copyright. Second, assume that any character from one of these works who is interesting enough to include in a fan work is also sufficiently delineated to be protected by copyright and that the same holds true for important story elements. Third, make sure the fan work is more transformative than it is derivative. Finally, be aware of the four fair use factors; in particular, avoid using too much of the underlying work and never make a fan work commercial, let alone a marketplace competitor for the original, without first seeking legal advice. And if a work seems likely to be infringing, take it down right away, without waiting for a reaction from the content owner.

For the content owner, there are also certain steps to avoid chilling fandom's expressions of admiration for the work and possibly alienating the consumer base. First, understand that most fan works are probably not infringing and that whether a work is infringing is determined by objective legal standards rather than by how much it upsets the copyright owner.

Second, before sending a cease and desist letter or otherwise instituting legal action, ensure that the original work and characters are protected. Third, also ensure that the fan work is not transformative or otherwise fair use. Finally, avoid Pyrrhic victories; a lawsuit, even where the fan work in question is in fact infringing, can harm a content owner's credibility with the fandom, which can end up costing more than the harm, if any, done by the fan work.

The relationship between fan work creators and the owners of the content on which those fan works are based has been, despite a few hiccups, relatively free of trouble; content owners have avoided the disastrous scorched-earth tactics of the music industry. With a bit of mutual consideration, this peaceful coexistence should be able to continue indefinitely.

References

Burroughs v. Metro-Goldwyn-Mayer, Inc., 683 F.2d 610 (2d Cir. 1982).

Campbell v. Acuff-Rose Music, Inc., 510 U.S. 569, 582–583 (1994).

Constitution of the United States, Article I, Section 8, Clause 8.

Convention Concerning the Creation of an International Union for the Protection of Literary and Artistic Works (Berne Convention), September 9, 1886, as last revised at Paris, July 24, 1971 (amended 1979), 25 U.S.T. 1341.

Copyright Act of the United States, 17 U.S.C. §§ 101 et seq., esp. § 102, 105, 106, & 107 (2012).

DC Comics v. Towle, 802 F.3d 1012 (9th Cir. 2015); cert. denied, *Towle v. DC Comics*, 2016 WL 361575 (March 7, 2016).

Hammett, D. (1934). *The Maltese Falcon*. New York: Modern Library.

New Line Cinema Corp. v. Easter Unlimited Inc., 17 U.S.P.Q. 2d 1631, 1633 (E.D.N.Y. 1989).

Nichols v. Universal Pictures Corporation, 45 F.2d 119 (2d Cir. 1930), cert. denied, 282 U.S. 902 (1931).

Suntrust Bank v. Houghton Mifflin Co., 268 F.3d 1257 (11th Cir. 2001).

Tolkien, J. R. R. (1966). *The Tolkien Reader*. New York: Ballantine.

Walt Disney Prod. v. Air Pirates, 345 F. Supp. 108 (N.D. Cal. 1972).

Warner Bros. Pictures v. Columbia Broadcasting Sys., 216 F.2d 945, 950 (9th Cir. 1954).

Further Reading

Elliott, J. (2001). "Copyright Fair Use and Private Ordering: Are Copyright Holders and the Copyright Law Fanatical for Fansites?" *The DePaul-LCA J. Art & Entertainment Law & Policy*, 11, 329.

Foley, K. M. (2009). "Protecting Fictional Characters: Defining the Elusive Trademark-Copyright Divide." *Connecticut Law Review*, 41, 921.

Gaiman v. McFarlane, 360 F.3d 644, 660 (7th Cir. 2004).

Halicki Films, LLC v. Sanderson Sales & Mktg., 547 F.3d 1213, 1224 (9th Cir. 2008).

Helfand, M.T. (1992). "When Mickey Mouse Is as Strong as Superman: The Convergence of Intellectual Property Laws to Protect Fictional Literary and Pictorial Characters." *Stanford Law Review*, 44, 623.

Hirtle, P. B. (2016). "Copyright Term and the Public Domain in the United States." January 1, 2016. Retrieved from http://copyright.cornell.edu/resources/publicdomain.cfm (visited April 23, 2016).

Nemetz, S. L. (1999–2000). "Copyright Protection of Fictional Characters." *Intellectual Property*, 14, 59.

Nevins, Jr., F. M. (1992). "Copyright + Character = Catastrophe." *Journal of the Copyright Society of the U.S.A.* 39, 303–304.

Nimmer, M., & Nimmer, D. (2016). *Nimmer on Copyright*. New York: LexisNexis.

Niro, D. D. (1992). "Protecting Characters Through Copyright Law: Paving a New Road Upon Which Literary, Graphic, and Motion Picture Characters Can All Travel." *DePaul Law Review*, 41, 359.

Robida, A. (1879). *Voyages Très Extraordinaires de Saturnin Farandoul dans les 5 ou 6 Parties du Monde et dans tous les Pays Connus et Même Inconnus de M. Jules Verne*. Paris: Imp. D. Bardin.

Schwabach, A. (2011). *Fan Fiction and Copyright: Outsider Works and Intellectual Property Protection*. Farnham and Surrey, UK: Ashgate Publishing.

Scliar, M. (1980). *O Centauro no Jardim*. Rio de Janeiro: Nova Fronteira.
Tushnet, R. (2007). "Copyright Law, Fan Practices, and the Rights of the Author." In J. Gray, C. Sandvoss, & C. L. Harrington (Eds.), *Fandom: Identities and Communities in a Mediated World*. New York: New York University Press.
United States Copyright Office, Circular 15a, Duration of Copyright. (2011). Retrieved from www.copyright.gov/circs/circ15a.pdf (visited April 23, 2016).
United States Copyright Office, Compendium of U.S. Copyright Office Practices 36–37 (3d. ed. 2014).
Warner Bros. Entm't v. RDR Books, No. 07 Civ. 9667 (RPP), 2008 U.S. Dist. LEXIS 67771 (S.D.N.Y. Sept. 8, 2008).

Part II

STAKEHOLDERS IN COPYRIGHT EDUCATION

7

COPYRIGHT LITERACY IN THE UK

Understanding Library and Information Professionals' Experiences of Copyright

Jane Secker and Chris Morrison

This chapter is based on research to investigate UK librarians' knowledge and experiences of copyright in their professional lives. A survey was undertaken in late 2014 following significant changes to UK copyright law. The survey originated in Bulgaria (Todorova et al. 2014), and the UK was one of ten countries that took part in the second phase of the project.

The survey aimed to investigate the level of copyright literacy among UK librarians and others working in related sectors; to identify any gaps in knowledge and training requirements in the sector; and to provide data to compare copyright literacy levels in other countries participating in the survey.

The authors were particularly interested in attitudes towards copyright education, which includes both professional qualifications for librarians and related professionals and continuing professional development (CPD) opportunities.

In light of the survey findings, the authors recommended that more detailed qualitative data was collected to further explore librarians' experiences. Consequently, three focus groups with librarians in higher education were undertaken in early 2016. This chapter highlights the valuable role that librarians play in providing copyright education to others, including formal teaching, as well as answering a range of queries. However, it also reveals that copyright can be a source of anxiety, and many librarians would like additional training and support to feel more confident. They perceive copyright to be a complex subject, and queries often involve an element of risk assessment. Many librarians feel uncomfortable providing guidance in an area where there are considerable grey areas. This leads to the belief that copyright is unlike other areas of library work and an imposition on them; many did not enter the profession thinking that this would be a significant aspect of information work. The research recognizes the value of learning more about copyright in a supportive, safe environment and the use of games-based learning.

The findings from the focus groups are only indicative inasmuch as additional data analysis was still being undertaken at the time of completing this chapter. However, it is anticipated that this research will be of interest to those developing copyright education for librarians and understanding their role in providing advice and support to others.

Definitions

'Copyright literacy' is used to signify the knowledge, skills and behaviors that individuals require when working with copyright content. Copyright laws around the world are constantly trying to keep pace with the practices that digital technology now allow. Consequently, infringing copyright in a digital world is increasingly easy to do, and librarians regularly encounter copyright challenges in their professional work.

The term 'copyright literacy' is also an attempt to place an understanding of copyright into a wider framework of digital and information literacy initiatives. Knowing how to use and share information ethically and legally are part of many major frameworks for digital and information literacy. In the United States, the ACRL Information Literacy framework and competency standards are widely used in higher education (ACRL 2015). The frame "information has value" expects students to understand not only issues such as attribution and plagiarism but also issues related to copyright. In the UK, A New Curriculum for Information Literacy (ANCIL) (Secker & Coonan 2012) includes an entire strand on the ethical use of information, including an understanding of copyright. However, teaching copyright as part of information literacy is relatively uncommon, and Smith and Cross (2015) explored whether copyright was the "third rail" (e.g., the controversial "charged" issue that people want to avoid touching) in information literacy. They discussed the difficulties and risks of introducing copyright into information literacy teaching and the concerns of librarians about giving what could be construed as legal advice.

Library and Information Professionals

Library and information science (LIS) professionals and those who work in related cultural heritage sectors such as museums, galleries and archives are increasingly grappling with copyright issues. Copyright issues are particularly pertinent with the shift towards delivering traditional services such as interlibrary loan and course readings for students in digital format. As more resources are purchased in electronic format, librarians need an understanding of the licensing arrangements. Many libraries and archives undertake projects to digitize their collections to both preserve them and to open up access to the collection. In addition, librarians in higher education are often tasked with managing collective licensing on behalf of their organization; for example, in the UK this involves coordinating the relevant Copyright Licensing Agency (CLA) license. Librarians' role in providing access to information means they are often called upon to offer advice when users want to copy materials. In a study carried out in France, Boustany (2014) argued that evidence was needed to explore the "readiness" of the profession to deal with copyright issues that were arising due to new technologies. Boustany argued that in France, where authors' rights are strong, there is an important need for librarians to develop their understanding of copyright to help redress the balance.

Professional qualifications in the library and related sectors have traditionally included some awareness of copyright law as part of legal and information governance issues. Copyright underpins some of the core document supply services that libraries operate and the copying facilities they offer. However, users increasingly copy library materials using their own devices, such as tablets and smartphones, so monitoring these activities has become more difficult. It is important for librarians to strike a balance between 'policing' copying activities and offering timely advice and support.

In UK higher education, much copying takes places under a blanket license purchased from the Copyright Licensing Agency (CLA), which covers photocopying, scanning from print, and digital copying. The reporting requirements of this license have led many academic libraries to establish centralized digitization services to support teaching. Some librarians and e-learning staff have taken on a compliance role to ensure that copyright material uploaded to the virtual learning environment (VLE) meets the terms of the CLA license.

Arguably, these developments all require UK librarians to develop a more nuanced understanding of copyright than they did before the widespread adoption of digital technology, but this study is the first to examine copyright literacy in detail.

Methodology

This research is based on both quantitative and qualitative research methods, including a survey and focus groups. In order to allow cross-country comparisons, the survey instrument developed by the Bulgarian research team was distributed in the UK with only minor amendments. It was made available online and included closed, half-open (using a five-degree Likert scale) and open questions.

The first part of the survey aimed to establish the knowledge and awareness of the respondents on issues of copyright. Section two explored attitudes towards copyright policies in libraries and cultural institutions. Section three examined attitudes towards formal copyright education and CPD, for example in library, archival and cultural heritage professional qualifications. Finally, the survey gathered demographic information from the respondents.

The survey was undertaken in December 2014 and promoted via e-mail discussion lists and social media, such as Twitter and LinkedIn. Twitter proved to be an effective way to promote the survey across the sectors, and it was promoted by the UK professional library body, the Chartered Institute of Library and Information Professionals (CILIP). The intention was to collect data from the profession as a whole, not just from those with specific responsibility for copyright.

Following the analysis of the survey findings, it was agreed that additional qualitative data would be collected to gain a greater understanding of the issues raised. Furthermore, because the survey relied on self-reported data on levels of knowledge about copyright, the qualitative analysis would allow participants' knowledge to be explored in more depth. This led to the decision to undertake a phenomenographic study, using focus groups to understand and explore the variations in experiences noted in the survey. The data was still being analyzed at the time of writing this chapter; however, phenomenography has provided insights into how copyright is experienced and dealt with and how it affects library and information professionals.

Phenomenography is a research method developed in Sweden in the late 1980s, and it has been used recently in information literacy research (Yates, Partridge, & Bruce 2012). It is concerned with exploring questions relating to learning and understanding, including how people learn and see knowledge in a particular context. It is underpinned by the idea that people collectively experience and understand phenomena in a number of qualitatively different but interrelated ways. It is based on a nondualist view of the world and sees experience as the relationship between people and the world.

Whilst it is beyond the scope of this chapter to discuss the various definitions of dualism, the aspect of this that particularly relates to copyright literacy is the splitting of reality into the objective and the subjective. This view of the world would assume that there is an objective truth about the nature of copyright in an information environment, to which subjective experiences can be compared. Phenomenography takes a different view whereby the variation in people's experience is said to represent "collective consciousness" about phenomena (Marton & Booth 1997). This methodology seemed to be particularly appropriate to explore the copyright experiences of librarians, given the variations in experience noted in the survey and by the authors in their professional work. It seemed likely that if these variations in experiences did exist, they might be related to the different roles and responsibilities of LIS professionals.

The focus groups also presented an opportunity to explore questions about how copyright was experienced by librarians. The questions were open-ended, and participants were asked about what they did rather than why, with minimal steer from the facilitator. Typically a phenomenographic study will lead to the development of what is known as an Outcome Space with a hierarchy of Categories of Description that relate to the variation in experience. The analysis starts with a detailed examination of the data, which is searched specifically for variations in experiences. High-level themes are reduced to so-called utterances, and as few categories as possible are generated. As this research is ongoing, the Categories are not presented in this chapter; however, indicative themes emerging from the data are presented.

Findings

The survey findings are described in greater detail in Morrison and Secker (2015), so this chapter provides a summary. There were over 600 responses in total; however, the questions were optional, which meant that different numbers of people answered each question. For ease of comparison, the responses are provided as percentages, but the number of respondents to each question has been included in the figures. Overall engagement with the survey was high, and over 100 respondents provided an e-mail address and expressed a wish to be kept informed about the results.

Demographic data helped to provide a useful context for the findings. Of those who completed this question, 76% were female and 24% were male, which is not atypical given the professions being surveyed. Participants ranged in age, including 8% under 30, 25% aged 30–39, 28% aged 40–49, 32% 50–59 and 7% over 60.

A large percentage of the respondents (57%) worked in the academic library sector. The breakdown of respondents by sector includes 57% from academic libraries, 10% from school libraries, 8% from public libraries. Museums and archives made up 5% of responses, and the remainder were from scientific, national or other specialist libraries.

General Knowledge and Awareness of Copyright

The first section of the survey asked respondents to comment on their overall familiarity with copyright and IPR issues. The survey used a five-point Likert scale for these questions, which ranged from extremely aware through to not aware at all.

Most respondents (40%) described themselves as "moderately aware" of copyright issues, with 17% saying they were "extremely aware" (a total of 57% either moderately or extremely aware). Twenty-seven percent were "somewhat aware" while just 3% of people were not aware at all of copyright and IPR issues. This data suggests that the survey was completed by librarians and professionals in generalist roles, not just the copyright officers within institutions. However, the survey reported on people's perception of their knowledge in the field.

The levels of perceived copyright literacy were also compared by gender and age. The analysis of age did not appear to be statistically significant, with a relatively stable spread of confidence across the different age groups. The analysis of gender highlighted some differences in perception, with a larger proportion of males (65%) identifying themselves as "extremely" or "moderately" aware of copyright, compared to 54% of females. The authors carried out a Chi-square test to see if there is a correlation between gender and confidence in copyright literacy knowledge. The results showed that there was a statistical difference and that men report higher levels of confidence in copyright literacy than women. These findings have some parallels with studies of library and information students and the differing self-efficacy levels between men and women in information retrieval skills (Bronstein & Tzivian 2013). Although the findings suggest significance worthy of further investigation, the authors felt that there was insufficient evidence to draw any conclusions on the relationship between copyright literacy and gender at this stage.

Familiarity With the Copyright Framework

Using the same five-point scale, respondents were asked to indicate their perceived knowledge and awareness of various aspects of the copyright framework, both nationally and internationally. The findings suggest that knowledge of UK copyright law is an area where respondents had the greatest confidence. International copyright law and international copyright organizations were the two areas where there was the least perceived knowledge.

There was also less experience of clearing rights amongst the respondents than might be expected. More than half of all respondents felt they were not at all familiar or only slightly familiar with this practice. Finally, knowledge of collective rights management (and organizations such as the CLA) was fairly evenly spread. Further details can be seen in Figure 7.1.

Respondents were asked about their perceived knowledge of licenses, copyright exceptions and several related copyright issues. It asked about their familiarity with topics such as Creative

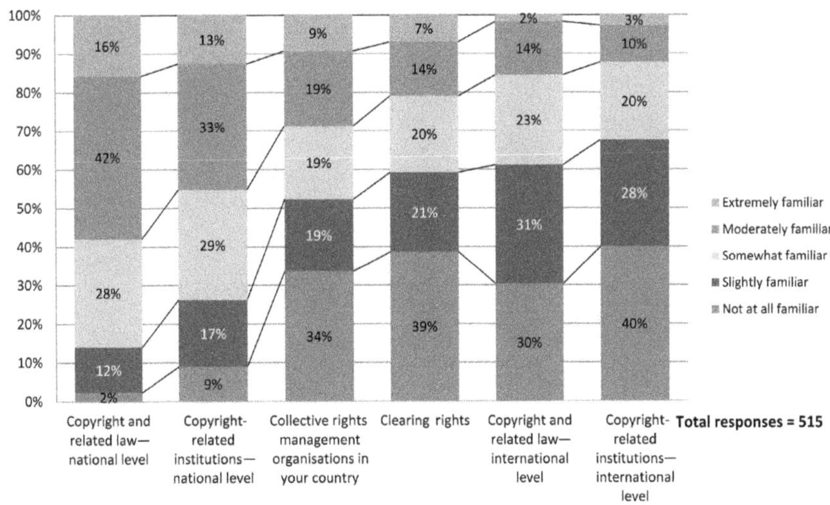

Figure 7.1 Familiarity With the Copyright Framework

Commons licenses, fair dealing, open access, licenses for electronic resources and issues related to e-learning. Licensing conditions in their own institution, licensing of digital resources, fair dealing and Creative Commons were all areas where many respondents reported being extremely or moderately aware.

Open access was another issue that almost half (44%) of respondents felt they were extremely or moderately aware of. Copyright and e-learning was an area where there were mixed levels of perceived knowledge: 34% of the people believed they were moderately or extremely familiar with the issues, but 46% felt they were either not at all or only slightly aware. Further details are provided in Figure 7.2.

The survey asked about familiarity with digitization issues, out-of-print works, public domain materials and orphan works (see Figure 7.3). These topics appear to be ones where there is considerable variation in perception, with some members of the profession believing they have a greater level of expertise than others. That expertise is likely to be related to their specific roles and to the nature of the organizations in which they work. For example, an archivist may be more familiar with public domain or orphan works issues than an academic librarian who deals with copyright to provide access to scanned readings.

The survey also asked how respondents kept up to date with copyright and IPR issues in the context of their work. Websites (cited by 76% of respondents) and colleagues (70%) were by far the most frequently cited sources of information. Books were also an important source of copyright information (cited by 62% of people), as were professional bodies (59%) and e-mail discussion lists such as the UK JiscMail list, LIS-copyseek (47%). Unfortunately, this part of the survey did not allow for free text comments to ask about the types of websites that people used for copyright information. For example, it would be useful to know if the UK Intellectual Property Office (IPO) website was an important source of information. It is also interesting to see that lawyers were relatively low down on the list of sources (at 10%), suggesting there is a benefit to having copyright advice available at the point of need and at a low cost.

Respondents were asked about their levels of interest in copyright initiatives from national libraries or from professional associations such as CILIP (the Chartered Institute of Library and Information Professionals) or LACA (the Libraries and Archives Copyright Alliance). The

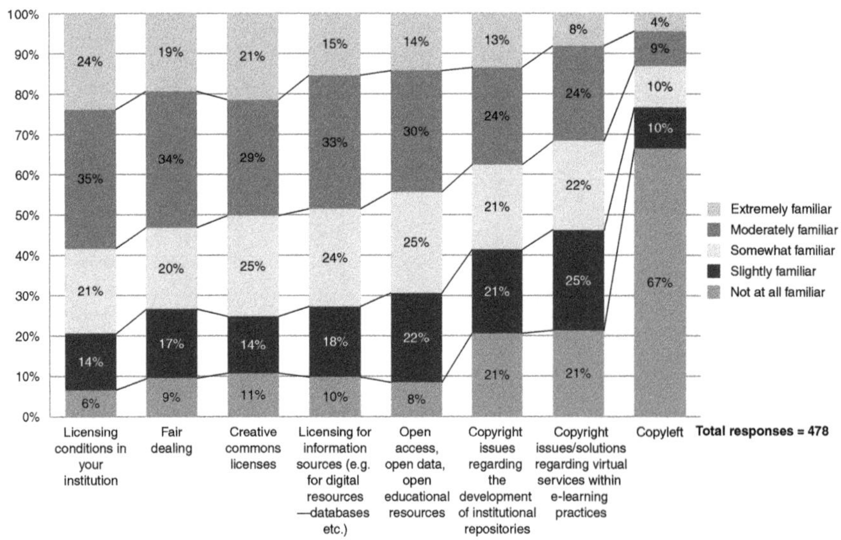

Figure 7.2 Familiarity with Licenses, Exceptions and Other Issues

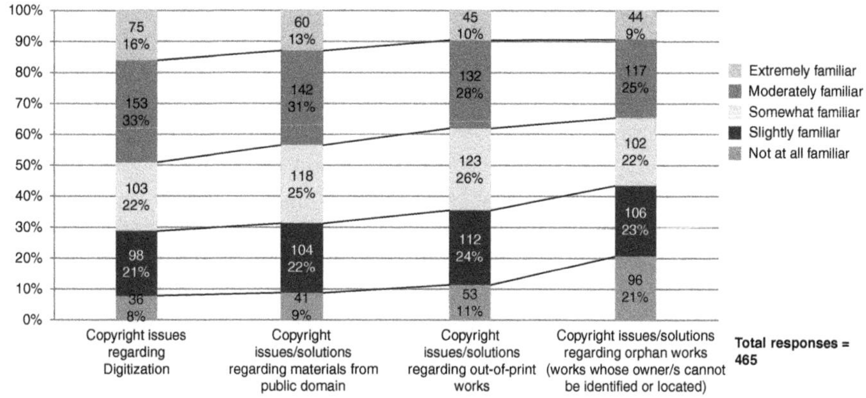

Figure 7.3 Familiarity with Digitization-Related Copyright Issues

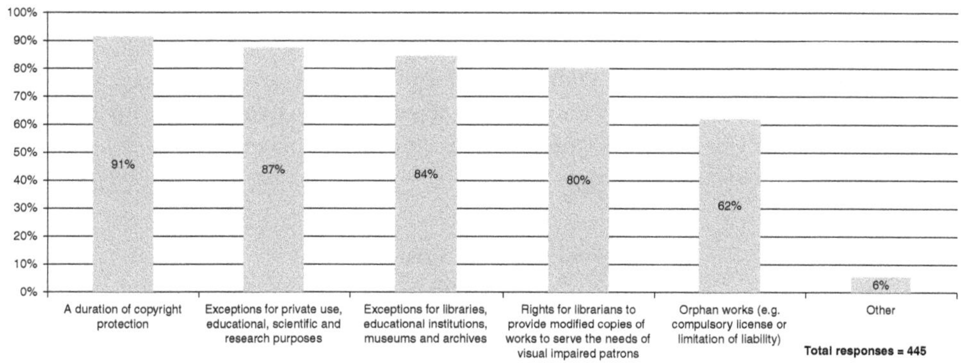

Figure 7.4 Percentage of Respondents Who Were Aware of Specific Provisions in UK Copyright Legislation

results suggest that most people (56%) were moderately or somewhat interested in these initiatives, but only 19% said they were extremely interested.

The survey queried respondents' understanding of specific aspects of UK copyright law, asking to answer yes/no/don't know to a series of statements. They were asked if there was a national strategy for copyright in the UK, and the results reveal a level of uncertainty in this area with 49% of people not knowing if such a strategy existed. This section asked them if the UK had a provision for the duration of copyright protection, their knowledge of specific copyright exceptions and the existence of a provision for orphan works. Figure 7.4 shows that 91% of respondents were aware there was provision in the law for the duration of copyright. However, knowledge of the UK's Orphan Works Licensing Scheme (launched in October 2014) had clearly not reached all professionals, as only 62% knew it existed.

The final question in this section asked people whether they agreed with a series of statements related to copyright reforms. These questions also tested their knowledge of attempts by the World Intellectual Property Organization (WIPO) to harmonize education-, library- and accessibility-related copyright provisions. The findings show broad support for greater harmonization of copyright laws and exceptions for libraries and education across the sector.

Copyright Policy at the Institutional Level

The survey examined copyright issues and policies at an institutional level. Unsurprisingly, almost all respondents (94%) agreed that their institutions owned resources protected by copyright and related rights. The majority of respondents (76%) thought that institutional copyright policies are necessary for libraries, although 21% said they were uncertain about the need for such policies. The survey went on to ask if the institution had a copyright policy or internal regulations. Sixty-three percent said they did, but interestingly nearly a quarter (24%) of those who answered the question were not sure if their institution had a copyright policy. The wording of this question was ambiguous, and so those who did not know may have been unsure if a copyright policy meant a policy on whether the employer owns the copyright in materials made by staff in the course of their employment or a policy on employees' use of third-party copyright materials.

Sixty-four percent of respondents stated that they had a person in their organization responsible for copyright issues. This question was of some interest to the authors, both of whom are copyright specialists in their own institution. Twenty percent of respondents said there was no dedicated person dealing with copyright, and 16% did not know. Further analysis was undertaken to explore whether the existence of a person responsible for copyright differed across the sectors.

A comparison was also undertaken across the sectors to see if the institutions had a copyright policy. There were some differences, with schools and public libraries slightly less likely to have a copyright policy than other sectors. However, 41% of public libraries and 53% of school libraries had a copyright policy or internal regulations, compared to 63% of all respondents. Some sectors were far more likely to have a copyright policy, with 64% of university libraries having one.

Copyright and Education

The final section of the survey asked respondents about the need for copyright and IPR to be included in formal education (such as LIS or archive administration master's courses) and CPD for library professionals. In both cases, the majority of respondents (over 90%) believed that copyright and wider IPR issues should be included in the curriculum. The survey asked which topics should be included, and respondents were able to include free text comments. The data was analyzed and categorized into over fifty unique topic categories, all of which were mentioned by at least one respondent. The twenty most frequently cited topics for both formal education and CPD are listed in Table 7.1. Fairly unsurprisingly, for formal education an overview of UK copyright law was suggested most frequently, followed closely by an understanding of copyright exceptions and how these relate to the licenses an organization held. Many respondents wanted the focus of formal education to be on understanding the law in practice. Digital copyright was also an important topic, as well as Creative Commons.

The free text comments were particularly interesting and a selection are included here. Many respondents expressed the need to understand a wide variety of copyright issues and to have them explained clearly and in an engaging way. One respondent listed an extensive list of topics and then added:

> Whatever it is it needs to be clear and as jargon free as possible to stop people glazing over.

Another participant stated copyright education should:

> reflect the fact that most LIS practitioners have significant exemptions [*sic*] and freedoms as regards copyright. Much existing copyright education is effectively written from a commercial rights holder perspective and tends to be unduly dogmatic as a result.

Table 7.1 Topics for Inclusion in the Formal Education and Continuing Professional Development of LIS and Cultural Heritage Sector Professionals

Topic	*Number of Responses for Formal Education*	*Number of Responses for CPD*
Recent updates to the law	—	67
Overview of UK copyright legislation	68	48
Copyright exceptions/relation to licenses	43	23
Practical application of copyright law	34	30
Digital copyright/copyright and the Internet	33	20
Creative Commons/copyleft	31	15
Fair dealing	27	16
Specific licensing schemes e.g. CLA, ERA	27	15
Exceptions for libraries	24	15
Open access and institutional repositories	23	15
Copyright of specific types of works e.g. images, music, unpublished works	21	9
International copyright law	20	14
Licensing of digital resources	20	13
Copyright duration/out of copyright work	20	—
Copyright and digitization/preservation	18	9
Exceptions for educational use	17	—
How to protect IP	16	17
Knowing how to stay up to date/good sources of copyright info	15	—
Clearing rights/tracing rights holders	14	—
What copyright covers/limitations	13	12
Copyright issues affecting particular user groups e.g. academics, students, members of the public, commercial uses, National Health Service	13	13
Case studies of impact on libraries and LIS bodies	—	13
Orphan works	—	10
Copyright training/education for others	—	10

One respondent highlighted the apprehension and anxiety that some professionals have about copyright issues, saying:

> I think copyright can seem daunting if you are not familiar with it, and by encouraging an awareness at an early stage, this would reduce any anxieties.

Another respondent agreed with this, stating:

> I find that people are often scared of copyright, or uncertain, so a good solid grounding on your own country's copyright laws and exceptions would be good.

Some respondents did not believe their formal education prepared them adequately regarding copyright matters; for example, one participant said:

> I have just finished my MSc and we had limited information on copyright law provided, the little I know I know because colleagues have shared it with me.

Another respondent echoed this point, saying:

> I believe that this subject area should be dealt with in as practical a way as possible. What kind of issues are likely to face librarians in their day-to-day work? What are they allowed to do and for whom? I don't remember copyright issues being addressed at all in my Postgraduate course and I think this was unfortunate.

However, respondents were aware that copyright was challenging to teach, and three respondents suggested it should be embedded into different modules rather than delivered as a stand-alone topic. Several interesting topics are not listed in Table 7.1 because they were mentioned by only between five and ten respondents, although they are worthy of note. For example, eight respondents thought information about the ethics and philosophy underpinning copyright should be covered in professional qualifications, and several respondents felt there was a need to understand some of the main differences between copyright laws in countries outside the UK.

The second question in this section asked participants to identify any topics or issues they thought should be covered in a CPD program. Many of the same topics were mentioned, and these are also presented in Table 7.1. Slightly fewer respondents answered this question, and several people believed all the same topics they mentioned in their previous answer should be included in CPD. However, there are some key differences. An understanding of recent updates to the law was the most frequently cited topic. However, many people wanted knowledge of practical aspects of copyright related to their job and how to deal with common copyright queries. Comments related to CPD reveal the need to keep up to date with recent changes in the law, caused in part by technology, which was a particular concern. As one respondent said:

> I still need to know what I am allowed to do and for whom, especially as digitisation has changed the field completely. We need updates on how legislation has changed and what a difference this makes to our work.

Another topic, mentioned by ten people, was the role of librarians in providing copyright training and education for others in their organization. One respondent believed that CPD should:

> encourage more general awareness of copyright issues so librarians/info specialists can educate academics about complying with copyright law. Also practical awareness for students' creative work and using [copyright] material in their own work.

The survey asked for respondents' preferences for receiving CPD, and there was a preference for face-to-face training, followed by online resources and online courses. Training courses were cited by 85% of people, with online resources from websites as being the next popular (cited by 82% of people). Distance learning or e-learning was another popular choice (80%).

Focus Group Results

In early 2016, three focus groups were carried out to gather additional qualitative data using phenomenography. It was decided to focus on librarians working in higher education because they had formed the largest group to respond to the survey. As the data analysis was still ongoing at the time of writing, these are interim results. Recurring themes are presented here, which will form the basis of the Categories of Description as further analysis is undertaken.

Copyright as Experience

The focus groups were an opportunity to explore how librarians experience copyright, including how they approach and feel about dealing with copyright queries, how they learn more about copyright as part of their CPD and how copyright compares to other areas of professional expertise. Interview questions were drawn up to guide the discussions, but these were deliberately kept as open as possible. The focus groups were transcribed in full, and data analysis in the form of summarizing and categorizing the data to identify emerging patterns was undertaken. Ten themes have emerged from the data so far:

1. *Copyright is not a 'core' aspect of librarianship.* It is an area where librarians feel their expertise is more limited than other areas of professional knowledge, and consequently they are often less confident dealing with copyright queries from users when compared to other types of queries.
2. *It's hard for librarians to provide evidence to support points.* Copyright is an area where librarians feel the need for evidence to back up their responses to queries from library users or colleagues. They are concerned not to be seen as 'making it up' particularly if different licenses have different terms and conditions. In each focus group, at least one librarian mentioned having felt challenged by a library user for making up 'rules' about copyright.
3. *It's challenging to communicate.* Copyright is complex, difficult to understand and remember, and consequently it was often difficult to explain to users. Many librarians also worried about keeping up to date with the law, as they were conscious that changes occurred relatively frequently.
4. *Librarians have a higher-level perspective on copyright but on uncertain foundations.* Copyright is an area in which librarians often have greater knowledge and expertise than library users, such as faculty, but this makes them feel uncomfortable. It is often surprising to them to have this greater knowledge, particularly because many academics sign copyright agreements and contracts as part of the publication process.
5. *Copyright is an imposition.* Some librarians believe they didn't have to deal with copyright in the past, prior to digital resources and the Internet. There was a sense from librarians that the burden of dealing with copyright should be shared. However, library users tend to see copyright as an irritation or impediment to their work, for which librarians are somehow more responsible. There was an overwhelming sense that librarians do not like feeling responsible for copyright or acting as an arbiter of what the law permits. Many librarians were aware that copyright law has many grey areas, making it difficult to give concrete answers, and they felt giving copyright advice could be risky for them personally.
6. *Copyright knowledge is contextual.* Almost all participants mentioned that copyright knowledge needed to be specific to their day-to-day role and highly practical rather than theoretical. This suggests that expertise in and knowledge of copyright exist in pockets. Issues such as open access policies and the CLA license were areas where some types of librarians expressed greater confidence, but there were considerable variations.
7. *Addressing copyright as a community.* Librarians believed that learning about copyright through case studies and real examples was helpful, and there were benefits to sharing copyright problems to help find solutions. Underlying this was the cooperative,

supportive nature of the library community where sharing knowledge about copyright was beneficial, but in practice they believed this happens less than it could.

8. *Copyright requires specialist support.* There was a strong sense that copyright is not like other areas of library work. It requires more specific legal expertise than librarians often feel comfortable with offering, so it was important to have a backup in the form of a dedicated expert within the organization.
9. *Effective copyright support needs an understanding of risk.* The risk element to copyright was seen as different to other aspects of library work, where librarians are less worried about the consequences if they get things wrong. However, when pressed on this, several librarians did admit that other aspects of information work could be dangerous, for example if they supplied inaccurate health information. But the sense remained that offering copyright advice could be potentially putting the librarian at risk of legal action.
10. *Copyright is perceived as an area of conflict and not simply a tension.* Not only did some librarians describe copyright as an area of tension; some went as far to suggest copyright as a "war" or dispute where they sat in the middle of publishers and academics. Some librarians felt their profession should be bolder and take more of a defensive stand against the current copyright regime. This attitude doesn't necessarily fit comfortably with the way in which many librarians might perceive themselves as a neutral conduit in a user's information journey. (Elmborg 2004)

The next stage of the data analysis will be an attempt to refine these emerging themes into Categories of Description and place them into an Outcome Space. The findings to date suggest there is a significant variation in experiences of copyright, related in part to the role of the librarian but also their ideological stance, confidence and professional knowledge. Nevertheless, what emerges is a clear sense that copyright plays an increasingly important role in the work of librarians, that they have considerable expertise, but that it is a challenging area of work.

Discussion

The survey suggests that levels of copyright literacy amongst UK librarians are high, in particular when compared to other countries. The survey was not without limitations, asking mainly closed questions. It may also be skewed in that the highest number of respondents came from academic libraries. However, comparing the levels of confidence in copyright issues between the sectors suggests that public and school librarians are less confident. Similarly, their institutions are less likely to have an individual with specific responsibility for copyright matters or copyright policy.

The findings suggest that in the UK there is a recognized need for copyright expertise within an organization, although it is not always the case that a dedicated post exists. Respondents expressed a desire to learn more about copyright in their professional qualifications and also to be kept up to date through CPD. The comments from the participants about copyright education suggest that many professionals feel they still do not know enough about copyright and have some level of anxiety over dealing with copyright queries. The data also suggests that, while many UK professionals are reasonably confident about their knowledge of UK copyright law, international issues and recent changes to the law have heightened awareness about the need to keep up to date.

Comparing the UK data to the findings from the first phase of the project (Todorova et al. 2014, 143) reveals interesting differences, and in general levels of copyright literacy appear to be higher in the UK compared to Turkey, France, Bulgaria and Croatia. Additional work is currently being undertaken to compare all fourteen countries who took part in the study; however, one point to note is that only 15% of institutions surveyed in Croatia, Bulgaria, Turkey and France had a person responsible for copyright, whereas in the UK this figure was 64%. The differences in the UK data are marked. The relatively high number of copyright officers in UK libraries and related organizations suggests that the UK takes copyright issues seriously; however, further research is recommended.

The findings suggest that copyright can be a cause of concern and anxiety and is an area where confidence in the advice being given is more limited. Copyright is seen as complex; it can be seen as an imposition, and it is potentially risky. Through further analysis, it is hoped that appropriate copyright education programmes can be developed. For example, it may be that games-based learning might be an effective way to teach librarians about copyright in a safe but engaging way (Morrison 2015).

Conclusion

This chapter examines the experience of copyright in the professional lives of UK librarians. The tension and anxiety it creates are clearly issues that could be tackled through education and CPD. However, it may also be helpful to view copyright as a key component in digital and information literacy. Increasingly when teaching information literacy, librarians are required to move away from a role of neutral conduit to critical partner in a user's information journey (Elmborg 2004). Yet currently copyright education has remained largely peripheral to the information literacy support offered by libraries and information services. If a more critical approach to teaching information literacy is developed, then arguably librarians might feel more comfortable with their role as a guide and source of advice for copyright queries rather than as arbiters or judges of what can and cannot be copied.

The authors have found games-based learning particularly effective when teaching librarians about copyright. Games can be helpful when teaching difficult subjects because they create a safe space for users to experiment, play and even fail. A copyright snakes and ladders game developed at the University of Sussex (Moore 2014) inspired the authors to develop a copyright game based on a set of cards. Copyright Card Game (Morrison 2015) has proved effective not only in teaching UK librarians about recent changes to the law in the UK but also in equipping them with a framework for approaching copyright queries. The team-based nature of the game also helps to develop a shared understanding of copyright issues and taps into a sense of community around copyright knowledge. Work is currently being undertaken to adapt this for U.S. copyright law.

In conclusion, it is important for librarians to work to embed copyright more fully into the information and digital literacy programs that they teach to both staff and students within their institutions. This proactive approach shifts copyright away from simply reacting to user queries. Additional analysis is being undertaken, but the use of phenomenography is helpful in better understanding how librarians experience copyright and in developing ways of teaching them about copyright in order to improve the advice and support librarians provide to others.

References

ACRL. (2015). "Framework for Information Literacy for Higher Education." Retrieved from www.ala.org/acrl/standards/ilframework

Boustany, J. (2014). "Copyright Literacy of librarians in France." [Online]. Paper presented at the European Conference of Information Literacy. Dubrovnik, Croatia, October 2014. Retrieved from http://ecil2014.ilconf.org/wp-content/uploads/2014/11/Boustany.pdf

Bronstein, J., & Tzivian, L. (2013). "Perceived Self-Efficacy of Library and Information Science Professionals Regarding Their Information Retrieval Skills." *Library and Information Science Research*, 36(2), 151–158.

Elmborg, C. (2004). "Literacies Large and Small: The Case of Information Literacy." *International Journal of Learning*, 11, 1235–1239.

Marton, F., & Booth, S. (1997). *Learning and Awareness*. Mahwah, NJ: Lawrence Erlbaum Associates.

Moore, A. (2014). "Can I Copy? A Snakes and Ladders Game for Copyright Do's and Don'ts." [Open education resource]. December 1, 2014. Retrieved from http://find.jorum.ac.uk/resources/19277

Morrison, C. (2015). "Copyright the Card Game: Shaking Up Copyright Training." *ALISS Quarterly*, 10(4), 25–28.

Morrison, C., & Secker, J. (2015). "Copyright Literacy in the UK: A Survey of Librarians and Other Cultural Heritage Sector Professionals." *Library and Information Research*, 39, 121–145.

Secker, J., & Coonan, E. (2012). *Rethinking Information Literacy: A Practical Framework for Supporting Learning*. London: Facet Publishing.

Smith, K., & Cross, W. (2015). "Is Copyright the Third Rail in Information Literacy, or a Common Denominator?" [Online]. ACRL Webcast, February 25, 2015. Retrieved from www.ala.org/acrl/intersectionswebcast

Todorova, T., Trencheva, T., Kurbanoğlu, S., Dogan G., & Horvat, A. (2014). "A Multinational Study on Copyright Literacy Competencies of LIS Professionals." Presentation given at 2nd European Conference on Information Literacy (ECIL) held in Dubrovnik, October 2014. Retrieved from http://ecil2014.ilconf.org/wp-content/uploads/2014/11/Todorova.pdf

Yates, C., Partridge, H., & Bruce, C. (2012). "Exploring Information Experiences Through Phenomenography." *Library and Information Research*, 36, 96–119. Retrieved from www.lirgjournal.org.uk/lir/ojs/index.php/lir/article/viewFile/496/552

Further Reading

Copyright the Card Game. (2015). "Open Educational Resource Download." Retrieved from https://ukcopyrightliteracy.wordpress.com/about-2/copyright-the-card-game/

Copyright User. (2016). Retrieved from http://copyrightuser.org/

Cornish, G. (2015). *Copyright: Interpreting the Law for Libraries, Archives and Information Services*. London: Facet Publishing.

Padfield, T. (2015). *Copyright for Archivists and Records Managers*. London: Facet Publishing.

Secker, J., & Morrison, C. (2016). *Copyright and E-Learning: A Guide for Practitioners*. London: Facet Publishing.

Suits, B. (2014). *The Grasshopper: Games, Life and Utopia* (3rd ed.). Ontario: Broadview Press.

8

CODES OF BEST PRACTICES IN FAIR USE

Game Changers in Copyright Education

Patricia Aufderheide

Media literacy teachers were among the first communities of practice to pioneer an approach to fair use that made copyright their friend. What they did was simple: they created a Code of Best Practices in Fair Use for Media Literacy Education (cmsimpact.org/medialiteracy). They clarified for themselves what they considered to be best practices in their work when using other people's copyrighted materials, under the copyright doctrine of fair use. It was considerably less simple to get to the point where they did that.

Media literacy teachers and their students extensively employ others' copyrighted materials. Teachers teach using real-life examples such as TV shows, commercials, advertisements, newspaper articles, and so on. They ask their students to make work that critiques real-life materials, which directly quotes it. They build curriculum laced with examples of real-life media. They upload materials to the web, both in protected and in open contexts. They give conference presentations referring to and using examples of popular media.

Media literacy has grown as a field in company with the growth of mass media, popular culture, and pervasive advertising, and it exists in order to help participants in popular culture have some analytical understanding of and control over their absorption and use of it. Unfortunately, it has also developed in tandem with a growing concern of large media companies to maintain control of their product in a digital era—particularly within traditional business models. Along with expansion of copyright monopoly rights, assisted with energetic media industry lobbying, media literacy teachers have experienced a never ending barrage of industry-fed teaching materials discouraging digital copying of all kinds, including the legal kinds.

This has put copyright in the crosshairs of any kind of media literacy activity, as I discovered in 2007 when I ran into Renee Hobbs, with whom I had earlier worked on a media literacy conference. She told me that she had used work produced by the first community of practice to establish their own fair use best practices—documentary filmmakers—in deciding how to employ fair use in a recent media literacy web video project. The code had worked well to answer her questions about a media literacy project's documentary components. But so many other aspects of media literacy also needed guidance on best practices in fair use. "We need something like that fair use code for media literacy educators," she said.

What she had used was the Documentary Filmmakers' Statement of Best Practices in Fair Use (cmsimpact.org/documentary). Filmmakers had been hamstrung by their then-practice of getting permission for all copyrighted material that showed up in their movies—the posters in a kid's bedroom, music playing in the elevator, the ringtone on the mom's phone, everything. Peter Jaszi and I had conducted a study of documentary practices and were able to document a crippling level of self-censorship as a result of such constricted practice (Aufderheide & Jaszi 2004). Filmmakers were avoiding whole topic areas, such as politics (too much need for TV clips), popular culture (too hard to get permission for movies and music), and, of course, anything ironic (it's hard to get permission from the person you're poking fun at).

Documentarians were so alarmed by the results of the study that they worked through several national organizations, with our coordination, to deliberate in small groups across the country about what would be best practice in interpreting fair use. Their consensus was recorded in the Documentary Filmmakers' Statement. Many of them suspected nothing would come of it, except the chance to vent.

But their resulting document actually had a powerful effect on the decision of insurers to change their policy, to accept fair use claims made within the terms of the statement. It changed the practice of lawyers such as leading Los Angeles entertainment attorney Michael Donaldson. And it tipped off large media companies that they could save considerable money, particularly during the Great Recession (Aufderheide & Jaszi 2011).

The media literacy community's code was one of a clutch of professional codes of best practices in fair use, all of which have changed field practice. To understand why the codes work so well, it is important to understand the logic of fair use, and the role of communities in shaping the implementation of the law.

Transformative Use, Risk Assessment, and Communities of Practice

Articulating best practices in fair use has turned out to be useful to a variety of professional knowledge communities, in spite of not being a legal document or sanctioned in law, precisely because of the nature of fair use. Fair use is structured in copyright law (in section 107 of the Copyright Act) as a general permission to employ others' copyrighted work without licensing it if the use generates new cultural expression and uses an appropriate amount of the original to permit that new expression. This "transformative" use thus does not step into the established market for the original work. In this way, a fair use matches up well with the four "factors" that the law requires one to consider (as well as leaving the door open for other considerations): the nature of the original work, the nature of the new work, the amount taken, and the effect on the market.

If there were any doubt, in 2015, Appeals Court Judge Pierre Leval wrote the decision for the 2nd Circuit Court in *Authors Guild v. Google*, settling the question of whether Google Books' copying of sections of books still under copyright was fair use. The court's decision was unanimously yes. His decision went further to lay out the way judicial reasoning works and should work on fair use. He wrote, among other things, "The ultimate goal of copyright is to expand public knowledge and understanding. . . . Thus, while authors are undoubtedly important intended beneficiaries of copyright, the ultimate, primary intended beneficiary is the public." Google's copying of entire books in order to provide snippets of them on demand to the public was a clearly transformative purpose, and transformative purposes meet the standard of serving the public by generating new culture. This transformative purpose does not intrude on the book market for books written by Authors Guild authors. Leval wrote, inter alia, "[A] transformative use is one that communicates something new and different from the original or expands its utility, thus serving copyright's overall objective of contributing to public knowledge." He goes on to distinguish merely changing some things in the original from transformativeness and contrasts fair uses with derivative works, all in plain language. Leval's measured and graceful explanation of transformativeness as a core value in interpreting fair use will be a service to judges and to users of fair use far into the future.

So the law draws no hard and fast lines in how much you can take, precisely because that would inhibit the utility of fair use. No one knows what they might need from the law in the future, except the right to create. Copyright law in the United States is designed to foster cultural creation, both by offering perks to creators (such as limited monopolies) and by allowing access to currently copyrighted work in order to generate new work. The enormous flexibility of fair use has, in the eyes of many, permitted the United States to be a leader in tech innovation. It is fair use, after all, that permits Google to offer search results, since it has to copy a work in order to display it. The law permits but not does not require any particular way of limited copying.

That flexibility and open-invitation permission can be frustrating, however, especially given the high fines (statutory penalties) built into today's copyright law for guessing wrong about your fair use claim. Should someone challenge your fair use with a lawsuit (an extremely rare phenomenon and usually reserved for deep-pocketed entities because no one wants to sue someone who can't pay a lot, but still a widespread fear) and should the work you quoted be registered formally at the copyright office, it would be possible for the plaintiff to demand not just a license fee but tens of thousands of dollars or more in fines. At the end of the day, it is up to the judge to make the call in a lawsuit about whether a fair use claim really was fair. Even more frustrating is that there is little case law to turn to, since fair use is litigated infrequently. Meanwhile, there is usually little usable advice given to people in any field, and many attempt simply to avoid using fair use or avoid talking about their uses.

Without any sense of where one's professional peers would come down on a particular kind of choice, practitioners are often left without enough information to make an informed risk assessment. Accurate risk assessment is crucial in fair use because fair use is a right. Like all rights, it does not come with guarantees. It can, in theory, always be challenged, just like other expressive rights you have. What provides comfort in other situations where people make risk assessments about their expressive rights is their understanding of what most people would do in that situation. When people make harsh statements about public figures, they operate within what they understand to be acceptable boundaries, ones that will not result in triggering a libel suit. When they criticize the government, they again employ their general understanding of acceptable behavior in order to believe they are on the comfortable side of a treason charge. Often, in employing fair use, people do not have that familiarity with what their peers might do.

That is where best practices statements come in. If communities can describe, both for themselves and their interlocutors, what they do creatively that requires use of others' copyrighted materials and can describe the limits of their best practice in using that material, they can make the open invitation of the law into more specific and useful norms for themselves.

These best practices documents have not only proven useful to practitioners but have never received any formal criticism from large copyright holders. Furthermore, they are useful in establishing expectations throughout the ecology of a field. This is not only because they demonstrate a link between what the law permits and what the goals and missions of professional practice are but also because, when deciding cases, judges inevitably refer back to the actual cultural practice of a field (Madison 2004). This is simply because making a fair use decision is grounded in specific cultural practice and particularly in what new expression you are trying to achieve.

The best practices codes that media literacy teachers and others have created have all been designed to be as robust as possible in reflecting consensus in the field while staying within current judicial interpretation of the law. They:

- Are grounded in solid research into current practices in the field, garnered by surveys, long-form interviews, or both, with participants reached through representative member organizations in the field.
- Represent a consensus of views established by a series of confidential, small-group meetings of experienced practitioners selected with the help of national associations in the field. In these meetings, individuals speak not as representatives of their institutions but as individual, experienced professionals.
- Are synthesized by a small team, until now usually led by Peter Jaszi and myself, into a draft document that is structured around common practices in the field.
- Are reviewed by an independent board of experienced copyright lawyers in order to conform to current judicial interpretation and the statute.
- Are accepted or endorsed by the leading national member organizations.

Distinctively, they are never produced in negotiation with large copyright holders. This is because they are articulations of the best practice of a particular field, when employing copyright law while accomplishing core-to-mission activities. Vendors, even prominent vendors to the field, do not have the standing or indeed the ability to speak to what practitioners in the field do or believe is best practice to do. Fair use by definition does not require the approval of people who may not want you to use it; that is exactly why it is such a valuable expressive right. So people whose interests are aligned to your getting permissions are the least appropriate people to be deciding on what your best practices should be.

Impact of the Media Literacy Code of Best Practices

In the case of media literacy, we were able to execute the entire process with a substantial grant from the John D. and Catherine T. MacArthur Foundation. First, the research team of Renee Hobbs, Peter Jaszi, and me conducted an investigation into current practices using long-form interviews. The resulting study, *The Cost of Copyright Confusion* (Aufderheide, Hobbs & Jaszi 2007), demonstrated that teachers were avoiding fair use out of ignorance and misinformation. As a result, they were using less effective teaching techniques, teaching and transmitting erroneous copyright information, failing to share innovative instructional approaches, and not taking advantage of new digital platforms.

Media literacy teachers got to this parlous place with a lot of help. They were and are surrounded by well-meaning efforts to help them employ fair use or to keep them safe without thinking. Checklists, flowcharts, and strict numerical guidelines abounded, all of them typically much better—as legal scholar Kenneth Crews has shown—at inhibiting any creative teaching than in explaining the purpose, rationale, and reasoning needed to employ the law (Crews 2001). Ironically for the education profession, no one seemed to trust media literacy teachers to learn how to reason with fair use, even though they clearly made complex judgment calls daily, with potentially serious consequences, about many other free speech issues. Advice was couched with so many caveats that media literacy teachers often believed that they had been forced into the position of skulking into their classroom and sneaking in illegal materials—even though they were often fully within the law. Their fear had the further consequences that they failed to share successful teaching techniques in contravention of core educational principles.

This knowledge was helpful in designing a range of scenarios for discussion of how to interpret fair use in specific practices of media literacy. Hobbs and Jaszi continued the process by holding small-group meetings across the country with K–12 teachers and professors of education. In each group, individuals were given a brief backgrounder on fair use and then asked to consider what they thought would be the behavior appropriate to the mission or purpose of an activity. They were further asked what they thought would go beyond that mission or be excessive or inappropriate behavior. Discussants typically had vigorous discussions among themselves about where to draw the line; these discussions were crucial to establishing expectations to be synthesized into a code.

Jaszi and Aufderheide drafted the synthesis document with Hobbs and presented it to the independent lawyers' board for comment. The field research and ensuing small-group conversations had identified five common situations in which fair use was appropriate. The code discussed fair use and its limits within these situations:

- Teaching media literacy
- Creating curriculum materials
- Sharing curriculum materials, whether by publishing, informally sharing with colleagues, or making them available on open websites
- Creating student work
- Showcasing student work

In each case, the common practices involved were described, the rationale for employing fair use at all was explained, and the conditions and limits were specified.

The Code of Best Practices in Fair Use for Media Literacy Education was deliberately written in layman's language and was focused on the actual practice of media literacy teachers. For example, the first situation, "Employing copyrighted material in media literacy lessons," first describes the kinds of materials used (TV news, ads, movies, photos, websites, and much more) and common teaching activities with them. It then asserts the eligibility of fair use in bringing illustrative material of all kinds into teaching, both formal and informal. Then it discusses the limits to fair use in those situations: material should be germane to the project or topic, and as much should be used as is relevant to the teaching purpose. Teachers should provide credit or attribution (this is not actually relevant to fair use law, but it was a strong tenet of good practice in using others' material for the teachers). If the material is digital, teachers should take reasonable measure against third-party access and downloads. (The entire document with many related materials is at cmsimpact.org/medialiteracy.)

Major organizations in media literacy endorsed the document. They included the Action Coalition for Media Education, the Association of College and Research Libraries, the Media Education Foundation, the National Association for Media Literacy Education, the National Council of Teachers of English, and the Visual Communication Studies Division of the International Communication Association. Each of these then disseminated the Code to their members.

A Vehicle for Professional Education

Codes of best practice embody and enable peer-to-peer learning about how copyright and fair use apply to particular needs within a knowledge community. For the media literacy community, the code opened up conversation about employing this part of copyright law in ways that were directly relevant to practitioners. For the first time, the media literacy teachers were asked to think about what they actually thought was the best way to do their jobs and given a way to do that within the law. For the first time, they were getting solid, actionable, trustworthy advice on copyright from their peers who knew their mission and goals.

For anyone working in a school system, there was much that was counterintuitive about the Code. Hierarchies abound in school systems; there is always someone to say no. Expertise is delegated, often to the librarians or media specialists who themselves may be mired in the swamp of misinformation about fair use. Now, teachers themselves were in charge of teaching others in their systems about the way copyright law could align with educational mission. It took courage to take the first steps to employ the code; gradually, the code's tenets have been normalized, at least in some media literacy practices.

Tools were developed, including videos, an FAQ, and other explainers (Center for Media & Social Impact 2015). Hobbs' book, *Copyright Clarity: How Fair Use Supports Digital Learning* (2011) became a staple for workshops, trainings, and even a MOOC. In those workshops, teachers described, sometimes with amazement, the realization that fair use decision making was a reasoning process and that conversation could be education. One noted in the evaluations, "The 'aha' moment was [realizing] the need to have critical thinking conversations with and among students, teachers and administrators." Another wrote about "the possibilities for dialogues among teachers and between teachers and their students; to put critical thinking at the center of kids' understanding and use of digital tools." A third noted, "It was refreshing to hear about the power of what I CAN do instead of informing me about the FORBIDDEN."

The Code was incorporated into institutional practice. School systems in Wisconsin, Virginia, and Maryland have built it into their guidelines. The National Council for Teachers of English adopted it and features it in annual meetings. Competitions and awards programs for student work—for instance, the Alabama Council for Technology in Education, the National Writing Project, and some national student video competitions—have changed their requirements, so that students who work within the Code's requirements can submit work with third-party material in it. The Code is on many school and university library websites (unfortunately, usually along with a lot of other contradictory, confusing, and just plain inaccurate links).

Teachers have seen the difference it makes not only to their work but to their students' work. Media educator David Cooper Moore, an early user of the Code, noted that:

> students are easily able to grasp fair use concepts, and it can often improve the quality of their work. When students ask not just whether they can use copyrighted material, but WHY they should use the copyrighted material, they ask questions about creative choices that always seem to deepen their own creative work.
>
> (Personal communication January 6, 2016)

The analysis and reasoning skills are well aligned with the critical thinking skills involved in analyzing and creating media. Media literacy consultant Rhys Daunic values how the code helps teachers understand copyright and fair use:

> with the understanding that if their use is serving or enabling a teaching goal, they can proceed with confidence. Awareness of the Code allows educators to get on with using media to teach. Through this readable interpretation of what was previously scary and unapproachable for teachers, they now have a framework to reflect on how they use media in their pedagogy, and perhaps even understand their practice better as a result of that metacognition.
>
> (Personal communication February 16, 2016)

When educators understand the law, they appreciate its relevance and see how it improves the quality of teaching and learning. Thus, copyright becomes an opportunity for deepening learning instead of being conceptualized as just a matter of legal compliance.

Communities of Practice Claim Their Rights

Since the Code was created, other communities of practice have created codes of potential interest to the media education community. The Association of Research Libraries, the most prestigious of the library associations and a trendsetter, established a Code of Best Practices in Fair Use for Academic and Research Libraries. Its first situation explains how fair use can apply (far beyond what the TEACH Act permits) to making learning materials available for enrolled students online. Its third situation explains how fair use can permit copying from aging formats such as VHS to newer ones without having to wait for the material to decay (as the Copyright Act's section 108 would require). Its fourth situation concerns how to employ fair use in making collections of material available digitally, even on open websites. Its sixth situation concerns fair use in creating digital archives of an institution's own material (e.g., student work). All of these are directly relevant to media education activities.

Members of the OpenCourseWare movement created a code that also has direct implications for media education professionals. The code concerns how to incorporate third-party unlicensed material into curriculum materials made available openly on the web. Its situations are different uses for such material, for example critique, illustration, demonstration/explanation. These situations are familiar ones for anyone preparing texts or curriculum materials in media literacy. The logic of the OpenCourseWare professionals parallels closely that of media literacy professionals and provides further reinforcement for the logic in the media literacy code.

Journalists created a Set of Principles in Fair Use for Journalism, which should be a friendly tool for any journalistic teaching or student work, as well as for reinforcing the reasoning used in the media literacy code. For instance, situation three of the journalism code deals with using unlicensed copyrighted material in cultural reporting and criticism. Limitations include, among others, taking as much of the original material as is appropriate to enable news consumers to understand the point being made, contextualizing the material, and making the connection between the material and the criticism/commentary clear.

Visual arts professionals—fine artists, art historians, museum staff, editors of art publications, and writers on art—created a Code of Best Practices in Fair Use for the Visual Arts. Its situations concerning writing on art, teaching about art, and making art are all directly relevant and analogous to the work that media education professionals do with students in order to spur critical thinking about media.

Other codes of best practices concern poetry, dance libraries and archives, film teaching and scholarship, communication scholarship, and music libraries. They all participate in the same logic as that used to create the media literacy code. They ground practitioners in the basic reasoning to be used in making any fair use decision, and they explain the rationale and limitations in specific circumstances. They are all available at cmsimpact.org/fair-use.

Each of these codes has made a difference in how practitioners in the given community do their work. They permit imaginative freedom to succeed creatively in accomplishing a professional mission. None has permitted users of unlicensed material to steal market share from existing markets for the products they sample and use.

Perhaps the most important work of codes of best practices, however, is in educating the next generation. Young people are at least as poorly served with copyright misinformation as the adults who are struggling to teach them. They are taught in an atmosphere of fear and reproof about the very act of copying, which in itself is a basic tool of teaching. Educating young people to the rights they have to create new culture using elements from the copyrighted world around them is a gift, and codes of best practices in fair use permit them to carry that knowledge with them far beyond a teacher's classroom and exercises.

References

Aufderheide, P., Hobbs, R., & Jaszi, P. (2007). "The Cost of Copyright Confusion for Media Literacy." Retrieved from www.centerforsocialmedia.org/resources/publications/the_cost_of_copyright_confusion_for_media_literacy/

Aufderheide, P., & Jaszi, P. (2004). "Untold Stories: Creative Consequences of the Rights Clearance Culture for Documentary Filmmakers." Retrieved from www.cmsimpact.org/sites/default/files/UNTOLDSTORIES_Report.pdf

Aufderheide, P., & Jaszi, P. (2011). *Reclaiming Fair Use: How to Put Balance Back in Copyright*. Chicago: University of Chicago Press.

Center for Media & Social Impact. (2015). "Media Literacy." Retrieved Novemer 11, 2016, from http://archive.cmsimpact.org/fair-use/related-materials/codes/code-best-practices-fair-use-media-literacy-education

Crews, K. (2001). "The Law of Fair Use and the Illusion of Fair-Use Guidelines." *Ohio State Law Journal*, 62, 98.

Hobbs, R. (2011). *Copyright Clarity: How Fair Use Supports Digital Learning*. Thousand Oaks, CA: Corwin/Sage.

Madison, M. J. (2004). "A Pattern-Oriented Approach to Fair Use." *William and Mary Law Review*, 45(4), 1525–1690.

U.S. Court of Appeals for the 2d Circuit. (2015, October 16). 13–4829-cv *Authors Guild v. Google, Inc.*

9

CREATIVE COMMONS IN JOURNALISM EDUCATION

Ed Madison and Esther Wojcicki

Respect for people and their property is a basic principle of a civilized society. We are taught at an early age that it is wrong to borrow or take from others without permission. But social norms related to how we exchange and share items can shift over time. Disruptive technologies in our digital age are altering the definition of authorship and ownership. Google, Facebook, and Twitter are seen as sources of news when, more often than not, they are conduits for accessing materials produced by others. This is especially true as it pertains to media and more specifically to journalism.

Philip Graham, former publisher of *The Washington Post*, is credited with describing journalism as the "first rough draft of history" (Shafer 2010). Yet increasingly those drafts are the products of collaboration between individuals who may work in separate settings and never meet. A story can be shot by a videographer in Southeast Asia, include narration recorded by a reporter in New York, feature music recorded by a composer in Los Angeles, and be assembled by a video editor in Chicago. Once a collaborative work is completed, who is the author? We will revisit this question at the conclusion of this chapter.

Because digital media is malleable, the true nature of a work's origins can be subject to interpretation. Matters of ownership are often an afterthought for students focused on following their creative instincts. Remixing content is facilitated by mobile apps that allow users to morph media in unprecedented ways.

So just what are the rules of the road for journalism students who want to enhance their work with text, still images, videos, or music produced by others? And what if, as a content creator, you wish to share your work without involving expensive lawyers and complicated contracts? How might journalism educators and their students make the best use of Creative Commons licensing? How are journalism entrepreneurs thinking about copyright and fair use in new ways as they develop new business models?

In earlier times, reporting news involved documenting eyewitness accounts of events with technology no more complicated than a pen and notebook, and the guidelines were quite clear. If you did not witness breaking news firsthand, you were to find and cite two reliable sources. The practice of proper attribution continues to be one of journalism's primary lessons. Young journalists are also encouraged to be fair and unbiased.

However, these tenets can be tough topics for journalism educators who must also explain the misdeeds of high-profile professionals like NBC's Brian Williams and journalist Jonah Lehrer who were found to have stretched the truth and fabricated facts. The pressures of competition and the desire to advance one's career can tempt individuals to seek short-term gains that are out of alignment with one's long-term best interests. Small and seemingly insignificant fibs can slowly add up and potentially result in an avalanche of blatant and unredeemable lies.

Teaching ethical guidelines is also complicated in this digital era where students come to class with app-enabled mobile devices that empower them to mix and mash existing media—be it images, words, or music—in ways that are arguably distinct from the original sources. Administrators and teachers face complex challenges when attempting to manage and monitor activity on their students' personal devices.

Issues pertaining to equity and inclusion also become a factor. Technology changes at rates that exceed many school districts' budgets. And students can experience a sense of shame if their family's budget does not afford them the ability to upgrade their personal devices as frequently as their peers. Software incompatibilities become another factor. Incompatible operating systems with ever-changing program updates can create an uneven playing field. When students begin to intuitively swap and mix media, clarity about who owns what can become blurred.

This chapter explores how the limitations of U.S. copyright law led to the development of Creative Commons licensing, which shifted the traditional model of content ownership from "all rights reserved" to "some rights reserved." This distinction frees media creators to choose varying levels of restrictions for their works, which is an appropriate option given the pliable nature of digital media. Additionally, the chapter examines how new business models for journalism are emerging and benefiting from broader adoption of Creative Commons. ProPublica, the Huffington Post Investigative Fund, and GroundReport are among the many bold experiments, and several are proving to be sustainable. We explore how student journalists are benefiting by licensing their work through Creative Commons. The Paly Voice and News21 produce stories that are republished by mainstream media, enabling young people to establish portfolios, be credited for their work, and reach mass audiences. Finally, this chapter explores many of the nuances of ownership in a digital world, including scenarios that involve collaborative and jointly created works.

The Good Ol' Days?

Making media—and specifically practicing journalism—seemed simple prior to the 1980s. Reporters covered events, secured quotes, cited their sources, filed their stories, and called it a day. That was until the Internet surfaced and began to gain traction. Google emerged as a dominant source for seekers of information, and Craigslist displaced newspapers as the preferred medium for selling used and other classified items.

These disruptions were significant for newspapers. Ad sales plummeted, and news staffs shrunk. Several legacy news organizations consolidated, and others closed. More than a hundred newspapers shut their doors in 2009, print sales dwindled by 30%, and 10,000 newspaper jobs were cut (Dumpala 2009).

The 24-hour news cycle, ushered in by cable news, proliferated with the rise of the Internet, requiring news organizations to function around the clock. Not only did competition increase, but afflicted newsrooms were also left with fewer resources. The shift has left journalists with less time to verify facts, edit stories, and make sure their work is credible.

CNN conspicuously tarnished its brand in recent years by rushing to judgment on several major stories, including misidentifying the Boston Marathon bombers and misstating that President Barack Obama's healthcare law was overturned by the Supreme Court (Carr 2013). Facing an industry-wide firestorm of economic pressures, Howard Weaver, vice president for news at The McClatchy Company, lamented, "You can give up, you can hunker down and bleed, or you can fight back. Well, I want to fight back" (Smolkin 2006: 1).

Corporate owners often claim they were blindsided by sudden shifts in technology that have disrupted their business models. However, in 2005 News Corp Chairman Rupert Murdoch admitted, "I didn't do as much as I should have after all the excitement of the late 1990s" (Duyn 2005). Rather than embrace the innovation of the Internet, many news organizations ignored it, and most posted their content without a charge (Tofel 2012).

Futurist Stewart Brand coined the often quoted phrase, "Information wants to be free!" It is commonly cited from a speech he gave in 1984 at the first Hacker's Conference in Sausalito, California. *Forbes* editor Richard Siklos noted that Brand's words are frequently used to vindicate the practice of copying and sharing someone else's work—and as a rationale for why the future of many legacy media companies remains in jeopardy. Often omitted are Brand's additional remarks from that evening: "On the one hand, information wants to be expensive, because it's so valuable. The right information in the right place just changes your life" (Lai 2009).

Brand was really addressing a tension between the two: the transformative potential of information that is vital versus the plummeting costs of distributing it once it is digitized.

Also rarely referenced are Brand's subsequent statements about how this tension affects journalism. Unlike many observers, Brand does not blame the Internet, Google, or Craigslist for the plight of newspapers. Rather, he holds corporate owners accountable for the conundrum they face. Consumer appetite for news and information remains high. However, after decades of free access, until recently, much of the public has been apathetic about having to pay for it (Arbel 2015).

In 2010, Rupert Murdoch defiantly told a National Press Club audience: "We are going to stop people like Google or Microsoft or whoever from taking stories for nothing. . . [T]here is a law of copyright and they recognize it" (Harris 2010). At the time, Brand was consulting for *The Washington Post*, which rebuffed his recommendation that they should embrace the interactive immediacy of newly emerging platforms like Twitter. "They basically said to me, 'Thank you for your time, and where do we send the check?'"(Lai 2009).

Author and activist Cory Doctorow revisited Brand's thesis in his 2014 book, *Information Doesn't Want to Be Free*. Doctorow revealed how, in the Internet age, media conglomerates have lobbied for broader legal interpretations of copyright law that are Orwellian. One proposal would give corporations sweeping surveillance access to consumers' private computer files, simply to verify that the files were not pirated (Doctorow 2014). Such attempts illustrate the desperate measures that digital disruptions can provoke.

Yet as audience expectations and appetites for more news and information continue to rise, some news organizations are beginning to profit. *The New York Times* passed the one million digital-only paid subscriber mark in 2015, four and half years after establishing a paywall. When combined with its additional 1.1 million print-and-digital subscribers, the publication has more readers than at any time in its history (Baquet 2015).

If high-powered media moguls like Rupert Murdoch and then *Washington Post* owner Philip Graham were puzzled by the complexities of copyright and digital distribution, it's easy to understand why such matters continue to confuse educators and their students. Understanding the original intent of copyright law can provide some initial clarity. Hobbs (2010: 18) observes, "Most people think it protects owner's rights. They think it's about money and profit and control. But looking at the U.S. Constitution we see that this is not the real purpose of copyright."

The Constitution states: "Government can establish a copyright system to promote the progress of science and useful arts, by securing for limited times to authors and inventors the exclusive right to their respective writings and discoveries" (U.S. Constitution, 1789: Article 1, Section 8, Clause 8). The framers sought to encourage creative expression in a manner that would give artists confidence that their interests were protected. Copyright laws were established to foster productivity and to make artistic endeavors sustainable. Adding further clarification, Hobbs cites Carrie Russell of the American Library Association who notes, "That authors and inventors benefit from copyright is a side effect of encouraging the dissemination of knowledge, and not a direct intent of copyright" (Russell 2004 as cited in Hobbs 2010: 18). The intent of the law was to allow creative works to pass from private ownership into public domain at some reasonable point of time past the life of the artist. Thus, contemporary creatives are free to reimagine the works of Shakespeare, Dickens, and Beethoven without consequences. Originally, U.S. copyright protections were limited to twenty-eight years. However, during the mid-20th century, industry lobbyists succeeded in pressuring Congress to double the term to fifty-six years. Congress revisited copyright legislation in 1976, granting individuals lifetime protection plus an additional fifty years. Corporate-held copyright terms were lengthened to seventy-five years. Terms were subsequently modified and lengthened further, creating lucrative revenue streams for the heirs of great artists but preventing newer artists from reinterpreting those earlier works (Lee 2013).

The law has a special provision that allows for the fair use of copyrighted materials as a means to ensure that copyright supports creativity and the creation of new knowledge. Fair use provides balance to copyright's strong legal protections, ensuring that copyright law does not become a vehicle for private censorship, restricting the free flow of information as protected by the First Amendment. Under the doctrine of fair use, people are empowered to use copyrighted content without payment or permission when the social benefit of the uses outweighs the private costs to the copyright holder. The Copyright Act states that "fair use . . . for purposes such as criticism, comment, news reporting, teaching (including multiple copies for classroom use), scholarship, or research, is not an infringement of copyright." The law privileges the "transformative" use of protected materials, meaning commentary and criticism, not just copying words verbatim (Electronic Frontier Foundation 2016).

Since the 1980s, emerging digital technologies have disrupted conventional practices in ways never contemplated by copyright law. However, they have sparked a new era of unbridled innovation, allowing creativity to be expressed and shared with minimal costs.

Understanding Creative Commons

Creative Commons arose from the work of Lawrence Lessig, who imagined flexible licensing schemes that could meet the needs of content creators who desire to share their works without the burdens of the market-based licensing process (Lessig, 2004). Rather than be bound by the narrow "all rights reserved" provisions of copyright laws, Creative Commons licenses permit content makers to specify "some rights reserved" in varying degrees. As of 2017, there are six designations:

Figure 9.1 Attribution: CC BY

This license permits others to disseminate, alter, and add to your work and even profit as long as they acknowledge you as the source. It is the most versatile license.

Figure 9.2 Attribution–ShareAlike: CC BY-SA

This license permits others to disseminate, alter, and add to your work and even profit as long as they reciprocate by making their work available under the same terms. This license is used by Wikipedia.

Figure 9.3 Attribution–NoDerivs: CC BY-ND

This license allows resharing, commercial and noncommercial, as long as the work is not modified, and you are credited.

Figure 9.4 Attribution–Non-Commercial: CC BY-NC

This license permits others to disseminate, alter, and add to your work but not for profit. They must also credit you. However, derivative works must be licensed by the same terms.

Figure 9.5 Attribution–Non-Commercial–ShareAlike: CC BY-NC-SA

This license permits others to disseminate, alter, and add to your work but not commercially, and as long as they acknowledge you as the source. Also, they agree to make the resulting new work available under the same terms.

Figure 9.6 Attribution–Non-Commercial–NoDerivs: CC BY-NC-ND

This is the most restrictive of the six Creative Commons licenses. Others may download and share your work as long as they credit you. However, they cannot profit from or alter the work.

People who want to add still images, video, or music to enhance the overall quality of their stories with minimal effort can use work that has been licensed through Creative Commons. Over a billion Creative Commons–licensed works are now in circulation, nearly tripling those issued between 2010 and 2015 (Creative Commons 2015). As a practical matter, it is not financially feasible for most students to fly to Greenland when they wish to write about melting icebergs affected by climate change. Creative Commons licensing allows students to search sites like Flickr.com for appropriate images that will illustrate their words. They may also choose to create a slide show or video, set it to found music, and embed the edited new work alongside their written article within a blogpost. Creative Commons provides simple solutions that benefit all parties. However, at the professional level, the stakes can be higher.

New Economic Models for Journalism Rely on Fair Use

Investigative journalism, long considered vital to keeping government agencies and corporate interests in check, has suffered significant economic setbacks as a result of the rise of Internet culture. Bloggers and small town publications often lack the resources necessary to defend legal challenges from public figures who bristle when reporters hold them accountable for uttering words that are not aligned with their actions. Solid investigative journalism requires time, money, and a high level of professionalism that comes with experience. This is increasingly critical at a time when recently high-profile political figures openly mock the watchdog role of the press.

Pop culture likes to lionize journalism's role in uncovering bad deeds. From Watergate to more recent church sex scandals explored in the Oscar Award–wining film *Spotlight*, Hollywood relishes a great investigative story well told. However, cinematic characterizations fail to capture the often unglamorous real work required in revealing dark truths. Bob Woodward and Carl Bernstein spent three years deciphering the clues that led to President Richard Nixon's resignation (Watergate.info 1974). *The Boston Globe* reporting team that investigated sexual abuse by Catholic Church priests filed 600 stories before the cardinal in charge resigned (Boston Globe 2016).

Emerging journalists benefit from understanding not only the practice of journalism but also its economics. Rather than fear technological disruption, some entrepreneurs are embracing it through experimentation with Creative Commons licensing. Their choice facilitates broader distribution of stories and increases their impact.

ProPublica is an independent, philanthropically funded investigative news unit launched in 2008 by Paul Steiger, former managing editor of *The Wall Street Journal*. Its website allows unencumbered access to its stories. ProPublica's open-door policy gives major news outlets a window of free exclusivity, which makes stories accessible to all other interested publications. The sole stipulation is that the copied works carry a CC BY-NC-ND (attribution noncommercial, no derivatives) Creative Commons license, which means the user will credit ProPublica and will refrain from reselling or altering the content.

While running Huffington Post, Arianna Huffington also strongly advocated for advancing investigative journalism and Creative Commons licensing factors into her distribution model. In 2009, the Huffington Post invested $1.75 million to establish its watchdog fund (Huffington 2009). The team earned considerable credibility in 2012 when it was awarded a Pulitzer Prize for its coverage of the effects of war on severely injured veterans (Calderone 2013). Much like

ProPublica, Huffington Post's investigative stories are free to competing news organizations as long as they carry a CC BY-NC-ND (attribution noncommercial, no derivatives) license.

Crowdsourced journalism relies on flexible copyright licensing schemes. For example, GroundReport.com has a business model that benefits from several Creative Commons options. It is a nonprofit global news site that welcomes content from individuals regardless of their level of experience, making it an appropriate outlet for student-produced journalism. Approximately 2,000 contributors submit articles, photos, and videos that are then vetted by a team of editors. Rather than payment, contributors receive "recognition rewards" bestowed by volunteer editors. Contributors retain ownership rights and can share work according to their preferred choice of Creative Commons license (GroundReport 2016). This provides budding journalists with an authentic audience and byline.

Only time will tell whether crowdsourced journalism will be sustainable. Entrepreneurial journalists are also experimenting with crowdfunding, popularized by Kickstarter and similar project sponsorship web platforms. Conceptually, independent journalists supposedly benefit from cultivating a community of patrons who will support their work. However, results can be mixed. A number of crowdfunding platforms (including Spot.us, Uncoverage, and Sponsume) have had substantial philanthropic funding and yet failed to gain sufficient traction to achieve sustainability. Documentaries with compelling storylines tend to fare better than the written word on crowdfunding platforms. Still, a variety of major global news organizations are beginning to share content freely with the expectations of long-term benefit. For example, Al Jazeera is among the visual content producers that use Creative Commons licensing to bolster its brand by sharing content with media companies that would otherwise be viewed as competitors. The company has established an online repository that includes written text, photos, and video footage that is free for use, as long as Al Jazeera is credited.

Student Media and Creative Commons

Journalism education prepares students to be effective communicators and provides skills they can apply in any profession. A critical task for content creators who decides to pursue a career in journalism is assembling a compelling portfolio of work that will gain them employment. Yet historically, internships have provided students with more opportunities to observe than to practice journalism. News organizations that are presently challenged to work within smaller budgets now actively engage in partnerships with universities and high schools to create pipelines for student-produced journalism. Creative Commons licensing allows those works to find a broader audience.

In Northern California, Palo Alto High School's award-winning journalism program is acknowledged as being among the nations' largest. Nearly 500 of the school's 1,900 students participate, producing seven distinct publications, including a newspaper, an online news site, three feature magazines, a sports magazine, and a three-camera newscast (Madison 2012, 2015). These student-run publications often break news, and they make use of Creative Commons licensing to share their stories with local and regional media.

At the college level, News21 is a Carnegie Corporation and Knight Foundation–funded initiative that brings selected students to the Walter Cronkite School at Arizona State University each summer to collaborate with journalism professionals. Since 2005, more than 500 students have participated. Through Creative Commons licensing, the work produced is shared with numerous national media outlets, which has included *The Washington Post*, MSNBC.com, and the Center for Public Integrity (news21.com 2016).

University of Oregon School of Journalism and Communication researchers and students collaborate with regional media organizations to experiment with new forms of documentary storytelling and to measure the impact of video messaging on audiences. "Northwest Stories," produced in partnership with Oregon Public Broadcasting (OPB), is a multiplatform-distributed series of documentary profiles on interesting and eccentric people who reside in the region. The stories are promoted statewide on OPB's news sites, radio stations, and KOPB-TV.

Student producers use social media to share behind-the-scenes vignettes that invite audiences to witness and participate in the story-gathering process. The intent is to make the production process more transparent and to invite audience participation. In 2014, one story featuring Oregon's Josephine County Sheriff Gil Gilbertson shed light on local matters related to crime and taxation. A second story on filmmaker Tim Lewis investigated environmental activism through the eyes of the radical Earth First! movement.

In fall 2015, journalist Kathryn Schulz's *New Yorker* article "The Really Big One" prompted University of Oregon researchers and students to once again partner with Oregon Public Broadcasting to produce "Don't Wait for the Quake," a live interactive town meeting on the subject of earthquake preparedness. Schulz's article brought new awareness to scientific predictions that the Northwest region of the United States is overdue for a potentially devastating earthquake. For this project, the team used Harv.is, a mobile app created by Laura LoForti and Andrew DeVigal that measures audience engagement levels in response to live or recorded media—in this case, student-produced video stories, including a first-person narrative, a how-to video, and a traditional documentary story with voiceover narration. An in-studio audience, as well as home web viewers and radio listeners, swiped up or down on their mobile devices as the videos played. Swiping up indicated feeling "motivated to act," while swiping down indicated feeling overwhelmed. Results indicated that stories depicting resilience and community collaboration garnered the highest levels of engagement. Creative Commons licensing has allowed this content to reach a broader audience. "Don't Wait for the Quake" stories were shared via Eugene, Oregon–based KLCC airwaves and news site. The entire hour program was also shared with a public access cable channel in Roseburg, Oregon. Whether one is in college or high school, having your work published by a major news organization promotes self-efficacy and credibility within the profession.

Revisiting Ownership

We posed some important questions at the beginning of this chapter that require further exploration. If a video is shot by a person in Southeast Asia and narrated by another in New York, with music composed and added by another in Los Angeles, and the work is assembled by yet another person in Chicago—who owns it? The answer is that, as we will see, possibly all of the contributors are owners of their particular contribution.

Alternatively, if the project is a so-called work for hire, people may choose to waive any rights to ownership as a condition of employment. For many young media producers, this can occur, unless they are self-financing their own creative work or have the knowledge and skills to negotiate different contractual terms with the financier. This area of law deals with *intellectual property* rights, a matter that is seldom discussed or explored with students. As matter of practice, we prepare students for jobs where they will be paid for their labor rather than teaching them to become entrepreneurs where they maintain equity in what they create. The distinction is similar to owning a home that maintains some level of intrinsic value that can be bought, sold, traded, or handed down to heirs.

In earlier eras, when jobs were stable and futures were more secure, the need to think and act entrepreneurially was less essential. It was safe to place one's faith in a career path that would lead to retirement without peril. However, that era has passed. Creative Commons licensing was created to facilitate the sharing of content, not to negate the rights of ownership. It allows authors to set the terms by which their works are shared and used by others. This is a critical lesson students are entitled to learn, especially at a time when the low cost of technology enables them to produce high-quality content that can rival that produced by corporate-owned companies.

We typically think of journalism as disposable media, meaning news is valuable to the degree it is useful to us today. Whether printed on paper or published online, its worth diminishes over time. However, entrepreneurs think of creating lasting value, meaning content that is "evergreen" or that maintains an extended shelf life. They contemplate branding strategies that create memorable themes that will resonate with audiences indefinitely. Thus, CBS's *60 Minutes* stories come and go, but the *60 Minutes* program is an enduring and iconic brand.

Students engage in producing creative works before they enter the workforce. A significant gray-area question is who owns those works, especially when they are produced with school-owned cameras or are written and edited on school-owned computers? These questions can become more complicated for public institutions whose facilities are funded by tax dollars. Prince George's County Public Schools, in the state of Maryland, made headlines when it proposed a policy that works created by student newspapers and blogs would become the property of the school district, even if they were created on the students' own time with their own materials. The proposed policy would have also covered works created by all county employees (Harris 2013). *Washington Post* reporters talked with legal experts who suggested that the plan was revenue driven, given the emerging market for teacher's lesson plans. Administrators realized that software affords educators and students with the tools to create works that might have residual value, and they did not want wish to be left out. In this instance, the County intended to claim all rights and proceeds. However, it withdrew the plan once it was established it lacked legal standing (Wiggins 2013).

When students create media, their work is protected by copyright law, whether the work was produced for a school activity or not. There is no paperwork to complete_copyright protections are automatic. This means that the author need not affix a copyright symbol or submit federal forms to enjoy full protection under the law. Copyrights can be transferred only by way of a written agreement. Many universities explicitly take the position that students retain ownership of the works they produce as part of the fulfillment of their assignments and projects, regardless of whether they are made on school premises or with school-supplied equipment. For example, New York University's Tisch School of the Arts has established and posted a Student Ownership Policy. The policy notes the dual nature of student work, first to fulfill a student's educational experience and second as an item of property of value to its maker. The policy acknowledges that students retain full ownership of their work. However, notwithstanding entry in festivals or competitions, students are not allowed to profit financially from their work until after they have graduated (Tisch School 2016).

When students create media for public distribution, they are responsible for securing proper appearance releases and permissions for third-party materials contained in the work. Further, the policy protects students from potential co-ownership claims from professors and instructors who may have advised students during the process of making the work. An additional provision grants the university the right to make copies, display, publicize, and add its name to the work. Any associated costs are borne by the university without a price markup (Tisch School

2016). Such policies honor a student's right to ownership while considering the institution's role in facilitating learning. The two are not mutually exclusive.

Circling back to our original hypothetical scenario: what if the collaborative work, created by four parties in distinct locales, was a speculative endeavor? In other words, what if the work wasn't performed for an employer, and there was no written agreement in place. Rather, members of the team contributed to the production on their own time and with their own resources? The answer in this instance is complicated. U.S. copyright law states that in the case of *collective works*, each person retains ownership in his or her contribution (Copyright.gov 2016).

Copyright in the contribution is considered distinct from copyright in the collective work in its entirety. If no written transfer of rights is in place, the holder of ownership in the whole collective work is presumed to have acquired only the rights to reproduce and distribute the contribution as part of that collective work, plus revisions and extensions of the same series. An example would be an essay anthology written by contributing authors. Unless otherwise transferred, each author retains his or her copyright interest in the individual contribution. However, the anthology's publisher may hold the copyright on the overall collective work.

Another category of ownership is a *joint work*, where parties establish a relationship of co-authorship. Specifically, a joint work is defined by the law as "work prepared by two or more authors with the intention that their contributions be merged into inseparable or interdependent parts of a unitary whole" (Copyright.gov 2016). Thus, ownership is undivided. As collaboration becomes increasingly normative in multimedia production, a good understanding of the legal rights of digital authorship will be an important dimension of media literacy.

Conclusion

Journalism education is vital in preparing young people to become effective communicators and informed citizens who can play an active role in a democratic society. Technology affords students and their teachers with powerful tools with which to capture stories and influence change. Harnessing that power requires a basic understanding of rules of ownership and fair use, especially as it relates to sharing one's content and when making use of content produced by others.

Journalism continues to be in a state of flux with new and emerging platforms disrupting the status quo. Yet the principles of journalism remain solid. Regardless of how news and information are consumed, readers and audience value accuracy, credibility, and transparency.

Immersive learning opportunities provide educators and their students with a wealth of applied knowledge and experience that strengthens their ability to chart their futures in these uncertain times. Whether one's creative contributions are done "for hire," speculation, or just plain fun, "collaboration" is the word that defines working relationships in this digital era, and Creative Commons licenses provide a mechanism for trouble-free exchange.

References

Arbel, T. (2015, September 30). "Forty Percent of Millennials Pay for Print, Online News." Associated Press. Retrieved from http://bigstory.ap.org/article/111f65247a564fb48816ada08d396803/40-percent-millennials-pay-print-online-news

Baquet, D. (2015, April 5) "The New York Times Reaches a Milestone, Thanks to Our Readers." *New York Times*. Retrieved from www.nytimes.com/2015/10/05/business/the-new-york-times-reaches-a-milestone-thanks-to-our-readers.html

Boston Globe. (2016, March 6). "Key Reports From Globe's Spotlight Team on Clergy Sex Abuse." Retrieved from www.bostonglobe.com/metro/2016/03/11/key-reports-from-globe-spotlight-team-clergy-sex-abuse/s7qc7M3W2nmLs5ULN8ILHJ/story.html

Calderone, M. (2013, January 14). "Huffington Post Awarded Pulitzer Prize." *Huffington Post*. Retrieved from www.huffingtonpost.com/2012/04/16/huffington-post-pulitzer-prize-2012_n_1429169.html

Carr, D. (2013, April 21). "The Pressure to Be the TV News Leader Tarnishes a Big Brand." *New York Times*. Retrieved from www.nytimes.com/2013/04/22/business/media/in-boston-cnn-stumbles-in-rush-to-break-news.html?_r=0

Copyright.gov. (2016). "Help, Type of Work." Retrieved from www.copyright.gov/eco/help-type.html#collective

Creative Commons. (2015). "State of the Commons." Retrieved from https://stateof.creativecommons.org/2015/

Doctorow, C. (2014). *Information Doesn't Want to Be Free: Laws for the Internet Age*. San Francisco: McSweeney's.

Dumpala, P. (2009, July 4). "The Year the Newspaper Died." *Business Insider*. Retrieved from www.businessinsider.com/the-death-of-the-american-newspaper-2009-7

Duyn, A. (2005, April 14). "Papers Must Embrace the Internet, Murdoch Tells Editors." *Financial Times*. Retrieved from www.ft.com/content/0fbebe38-ac45-11d9-bb67-00000e2511c8

Electronic Frontier Foundation. (2016). "Legal Guide for Bloggers: Intellectual Property." Retrieved from www.eff.org/issues/bloggers/legal/liability/IP

Groundreport.com. (2016). "Tell Your Story on Ground Report: Learn the Trade: Get Noticed by Media Outlets." Retrieved from www.groundreport.com/about-us/

Harris, E. (2013, February 6). "Copyright Ownership in Students' Work." *Copyrightlaws.com*. Retrieved from http://xigentinc.com/copyright-ownership-in-students-work/

Harris, P. (2010, April 7). "Rupert Murdoch Defiant: 'I'll Stop Google Taking Our News for Nothing.'" *The Guardian*. Retrieved from www.theguardian.com/media/2010/apr/07/rupert-murdoch-google-paywalls-ipad

Hobbs, R. (2010). *Copyright Clarity: How Fair Use Supports Digital Learning*. Thousand Oaks, CA: Corwin/Sage.

Huffington, A. (2009, April 29) "Announcing the Launch of the Huffington Post Investigative Fund." *Huffington Post*. Retrieved from www.huffingtonpost.com/arianna-huffington/announcing-the-launch-of-_b_180543.html

Lai, J. (2009, July 20). "Information Wants to Be Free and Expensive." *Forbes*. Retrieved from http://fortune.com/2009/07/20/information-wants-to-be-free-and-expensive/

Lee, T. (2013, October 25). "15 Years Ago, Congress Kept Mickey Mouse Out of the Public Domain. Will They Do It Again?" *Washington Post*. Retrieved from www.washingtonpost.com/news/the-switch/wp/2013/10/25/15-years-ago-congress-kept-mickey-mouse-out-of-the-public-domain-will-they-do-it-again/

Lessig, L. (2004). *Free Culture: How Big Media Uses Technology and the Law to Lock Down Culture and Control Creativity*. New York: Penguin Press.

Madison, E. (2012). "Journalistic Learning: Rethinking and Redefining Language Arts Curricula." Doctoral dissertation, University of Oregon.

Madison, E. (2015). *Newsworthy: Cultivating Critical Thinkers, Readers and Writers in Language Arts Classrooms*. New York: Teachers College Press.

News21.com. (2016). "About Us." Retrieved from http://news21.com/about-news21/

Russell, C. (2004). *Complete Copyright: An Everyday Guide for Librarians*. Washington, DC: American Library Association, Office for Information Technology Policy.

Shafer, J. (2010, August 30). "Who Said It First? Journalism is the First Rough Draft of History." *Slate*. Retrieved from www.slate.com/articles/news_and_politics/press_box/2010/08/who_said_it_first.html

Smolkin, R. (2006). "Adapt or Die." *American Journalism Review*. Retrieved from http://ajrarchive.org/Article.asp?id=4111

Tisch School. (2016). "Student Ownership Policy." Retrieved from https://tisch.nyu.edu/about/intellectual-property-rights/student-ownership-policy

Tofel, R. (2012). "Why American Newspapers Gave Away the Future." *Now and Then Reader*. Retrieved from www.nowandthenreader.com/why-american-newspapers-gave-away-the-future/

U.S. Constitution. (1789). "Article 1, Section 8, Clause 8." Retrieved from www.copyright.gov/title17/92preface.html

Watergate.info. (1974). "Brief Timeline of Events." Retrieved from http://watergate.info/chronology/brief-timeline-of-events

Wiggins, O. (2013, February 2). "Prince George's Considers Copyright Policy That Takes Ownership of Students' Work." *Washington Post*. Retrieved from https://www.washingtonpost.com/local/education/prince-georges-considers-copyright-policy-that-takes-ownership-of-students-work/2013/02/02/dc592dea-6b08-11e2-ada3-d86a4806d5ee_story.html?utm_term=.04878a762e1e

Further Reading

Creative Commons. *Copyright Basics*. [Video]. Retrieved from https://youtu.be/Uiq42O6rhW4

"Creative Commons Images and You: A Quick Guide for Image Users." Ars Technica. Retrieved from http://arstechnica.com/tech-policy/2011/08/creative-commons-images-and-you/

"Get Creative Commons Savvy." P2PU. Retrieved from https://courses.p2pu.org/en/groups/get-cc-savvy/content/elements-of-a-cc-license/

"Legal Guide for Bloggers." Electronic Frontier Foundation. Retrieved from www.eff.org/issues/bloggers/legal

10

BLURRED LINES AND SHIFTING BOUNDARIES

Copyright and Transformation in the Multimodal Compositions of Teachers, Teacher Educators, and Future Media Professionals

J. Patrick McGrail and Ewa McGrail

> Fair use should not be considered a bizarre, occasionally tolerated departure from the grand conception of the copyright monopoly. To the contrary, it is a necessary part of the overall design.
>
> (Leval 1990: 1110)

What's the difference between a media professional and an amateur producer? The rapid proliferation of better-quality "prosumer" (Anderson 2003) equipment and of powerful yet inexpensive editing software has helped to erode the long-standing distinction between professional media producers and amateurs (Jenkins 2006; Dush 2009). High-definition cameras, digital audio recorders, and powerful editing and visual effects software are now available for relatively little money to the average aspiring audiovisual artist (Lessig 2004; Williams & Zenger 2012). When the Internet became searchable via browsers, the text, graphics, images, audio, and video of websites became downloadable elements that could be copied and reused. In addition, the rise of social media has greatly accelerated the practice of sharing and distributing audiovisual content among the digitally literate (Palfrey et al. 2009).

A perhaps less anticipated result of this greatly enhanced access to digital media is the desire on the part of contemporary creators—a term that now regularly encompasses teachers, teacher educators, and media professionals (Bishop 2009; Bruce & Chiu 2015; Cremin & Baker 2014; Hundley & Holbrook 2013)—not only to use today's digital tools to create original productions but also to use these tools to augment their originally authored work with previously authored media and to comment upon, satirize, parodize, or enhance and thus to *transform* this previously existing creative material (Burwell 2013; Jenkins 2006; Knobel & Lankshear 2008; Palfrey et al. 2009). Much of this preexisting material is part of our audiovisual culture, including samples of pop songs, news broadcasts, popular films, television shows, and iconic images.

Simply put, a predominant cultural practice in our time has facilitated a vast and fruitful commentary on both the past and present (Lessig 2008; McCorkle 2015; Porter 2015). As Fisher and colleagues (2012: 296) argued *in re* the Shepard Fairey case:

> [I]t is only in the past decade that all of the elements have come together to create an Internet-based ecosystem that is making the collective photographic record of the world accessible and usable by artists as common reference material. The components of this ecosystem include:
>
> (a) Digital cameras;
> (b) Ubiquitous broadband connectivity;
> (c) Standardized digital image formats;
> (d) Photo databases and consumer photo sharing sites;
> (e) Image search;
> (f) Photo editing and manipulation tool sets.

Since the preexisting materials appropriated for social and intracultural commentary (Knobel & Lankshear 2008; Lessig 2008) are copyright protected (McCorkle 2015; Porter 2015), understanding fair use and, more specifically, the construct of transformation underpinning fair use within copyright law is a crucially important skill to acquire (Aufderheide & Jaszi 2011; Hobbs, Jaszi, & Aufderheide 2007). Fair use grants creators, under certain circumstances, "the right to use, transform, and critique cultural materials" without permission or payment (Burwell 2013: 209). Heymann (2008: 466) points out, however, that just because "virtually everything is transformative," it does not necessarily follow "that nothing is infringing."

Determining whether a given use of copyrighted material in one's creative work is *transformative* is a difficult question, but it is a question that must first be answered, at least to an ethically satisfactory degree, by the end user of the material. Today's websites, photos, videos, and other material are frequently available for downloading without technical barriers (Cobia 2009); therefore, if the use of a copyrighted work is contemplated by end users, the users should articulate—at least for themselves—that the use is fair. This is because "transformativeness in itself can be broadly interpreted" (Aufderheide & Jaszi 2011: 93) and transformative use can vary across subject matter. For example, case law shows us that a transformative use has not as often been found in cases that involve musical sampling (Landau 2015). Hence, any decision making that concerns transformation requires a nuanced understanding of its relation to the other analytic factors under the fair use exception. These are, generally, the nature, amount, and effect of the appropriation on the original work, as stipulated in the Copyright Act's Section 107 (Copyright Act 1976).

Copyright education is now an essential component of both the disciplines of communication and education. Today, both preservice teachers and aspiring media professionals must pay close attention to the copyright implications of the multimedia work they create. They must take special care that the copyrighted content they select for use, manipulation, and reframing meets the standards for fair use and transformation as provided in the Copyright Act (McKenna 2000). In this chapter, we discuss the doctrine of fair use and in particular the concept of transformation. We consider how to best use its freedoms and assess its limits in the creation of new digital media objects and creative classroom tools.

The Doctrine of Transformation

The doctrine of transformation begins with a 19th-century case, *Folsom v. Marsh* (1841). The Reverend Charles Upham had copied over 300 pages from the plaintiff's author, Jared Sparks. (Sparks and Upham were both authors; the case title's name comes from their respective publishers.) Because the copying, while egregious by today's standards, was not complete, the defense suggested that it was an abridgment, which was not considered a violation of copyright during that period. Judge Story (1845) dismissed this argument and declared:

> It is certainly not necessary, to constitute an invasion of copyright, that the whole of a work should be copied, or even a large portion of it, in form or in substance. If so much is taken, that the value of the original is sensibly diminished, or the labors of the original author are substantially to an injurious extent appropriated by another, that is sufficient, in point of law, to constitute a piracy pro tanto.
>
> (115)

At the same time, however, Judge Story (1845) laid out in rough form the doctrines of fair use, which, with some changes of language, were statutorily encoded in the 1976 federal Copyright Act as 17 U.S.C. § 107. He wrote:

> In short, we must often, in deciding questions of this sort, look to the nature and objects of the selections made, the quantity and value of the materials used, and the degree in which the use may prejudice the sale, or diminish the profits, or supersede the objects, of the original work.
>
> (Story 1845: 116)

Compare this language to what has been enshrined in the Copyright Act and important differences may be noted. The applicable parts of Section 107, the doctrine of fair use, are:

> (1) the purpose and character of the use, including whether such use is of a commercial nature or is for nonprofit educational purposes;
> (2) the nature of the copyrighted work;
> (3) the amount and substantiality of the portion used in relation to the copyrighted work as a whole; and
> (4) the effect of the use upon the potential market for or value of the copyrighted work.
>
> (Copyright Act of 1976)

As the reader can see, if anything, the language adopted in the Act is somewhat softer in tone than that provided by Story. Because it is fundamentally situational and contextual, perhaps more than in any other area of copyright, fair use continues to bedevil copyright attorneys, defendants (Porter 2015), and those who wonder if they can use some portion or modicum of a preexisting work and at what point their new creative works become transformed (Abruzzi 2012). The answer to whether a particular use of a copyrighted work is a fair use is generally, "It depends."

The doctrine of fair use was enshrined in law because reasonable people realized that if it were not permitted as a defense, works of journalism, scholarship, and criticism could not quote protected works, and many other quotidian uses of copyrighted work would become legally suspect (United States 2005). Political speech would also be severely restricted; after all, if copyright law were absolute, how could one candidate mention or make reference to the written remarks of another (Abruzzi 2012)? Moreover, as the ambit of protected expression has grown, it might become difficult in the future to create works not tainted by the specter of infringement (McGrail & McGrail 2010). Fair use is therefore an affirmative defense that offers essential balance to the law of copyright itself.

As early as the mid-19th century, a tension existed between those who sought to earn a living from their creativity and those who required work that had gone before to provide context and perspective for the mounting of their own work (Lee 2009). In *Emerson v. Davies* (1845), the court remarked:

> [In] truth, in literature, in science and in art, there are, and can be, few, if any, things, which in an abstract sense, are strictly new and original throughout. Every book in literature, science and art, borrows, and must necessarily borrow, and use much which was well known and used before.
>
> (The Federal Cases 619)

Two major difficulties may occur when a judge makes a decision about whether a particular use of copyrighted works is (or is not) a fair use. The first difficulty is that, in some cases, the transformation in the secondary work is fully evident, but it may not be sufficiently different from the original work to be considered a new work in its own right. The second is that one court may find that a sufficient transformation has occurred, and a higher court may reverse or vice versa. For example, in *Cariou v. Prince* (2011), a federal District Court case, an artist manipulated the photographs of a photographer, and the question before the District Court was whether the processes undertaken were sufficient to transform the works to new, original works. The court found that, for a work to be transformative, it must "in some way comment on, relate to the historical context of, or critically refer back" to the original work (Nguen 2015: 127). In *Cariou*, the federal court did not find that such a transformation had occurred, but when the case was appealed to the Second Circuit (*Cariou v. Prince* (2013)), a transformation was found for twenty-five of the thirty photographs in question, and those works were adjudged not infringing. The Second Circuit remanded the case to the District Court for findings on the remaining five photographs, and the parties settled out of court (Nguen 2015).

Generally, transformation is now connected most strongly to the first of the four factors of fair use, the purpose and character of the use (Lee 2009). Prior to the *Campbell v. Acuff-Rose* (1994) case, the third factor probably had primacy ("the amount and substantiality" of a secondary use). Since then, *Campbell* (1994) has become the flagship for contemporary transformation theory in fair use. In 1993, the controversial rap group 2 Live Crew created a version of Roy Orbison's classic 1964 hit, "Oh, Pretty Woman," which they called "Pretty Woman." In it, they borrowed the iconic opening guitar phrase, and the melody and lyrics that, in poking fun at the original, used a significant portion of Orbison's original song. Prior to this, fair use cases had generally turned on how much of an earlier work had been borrowed (Supreme Court of U.S., "Syllabus" 12–16). In their case, however, 2 Live Crew had borrowed liberally from the preexisting song and could not argue for a triviality of appropriation. The court emphasized that if the intent had not been parodic, the group would have indeed run afoul of the third fair use factor, the amount and substantiality of the portion of the work used. Instead, the court found that parody was a bona fide transformative factor. While 2 Live Crew borrowed heavily from the original, the result did not supplant the original work, because it parodized it. Parody, the court ruled, if found to be legitimate, is then per se transformative (Supreme Court of U.S., "Syllabus" 17–20). In other kinds of appropriation, for a secondarily used work to be found transformed, it too must create something sufficiently original in meaning; the resulting work must stand on its own.

A number of modern artists, including Jeff Koons and Shepard Fairey, have perhaps taken transformation into the realm of context (McCorkle 2015). Shepard Fairey took a photograph of then-presidential candidate Barack Obama and attached below his image the legend, "Hope." The photographer Manny Garcia, who took the photo for the Associated Press (AP), threatened to sue Fairey, who, in association with the Stanford Fair Use Project, then sought a declaratory judgment against the AP (*Shepard Fairey v. Associated Press* (2010)), but the parties settled out of court, in a sense depriving us of further court guidance in this area (McCorkle 2015). However, Fairey teamed with a number of legal experts and wrote a lengthy monograph on his own case, noting that Garcia's aim had been to take a realistic portrait of then-Senator Obama. Indeed, the primary purpose of all of the AP's photographs is (in the AP's own words) to provide "a truthful, unbiased report of the world's happenings." In keeping with that general commitment, Garcia had testified that he had no intention of promoting Obama's candidacy. By contrast, Fairey's primary objective in creating the Hope Poster was to promote Obama's candidacy (Fisher et al. 2012: 262). Thus, as political speech, Fairey and his colleagues argued that his poster should be accorded the highest possible protection, for, as the Supreme Court has observed, "the First Amendment has its fullest and most urgent application to speech uttered during a campaign for political office" (Citizens United 2010: 23).

Jeff Koons has been involved in a number of court cases that have turned on transformation and fair use. He has won some and lost some and often on legally similar sets of facts. In *Rogers v. Koons* (1992), the Court ruled against him for his sculpture of puppies based on a photograph of the same. He lost two other court cases before winning in *Blanch v. Koons* (2006), in which he once again used an advertising photograph for a sculpture he made of legs. In doing so, he used material in what the courts call a "secondary" way, in order to comment upon the original, advertised material. In the holding in *Blanch*, the court quoted celebrated fair use scholar and jurist Pierre Leval, who wrote:

> If . . . the secondary use adds value to the original—if the quoted matter is used as raw material, transformed in the creation of new information, new aesthetics, new insights and understandings—this is the very type of activity that the fair use doctrine intends to protect for the enrichment of society.
>
> (Leval 1990: 1111)

Both Fairey and Koons have thus performed a valuable societal service by helping us understand both the boundaries of copyright and where it sometimes comes into conflict with free speech and cultural investigation. Even when they have lost or have been forced to settle, they have helped maintain the vitality of artistic expression (McCorkle 2015). In Koons' case, he has revealed that the advertisements and popularly available graphical material that he frequently uses to create his objets d'art, have an effect on people, an effect that should be explored and commented upon. In Fairey's case, he made a simple politically motivated observation that served to rally followers of then-Senator Obama. In each case, their commentary could never have been so vivid or so effective without the secondary use of a protected work, sublimely transformed. In the next section, we will examine how this commentary has come to be popular with teachers, teacher educators, and media professionals.

Transformation, Remix, and Multimodal Creativity for Educators and Media Professionals

Although digital content creation practices and the resulting products will continue to evolve, remixes and mashups have become the prevalent modes of communication and collaboration, as well as the means of expression for the social and cultural commentary contained in these creations among students, educators, and media professionals (Edwards 2016; Stedman 2012).

There are many reasons that someone in the teaching and media production professions might wish to create a remix or mashup in the 21st century. First, it is often an exercise where creativity is pressed into service for a specific pedagogical purpose (Cremin & Baker 2014; Hundley & Holbrook 2013). Using the vividness and reflexivity of preexisting works helps orient the works symbolically and create connections between them and existing works that, as "cultural tokens" or memes, have emotive meaning to people (Lessig 2008: 75). This aids the process of meaning-making for the students of a teacher, teacher educator, or teaching media professional and situates the meaning in a real-world reference. It also locates the sociocultural context in which the creation dwells (Lankshear & Knobel 2010). Secondly, a teacher's own facility with the building tools of remixing and mashups is improved with each remix, no matter the specific purpose of the piece. Thirdly, it may be the pedagogical point of the piece to actually convey how to make a mashup itself to students, aspiring artists, and media professionals. Finally, teachers and teaching media professionals may feel they need to "keep their hand in it," as the saying goes, and keep skills, interest, and creative vim fresh and current.

Collages, montage, and sampling are examples of popular remix forms, which as a genre "use one or many materials, media either from other sources, art pieces (visual arts, film, music, video, literature etc.) or one's own artworks through alteration, re-combination, manipulation, copying etc. to create a whole piece" (Sonvilla-Weiss 2010: 9). In remix and related creations, "the sources of origin may still be identifiable yet not perceived as the original version" (Sonvilla-Weiss 2010: 9). Mashups, on the other hand, as Sonvilla-Weiss explains, "put together different information, media, or objects without changing their original source of information, i.e. the original format remains the same and can be retracted as the original form and content, although recombined in different new designs and contexts" (2010: 9).

As evident in these definitions of remix and mashup, there are many ways in which a portion of an original work can be transformed into something that helps make a new creative piece. Changes that lead to creative transformation can be for many reasons and via many methodologies, including the following:

1. Content, changing message, meaning or position (Burwell 2013; Nguen 2015; Rife 2009)
2. Expression and means of expression (Aufderheide & Jaszi 2011; Lessig 2008)
3. Production process or technical aesthetics (Burwell 2013)
4. The source of the words or content (McIntosh 2012)
5. Text form and structure (Cope & Kalantzis 2000; Mills & Exley 2014)
6. The audience and context (Aufderheide & Jaszi 2011; Edwards 2016; Nguen 2015)
7. "Purpose, delivery, design, and style" (Edwards 2016: 42; Hobbs & Donnelly 2011; Hobbs 2010)

The key question is, then, how to determine at what point something is or is not new, when it is transformed or changed enough, and what criteria or indicators one should use to make such a determination. Fortunately, we are not without guidance in this area.

First of all, teachers, teacher educators, and teaching media professionals typically do not create digital multimodal creations that feature externally authored material without having a prevailing pedagogical purpose. Moreover, educators need to remember that statutorily, they may display any material they wish, as long as it is in a face-to-face classroom situation (U.S. Code Title 17; McGrail & McGrail 2010; Westbrook 2011). For educators, a fair use analysis would be necessary if the work in question became available to the public, such as on a public site like YouTube or through social media such as Instagram, Snapchat, Facebook, or Twitter (Westbrook 2011). Nevertheless, in today's educational milieu, such a circumstance might well be often encountered (Purcell et al. 2013; Thibaut 2015), and in that event, the reuse of externally authored material should be examined. Educators and students can learn how to make a fair use determination by using a reasoning process that considers the balance between the rights of the copyright holder and the rights of the user.

Although there is not and there never will be an exhaustive or "bulletproof" list of criteria for the fair use of protected works, we can derive some general understanding of and arrive at guidelines based on the statutory definitions of fair use, relying on previous key court decisions, as well as exemplars of practice in the professional literature (e.g., McIntosh 2012; Navas 2009). Because every court case is different—both in the material being argued over and the legal personnel arguing it—similar facts can lead to dissimilar results (compare the court decisions from 2011 and 2013 for *Cariou v. Prince*).

Therefore, the first fair use analysis undertaken should *not* be the one that takes place in a courtroom. Teachers, teacher educators, and teaching media professionals should embark on this analysis with every digital multimodal composition that they create. Recently, Porter (2015: 269) has argued:

> What is needed, I would argue, is a rhetorical frame of thinking about context and a heuristic methodology—that is, a critical procedure for making ethical and legal judgments about the use of others' intellectual property. This type of ethical reasoning is what Aristotle called *phronesis*, or the art of practical judgment. Such as approach would include some broad principles and guidelines, some heuristic questions, and some case examples—of clear-cut fair uses, clear-cut infringements, and the vast of gray area in between.

Practical Wisdom: Exploring Transformative Use of Copyrighted Content

We believe that acting on the basis of practical judgment, reasoning, or phronesis, is essential to understanding fair use transformativeness. In order to acquire such a mode of thinking, a process should be developed of asking specific and pointed questions about and interrogating proposed actions with respect to the use of appropriated material for multimodal composition. Here are some preliminary questions and "food for thought" that should push forward the concept of phronesis for teacher educators and teaching media professionals interrogating their proposed use of externally authored material for new and creatively transformed works.

1. *Is my secondary use a direct appropriation of material, as with sampling, or merely based on existing material, such as using characters from an existing novel?* Each of these exigencies invites different fair use issues.
    a. In the first instance, sampling, current copyright law permits free "soundalike" recording, as long as composers, if any, are compensated (Copyright Law 17 U.S.C.

§ 114 (b)(2)). Therefore, if the sample is not particularly distinctive, it may be wiser and legally safer to make a soundalike version of it.

b. The second instance deals usually with so-called fan fiction, in which fans of a game, book, graphic novel, movie, or the like take the recognizable characters, usually with their names, histories, and situations intact (Stedman 2012). If this is done privately, there is usually no fair use issue. If, however, these are distributed widely, litigation may result, even if there is no commercial gain proposed or realized. This is because such work may weaken or supplant the ambit of the original characters or situations. The more distinctive such characters, situations, or events are, the more likely they are to be protected by copyright, even if no words or images are exactly appropriated. If, however, your characters are merely loosely based on others, it is likely not an infringement. For example, it is fine to have a caped flying character who has super powers; there are dozens, perhaps hundreds of such characters. Described thus, it is insufficiently distinctive to replace any former work. Having one who is vulnerable to kryptonite or who is called the Man of Steel, on the other hand, would likely not be a fair use because it would be too similar to the protected character of Superman. Details matter.

2. *If my use is a direct or exact appropriation, is it necessary for the point I am trying to make?*

   a. If you seize an image because it is convenient, you should inquire as to whether it is *absolutely necessary* for the point of the remix you are building. If it is not absolutely necessary, while it still may be legal to appropriate it, you need to be aware that the copyright holder may avail themselves of remedies, such as a DMCA takedown notice, cease and desist letter, or formal legal notice (Cobia 2009).

   b. If it is necessary, the question falls to the amount of the appropriation (the third factor in fair use, 17 U.S.C., § 107). The greater the degree or amount of appropriation, the more it is incumbent upon the appropriator to show how the amount of the seizure is justifiable. Since there is no "bright line" rule, proportionality and reasonableness are key. Rife (2009: 149) elaborates on this point further in this advisory statement: "Use as little as possible (either in size, amount. . .) in order to accomplish your own writerly goals, but do not be afraid to *use what you need to make your point*."

3. *If it is a direct appropriation, what is its specific purpose in my oeuvre as a whole?* The piece taken from a copyright-protected work should have a *specific* purpose in the remix.

   a. One purpose enshrined in case law is parodic intent (see *Campbell v. Acuff Rose* (1994)). If a work is seized for the purpose of a parody of the original work, the courts generally assume that the amount of the appropriation is far less relevant to fair use.

   b. You may feel that it is necessary to seize a portion of a work to comment upon it in another way, perhaps to offer criticism of it, whether journalistic or otherwise. One of the most common uses of this kind is to select a portion of a work to comment upon it for purposes of scholarship, criticism, or commentary. This may be done with any sort of work. In the case of audio, video, or text, a small but relevant portion may be used. Again, no bright line rule exists for guidance, especially in light of the 11th Circuit Court's decision to specifically decline to use the 10% rule in the Georgia State copyright case (*Cambridge University Press et al. v. Patton et al.* (also captioned as *v. Becker* 2014)). In the case of still images, since a portion or detail of a protected photograph is often insufficient to comment upon, case law suggests that the reproduction of a protected work be at a lower level than the original, sufficient for commentary, but that does not facilitate illicit copying (*Kelly v. Arriba Soft Corporation* 2003). In such a case, the transformation is to a form that cannot serve to replace the original.

4. *If it is a direct appropriation, is the use proportional to the amount needed for me to make the point, observation, or aesthetic trope of my piece?*

    a. Copyright law does not make a per se distinction between a journalistic use, which comments upon a work, and a purely aesthetic use, which may attempt to use found digital objects for aesthetic elaboration. Because of this, even bona fide journalists generally may not reproduce an entire copyrighted work in service of their own work. The third factor of fair use—the amount and substantiality factor—weighs in here. One of the most important cases as to "how much is too much" is the J. D. Salinger case (*Salinger v. Random House, Inc.* 1987), where letters from the renowned but reclusive author were commented upon and heavily quoted prior to publication. It resulted in the important finding that whether a work is unpublished does not absolutely bar a fair use analysis but compels its strict observation. Commensurate language on this point was added to U.S. Code (Copyright Act, Title 17 1992).

5. *If it is a direct or exact appropriation, as with a musical sample, is the portion borrowed the most recognizable part of the work, the "heart" of the work?*

    a. The heart of a work refers to the most recognizable portion of a copyrighted work, the part of the work that produces its greatest artistic or economic service to the author (*Campbell v. Acuff-Rose* 1994). Consider that many books, movies, or songs may elaborate on more than one element. For example, *Star Wars* features dozens of major characters appearing over the course of many movies, books, games, and other creative forms. If one were to appropriate, for example, the character of Luke Skywalker, it would be disingenuous to argue that this was a minor character because there were so many others. While the actual "time" of Skywalker's entrance and exit in the story may be, as a proportion of the whole, brief, Skywalker, along with a handful of other characters, such as Princess Leia and Han Solo, is part of the "heart" of the franchise. Skywalker forms one of the most important characteristic elements of the story, and much of the narrative arc depends on his existence. If you were to appropriate the Skywalker character—including his history and character arc—you might materially diminish his artistic puissance in the original work. It is therefore likely to arouse litigation on the part of the copyright holder.

6. *If it is a direct appropriation, what kind of work is it from? Is it more factual or more creative?*

    a. The Supreme Court has materially abandoned the "sweat of the brow" standard in copyright, which means that the amount of effort (as opposed to the novelty or creativity) in assembling elements to make a work of copyright is not relevant to its protected status (see in particular the Feist case, *Feist Publications Inc. v. Rural Telephone Service Co.* 1991). Thus, it is expected that scientific, historical, and other nearly completely factual accounts depend upon earlier factual accounts for their scholarly worthiness. Facts cannot be protected by copyright. Therefore, the courts accept a more relaxed standard in the application of fair use to these works than to those that are more purely creative, such as musical works, novels, fictional motion pictures, and the like (Rife 2009). So the use, for example, of a scientific finding, formula, or equation is rarely the cause of litigation.

b. This doesn't mean that a factually based work is entirely open for free appropriation. Many scientific or factual works contain new findings or new assertions, and the copying of these may expose you to litigation. On the whole, however, a more liberal use of preexisting protected material would probably be acceptable to the courts.

c. It is also true that one may use anything in the public domain as liberally as one chooses, even if another, protected work uses the same selection.

7. *If it is an appropriation, have I altered or processed the portion to change it to fit the artistic raison d'etre of my work?*

   a. If you wish to use some aspect of a protected work but you wish to alter it significantly in order to fit the new work, this is not only creative but prudent. If preexisting material is altered sufficiently that it is not recognizable, there is no infringement. This is because the recognition of the earlier protected work in listeners or viewers is key to whether the latter work is in danger of supplanting it. If a picture, drumbeat, graphic, or the like is so altered, it is considered transformed for the purposes of fair use, and so it forms a completely different kind of work.

8. *If it is an appropriation, have I changed the audience and purpose for my creative work?*

   a. This can happen in a number of different ways. Jeff Koons, previously mentioned several times, repurposed work as to both genre and audience. In the case of audience, it is likely that those who look at and admire his provocative sculptures would not have studied the advertising art and other quotidian ephemera of mass communication from which he appropriates images so intently (Farago 2014, June 25). This is also a form of transformation. Koons' sculptures are hardly replacements for the persuasory commercial work from which he has borrowed certain elements.

9. *If it is an appropriation, have I changed the genre of an appropriated work?*

   a. A change of genre can be that across a medium, such as a change from a book to a movie, or it can involve a change from a comedy to a more serious work. It can also involve both of these changes. When *Buffy the Vampire Sla*yer (Kuzui 1992) was made into a movie, the movie decided to take an overtly comical and spoofing look at the subject matter, a cheerleader who had been anointed to kill vampires. However, when the popular television program of the same name *Buffy the Vampire Sla*yer (Whedon 1997) was developed using the movie as a stem, the entire tone of the piece changed to that of very serious speculative fiction.

Discussion and Conclusion

Teachers, teacher educators, and those who teach future media professionals need to assert themselves in the copyright sphere more forcefully than they have been doing (Aufderheide & Jaszi 2011). In many cases, more conservative members of this cohort have assumed that any use of exterior work requires a raft of written permissions (Hobbs, Jaszi & Aufderheide 2007; Rife 2009). Of course, large copyright holders wish to preserve this status quo because it serves their financial interests (Grimmelmann 2009). The truth is that the constantly evolving court guidelines for fair use and copyright require a full-throated and aggressively creative approach by those who seek to use protected work, especially in the education and media literacy professions. A timid approach will only result in the goal line being moved back (Aufderheide & Jaszi 2011). Because Congress has increased the period of protection for copyrighted works so extensively (17 U.S.C. 2011; Lessig 2004), fair use is extremely important not just for commentary but for more artistic projects as well (Aufderheide & Jaszi 2011; Lessig 2008).

In many cases, even a fairly liberal use of earlier works has been tolerated if the result is a completely new work. A good example is DJ Danger Mouse's *Grey Album*, which is a mashup of the Beatles' *White Album* and Jay-Z's *Black Album*. Both Jay-Z and the two surviving Beatles highly praised the result (Gross 2010), which in the current litigious atmosphere, is particularly surprising. However, again, as we have emphasized, the parts created by the Beatles and Jay-Z, while evident and obvious throughout the transformed work, do not supplant or stand in for the work of their preexisting musical art. Instead, the album forms a kind of homage to them, even as it comments upon them, and demonstrates that further aesthetic purposes exist for the music it builds upon. The music of the Beatles and hip-hop star Jay-Z have thus been commented upon in a completely creative way, even though the *Grey Album* consists mostly of their earlier work (York 2014). It has been transformed, and a thing of new value has been created.

Teachers, teacher educators, and teaching media professionals are already in a presumed "good" group of copyright "citizens." As educators, the first of the four factors of fair use already supports them, as written in the statute (Copyright Act of 1976, section 107). Moreover, the Register of Copyrights has recognized the special status of media literacy educators in permitting the unlocking of protected DVD content for fair use purposes (Hobbs 2011), even when such use violates technological barriers that have been secured by the Digital Millennium Copyright Act (1988). However, to keep the goodwill of legislators and the courts, educators must make good faith efforts to create work that errs on the side of creativity and transformation (Rife 2009) and away from mere copying. Engaging in a prior fair use analysis goes a long way toward this good end. Teachers are uniquely positioned to do the work of moving the goal line back to a more balanced ambit between copyright owners and end users. The law and practice are ours to use and amend. Hayek (2010: 62–63) wrote:

> The fundamental contrast between government by rules, whose main purpose is to inform the individual what is his sphere of responsibility within which he must shape his own life, and government by orders which impose specific duties has become so blurred in recent years that it is necessary to consider it a little further. It involves nothing less than the distinction between freedom under the law and the use of the legislative machinery, whether democratic or not, to abolish freedom.

The interpretation of fair use in the last twenty years has been, in the view of Lessig (2008) and others, moved to a position out of balance. It is important that we use our understanding of transformation—and the "legislative machinery" Hayek mentions—to assure that copyright and fair use, which specifically exist for our commonwealth, remain balanced as to what accepted practice is. This does not necessarily mean that we must change the law; rather, we must ensure that others outside the field of media education accept the good faith practices of those of us within it, that is, educators and media professionals. From this, we can change what the courts and society will find to be infringing and what they will deem a just yet creative use.

References

Abruzzi, B. E. (2012). "Copyright and the Vagueness Doctrine." *University of Michigan Journal of Law Reform*, 45(2), 351–404.

Anderson, D. (2003). "Prosumer Approaches to New Media: Consumption and Production in Continuum." *Kairos, 8*(1). Retrieved from http://kairos.technorhetoric.net/8.1/binder2.html?coverweb/anderson/index.html

Aufderheide, P., & Jaszi, P. (2011). *Reclaiming Fair Use: How to Put Balance Back in Copyright*. Chicago: University of Chicago Press.

Bishop, J. (2009). "Pre-Service Teacher Discourses: Authoring Selves Through Multimodal Compositions." *Digital Culture and Education*, 1(1), 31–50.

Blanch v. Koons. (2006). 467 F. 3d 244 2d Cir.

Bruce, D. L., & Chiu, M. M. (2015). "Composing With New Technology: Teacher Reflections on Learning Digital Video." *Journal of Teacher Education*, 66(3), 272–287. Burwell, C. (2013). "The Pedagogical Potential of Video Remix: Critical Conversations About Culture, Creativity, and Copyright." *Journal of Adolescent & Adult Literacy*, 57(3), 205–213. doi:10.1002/JAAL.205

Cambridge University Press et al. v. Patton et al. (2008). Cv.01425.

Cambridge University Press et al. v. Becker et al. (2014). D.C. Docket No. 1:08-cv-01425-ODE

Campbell v. Acuff-Rose Music, Inc. (1994). 510 U.S. 569, 583–585.

Cariou v. Prince. (2011). 784 F. Supp. 2d 337.

Cariou v. Prince. (2013). 714 F. 3d 694 2d Cir. *Citizens United v. Fed. Election Comm'n*. (2010). 130 S. Ct. 876, 898.

Cobia, J. (2009). "The Digital Millennium Copyright Act Takedown Notice Procedure: Misuses, Abuses, and Shortcomings of the Process." *Minnesota Journal of Law, Science and Technology*, 10(1), 387–411.

Cope, B., & Kalantzis, M. (Eds.) (2000). *Multiliteracies: Literacy Learning and the Design of Social Futures*. New York: Routledge.

Copyright Act of 1976. Pub. L. 94–553.

Copyright Act of 1992. Pub. L. No. 102–492, 106 Stat. 3145, amending §107.

Copyright Law of the United States of America, Title 17. Circular 92.

Cremin, T., & Baker, S. (2014). "Exploring the Discursively Constructed Identities of a Teacher–Writer Teaching Writing." *English Teaching: Practice and Critique*, 13(3), 30–55.

Digital Millennium Copyright Act (DMCA). (1998). "U.S. Copyright Office." Retrieved from www.copyright.gov/legislation/dmca.pdf

Dush, L. (2009). "Beyond the Wake-Up Call: Learning What Students Know About Copyright." In S. Westbrook (Ed.), *Composition and Copyright: Perspectives on Teaching, Text Making, and Fair Use* (pp. 114–132). New York: State University of New York Press.

Edwards, D. W. (2016). "Framing Remix Rhetorically: Toward a Typology of Transformative Work." *Computers and Composition*, 39, 41–54.

Emerson v. Davies. (1845). 8 F. Cas. 615, 619 (No. 4,436). CCD Mass.

Farago, J. (2014, June 25). "Jeff Koons: A Retrospective Review—Great, Good, Bad and Terrible Art." *The Guardian*. Retrieved from www.theguardian.com/artanddesign/2014/jun/25/jeff-koons-retrospective-review-whitney-museum-good-bad-art

The Federal Cases [Book 8]. (1895). St. Paul, MN: West Publishing Company.

Feist Publications, Inc., v. Rural Telephone Service Co. (1991). 499 U.S. 340.

Fisher, W. W. III, Cost, F., Fairey, S., Feder, M., Fountain, E., Stewart, G., & Sturken, M. (2012). "Reflections on the Hope Poster Case." *Harvard Journal of Law & Technology*, 25(2), 243–338.

Folsom v. Marsh. (1841). 9. F. Cas. 342 (C.C.D. Mass). Grimmelmann, J. (2009). "Ethical Visions of Copyright Law." *Fordham Law Review*, 77(5), 2005–2037.

Gross, T. (2010). "Jay-Z: The Fresh Air Interview." Retrieved from www.npr.org/templates/transcript/transcript.php?storyId=131334322

Hayek, F. A. (2010). *The Abuse and Decline of Reason*. Abingdon, UK: Routledge.

Heymann, L. A. (2008). "Everything Is Transformative: Fair Use and Reader Response." *Columbia Journal of Law and the Arts*, 31(4), 445–466.

Hobbs, R. (2010). *Copyright Clarity: How Fair Use Supports Digital Learning*. Thousand Oaks, CA: Corwin and NCTE.

Hobbs, R. (2011, April). "Unlocking the Power of Film for Education: Seeking a DMCA Exemption for Media Literacy Education." Keynote presented at the Conference on College Composition and Communication, Atlanta, Georgia. Abstract. Retrieved from http://mediaeducationlab.com/unlocking-power-film-education-seeking-dmca-exemption-media-literacy-education

Hobbs, R., & Donnelly, K. (2011). "Toward a Pedagogy of Fair Use for Multimedia Composition." In M. C. Rife, S. Slattery, S., & D. N. DeVoss (Eds.), *Copy(Write): Intellectual Property in the Writing Classroom* (pp. 275–294). Fort Collins, CO: WAC Clearinghouse.

Hobbs, R., Jaszi, P., & Aufderheide, P. (2007). *The Cost of Copyright Confusion for Media Literacy*. Washington, DC: Center for Social Media.

Hundley, M., & Holbrook, T. (2013). "Set in Stone or Set in Motion? Multimodal Digital Writing With Pre-Service English Teachers." *Journal of Adolescent & Adult Literacy*, 56(6), 500–509.

Jenkins, H. (2006). *Fans, Bloggers, and Gamers: Media Consumers in a Digital Age*. New York: New York University Press.

Kelly v. Arriba Soft Corporation. (2003). 280 F.3d 934. (9th Cir.), withdrawn, refiled at 336 F.3d 811 (9th Cir.).

Knobel, M., & Lankshear, C. (2008). "Remix: The Art and Craft of Endless Hybridization." *Journal of Adolescent & Adult Literacy*, 52(1), 22–33.

Kuzui, F. R. (Director.) (1992). *Buffy the Vampire Slayer* [Motion picture]. Los Angeles: Twentieth Century Fox Film Corporation.

Landau, M. B. (2015). "Are the Courts Singing a Different Tune When It Comes to Music? What Ever Happened to Fair Use in Music Sampling Cases?" *IP Theory*, 5(1). Retrieved from www.repository.law.indiana.edu/ipt/vol5/iss1/1

Lankshear, C., & Knobel, M. (2010). *DIY Media: Creating, Sharing and Learning With New Technologies*. New York: Peter Lang.

Lee, S. (2009). "Fair Use and Criticism on the Internet." In S. Westbrook (Ed.), *Composition and Copyright: Perspectives on Teaching, Text-Making, and Fair Use* (pp. 31–49). Albany: State University of New York Press.

Lessig, L. (2004). *Free Culture: The Nature and Future of Creativity*. New York: Penguin.

Lessig, L. (2008). *Remix: Making Art and Commerce Thrive in the Hybrid Economy*. New York: Penguin Press.

Leval, P. N. (1990). "Toward a Fair Use Standard." *Harvard Law Review*, 103, 1105–1136.

McCorkle, B. (2015). "Hindered Hope: Shepard Fairey, the Associated Press and the Missed Opportunity to Help Clarify U.S. Copyright Law." In D. N. DeVoss & M. C. Rife (Eds.), *Cultures of Copyright* (pp. 54–63). New York: Peter Lang.

McGrail, J. P., & McGrail, E. (2010). "Overwrought Copyright: Why Copyright Law From the Analog Age Does Not Work in the Digital Age's Society and Classroom." *Education and Information Technologies*, 15(2), 69–85. doi 10.1007/s10639-009-9097-9

McIntosh, J. (2012). "A History of Subversive Remix Video Before YouTube: Thirty Political Video Mashups Made Between World War II and 2005." *Transformative Works and Cultures*, 9. doi:10.3983/twc.2012.0371

McKenna, T. (2000). "Where Digital Music Technology and Law Collide: Contemporary Issues of Digital Sampling, Appropriation and Copyright Law." *The Journal of Information, Law and Technology (JILT)*, 2000(1). Retrieved from https://www2.warwick.ac.uk/fac/soc/law/elj/jilt/2000_1/mckenna/

Mills, K. A., & Exley, B. (2014). "Time, Space, and Text in the Elementary School Digital Writing Classroom." *Written Communication*, 31(4), 434–469.

Navas, E. (2009). "Regressive and Reflexive Mashups in Sampling Culture." [2010 revision]. Retrieved from http://remixtheory.net/remixImages/NavasMashups_2010.pdf

Nguen, N. (2015). "No Copyright Intended." In D. N. DeVoss & M. C. Rife (Eds.), *Cultures of Copyright* (pp. 125–139). New York: Peter Lang.

Palfrey, J., Gasser, U., Simun, M., & Barnes, R. F. (2009). "Youth, Creativity, and Copyright in the Digital Age." *International Journal of Learning and Media*, 1(2), 79–97.

"Paul McCartney Is Down With Hip-Hop." (2011). Retrieved from https://cbswods2.wordpress.com/2011/02/24/paul-mccartney-is-down-with-hip-hop/

Porter, J. E. (2015). "Response to Part II: Being Rhetorical When We Teach Intellectual Property and Fair Use." In M. C. Rife, S. Slattery, & D. N. DeVoss (Eds.), *Copy(Write): Intellectual Property in the Writing Classroom* (pp. 263–272). Fort Collins, CO: WAC Clearinghouse.

Purcell, K., Heaps, A., Buchanan, J., & Friedrich, L. (2013). *How Teachers Are Using Technology at Home and in Their Classrooms*. Washington, DC: National Writing, College Board, and Pew Research Center.

Rife, M. C. (2009). "Ideas Toward a Fair Use Heuristic: Visual Rhetoric and Composition." In S. Westbrook (Ed.), *Composition and Copyright: Perspectives on Teaching, Text-Making, and Fair Use* (pp. 133–153). Albany: State University of New York Press.

Rogers v. Koons. (1992). 960 F.2d 301. 2d Cir.

Salinger v. Random House, Inc. (1987). 811 F.2d 90 2nd Cir.

Shepard Fairey v. Associated Press. (2010). No. 09–01123. S.D.N.Y.

Sonvilla-Weiss, S. (2010). "Introduction: Mashups, Remix Practices and the Recombination of Existing Digital Content." In S. Sonvilla-Weiss, (Ed.), *Mashup Cultures* (pp. 8–24). Germany: Springer-Verlag Wien.

Stedman, K. D. (2012). "Remix Literacy and Fan Compositions." *Computers and Composition*, 29, 107–123.

Story, W. W. (1845). *Reports of Cases Argued and Determined in the Circuit Court of the United States for the First Circuit*, Vol. 2. (2nd ed.). Boston: Little & Brown.

Supreme Court of U.S. (1994). "Syllabus." *Campbell v. Acuff-Rose Music, Inc.* 510 U.S. 569, 583–585.

Thibaut, P. (2015). "Social Network Sites With Learning Purposes: Exploring New Spaces for Literacy and Learning in the Primary Classroom." *Australian Journal of Language and Literacy*, 38(2), 83–94. United States. (2005). "Cong. House Committee on Energy and Commerce: Subcommittee on Commerce, Trade, and Consumer Protection." In *Fair Use: Its Effects on Consumers and Industry*. 109th Cong. 1st Sess. H.R. Washington, DC: GPO.

Westbrook, S. (2011). "What We Talk About When We Talk About Fair Use: Conversations on Writing Pedagogy, New Media, and Copyright Law." In M. C. Rife, S. Slattery, & D. N. DeVoss (Eds.), *Copy(Write): Intellectual Property in the Writing Classroom* (pp. 159–177). Fort Collins, CO: WAC Clearinghouse.

Whedon, J. (Producer.) (1997). *Buffy the Vampire Slayer* [Television show]. New York: Fox.

Williams, B. T., & Zenger, A. A. (Eds.) (2012). *New Media Literacies and Participatory Popular Culture Across Borders*. New York: Routledge.

York, J. C. (2014, April 24). "The Fight to Protect Digital Rights Is an Uphill Battle, but Not a Silent One." *The Guardian*. Retrieved from www.theguardian.com/commentisfree/2014/apr/24/the-fight-to-protect-digital-rights-is-an-uphill-battle-but-not-a-silent-one

Further Reading

Aufderheide, P., & Jaszi, P. (2011). *Reclaiming Fair Use: How to Put Balance Back in Copyright*. Chicago: University of Chicago Press.

Hobbs, R., & Donnelly, K. (2011). "Toward a Pedagogy of Fair Use for Multimedia Composition." In M. C. Rife, S. Slattery & D. N. DeVoss (Eds.), *Copy(Write): Intellectual Property in the Writing Classroom* (pp. 275–294). Fort Collins, CO: WAC Clearinghouse.

Lessig, L. (2008). *Remix: Making Art and Commerce Thrive in the Hybrid Economy*. New York: Penguin Press.

Porter, J. E. (2015). "Response to Part II: Being Rhetorical When We Teach Intellectual Property and Fair Use." In M. C. Rife, S. Slattery & D. N. DeVoss (Eds.), *Copy(Write): Intellectual Property in the Writing Classroom* (pp. 263–272). Fort Collins, CO: WAC Clearinghouse.

11

AUTOMATED PLAGIARISM DETECTION AS OPPORTUNITY FOR EDUCATION ON COPYRIGHT AND MEDIA

Clancy Ratliff

In George Landow's 1992 speculative fiction short story "Ms. Austen's Submission," the protagonist, Jane Austen, is an Apprentice Author in a dystopian society with strict controls on authorship. She gets three attempts to submit a piece of writing to a computer, named Evaluator, and if she is rejected on all three attempts, she fails in her author apprenticeship. She has been rejected once already. The feedback from Evaluator, delivered instantly, is this:

> Ah, yes, Ms. Austen, a story on a young author, another one. Let's see, that's the eighth today—one from North America, one from Europe, two from Asia, and the rest from Africa, where that seems a popular discovery of this month. Your ending, like your concentration on classroom action and late-night discussions among would-be authors, makes this a clear example of Kunstlerroman type 4A.31. Record this number and check the library, which at the last network census has 4,245 examples, three of which are canonical, 103 Serious Fiction, and the remainder ephemera.
>
> Your submission has been erased, and the portions of your Authorpad memory containing it have been cleared, thus allowing you to get on with more promising work. Thank you for your submission. Good day, Apprentice Author Austen.
>
> (Landow 1995)

The story reveals Ms. Austen's fear of Evaluator, which is simultaneously a scoring system and a text-matching system, and the stakes of its decision about this submission, which, if accepted, could result in a promotion to Author.

Originally a piece of hypertext fiction with five different endings, the story was published in the anthology *Rhetoric: Concepts, Definitions, Boundaries*, where I first encountered it. "Ms. Austen's Submission" is an example of literary media education: it aims to elucidate the ways that technological tools can result in calibrations of culture as people interact with them. In 1994, Andrea Lunsford contextualized Landow's story, remarking that it "sketches in the outlines of what is sure to be a bitter fight of global proportions over the control, ownership, and system of rewards surrounding the economies of intellectual property, copyright, and related rights," adding that "Landow makes such problems most concrete in his closing story, 'Ms. Austen's Submission,' a not-so-futuristic look at what could become of 'authors' and their 'works' if democratization, decentralization of power, and openness fail to emerge as the hallmarks of an electronic information society" (Lunsford 1994: 277). In the educational context, there are many versions of Evaluator now that check for originality and that give instantaneous feedback on writing once submitted and even in the act of writing.

Media education is generally thought of as cultivating a critical, informed perspective about the rhetorical strategies of media artifacts, particularly images, film, and video—documentary film, narrative film, and advertisements, for example—but also those media artifacts that involve user interaction, such as mobile apps and video games. Producing media compositions (machinima, supercuts, mashups, etc.) is often included in this education. Lessig (2001) would call this engagement with the *content layer* of media. Along with that is the *logical layer*, or the software code that enables the production of such media, and the *physical layer*, the fiber, routers, and other basic infrastructure of Internet access. My focus is situated at the intersection of the content and logical layers: automated essay scoring (AES) and plagiarism detection services (PDS), software that scores and text-matches documents with others in large databases. These are real-world digital education tools, now in use in K–12 and higher education that are not unlike Landow's Evaluator.

With major educational reform at the K–12 level, the scholarly and public conversation about AES has increased. However, as early as 2006, scholars in composition studies were writing about AES (see the edited collection *Machine Scoring of Student Essays: Truth and Consequences*). That same year, the Conference on College Composition and Communication's Intellectual Property Caucus began drafting a position statement on PDS, objecting to them on pedagogical grounds but also on legal grounds, given students' rights under copyright law. These critiques of AES and PDS, with the interests of students at the forefront, have proceeded *pari passu* for over ten years, even as the technology has changed and the user base has grown. While it's easier for most to see the problems that come with taking human readers away from students, many teachers routinely, even enthusiastically, use Turnitin, which is also essentially a machine reading tool. I want to bring these two critical conversations together by using the frame "automated plagiarism detection" (APD).

Copyright Issues With Plagiarism Detection Platforms

Though several automated plagiarism detection services, or, as they're also called, plagiarism prevention tools, exist (including tools like SafeAssign, iThenticate, etc.), Turnitin is the most successful and has the largest institutional presence, with contracts with over 15,000 institutions. Turnitin is a large database of student writing, scholarly articles, and webpages: 60 billion webpages and 600 million student papers. When teachers encounter a phrase or sentence that is written in a dramatically different style from the rest of the writing assignment, they can use these services, which search from among many documents that are publicly available online. Turnitin, however, doesn't just search the Internet: it searches from within its own database, as well as the web, for matches with all the text in a student's writing assignment. The more student papers the database contains, the more capacity it has to detect potentially problematic uses of outside sources. According to Elijah Mayfield, Vice President of New Technologies for Turnitin, the product "is used by 30 million students in 149 countries, including more than half of all American universities" (personal communication).

In 2007, Turnitin's uses of student work were brought into question by copyright experts. Under U.S. copyright law, anyone who does a piece of writing automatically owns the copyright to that writing when it is in a fixed medium: a saved document on a computer, for example. Those who want to use that writing, especially for profit, usually have to ask permission and pay royalties. Turnitin, however, has not paid students for the 600 million writing assignments it has saved in its database. The primary legal challenge took place when students from McLean High School in Virginia and Desert Vista High School in Arizona sued iParadigms, the parent company of Turnitin, for copyright infringement. The court ruled in iParadigms' favor, with the reasoning that Turnitin's use of students' work was transformative and that it did not affect the market value of their work; in other words, it did not prevent the students from making money on their own writing (Zimmerman 2008, Povejsil 2009). This ruling is interesting in that fair use is not interpreted conventionally, with not-for-profit use considered more fair and for-profit use less fair, and protecting corporations and individuals alike, for purposes not limited to what we may think of as the reasoning behind fair use: encouraging art, creativity, and free expression. The common purposes of fair use tend to be for education, art, or free civic expression, but with the iParadigms ruling, corporate for-profit use became grouped in as well.

How Automated Plagiarism Detection Platforms Work

Currently Turnitin offers three services:

1. **Feedback studio.** Plagiarism checking, online feedback and grading
2. **Revision assistant.** Instant formative feedback on student writing
3. **Scoring engine.** Automated essay scoring

The text-matching service that provides "originality reports" to inform judgments about plagiarism is folded into Turnitin's grading service, which is popular among teachers.

To explore the Turnitin grading features, I submitted one of my own papers to the database. As a side note, this was one of my papers for my undergraduate degree, which I wrote in 1997 for an advanced composition course, and it's probably the paper I'm the most proud of, as it won a Phi Kappa Phi Scholars Forum award. Titled "Eudora Welty: Social Significance in 'A Piece of News' and 'Where Is the Voice Coming From?'" this paper examines gender roles and racism in two of Welty's short stories. Embedded in this paper is a great deal of intellectual engagement, which is baked into the process of completing any writing project: hours of library research and reading, thinking, drafts and feedback in class, as well as conferences with the professor in her office, particularly as I revised it after she nominated it for the award.

Turnitin found my essay to be 19% similar to other works in its database, so 81% was my original work, a flattened quantification of this intellectual process. Evidently, many other students have been as interested in these two stories—and the quotations we all decided to use from them—as I was. I directed my attention to GradeMark, Turnitin's grading feature, which includes prewritten comments that can be dragged and dropped into the student's paper. These are general notes having mostly to do with superficial features of the text, not larger questions of content, as shown in Figure 11.1.

Figure 11.1 Grading Tools in Turnitin

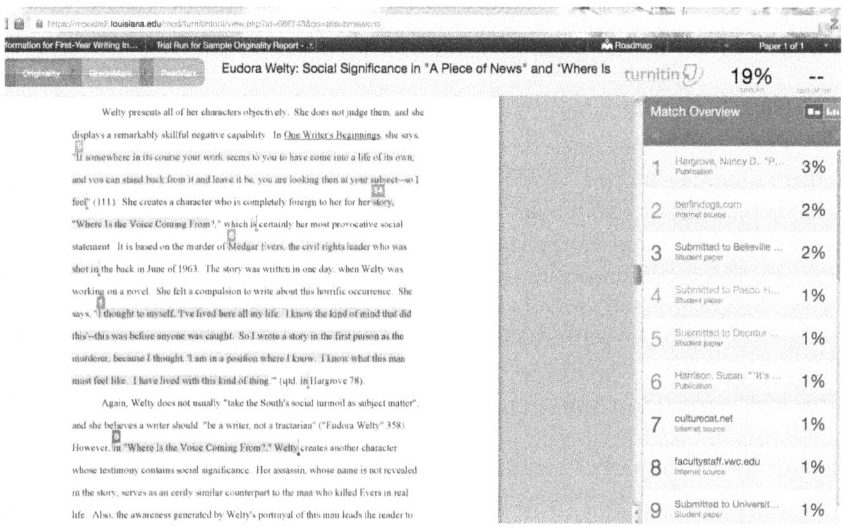

Figure 11.1 Continued

As Figure 11.1 shows, when I highlighted part of my text and clicked the "Vague" tag, it made this comment appear in my paper.

> **Unclear:**
>
> When making a point in one of your body paragraphs, one of the most common mistakes is to not offer enough details. A paragraph without much detail will seem vague and sketchy. A paper is always strengthened when your claims are as specific as possible. The more detailed evidence you offer, the more reference points your reader will have. Remember that you are communicating your argument to a reader who has only your description to go by. Someone who reads your essay will not automatically know what you mean to express, so you have to supply details, to show the reader what you mean, not just tell him or her.

The "Tone" tag gave me this prewritten feedback:

> **Inappropriate Tone:**
>
> The way you say something can be just as meaningful as the content of what you say. In an academic essay, there is a danger of being too informal. As you write, you must have a clear sense of the kind of reader (audience) you are writing for, and adjust the formality, complexity, sincerity, and depth of your writing accordingly. In short, your tone is your overall attitude toward your reader. Your tone should in all circumstances be consistent and respectful. Problems with tone arise most often from the use of slang expressions, which you must avoid in academic writing.

Decontextualized feedback like this is of little value to student writers. In my own teaching, one test I give myself when I respond to students' writing assignments is this: I write my comments, and then I do something else for a while. Then I look back at the student's paper, without looking at the student's writing, only my comments. If I can't tell, based only on my comments, what the subject matter of the paper is, I write more comments. Here's a comment I wrote on one student paper:

> From this essay, it's not really clear why Germany is letting in so many refugees relative to other European countries. It's OK for this question to be outside the scope of your project here, because most of what you're saying does focus on your main question, which is what life in Germany is like for Syrian refugees. Still, I'd like you to make the point explicitly that the Merkel administration [Angela Merkel, the Chancellor of Germany] obviously has reasons they are choosing to take in many refugees, but that the citizens of Germany are divided in how they feel about supporting and resettling Syrian refugees. Also, it's up to you whether you do this or not, but I'm interested in your reasons for choosing this topic. It would be nice to see you say a little about that in either the introduction or conclusion.

From reading my comments, I see that they engage directly with her research question: what Syrian refugees' experiences have been. Here is an additional example from a different student paper about mental health care in Hungary:

> Somewhere in the essay, if possible, it would be helpful to have a brief sentence or two of explanation of how mental health care in Hungary is funded. The country's health care system is funded mostly by taxes (universal health care), but I don't know if mental health care is included in that—I'm guessing it probably isn't.
>
> Here is a suggestion for the conclusion, because it's a logical place in the essay where you can look toward the future: MANY of the Syrian refugees are going into and through Hungary. Actually, if I understand correctly, they have closed their borders now, but before that happened, large numbers of people entered the country. These are people who have all suffered physical and mental trauma, and I believe that in general, people who have experienced trauma/have PTSD can be triggered by a variety of things, including seeing and hearing about tragedies such as theirs, so it creates more need for Hungarian citizens to have appropriate help as well. That's a point you might want to make.

Rather than concern myself with what percentage of these students' papers was similar to other texts in Turnitin's database, I put my time into engaging with the process of meaning-making, both in conferences with students and with my comments. I was following research-based practices of responding to student writing, which call for teachers to respond as readers, demonstrating a thinking, active audience that is affected by the student's writing, helping students see themselves as writers whose words can make real impressions; I was not passively, absently marking for grammar, punctuation, and basic conventions.

In order to do this time-consuming, labor-intensive work of helping students complete writing projects and then responding to that writing, teachers need support. The National Council of Teachers of English has recommended smaller class sizes for writing courses in order to enable teachers to give student writing the proper amount of attention. Its statement "Principles for the Postsecondary Teaching of Writing" argues that "no more than 20 students should be permitted in any writing class. Ideally, classes should be limited to 15. Remedial or developmental sections should be limited to a maximum of 15 students." Small class size can help faculty members teach writing. However, hiring more teachers is expensive, and some institutions have chosen not to lower—even to increase—class size and buy software that purports to do some of the teachers' work for them automatically.

How Automated Essay Scoring Platforms Work

While faculty in departments of English, writing, and composition are familiar with the rise of automated scoring tools, those outside the field may be unaware of the rapid spread of these tools in K–12 and higher education. Automated essay scoring (AES), or machine reading, became available as a commercial product in the late 1990s. A prominent one is ACCUPLACER, which is part of The College Board, and its essay scoring tool, WritePlacer Plus, which is intended to help place students into the college writing course that best suits their needs. Another is the Intelligent Essay Assessor, which is part of WriteToLearn, a Pearson Education product for grades four through twelve, similar to Turnitin's Revision Assistant and Scoring Engine. Educational Testing Services (ETS) has a similar product called Criterion, and Measurement Incorporated has PEG Writing (PEG stands for Project Essay Grading).

Such tools can be highly sophisticated not only in checking for sentence-level errors but also in emulating the response of human readers. One such system is the Enhanced AI Scoring Engine (EASE), which learns instructors' styles: "A professor scores a series of essays according to her own criteria. Then the software scans the marked-up essays for patterns and assimilates them." The goal is to "create a tireless, automated version of the professor" that can grade more quickly and at lower cost (Kolowich 2014, The Prof in the Machine section, para. 3).

However, the organizations that make AES tools are aware of how these tools are perceived by educators, and they are careful to qualify what the software can and cannot do. A joint report by The College Board, Pearson Education, and ETS notes:

> Automated essay scoring systems do not measure all of the dimensions considered important in academic instruction. Most automated scoring components target aspects of grammar, usage, mechanics, spelling, and vocabulary. Therefore, they are generally well-positioned to score essays that are intended to measure text-production skills. Many current systems also evaluate the semantic content of essays, their relevance to the prompt, and aspects of organization and flow. Assessment of creativity, poetry, irony, or other more artistic uses of writing is beyond such systems. They also are not good at assessing rhetorical voice, the logic of an argument, the extent to which particular concepts are accurately described, or whether specific ideas presented in the essay are well founded.
>
> (Williamson et al. 2010: 2)

On its website, The College Board explains WritePlacer: "WritePlacer® asks students to write an essay that is then scored to measure their writing skills. The student's response is scored electronically using an automated system, and scores are returned within seconds " (The College Board 2017: Writing Assessments section, para. 1). Their messaging is different, however, when it is directed toward students. In a guide intended for students in which The College Board explains to students how to prepare for a WritePlacer exam, The College Board does not disclose that students are writing to a computer that scores the essays; they elide this by using the passive voice, as in, "Your essay will be given a holistic score that represents how clearly and effectively you expressed your position" (The College Board 2008: 1).

Since 2011, with the implementation of the Common Core State Standards Initiative, automated scoring has been incorporated into the testing regime of American public education. Because the Common Core standards needed new assessments for "college and career readiness," any writing components had to be scored in a way that was consistent, economical, and comparable across states. Enter AES. Debate and planning about how AES would be used in the Common Core assessments has been ongoing since then, but for 2017, the terms of the contract between the Common Core states and Pearson are that 100% of the writing assessments used by the Partnership for Assessment of the Readiness for College and Careers (PARCC) will be scored by software and that 10% of those will be rescored by human readers, where human readers act as a spot check for validity. For states that participate in the Smarter Balance Assessment Consortium (SBAC), which provides an online assessment that offers research, writing, and problem-solving tasks that measure critical-thinking and problem-solving skills, all the writing assessments will be scored by software, but 25% will be rescored by human readers (Strauss 2016, para. 3–6).

Educator Perspectives

Teachers have issued responses to developments in AES and PDS over the years in articles in scholarly journals, books, and articles and letters in mainstream news publications (Herrington & Moran 2001; Ericsson & Haswell 2006). Regarding AES, teachers have expressed serious concerns about machine-scored writing assessments as part of a broader conversation objecting to high-stakes testing, faculty working conditions including class size and grading load, and research-based best practices for writing assessment. Some teachers have also made arguments against PDS, which I will review, but the case remains that the resistance to PDS is not as strong or widespread as that to AES and that Turnitin in particular is still a popular tool in secondary and postsecondary education. In an e-mail to the Writing Program Administration listserv in 2013, Rebecca Moore Howard wrote (emphasis in original):

> Turnitin has become like abortion and the death penalty: A topic on which people are making decisions based on deeply held beliefs inaccessible to logos. I visit faculties at several campuses every year, and in each audience are instructors who cannot imagine teaching without Turnitin. I am in a post-debate state with such people, unwilling any longer to search for the common ground on which we will exchange principles and consider possibilities, at the end of which these folks will return to Mother Turnitin against all reason. I just tell folks why I don't use it, and turn to another topic. *No one* has ever said to me, "You know, I thought about what you said, and I changed my practice." No one.

Howard is a distinguished scholar in the writing and composition community who for decades has studied plagiarism and argued against the use of PDS, but these educators are in the minority. Still, the movement against AES has gained traction with teachers, as well as with parent organizations like the Parent Coalition for Student Privacy, Network for Public Education, FairTest, and Parents Across America. College writing faculty created a petition in 2013 asking faculty, students, parents, and the public to support assessments using human readers. Called humanreaders.org, it currently has 4,309 signatures (Haswell & Wilson 2013).

As far back as 2001, the editors of *College English* published "What Happens When Machines Read Our Students' Writing?" by Anne Herrington and Charles Moran, who experimented with Vantage Learning's IntelliMetric and with Intelligent Essay Assessor by writing essays and having the tools score them. They reflected on their experience and concluded that there is an important distinction between writing on the machine and writing to the machine. E-mail, they argue, "mediates and facilitates communication between and among human beings. Writing to the machine, however, as we found ourselves doing as we experimented with WPP and IEA, creates what is for now an unprecedented and unnatural rhetorical situation" (Herrington & Moran 2001: 496). They continue:

> We believe this expectation of active response is fundamental to the act of writing. Even if the response is not communicated by the reader to the writer, as is the case in a placement-testing situation, the writer assumes she will have some impact on a reader's thoughts and feelings. Writing to a machine—particularly over multiple occasions, particularly for instructional purposes—desensitizes us as writers. As we wrote to the machine, we felt less investment in figuring out something we wanted to say than we do when we are writing to human readers. We thought less of rhetorical, affective, and interpretive interests that human readers may have.
>
> (Herrington & Moran 2001: 497)

In this writing situation, the reader, so important for the communication and meaning-making involved in the process of writing, is taken away from the writer. Herrington and Moran reprised their 2001 research in a chapter in a 2006 collection titled *Machine Scoring of Student Essays: Truth and Consequences*, in which they interviewed students soon after they had taken a placement test that had been scored automatically. Students were surprised to learn about automatic scoring, and they felt dissonance about the experience. They thought they would have approached the writing task differently, though the specific differences were inchoate, if they had known it would be assessed by a computer and not read by a teacher (Herrington and Moran 2006: 120 *ff.*). The concept of audience, which is a powerful affective and pedagogical motivator, is removed from student writers who are writing for machine-scoring platforms. Herrington and Moran emphasize that these tools continue to be used in underfunded public universities and community colleges because "[o]n the list of institutions using WritePlacer Plus or Criterion there is no Harvard or Princeton, no Williams or Oberlin or Amherst" (Herrington and Moran 2006: 126). They argue that "[t]he distribution of this product suggests to us an extension of the social and economic stratification that has been such a feature of the past decade: the wealthy and connected learn to write to make meaning and to achieve their rhetorical purposes; the poor and unconnected learn to write to scoring engines" (Herrington and Moran 2006: 126). William Condon also pointed out that AES goes against all the best known, research-based assessment practices, particularly portfolios that are evaluated in a local context using local standards (2006: 215). In 2013, the National Council of Teachers of English published a position statement against AES. It sets forth a list of reasons for the position, such as stifling teachers' innovation and creativity because in machine-scored assessments the software is designed for the specific prompts in the assessment construct. NCTE (2013: Machine Scoring Fails the Test section, first bullet point) further argues that:

> Using computers to "read" and evaluate students' writing (1) denies students the chance to have anything but limited features recognized in their writing; and (2) compels teachers to ignore what is most important in writing instruction in order to teach what is least important. . . . Computer scoring removes the purpose from written communication—to create human interactions through a complex, socially consequential system of meaning making—and sends a message to students that writing is not worth their time because reading it is not worth the time of the people teaching and assessing them.

Although the field's response to automated scoring has been unequivocally critical on a large scale, I am suggesting that the same cannot be said for plagiarism detection platforms. Powerful cultural notions of authorship, which shape copyright law as we know it, also shape the context for writing instruction. Because plagiarism is considered to be such a shocking transgression, many teachers have embraced PDS in the service of justice: these platforms serve as a sheriff (of sorts), keeping everyone honest. This promise of deterrence has successfully persuaded administrators and faculty at many institutions, who have been convinced that plagiarism is rampant (Vie 2013a; 2013b).

To be sure, there have also been some scholars who have written critiques of PDS. The Conference on College Composition and Communication (CCCC) has an Intellectual Property Caucus, which has kept a critical stance toward PDS and, in 2006, crafted a position statement against the use of PDS on college campuses. Eventually, the CCCC adopted a shorter version of the statement as a resolution in 2013. This resolution lays out the pedagogical case against PDS, arguing that they "can compromise academic integrity by potentially undermining students' agency as writers" by "treating all students as always already plagiarists, creating a hostile learning environment, shifting the responsibility of identifying and interpreting source misuse from teachers to technology, and compelling students to agree to licensing agreements that threaten their privacy and rights to their own intellectual property" (CCCC 2013: Resolution 3 section, para. 2). Stephanie Vie has analyzed Turnitin's marketing rhetoric, noting that the company no longer relies so heavily on the appeal to preserving academic integrity, perhaps as a consequence of the 2007 lawsuit, but now has pivoted to emphasizing their grading and peer review tools, GradeMark and PeerMark, the former of which I demonstrated earlier, and how iParadigms uses the eco-friendliness involved in electronic, paperless grading to shift the conversation away from critiques of their problematic use of students' intellectual property (Vie 2013a). Not only does their product save trees, Turnitin claims, it also saves time:

> Jiansheng Guo, a professor and interim associate dean at California State University East Bay, reflects on his grading practices before Turnitin, stating that he would previously collect stacks of paper in hard copy and take 20–30 minutes per paper to finish grading. After Turnitin, Guo stated he could finish each paper in five minutes using the rubrics and drag-and-drop comments available in GradeMark "and that's why I can cope with 120 students as if they were 30 students." Even though the video uses the phrase "faster grading, richer feedback" (2:19), the richness of the feedback is never addressed; instead, some of the words and phrases Guo uses are easy, saves time, focus, concentrate, and productivity. His discussion of how the rubric allows for him to explain why students received the grade they earned emphasizes assessment (and rubrics) as a way of defending a grade rather than as a tool to guide students in later writing assignments by showcasing strengths and weaknesses and giving suggestions for continued growth.
>
> (Vie 2013a, Other People's Papers, Part 2 section, para. 7)

Admittedly, we don't see Guo's rubric or comments, but a change from 20–30 minutes per student writing project to five minutes is significant; it limits the capacity of the reader response considerably. Here we see the grading tool highlighted, but the plagiarism detection is always present as well.

The Convergence of Automatic Scoring and Plagiarism Detection

I have been arguing that AES and PDS are connected, but not in a way that is recognizable to most writing teachers. Machine scoring has a negative association with high-stakes testing and can be understood as an issue of deprofessionalization for faculty: the day may come when an online course taught and graded by Professor Siri or Alexa could eliminate the need for teachers entirely. Turnitin, however, is the teacher's aide—the friendly assistant who is an ally in the struggle against would-be cheaters.

To clarify: what do AES and PDS have in common?

- Both lack human judgment.
- Both rely on databases of student writing without compensation for students.
- Both make money on student writing.
- Both compromise student privacy.
- Both go against best pedagogical practices of writing as making meaning for an audience in a local context.
- Both appeal to saving teachers' time (and institutions' money).

What is to be gained, then, from understanding these connections? I suggest that it can make both arguments stronger: nor does it strengthen the case against PDS but against AES as well. The CCCC Resolution against automated plagiarism detection cites several reasons for its position, as do the critical scholarly analyses of Turnitin, but not the implications for machine scoring and the overlap of PDS and AES. By seeing the similarity between machine scoring and automated plagiarism detection, we focus attention on the political economy of these digital platforms because machine-scoring software companies, like PDSs, profit from student writing and deprofessionalize teachers by compromising their authority and judgment.

The outcome of the 2007 lawsuit against Turnitin hasn't kept institutions from using PDSs and many from making it mandatory over teachers' and students' objections. At my university in November 2007, I attended a talk by a consultant who had been asked to give a lecture about plagiarism. The talk was titled "Plagiarism 101: Keys to Preventing Academic Misconduct," and after the session ended, the then-provost expressed interest in adopting Turnitin. Another professor and I explained our reservations about PDSs, particularly that they violate students' copyright. The provost guffawed.

A large part of media education is knowing one's own rights under the law: the right to one's own intellectual property and the right to use writing, art, music, and additional works by others in order to make creative and critical statements. As fraught as copyright law is, it does empower creators with its lengthy terms of years and the restrictions on legal uses of others' works. It grants creators, including students, a powerful array of legal rights as soon as the work is in a fixed medium, with no application process required. In that regard, the awareness raised by plagiarism detection platforms can be generative: plagiarism detection platforms remind us that there are no Apprentice Authors as in Landow's story. Students are authors and should be as respected as such, under the law, in the classroom and in public discourse.

References

The College Board. (2008). "WritePlacer® Guide With Sample Essays." Retrieved from https://secure-media.collegeboard.org/digitalServices/pdf/professionals/accuplacer-writeplacer-sample-essays.pdf

The College Board. (2017). "Accurate Placement—ACCUPLACER." Retrieved from https://accuplacer.collegeboard.org/educator/accurate-placement

Condon, W. (2006). "Why Less Is Not More: What We Lose by Letting a Computer Score Writing Samples." In P. F. Ericsson & R. Haswell (Eds.), Machine Scoring of Student Essays: Truth and Consequences (pp. 211-220). Logan: Utah State University Press.

Haswell, R., & Wilson, M. (2013). "Human Readers: Professionals Against Machine Scoring of Student Essays in High-Stakes Assessment." *Human Readers*. Retrieved from http://humanreaders.org/petition/

Herrington, A., & Moran, C. (2001). "What Happens When Machines Read Our Students' Writing?" *College English*, 63(4), 480–499.

Herrington, A., & Moran, C. (2006). "WritePlacer Plus in Place: An Exploratory Case Study." In P. F. Ericsson & R. Haswell (Eds.), Machine Scoring of Student Essays: Truth and Consequences (pp. 114–129). Logan: Utah State University Press.

Kolowich, S. (2014). "Writing Instructor, Skeptical of Automated Grading, Pits Machine vs. Machine." *Chronicle of Higher Education*. Retrieved from http://www.chronicle.com/article/writing-instructor-skeptical/146211

Landow, G. (1995). "Ms. Austen's Submission." In W. A. Covino & D. A. Jolliffe (Eds.), *Rhetoric: Concepts, Definitions, Boundaries* (pp. 785–790). New York: Allyn & Bacon.

Lessig, L. (2001). *The Future of Ideas: The Fate of the Commons in a Connected World*. New York: Vintage.

Lunsford, A. (1994). "Review of Hypertext: The Convergence of Contemporary Critical Theory and Technology by George P. Landow." *Modern Philology*, 92(2), 272–277.

National Council of Teachers of English. (2013). "NCTE Position Statement on Machine Scoring." Retrieved from http://www.ncte.org/positions/statements/machine_scoring

Pearson. (2011). "WriteToLearn: Demonstrating Reading & Writing Performance Gains." Retrieved from http://cdn2.hubspot.net/hubfs/559254/WTL/resources/WTL_EfficacyReport.pdf?t=1470271884493

Povejsil, K. (2009). "US Court of Appeals Unanimously Affirms Finding of 'Fair Use' for Turnitin." Retrieved from https://turnitin.com/static/resources/documentation/turnitin/sales/Turnitin_RELEASE_042709_Appeals_Court_Affirms_Fair_Use.pdf

Strauss, V. (2016, May 5). "Should You Trust a Computer to Grade Your Child's Writing on Common Core Tests?" *Washington Post*. Retrieved from http://www.washingtonpost.com/news/answer-sheet/wp/2016/05/05/should-you-trust-a-computer-to-grade-your-childs-writing-on-common-core-tests/

Vie, S. (2013a). "Turn It Down, Don't Turnitin: Resisting Plagiarism Detection Technologies by Talking About Plagiarism Rhetorically." *Computers and Composition Online*. Retrieved from http://www2.bgsu.edu/departments/english/cconline/spring2013_special_issue/Vie/

Vie, S. (2013b). "A Pedagogy of Resistance Toward Plagiarism Detection Technologies." *Computers and Composition*, 30(1), 3–15.

Vie, S. (2015). "Don't Fear the Reaper: Beyond the Spectre of Internet Plagiarism." In L. C. Lewis (Ed.), *Strategic Discourse: The Politics of (New) Literacy Crises*. Logan, UT: Computers and Composition Digital Press/Utah State University Press.

Williamson, D. M., Bennett, R. E., Lazer, S., Bernstein, J., Foltz, P. W., Landauer, T. K., . . . Sweeney, K. (2010). "Automated Scoring for the Assessment of Common Core Standards." Retrieved from http://www.ets.org/s/commonassessments/pdf/AutomatedScoringAssessCommonCoreStandards.pdf

Zimmerman, T. (2008). "McLean Students File Suit Against Turnitin.com: Useful Tool or Instrument of Tyranny?" *The CCCC Intellectual Property Annual*. Retrieved from www.ncte.org/cccc/committees/ip/2007developments/mclean

Further Reading

Canzonetta, J., & Kannan, V. (2016). "Globalizing Plagiarism & Writing Assessment: A Case Study of Turnitin." *The Journal of Writing Assessment*, 9. Retrieved from http://journalofwritingassessment.org/article.php?article=104

Ericsson, P. F., & Haswell, R. H. (2006). *Machine Scoring of Student Essays: Truth and Consequences*. Logan, UT: Utah State University Press.

Gillis, K., Lang, S., Norris, M., & Palmer, L. (2009). "Electronic Plagiarism Checkers: Barriers to Developing an Academic Voice." Across the Disciplines, 20. Retrieved from https://wac.colostate.edu/journal/vol20/gillis.pdf

12

YOUTH, BYTES, COPYRIGHT

Talking to Young Canadian Creators About Digital Copyright

Catherine Burwell

Canada's most recent copyright legislation is the Canadian Copyright Modernization Act. The Act was passed in Canadian Parliament in 2012, after three earlier attempts at passing bills in 2005, 2008, and 2010 failed. All three bills were abandoned for procedural reasons rather than because of their content. Nonetheless, these were highly contentious bills that brought copyright to the attention of the wider public. Indeed, as Laura Murray and Sam Trosow write, the early bills produced a number of "dramatic moments" that made copyright "a topic of discussion in bars and coffee shops all over the country" (Murray & Trosow 2013: xi).

These dramatic moments included controversies over digital rights management (DRM) and the role of Internet service providers (ISPs) in copyright infringement. However, over the course of those years—from 2001 when the government first announced its intention to amend the bill until 2012 when the Modernization Act was finally passed—the shape and content of the bill shifted considerably. During that time, the voices of consumers became more audible, and a discourse of users' rights more distinct. The bill that was passed in 2012 ultimately expanded consumer and educational uses of copyright material but retained the earlier DRM restrictions.

As both consumers and creators, young people confront, negotiate, and resist copyright laws on a regular basis, yet we know little about their experiences and impressions of copyright. This chapter attempts to fill that silence by reporting on a qualitative study undertaken to talk to young Canadian creators. Drawing on interviews with twenty-five creators across five provinces, I describe activities such as sharing, copying, and transforming in order to paint a picture of young creators' encounters with copyright and their efforts to engage in ethical dealings with digital materials and with other cultural producers.

I begin by outlining distinctive histories and features of Canadian copyright law and compare fair use with fair dealing. I then lay out the cultural studies approach used in this project, which places value on the study of copyright within local communities and everyday contexts. I explain how the research was conducted and follow with the results, which are presented as a series of practices common to many of the participants. Finally, I end with a few closing thoughts about the implications of these findings for media education.

Background to Copyright in Canada: What's the Deal With Fair Dealing?

Canadian copyright law has its basis in British, French, and American law and is thus different from U.S. law, with which it is sometimes confused (including by Canadians themselves). One of the significant differences lies in Canadian law's *fair dealing* exceptions, a feature it shares with other Commonwealth countries, such as the United Kingdom and Australia. Under the Copyright Modernization Act, fair dealing—those uses of copyright-protected material that are exceptions to infringement—falls within eight categories. These are the right to use content for research, private study, education, parody, satire, criticism, review, and news reporting. If a use falls within one of these categories, then it is subject to five further tests for fairness. These include considerations such as the amount of work used, the possible alternatives to the use, and the effect that the use has on the original work. Essentially, then, fair dealing puts in place a two-step process. Use—or dealing—must first fall within at least one of the eight predetermined categories. If it is deemed to fit within one (or more) of these purposes, then a number of other considerations for determining fairness are taken into account.

At one time, fair dealing was a provision with little power. However, a series of influential court cases over the past several years have changed that. In the case of *Théberge v. Galerie d'Art du Petit Champlain* (2002), the Supreme Court stated, "Excessive control by holders of copyrights and other forms of intellectual property may unduly limit the ability of the public domain to incorporate and embellish creative innovation in the long-term interests of society as a whole" (para. 32). This announcement signaled a new framework for copyright analysis, one that emphasized copyright's role in making cultural goods available for use. Two years after that decision, another influential ruling heightened the importance of fair dealing. In *CCH v. Law Society of Upper Canada* (2004), the Supreme Court stated that fair dealing should be understood as an "integral part" of the *Copyright Act*. It went on to say that fair dealing is a "user's right" and that, in order to balance the rights of copyright owners and users, fair dealing "must not be interpreted restrictively" (para. 48). In 2012, the significance of users' rights and fair dealing was further reinforced through two events. The first was the passage of the new Copyright Act and with it the addition of three new categories of fair dealing (education, parody, and satire). The second was the delivery of five Supreme Court rulings (issued on a single day) that unequivocally affirmed fair dealing as the right of every user.

Despite their similar names, fair dealing and fair use are not the same. Fair use models, which have been adopted in countries such as Israel, the Philippines, and the United States, are generally considered to be more open and flexible than fair dealing. This is because fair use, unlike fair dealing, does not set out a series of categories that work must fall within (e.g., research, review, or parody). Instead, any use may, potentially, qualify as fair use. As Michael Geist (2013) notes, the fair use approach is most closely associated with the United States. The U.S. provision points toward teaching, scholarship, research, reporting, comment, and criticism as illustrations of possible fair uses but leaves open the possibility of others.

Fair dealing, on the other hand, is more limited in its scope, given that dealing must fit within one of the enumerated purposes and must pass through a two-step analysis. Nonetheless, a number of scholars have commented on the "dynamic" nature of fair dealing within Canada. Michael Geist argues that recent court cases broadening the scope of fair dealing and changes to the

Copyright Act have "effectively turned the Canadian fair dealing clause into a fair use provision," one that seeks to provide balance between creators' rights and users' rights (Geist 2013: 159). In their "manifesto for a robust culture of fair dealing," Rosemary Coombe and her coauthors write about fair dealing not as a legal regime but rather as processes undertaken by digital users. These processes, they argue, need to be seen as "dynamic, complex, contingent and shifting" (Coombe, Wershler, & Zeilinger 2014: 3). They call for a broader understanding of fair dealing that shifts the emphasis away from legal abstractions and toward human capacities, relationships, and practices. Similarly, Laura Murray (2014a), reflecting on the concept of "dealing," reminds us that dealing is always active, relational, and process based. Casting our vision on fair dealing and recognizing it as complex and ongoing human activity returns us to the social relationships and activities at the heart of copyright law. This is a way of approaching copyright and fair dealing that I expand on in the next section, as I consider the frameworks that guide this study.

Theoretical Framework: Approaching Copyright in Context

Many Canadian scholars have advocated for considering copyright in a contextualized and interdisciplinary way rather than relying solely on a legal lens. We can see this approach especially clearly in Rosemary Coombe's groundbreaking book, *The Cultural Life of Intellectual Properties*. In it, Coombe undertakes an ethnographic study to explore how intellectual property (IP) works in everyday life. Her study approaches law as a "diffuse and pervasive force shaping social consciousness and behaviour" while also taking into account the ways in which public practices and perceptions of legal regimes may shape the law itself (Coombe 1998: 12). This means considering the relationship of a wide range of cultural practices and local knowledges to copyright law and acknowledging the multiple ways in which citizens negotiate, interpret, misinterpret, and disregard the law.

This situated approach has been fruitfully taken up both in Canada and elsewhere. Alexandra Boutros (2014), for example, explores the tensions between Canadian copyright law and the production practices of Canadian hip-hop artists. She notes how these young artists draw on an African American history of sampling, collaboration, and intertextuality that sits uneasily with the Western notions of individual authorship encoded in Canadian law. Katharina Freund (2016) conducts ethnographic research of online fanvidding communities in order to understand how remix artists make sense of U.S. copyright law. Her work portrays communities that don't simply react to manifestations of copyright law (e.g., in the form of YouTube takedown notices) but rather educate their members and engage in strategies to protect themselves against infringement suits. And in her work on the legal rules that govern flows of information, Julie Cohen pushes against legal scholarship's tendency toward immateriality and disembodiment, and instead advocates for a model that focuses on processes of cultural participation and on understanding "what it is that the people we call authors actually do on a day-to-day basis" (Cohen 2012: 62).

This study draws on just such a model. As I outline in this chapter, by talking to young creators about their creative practice, their use of digital materials, and their everyday interactions with others, I hoped to provide insight into fair dealing and the ways that young Canadians perceive, negotiate, and sidestep copyright law.

The Study: Interviewing Young Creators

This research was prompted by my own long-standing interest in young people's creative pursuits. As a high school English and media studies teacher between 1997 and 2011, I observed firsthand young people's increasing engagement with digital media, much of it highly creative in nature. In doctoral research conducted in the later years of my teaching career, I explored the relationship between media corporations and young digital users, largely through online research. There, on discussion boards, fan fiction sites, video-sharing platforms, and social networking sites, I noted the presence of animated conversations related to authorship, ownership, and copyright. Young people were discussing the circulation of digital materials, remix practices, corporate power to remove user-generated content, and, occasionally, copyright law itself (Burwell 2010). My preliminary research with focus groups confirmed that young people—particularly those who identified as artists or creators—had experience negotiating the ethical use of digital materials and were interested in talking about the topic.

The qualitative study discussed here, then, explores young Canadian creators' experiences of copyright and their creative practices, particularly in regard to their uses of digital media. I conducted individual interviews with twenty-five young Canadians between the ages of 18 and 28 in five Canadian provinces: British Columbia, Alberta, Saskatchewan, Ontario, and Québec. Most participants lived in cities, including Calgary, Edmonton, Toronto, and Montréal, but a few also lived in more rural regions of these provinces. Of the twenty-five participants, one was agender, eleven were female, and thirteen were male.

I was interested in speaking with young people participating in a wide range of creative practices. The final list of participants included musicians, game developers, visual artists, comic creators, spoken word poets, creative writers, photographers, podcast creators, and makers of wearable technology. While I especially wanted to understand more about how young people encountered copyright within the context of digital media, not all of the participants considered themselves "digital creators." Nonetheless, all of them used digital technology in some way to participate in creative communities or to promote and circulate their work. And in fact for the majority of the participants, digital media formed the backbone of their creative practice.

With the help of research assistants Tom Miller and Heather Osborne, interview subjects were identified through online searches, events listings, and word of mouth. All participants had made their work public in some significant way, whether that meant performing in front of audiences, posting work online over a sustained period, publishing in print, displaying in galleries, or participating in events such as maker faires. This was an important factor in selection, as it meant that all participants had faced the challenges that come with having an audience, challenges that, in the context of copyright, mean that one's work is open to scrutiny from others—and also to reuse. Although all creators had exhibited, performed, published, or practiced their work in public spaces (whether digital or physical), less than a third of them made their living from their creative labor. In the majority of cases, they were either students (undergraduate or graduate), worked in a job unrelated to their creative practice (e.g., as a clerk in a bookstore), or worked in a job related to arts or media (e.g., as a facilitator in a "maker" program in a museum). In every case, the participants devoted a significant amount of their time to their creative labor and to promoting their work and building a public profile.

In inviting and later speaking with participants, I took important cues from previous research conducted by Laura Murray. In 2006, she undertook a study to speak to Canadian visual artists about their experiences and impressions of copyright. As Murray later explains, "the framing of the project was too narrow," and many artists declined the invitation because of a lack of confidence or interest in the topic (Murray 2014b: 135). Those who did take up her invitation had frequently had negative experiences with copyright, skewing her research in a particular direction. In subsequent research on cultural labor and IP with practicing artists, Murray (2014b) chose not to declare a focus on copyright. Instead, she brought up the topic only at the end of interviews, an approach guided by the increasingly common observation, previously mentioned, that IP law is best understood in the context of everyday cultural and economic life.

In relation to these instructive experiences, I attempted to choose a middle path. In my invitations, I made clear my interest in talking to interview subjects about copyright and fair dealing. At the same time, I reassured potential participants that they didn't need to be experts on these subjects. I also explained that I wanted to talk to participants about their current projects, their creative practices, and some of challenges they and others of their generation faced as they undertook cultural work in contemporary economic conditions. In short, I hoped that our discussions of copyright would unfold within the context of broader conversations about their experiences, interests, and ways of thinking about creativity.

The interviews lasted anywhere between 45 minutes and 2 hours and took place either in person, on Skype, or over the telephone. The interviews were semistructured, enabling me to respond to the participants' varied experiences and to follow particularly fruitful leads in the conversation. Nonetheless, most interviews took a fairly similar shape. They began broadly, with participants talking about their personal histories and their paths toward their current creative work. In most cases, I was able to watch, read, listen to, or learn about their work beforehand and so pose specific questions about it. Sometimes, if the interviews were face-to-face, we looked at their work online as we talked about it.

After establishing this personal history, I asked about some of the challenges they faced in their current creative activities and the role digital technology played in the creation, promotion, circulation, and response to their work. In many cases, particularly when the participants' creative work was primarily digital, these questions led us naturally into talking about issues related to copyright and fair dealing, such as the participants' own appropriation of digital materials, the reuse or theft of their work by others, or incidents of having work removed from sites like YouTube. In interviews where the participants had not already voiced experiences and opinions related to topics such as copyright, appropriation, or ownership, I deliberately shifted to that topic in the second part of the interview. While my questions varied in response to each participant's practices and previously expressed ideas, some of the most common questions in this second half of the interview were as follows:

- Do you copy, borrow, sample, or reuse (digital) material in your own work? What is your attitude to this reuse? Have you ever had any reactions to this reuse (e.g., take-down notices)?
- Have you ever had your work copied, borrowed, sampled, reused, or circulated with or without your permission? What has been your reaction to this reuse?
- What kinds of issues related to copyright do creators working in the same area as you typically face?
- If you had to define copyright for someone younger than you, what would you say?
- Have you ever heard of the terms "fair use" or "fair dealing"? If yes, what do they mean to you? If no, what do you think the word "fair" means in relation to copyright?
- Think about what you've told me about copyright in this interview: where or how have you learned this?

Because participants took part in a wide range of artistic practices with diverse processes and norms for creation, appropriation, and adaptation, as well as very different histories and industry expectations (e.g., norms for modding games versus sampling in hip-hop music), these kinds of questions provoked a wide range of responses. Nonetheless, as I outline later in the chapter, a number of broad themes related to their creative practices emerged.

Research Findings: Dealing With Copyright

Coombe, Wershler, and Zeilinger write that, in order to understand "the legal, social, and practical contours of cultural life in a digital era," we need a much better understanding of what people "actually *do* in digital environments" (Coombe et al. 2014: 3, italics in original). Similarly, Murray notes that in fair dealing there "is an emphasis on human *activity*" (Murray 2014a: 350). In keeping with their injunction to consider activity, I present some of the results from the study as *a series of actions* that brought the participants into contact with issues related to copyright. This presentation also seems appropriate because it reflects the focus of our conversations. Young creators were eager to tell me about what they were doing—and also, in many cases, what had been done for them or to them.

The actions that I focus on here—copying, transforming, sharing, and setting norms—were those most frequently cited by the participants. The boundaries between copying and transforming were an issue of concern for many of the participants, for example, and were particularly prominent in discussions of sampling in hip-hop and electronic music. There were similarly porous borders between sharing and copying. As one participant pointed out, sharing in the Internet culture is "supposed to be a good thing." Yet at what point does the sharing of one's work become less of an opportunity for recognition and more of a worry about uncontrollable reproduction? If anything, the blurry nature of these categories should remind us of how challenging it is for these young creators to navigate the complex terrain of contemporary digital production.

Copying: Throwing Shade

Copying was one of the practices participants referred to most frequently. Despite the seeming straightforwardness of the act, copying within their conversations held many nuances. It was an activity that many participants saw as necessary for reasons of learning or finance. In other cases, copying was a criticism leveled against participants, one they rejected. Copying was most likely to be vilified if it led to others making profit from an independent artist's work.

Many participants referred to copying as a crucial aspect of creating. They freely copied the musical, visual, or literary styles of others, often as a way of learning. "I am kind of like a pro copier," said Jennifer, a comic book artist. "I think there is a lot of good that comes artistically from copying." Similarly, Sharon, a spoken word artist, said that she would intentionally try to emulate another poet's style as a way of determining her own. "I think it's always okay to kinda try on their shoes for a little bit. And just see which parts of them are comfortable." And two participants, one a creator of large-scale sculptures and the other a maker of wearable technology, noted that within the maker movement where they worked, copying was not only acceptable but expected. For many projects, being able to understand templates and follow instructions was what led to a functioning finished product.

In these cases, copying was a matter of emulating, recreating, or following a pattern rather than a technical process of digital reproduction. Yet learning was also evident within instances of digital copying. For Jorge, a hip-hop artist, and his friends, downloading music from Napster was a road to creative learning and, in Jorge's case, a professional musical career. Jorge explained:

> When I was 14 or 15, I created my first disc. Which is kind of interesting as far as copyright goes because none of the music was actually mine. What we would do is we would download these songs and then—it wasn't even in a studio—we'd play one track over the

> computer microphone and then we would rap over these songs. And we burned them on the discs. And then, we would just take these to school and sell them for five bucks a pop.

Jorge noted that a lot of "people with musical pedigrees" would "throw shade" on him and his friends because they were just copying tracks and rapping over top of them. Looking back at his beginnings, Jorge laughs and says it was "crazy." But he also acknowledges that it was through these experiences that he and his friends learned to how make and produce music and how he himself became a poet and arranger. Jorge also pointed out that this process developed in response to a "lack of mentorship and a lack of creative guidance." In their absence, a combination of community, technological resourcefulness, and copying led to a process of appropriation that, as Henry Jenkins (2006) has suggested, might well be seen as a kind of creative apprenticeship.

Sampling was also raised in relation to the practice of copying. Most of the musicians I spoke with were quick to point out that sampling should be considered as transformative (and I will return to the practice in my discussion of transformation) but that many others saw sampling as copying—and thus stealing. This interpretation of sampling was a source of frustration. Alec, a new media artist and composer of electronic music, noted that he made most of his music through sophisticated processes of sampling and argued that it should be seen as a kind of musical instrument. Nonetheless, he felt he had to hide or bury his primary method of production not only because of copyright claims but also because of audiences.

> In this climate, if you sample, you're seen as a monster. You're taking away from the people who are working so hard to create content, their blood, sweat and tears going in to it. It's scary times.

Alec expressed deep concern for the kinds of relationships that were created through this view of sampling, in which artists were pitted against one another and made to feel shame for the processes they used to create their art. This view of sampling also overlooked the idea that, in Alec's words, "sampling democratizes. You don't have to have a guitar or a nice mic and all that other shit. You just need to have a sampler." Sampling in his view and in the view of the hip-hop musicians interviewed makes a space for young creators with few resources.

Aside from sampling, most of the participants agreed that there was a point at which copying became stealing. Frequently, this was associated not only with the digital reproduction of one's work but also with profit making. Many participants, especially those in the visual arts, raised the worry of having their images reproduced on T-shirts or tote bags for sale online. While this had happened to only one of the participants, many more raised this as, in Jennifer's words, "the nightmare scenario I hear of most often." The amount of work copied was also used as a way to distinguish coping from stealing. "In web development," Kaitlyn said, "you could copy code. Taking code is fine. But you wouldn't recreate all of what someone did."

Transforming: You're (Not) Always Recombining Ideas

The act of transforming or adapting digital or analogue materials figured prominently in participants' accounts of their creative practices. I have used the word "transform" in an attempt to gather together these varied practices. However, the participants' own phrases were far more vivid and revealing and serve as a good introduction to their varied activities.

These phrases included modding, modifying, mashing-up, mixing, combining, recombining, recontextualizing, repurposing, rearranging, recycling, remixing, reinterpreting, satirizing, and sampling.

Many—but not all—participants held to a view that all creativity was made up of acts of transformation. A number of them, like Kaitlyn, voiced the opinion that "there is no complete originality—you're always recombining ideas." Perhaps unsurprisingly, this view was most often voiced by those working in areas of new media, such as game development, electronic music, or like Kaitlyn, wearable technology. Many of these young creators spoke about their projects in terms of combining and remaking, processes they viewed as inherently imaginative.

Mark, for example, described his current game development project as "a lovechild" created out of his three favorite childhood games—Legend of Zelda, Secret of Mana, and Diablo. "I just want to take everything I love about video games and pour it into one piece of content," he said. Such an undertaking was anything but easy:

> It's going to be a big challenge for me to take some of these ideas and combine them. On the one hand, you have a very story-driven static RPG, very linear, start to finish. And then you have something like Diablo, which is a lot less story heavy and it's more game play. . . . And then there's Legend of Zelda, which implements things that neither of the other two games have. Like puzzles and sort of, requirements to be able to advance in the game. . . . It's going to be very interesting for me to come up with a way to sort of mix everything I like about them.

When I asked Mark whether such a project was original, he too stated that he didn't believe there was "anything that's truly original anymore." What he did believe is that the final game would be considerably different from the ones it was influenced by and that the reason he would be able to pour all his energy into the project was because it was based on cultural properties that he already felt strongly connected to.

Corey, a video game music composer, described his process of music creation as rearranging, given that he created most of his sounds himself, even if they were inspired by others' compositions. One of Corey's most instructive musical experiences was having his own music rearranged by a more experienced musician:

> He took some of my tracks and completely redid them with some of his own samples and his own compositions—he just made it better. And that was cool because that was the first time that I got to hear another musician—a more experienced musician—take what I had been doing and reinterpret it into something better.

Jang, a video game designer, also produced some of his own videogame music through reworking existing anime compositions. He explained that he tried to imagine how the music would sound with additional layers of instrumentation. After he added them, he converted his reworked composition into 8-bit format. The final product, he explained, was "definitely a fair use" but at the same time expressed his love for the original score.

It should be noted, though, that not all the participants had such a positive view of remix and appropriation. Most of those who were skeptical about the value of transforming the work of others were young women. Allie, a blogger and creative writer, was deeply unimpressed by fan fiction. While she agreed that literary influence was undeniable and even valuable, she was uninterested in reading another person's take on an already existing character. "Maybe just leave it to the author that actually created that character," she advised. Nabila, a dancer and spoken word artist, summed up the sometimes superficial nature of digital remixing by joking, "I can just take a little bit of this and a little bit of that and make it mine. Ta-da."

Sharing: It's Kind of a Free-for-All

Sharing and spreading digital media could conceivably be included with the practice of copying. Yet in many conversations, it seemed to represent a separate strand of experience. It was more often described as something done to participants' work rather than something they did themselves. Perhaps because of this, sharing—despite its positive connotations—frequently became the source of frustration or worry.

Certainly, all participants wanted their creations recognized, whether that work was a blog post, a podcast, a videotaped performance, or an illustration. Depending on the nature of the work, they hoped for it to be mentioned, reposted, linked to, read, watched, listened to, looked at, or purchased. Especially for those living outside of Toronto and Montréal, a strong online presence was seen to increase their audience and their sphere of influence across the country. What many of the participants did not want, however, was for their work to be shared and spread widely without their permission, without attribution or, where it was appropriate, without payment.

Yet this is what happened to a number of participants. Nabila, for example, was alerted by a friend to a stanza from one of her poems that had been reposted to Instagram without her permission—and without attribution. It was an event that led her to make her own Instagram account private and to take more precautions with making her work public. Marie, who along with her partner ran a design studio and a vegan blog that featured their quirky illustrations, found one of their images used without permission or payment on another small company's site. After consulting with friends in a chat group for design professionals, she and her partner requested that the company remove their image. Still, she couldn't help but notice that since her request, the company had continued to post other artists' uncredited photos and illustrations in order to market their own products.

Jennifer's experiences of circulation were more dramatic. The creator of a web comic of some note, Jennifer discovered that one of her images had been "shared like a million times or something." This description was not hyperbole. Jennifer's image and the phrase that accompanies it have indeed become very widely recognized and can still be found circulating several years later. But what made Jennifer's experience notable was not simply the degree of sharing. It was also her response to the circulation of her image, which expresses feelings of depression and loneliness.

> I was just really kind of frustrated with this because I'm putting up this very personal work that for me was the first time admitting certain things I felt about myself or my world. It's not always how you want to present yourself.

Not only did the image go viral online, it also spawned costumes, products, and graffiti, some of which altered the emotional tone of the original content. As Jennifer suggested, the image as it first appeared on her own Tumblr page fit within "a context of other pieces that are all kind of a chorus describing this feeling. But in isolation, it becomes kind of a goofy thing."

Jennifer suggested that the circulation of her work was "nobody's fault" and that what she learned was that "anybody can own anything." This was a sentiment echoed by a number of other creators, who often spoke of a lack of control. Kevin, also a web comic creator, noted that "things can be shared so easily. If it's on the web, it can float anywhere. How can you control that?" Like Jennifer, most did not blame others for this widespread circulation. Even Marie, who noticed that the company she approached continued to post uncredited material, explained, "I really think they didn't know the difference between what is rebloggable and what is artistic property. That's not really clear so I don't blame them. It's kind of a free-for-all." While this lack of control over the use of their artistic property was widely accepted, sharing was nonetheless an emotionally fraught subject for many of the participants.

Setting Norms: Allowing Others to Do More

While the landscape of digital media might at times be "kind of a free-for-all," the young creators I spoke with nonetheless strove to understand, uphold, and help establish ethical practices within their own creative communities. Indeed, if it seems that the communication of my findings to this point have touched little on the actual matter of copyright, fair dealing, and users' rights, that is because, in their own descriptions of their experiences, these constructs were not raised frequently. When I asked participants if they had ever had any direct encounters with copyright law, in all cases but two, affirmative answers pointed toward remixed content being removed from YouTube or SoundCloud and amounted to no further action. None of the participants were familiar with the terms "fair dealing" or "users' rights," although certainly some knew fair use. During many interviews, the interviewees and I had brief exchanges about copyright law or about what might constitute fair dealing (after I shared the meaning of that term). Yet when it came to relating their own creative practices and experiences, few of them drew consistently on this language, even though, as I hope I have demonstrated, we had intelligent and reflective conversations about activities like remixing, sharing, and copying and about concepts such as property, profit, originality, and ownership, all of them intimately linked with copyright.

This lack of legal language, however, did not signal an absence of ethical behavior or attitudes. In fact, it was clear from many conversations that participants attempted to act ethically and that, along with others taking part in similar practices, they worked to establish norms for the principled use of others' work. Their concern and efforts to build and maintain ethical practices for fair dealing in concert with other creators points toward Julie Cohen's argument that "creative practice is relational at its core" (Cohen 2012: 84).

At its simplest and most informal, these efforts took the form of asking permission to reuse others' work. Many of the participants had asked for such permission and received it. Stephen, who created a popular science podcast, gave a detailed account of learning how to find music and slowly becoming socialized into the norms of the podcasting community.

> For [my podcast], before I started using the Free Music Archive, I had a friend who was, at the time, making a lot of ambient music. And I was like, "Hey, can I use your music?" And he's like "Sure." Because I saw that other podcasts seemed to do the same thing.

Later, Stephen started to use music from the Free Music Archive, a curated collection of audio downloads that rights holders have made available for reuse. When he decided that he wanted to use a song from the folk group the Mountain Goats, he contacted lead vocalist John Darnielle for permission and received it from Darnielle's agent. In turn, Stephen suggested that he would be willing to make his own content available to use for free, with permission: "I'm totally cool with people using it, but I'd prefer if you asked first." All of this, he said, is a kind of "correct etiquette" that creators slowly pick up as they learn their practice.

Attribution was considered to be another important ethical practice. For some, this was simply about respect, or, as more than one participant phrased it, "giving credit where credit is due." On the other hand, Mark explained attribution as an alternative form of payment in an attention economy. This was especially true for those like YouTube creators for whom attribution in the form of a link or "shout-out" might increase traffic to their own channel and thus raise revenues from advertising.

Of course, not all creative fields nor all creators understand ethical practice in the same way. As participants in an art form rooted in a culture of borrowing and yet deeply impacted by strictly enforced copyright protections, the electronic and hip-hop musicians I spoke with had a somewhat different vision. As a composer of electronic music, Alec had deeply held beliefs about the inadequacy of copyright to address new musical practices. Indeed, he was the interview subject most focused throughout the conversation on copyright, which he believed benefitted corporations but worked only to create animosity among artists. He longed for "a more sophisticated system for crediting artists whose work we've sampled and whose work we've been inspired by." Until that system comes into play, Alec believes musicians must be open to others using their work without permission or credit, a belief he enacts through allowing and even encouraging others to reuse his music. As a rapper, Jorge held similar views about the need for support between musicians, saying, "[W]e need to be able to stand on one another." Not yet in the position where his own had been work sampled, Jorge nonetheless worked toward building community and an ethic of collaboration and exchange among local hip-hop artists by hosting their music on his own website.

Finally, the use of Creative Commons licenses was another avenue that many participants, no matter what their practice, believed provided the possibility for ethical relations among creators, one that ran the middle ground between informal relations between artists and those more formally instituted through copyright law. Matt pointed toward a common practice of requesting reciprocity in the use of such licenses by asking others who used his work to release it under the same license. Tim believed that Creative Commons and copyleft licensing worked toward leveling the playing field of cultural production, so that those creators without the resources to pay for sounds or images had access to high-quality materials. And Stephen expressed the feelings of many participants across artistic fields when he said he was "eternally grateful" to people who made their work freely available through such licenses "because I think they allow other creative people to do a lot more." Through their everyday activities and decision making, the participants expressed—and enacted—an understanding of the ethical and reciprocal dimensions of copyright.

Final Thoughts: Talking About Copyright in Media Education

My time spent talking with these young people made it amply clear that through their cultural practices, young creators regularly encounter the fundamental notions underlying copyright law. By sharing, copying, appropriating, and remixing digital materials (or having their own materials used in a similar fashion), they engaged with ideas of originality, authorship, ownership, profit, permission, and the commons. But perhaps the verbs "encounter" and "engage" are too passive. In fact, these young people made continuous decisions related to these concepts. They decided whether to copy a piece of code, whether to make an image available to the commons, whether to request permission to use a sample. To borrow the language of Canada's copyright law, they had to *deal*. And in doing, deciding, and dealing, they made choices about what seemed fair and ethical. Sometimes these choices were based on what they knew or believed about copyright law. More often, though, these choices were made by talking to peers, by looking at common practices in their field, or by turning to solutions like Creative Commons. Their choices were also affected by their own values, which included beliefs about fair exchange, about encouraging others, about ensuring their work was properly valued, and about creating equitable conditions for cultural producers with fewer resources.

So what does this mean for media education? Alec, when asked about how we might move toward the more harmonious relationships among musicians that he envisioned, suggested talking—talking openly about copyright and about the kinds of artistic practices musicians use. For all the seeming simplicity of that statement, I would agree. In many of the interviews, participants expressed pleasure and even relief in being able to speak about these subjects. Jorge interrupted his story about learning how to make rap music with his friends to tell me, "This is really cool. I'm glad I get to talk to you about this." Talking about copyright, about fairness, and about cultural production practices seems like a good starting place for new visions to be enacted and new understandings to be generated. It may also be a good place for media education to begin.

Yet as a number of education scholars have noted, copyright is only rarely talked about in classrooms and lecture halls (Burwell 2013; Palfrey et al. 2009). It is, as Dustin Edwards writes, "the elephant in the room" that many educators would prefer to ignore, given the lack of familiarity that many of us have with what appears to be a bewildering area of law (Edwards 2016: 52). Yet this is an elephant we need to address not in a single voice but in many. Writing in the context of American copyright law, John Palfrey and his colleagues at the Berkman Center for Internet and Society argue that "the teaching of copyright law must not only discourage illegal use of content but also describe the creative activities the law is designed to enable" (Palfrey et al. 2009: 91), an approach that emphasizes a balanced understanding of user's rights and responsibilities to creators. Critiquing the restrictive way that plagiarism and copyright are addressed in classrooms, Lea Evering and Gary Moorman (2012) advocate for broader discussions of copyright that include examples of artistic influence and exploration of the gray area that exists between building on the ideas of others and stealing them.

Based on my own research, I would suggest that these much needed conversations about copyright might also be accompanied with an even more expansive approach that addresses the social relations of young people's everyday media practices. Whether or not they see themselves as creators, most young people take part in the circulation, production, and interpretation of digital materials. Considering the kinds of relationships these activities foster is one way to raise the ethical questions that were central to the decision making of many of the participants.

To give just one example, students and teachers might inquire into the kinds of connections that are created through the appropriation of an independent creator's digital image. What are the possible ways that creators might feel about the appropriation (e.g., honored, exploited)? What impact might it have on them (e.g., increased attention for their work, loss of profit)? What kind of benefits accrue to the person who appropriates the image? What kind of relationship is established between the two parties (e.g., collaborative, consumerist, commercial)? And how might those relationships be altered by permission, attribution, or payment? These sorts of questions do not yield easy answers, but they do ask young people (and their teachers) to probe their own digital activities and to reflect on the kinds of interactions they hope to have in digital spaces.

Of course, these kinds of inquiries needn't be based only in dialogue. As Renee Hobbs and Katie Donnelly (2011) suggest, by producing their own media in classroom situations, young people are engaged in a process that requires them to make careful judgments about their use of digital materials. Making these kinds of judgments, Stuart Poyntz (2011) reminds us, "is not something we do on our own, because to judge is to form points of view or positions regarding others." In this way, through media production and through asking questions about the ethical relationships to others that are established through use of copyrighted material, young people enact the mediation of social relations that is at the heart of copyright law.

References

Boutros, A. (2014). "'My Real'll Make Yours a Rental': Hip Hop and Canadian Copyright." In R. Coombe, D. Wershler, & M. Zeilinger (Eds.), *Dynamic Fair Dealing: Creating Canadian Culture Online* (pp. 317–326). Toronto: University of Toronto Press.

Burwell, C. (2010). "Rewriting the Script: Toward a Politics of Young People's Digital Media Participation." *The Review of Education, Pedagogy and Cultural Studies*, 32(4–5), 382–402.

Burwell, C. (2013). "The Pedagogical Potential of Video Remix: Critical Conversations About Creativity, Culture and Copyright." *Journal of Adolescent and Adult Literacy*, 57(3), 205–213.

CCH Canadian Ltd. v. Law Society of Upper Canada, 2004 SCC 13 (CanLII).

Cohen, J. (2012). *Configuring the Networked Self: Law, Code and the Play of Everyday Practice*. New Haven, CT: Yale University Press.

Coombe, R. (1998). *The Cultural Life of Intellectual Properties: Authorship, Appropriation, and the Law*. Durham, NC: Duke University Press.

Coombe, R., Wershler, D., & Zeilinger, M. (2014). "Introducing Dynamic Fair Dealing: Creating Canadian Digital Culture." In R. Coombe, D. Wershler, & M. Zeilinger (Eds.), Dynamic Fair Dealing: Creating Culture Online (pp. 3–40). Toronto: University of Toronto Press.

Edwards, D. (2016). "Framing Remix Rhetorically: Toward a Typology of Transformative Work." *Computers and Composition*, 39, 41–54.

Evering, L. C., & Moorman, G. (2012). "Rethinking Plagiarism in the Digital Age." *Journal of Adolescent & Adult Literacy*, 56(1), 35–44.

Freund, K. (2016). "'Fair Use Is Legal Use': Copyright Negotiations and Strategies in the Fan-Vidding Community." *New Media & Society*, 18(7), 1347–1363.

Geist, M. (2013). "Fairness Found: How Canada Quietly Shifted from Fair Dealing to Fair Use." In M. Geist (Ed.), *The Copyright Pentalogy: How the Supreme Court of Canada Shook the Foundations of Canadian Copyright Law*. Ottawa: University of Ottawa Press.

Hobbs, R., & Donnelly, K. (2011). "Towards a Pedagogy of Fair Use for Multimedia Composition." In M. C. Rife, S. Slattery, & D. N. DeVoss (Eds.), *Copy(Write): Intellectual Property in the Writing Classroom* (pp. 275–294). West Lafayette, IN: Parlor Press.

Jenkins, H. (2006). "Confronting the Challenges of Participatory Culture: Media Education for the 21st Century." Working paper, MacArthur Foundation. http://digitallearning.macfound.org/

Murray, L. J. (2014a). "Deal with It." In R. Coombe, D. Wershler, & M. Zeilinger (Eds.), *Dynamic Fair Dealing: Creating Culture Online* (pp. 349–353). Toronto: University of Toronto Press.

Murray, L. J. (2014b). "Cultural Labor in a Small City: Motivations, Rewards, and Social Dynamics." In L. J. Murray, S. T. Piper, & K. Robertson (Eds.), *Putting Intellectual Property in Its Place: Rights Discourses, Creative Labor, and the Everyday* (pp. 132–157). New York: Oxford University Press.

Murray, L. J., & Trosow, S. E. (2013). *Canadian Copyright: A Citizen's Guide* (2nd ed.). Toronto: Between the Lines Press.

Palfrey, J., Gasser, U., Simun, M., & Barnes, R. F. (2009). "Youth, Creativity, and Copyright in the Digital Age." *International Journal of Learning and Media*, 1(2), 79–97.

Poyntz, S. (2011). "Critical Citizenship and Media Literacy Futures." *A Manifesto for Media Education*. www.manifestoformediaeducation.co.uk/

Théberge v. Galerie d'Art du Petit Champlain Inc., 2002 SCC 34 (CanLII).

Further Reading

Bannerman, S. (2013). *The Struggle for Canadian Copyright.* Vancouver: University of British Columbia Press.

Campbell, M. (2013). *Out of the Basement: Youth Cultural Production in Practice and Policy*. Montréal: McGill-Queen's University Press.

Cohen, J. (2007). "Creativity and Culture in Copyright Theory." *UC Davis Law Review*, 40, 1151–1205.

13

FAIR USE AS CREATIVE MUSE

An Ongoing Case Study

Malin Abrahamsson and Stephanie Margolin

Traditionally, academic libraries don't *teach* students, staff, or faculty much about copyright; rather, by approaching copyright law as something to be enforced, libraries have often assumed the role of de facto enforcers. Faculty, in turn, rely on library reserves departments to interpret copyright regulations and help them determine how much content they are *allowed* to provide to students. There is a primacy to their role as consumers, along with an attitude that copyright limits consumers' access to the content that they want. For students, if they think of copyright at all, it is generally outside the context of schoolwork, and again it is seen as restrictive, limiting file sharing, for example. In a world transitioning from print to digital media, change is necessary in how we think about, talk about, and teach copyright.

When it comes to copyright and academia, these old rules and paradigms no longer apply. For faculty, compliance with copyright regulations has become both more urgent—with cases like Georgia State (United States Court of Appeals for the 11th Circuit 2014) looming large over academic use of copyrighted material—and increasingly complex, in part due to the advent of e-books, PDFs of journal articles, and other electronica. What's more, as faculty continue to move their classes to online spaces and consider "open" (as in open access, or OA) spaces for their work, there are new rules and challenges. Faculty's role as content creators in the public sphere has expanded. While the coin of the realm continues to be academic journal articles, blog posts, tweets, digital conference presentations, and open access syllabi and course materials necessarily require faculty to take a new look at their behaviors as both content creators *and* consumers. How do we help faculty navigate these two approaches to content?

For students, too, the rules are changing. As virtually every college and university requires a "plagiarism" statement of some sort on all syllabi, students tend to conflate the concepts of plagiarism and copyright—and to fear and abhor them both as restrictive. Student work, however, is becoming increasingly public, open (again, as in OA) and multimodal. This leaves the ethical and cultural definitions of plagiarism banging against the legal definitions of copyright. What do the two ideas have in common, and how do they differ? How do we help students understand lessons of copyright that apply to both their personal and academic lives, and how do we begin to introduce students to the idea that they not only consume content but also create it?

We live in interesting times, and both of us (authors) love a good challenge. How, then, do we begin to change ideas about copyright on our campus (and, with this chapter, beyond our campus), without making the regulations of copyright seem overly stifling, restrictive, and antiquated? We asked ourselves: is there a way that we can help faculty and students to see the opportunities that copyright provides, not merely to content producers (though we encourage that thinking as well) but also to content consumers?

In this chapter, we discuss the approaches that we have tried with faculty and students at our college. We are an interesting team. One author, Margolin, is the instructional design librarian but has little prior experience with or knowledge of copyright. Author Abrahamsson is not a librarian but is the library's acquisitions manager and copyright assistant. Her position is somewhat unique among libraries but helps to show that copyright is important because it affects all of us and that fair use is and should be accessible by anyone—including those of us who are not lawyers. Each in our own way feels that our job is to point people (faculty, staff, and students) to the necessary resources. In teaming up, we realized that we could build on one another's strengths and on our shared enthusiasm. The idea that propelled us to rethink our outreach was to a large part inspired by the publication of the Association of Research Libraries' Code of Best Practices in Fair Use for Academic and Research Libraries (www.arl.org/storage/documents/publications/code-of-best-practices-fair-use.pdf) and its radical take on transformative use. By explicitly extending the concept of transformation to also include the *contextual* use of copyrighted material, this guiding document effectively invites new thinking and supports creative solutions to old problems. We are fortunate to have been able to conduct this work in an intuitive and experimental fashion; there were few expectations put on us and our instruction, so we were free to improvise and even to fail. Our attempts have advanced our own thinking on these topics, and we hope that by discussing them in this work we will bring them to a still larger audience.

Our case study is divided into four different programs that we developed for faculty and students at Hunter College, a public higher education institution with 23,000 undergraduate and graduate students enrolled in more than 170 academic programs, located in New York City and part of the City University of New York (CUNY) system. As we will see in the pages that follow, it is only through courageous, collaborative, and creative approaches to teaching copyright that we can discover "what works" to advance the knowledge of faculty and students in making wise decisions about the use of copyrighted content in (and beyond) education. Through this process we have collaborated closely with faculty and staff with the goal of providing pragmatic and creative approaches to copyright and fair use.

Program 1: The Faculty Seminar

Hunter College's center for teaching and learning, known as the Academic Center for Excellence in Research Teaching (ACERT), sponsors a regularly scheduled Lunchtime Seminar series. This series provides a rare opportunity to speak directly to a small but interested group of faculty about various aspects of their pedagogy. Academic library faculty and staff occasionally use these sessions to share new ideas and programs within the broad realm of library instruction in the hopes of building interest and finding new faculty with whom we might collaborate.

During the 2014 spring semester, we felt the time was right for a new kind of conversation about copyright and fair use, and so we presented a Lunchtime Seminar entitled "How to Use (and Transform) Stuff That You Don't Own." The title signaled our (not so hidden) agenda, which was to begin to transform the way that Hunter College faculty saw the topic of copyright and fair use, moving beyond the traditional focus on compliance with copyright requirements. Unlike other programs, where librarians simply share a curated collection of resources, we instead modeled the reasoning and critical-thinking practices that are needed to make a fair use determination, showcasing fair use reasoning in the context of classroom instruction. As we were inviting faculty to think in new ways about "borrowing" materials—we believed that we would have to model our lesson, demonstrating transformative use, rather than simply talking about it. Ultimately, our demonstrations were twofold: we created a lesson using transformative use, and, within that, we presented material from a colleague's lesson, which was another example of transformative use.

First, we must describe our own transformative use of copyrighted materials for teaching and learning. As luck would have it, in early 2014, an episode of *The Good Wife*, a popular CBS legal drama, considered a case of copyright infringement (King, King, & Schellhaas 2014: "Goliath and David"; Season 5, episode 11; air date January 5, 2014). We decided to let the characters of the drama do some of our teaching for us, and this fictitious television case became the center of our presentation. In this episode, the plot includes a storyline about musicians who have created a pop cover of a rap song and now believe that their version of the song has been "stolen" by a popular television show. The musicians seek legal advice because they would like to sue for a portion of the profits on the song.

To prepare, we purchased a streaming license for the particular episode. We then watched several times to carefully select the necessary scenes. In our presentation, we alternated between showing the video clips and offering key ideas in our instruction, not only providing feedback and context for the ideas about copyright related to the TV show but explicitly outlining how, in order for this to be transformative use, we—as educators—needed to show only the relevant portions that contributed to our lesson, no more, but thankfully also no less. This is a great example of how there is no "magic number"; use the amount of content that is needed to tell your story.

Then, we addressed the pedagogical value of discussing copyright and fair use using the University of Minnesota Libraries' excellent interactive web tool, Thinking Through Fair Use (www.lib.umn.edu/copyright/fairthoughts). The website invites users to reflect on the four factors in considering how fair use may apply to their particular context and situation of use. Users complete the form, which encourages them to reflect on their particular use of copyrighted content. We believe that one strength of this tool is that it is not prescriptive; rather, it encourages users to *think* and *discuss*. It provides a scaffolding to help guide deeper thinking about one's use of copyrighted materials and to structure an argument. By highlighting the intentionally ambiguous legal formulation of fair use, the tool effectively validates the gray areas, helping users see where their usage supports and does not support fair use. As a result, users can formulate their own arguments as to whether their [usage] is fair use. It appropriately presents the gray areas of fair use evaluation and supports and scaffolds their arguments about whether a given example constitutes fair use.

Finally, in the context of pedagogy and innovations to one's teaching, we showed a second example of transformative use, created by a former librarian colleague, Danielle Becker. To demonstrate the complexity of bias in sources for an undergraduate research class, Becker illustrated her lesson with a carefully selected scene from the television drama, *The West Wing*. In this scene, the characters discuss and show examples of the biases inherent in maps ("Somebody's Going to Emergency, Somebody's Going to Jail"; Season 2, episode 16; air date February 28, 2001). We learn about a fictional professional organization of cartographers who want to replace the familiar Mercator projection map with an inverted version of the Gall-Peters projection map, arguing that the Mercator project map distorts the scale, location, and relative position of developing countries. The episode points out that even maps have a representational bias. We pointed out that Professor Becker included only the specific scenes of the television show that were relevant to the point she was raising with her students.

Fair use is, perhaps frustratingly, all about the gray areas. To illustrate this point, we showed a concluding scene from *The Good Wife* that appropriately muddies the copyright issues by introducing music experts who disagree on the satirical (and thus transformative) nature of the work.

At this point, we moved the discussion to situations where fair use will *not* apply: when people use others' copyrighted materials for decorative illustrations or when they use copyrighted music for the background of their videos, for example. Such cases provide the opportunity to introduce Creative Commons licensing and searching and to discuss some of the ways that open access materials can be useful for content consumers. As always, our goal is to empower, so we directed faculty to sources that they can legally use, often without seeking permission or paying any fees. However, we stress the importance of attribution, reminding faculty and staff of their role as creators who, in turn, want their own work to also serve as a building block.

Lessons Learned

Even when faculty are exposed to a presentation like this one, transformation of habits and attitudes takes a good deal of time. On the one hand, faculty response to our presentation opened eyes. Faculty likely attended our presentation because they may be using copyrighted materials, often in the development of their hybrid or online courses. Because they are learning a new pedagogy *and* new technology, their use of media and other copyright-protected materials is often haphazard. And, in several cases, their response was one of fear or hesitation. In fact, despite our assertions to the contrary, in the eyes of some, we became the "copyright police." A small number of attendees had experience with copyright-protected materials and habitually sought permissions rather than take advantage of the protection of fair use. For these users, too, we may have moved the needle, but it was slow and gradual. We continue to work with faculty in other ACERT settings, and this presentation is one we would like to offer on a semiannual basis because the needle is so slow to move. As contexts change, we have found that faculty may hear the same presentation with new ears. What's more, new faculty members who may benefit from the learning experience arrive on a regular basis.

Program 2: Hands-On Workshops for Faculty

Twice annually, ACERT offers a week-long intensive training aimed at faculty who will be teaching online or hybrid courses in the upcoming year. Faculty spend the week preparing an online module, either transforming a traditional face-to-face experience or developing a new wholly online one. Working with ACERT's instructional technologists and other guests, faculty are supported in their course design. The participants are introduced to a variety of organizational strategies and design tools that utilize a range of technologies in support of teaching and learning.

We are regularly asked to present a hands-on workshop as part of this curriculum, as faculty are often considering which materials they can use and how. This tends to be a small group, allowing us to be highly responsive to the individual needs of each cohort and consequently with our material changes with each presentation. We ask each faculty member to introduce themselves and describe their course, what types of materials they currently use, and whether there is a specific rationale for this use. We cover topics such as copyright, fair use, and suggested tools and information about how to find and use other people's materials without running into copyright problems.

It is a common misconception among faculty that, because online and hybrid college courses are educational, any copyrighted material used in them is categorically permitted and/or considered fair use. We begin by teasing out different types of use to address this misunderstanding and encourage a deeper analysis. For example, we might point to the difference between using a specific image because it illustrates a key concept in the course and using that image as a decorative banner. Participants then take a moment to consider the purposes of the materials they will be using in their course.

Decorative Use

Very often, we found that faculty wanted to find material for decorative purposes in order to make their website or PowerPoint slides more attractive. They sometimes use images or visual material merely to attract and hold attention. They were surprised to learn that this use also requires fair use analysis for copyrighted material. We then introduced Creative Commons and demonstrated how to search for images, sound, and video with limited or no copyright restrictions. We also asked faculty to explore how search results may vary depending on media and license settings in Creative Commons.

Educational Use

We next talked about where to find and how to use educational content that is accessible through the library (i.e., subscription databases). Thus far, we have only advised faculty designing online and hybrid courses aimed at Hunter students (restricted access behind a login). Consequently, for these courses, we have used material that is restricted to the Hunter community, explained how to find material using library tools, and how to correctly embed it in the course.

Transformative Use

The authors find the conversation about transformative use to be the most rewarding because this is where we can encourage faculty creativity. A conversation about intentionality may help people think about their purpose in a new way and understand that transformative use can be conceptual. Relevant and meaningful examples illustrate this point better than abstract discussion, and we have tried to give suggestions that were based on the topics and material that faculty members were already working with. For example, advertising can be used for the critical study of culture and gender, and popular Hollywood productions similarly can illustrate key concepts in a course. It is the recontextualization of the original intents behind these familiar works that constitutes the transformative aspect of fair use. What's more, in changing the context of these works for students, they can become powerful learning tools.

Lessons Learned

The most significant lesson we've learned from this scenario is to work with the faculty while they are actively creating. Rather than working with abstract what-ifs, we are able to make our instruction directly relevant as we listen and respond to the needs of our participants in real time.

Program 3: Student Workshops in Freshman Composition

Hunter offers over 100 sections of Freshman Composition (ENGL 120) each year, all of which conform to a standard curriculum including a scaffolded research paper assignment. Each section is required to have at least one session with a librarian, and, most often, these library sessions introduce students to college-level databases to prepare them for the research that they will be doing. Beginning in fall 2014, several Hunter instructors launched a small pilot ENGL 120 with a multimodal focus where, in addition to the required research paper, students also created a digital project to be publicly displayed (e.g., YouTube or Vimeo) at the student's discretion. Having identified that this student work would be publicly displayed, the authors reached out to an instructor of this initial pilot, Jack Kenigsberg, and we agreed to collaborate on fair use instruction.

The authors remember this pair of workshops (two sections of the same course, both taught by Kenigsberg) as initially disappointing. However, upon further reflection, there were several positive aspects to these two student-facing workshops. Most importantly, our relationship with Kenigsberg helped make this collaboration successful. Like us, Kenigsberg is willing to experiment. His teaching is innovative: he adopted the multimodal pilot, and he was eager for us to bring fair use instruction to his students. What's more, he understood that such instruction would take time. Not only did we work with his students for one full-class session, Kenigsberg also devoted additional class time to jointly developed fair use–related activities.

Our final curriculum for this class had three parts. First, Kenigsberg administered an in-class "pre-assessment" given via Google Form a few days before our scheduled visit. Both the authors and Kenigsberg were able to review results and assess student knowledge of the subject. Next, the authors came into the classroom to work with the students for one class period. Finally, several weeks later, Kenigsberg gave the students a "real-world" assignment where they completed an analysis of one of the objects they were using in their multimodal projects.

Pre-Assessing Student Knowledge

We asked students seven multiple-choice questions and one that required a short answer. We deliberately created questions that played on common perceptions and misperceptions about copyright. We provided more than one correct answer among our multiple choices, and in several cases, all answers were correct. However, by seeing the answers that students did select, we began to learn what they did and did not know about copyright. For example, one of our questions was, "What is the process of getting copyright?" Despite the fact that all of the answers we listed were correct, in looking at the answer that most students selected, we knew where to focus our teaching. (See the Appendix for a full list of copyright questions and answers.)

We included a short-answer question ("Why is copyright relevant to this class?") to provide a starting point for our in-person conversation with the students. Perhaps the most common response that we saw was students who conflated and confused the concepts of copyright and plagiarism, as well as the punishments associated with each. On the flip side, some students correctly identified positive aspects of copyright: it protects the author; it helps keep works safe from replication. Others noted that copyright related to their ability to use "outside" materials (e.g., materials that they did not create). A small number of students recognized themselves as content creators who were therefore protected by copyright. Interestingly, it was only a few students who correctly identified how copyright was relevant to the assignment in this particular class.

The pre-assessment helped us to see that our preparations were on target. The challenges included clarifying the differences between copyright and plagiarism and encouraging students to see themselves as content creators, producing work that was, in turn, copyrightable.

In-Class Curriculum

In addition to the content of our workshop, we were primarily concerned with effectively engaging with our students, a problem that author Margolin has often found in similar "one-shot sessions." As we prepared to meet the students, we tried to balance a curriculum that was informative, useful, and fun. We prepared our lesson with feedback from Kenigsberg, who prompted, "Personally, I'm less interested in finding materials that are 'safe' and more interested in how to use 'unsafe' materials with fair use or transformative use"(Kenigsberg, personal communication October 3, 2014). Kenigsberg's input helped us to fine-tune what would be most relevant to the students in this particular class.

The pre-assessment results provided an entry into our direct work with the students. We reassured them that, for the most part, they were on target and that *almost* everything is copyrightable. We began to wrestle with the confusion between copyright and plagiarism, pointing out the differences and thus further clarifying the importance of copyright in this class.

We discussed students' roles as both consumer and creator. We used a think-pair-share exercise for students to consider their interests in copyright from both perspectives. We also introduced the idea of Creative Commons licenses, which provided a nice transition, again, from a producer (who uses a CC license on her work) to a consumer, who might opt to search by CC license to find appropriate materials.

The bulk of our talk was about fair use and transformative use. We discussed the origins and rationale behind the concept of fair use, as well as the four factors. Since the students were to create their own short films using found materials, we illustrated our discussion of transformative use with a video mashup and then worked as a class to analyze the four factors in the context of this video.

Final Assignment

Several weeks after our visit, in conjunction with their video assignment deadline, each student had to select one item from her mashup and analyze its use with the Thinking About Fair Use analysis tool. It was here that we found a wrinkle in our collaboration. The authors had intended for this to be a brief writing assignment for the students, where they would apply what they had learned in class, with prompts from the tool. Instead, Kenigsberg assigned them to use the tool to reflect on one of the objects, with no writing assignment attached. This shifted the exercise from one of analysis and critical thinking to one more oriented toward button pushing and completing an online form. Students were not required to provide evidence and did not use this tool for its intended purpose: to develop an argument.

Lessons Learned

True collaboration is essential. One of the great strengths of this particular experience was the strong collaboration between the authors and the instructor, Jack Kenigsberg. He understood the importance of fair use and transformative use for his students, particularly in the context of their multimodal assignment. To that end, he was willing to collaborate with us on assignment design and provide feedback. That said, no collaboration is perfect. In our final assignment, we were unclear about the work product. We envisioned the follow-up as a written critical analysis of whether the use of one item from their project constituted fair use. We feel that our impact would have been greater and student learning would have improved with the follow-up assignment as we had designed it. However, Kenigsberg's feedback continued to be supportive. He said that his students' work "showed they understood the concepts and could apply them" (Kenigsberg, personal communication February 9, 2015). We look forward to trying the writing assignment in a future workshop.

We also learned that it is important to use every engagement strategy that you can think of. A presentation about fair use and copyright has all of the usual challenges of one-shot instruction, and more. Many students carry severe anxiety related to the punitive nature of plagiarism (e.g., harsh punishments for plagiarism that they may consider accidental or confusing). These students may also erroneously link plagiarism and copyright. This results in a class full of students who, at best, do not want to hear what librarians are teaching and, at worst, may have anxieties about it. We used humor. Our pretest, for example, contained silly answers designed to help alleviate some of the anxiety that students might be feeling. We presented a campy mashup based on the popular film *Top Gun* that transforms the narrative. We attempted to be approachable and to make the material so. In the end, we could have done even more: a lesson that promoted active learning would likely have enhanced the experience for students or perhaps a question–answer format where they were invited to ask us questions.

We learned the importance of linking lessons directly to assignment. Overall, our work was relevant to the students' multimodal assignments. However, our lessons lost some of their relevance: "when it came to actually making their movies, a lot of them were so clearly in violation of copyright that I could have made a small fortune in finder fees. . . . That's probably because I told them a few times that I didn't actually care that much how often they violated copyright. I should probably stop doing that" (Kenigsberg, personal communication February 9, 2015). His own goal for the course was to give students the intellectual experience of creating these multimodal projects, and, ultimately, no doubt like many of his fellow instructors, he decided that (in this case) copyright rules got in the way (though from his comments, perhaps he is reconsidering that approach). We also learned that it's hard to expand our target audience of faculty members within the institution. While adjustments are needed, we feel that we have the start of a solid and innovative copyright/fair use lesson for undergraduates that is well aligned with the nature of the undergraduate Freshman English course. However, it has proven difficult to get more faculty interested and to reach more students. We have therefore opted to aim even bigger—spreading the word *outside* our institution in the hopes that others might adapt our lesson ideas to their own campus needs.

Program 4: Student Workshops in Studio Art and Combined Media

In 2015, we received two separate invitations by art instructors Constance DeJong and Peter Dudek to speak to their students about fair use. In both cases, the instructors wanted us to follow up on previous class discussions. In preparation, we collaboratively selected a series of relevant readings about art and appropriation that the students completed before our visits.

In the early spring of 2015, instructor Peter Dudek invited us to visit his Studio Art (Art 101) class. These undergraduates were already somewhat familiar with copyright: after a class visit to a gallery showing work by Richard Prince, they had briefly discussed a couple of the most infamous art-related copyright cases (*Cariou v. Prince* and *Davidovici v. Koons*). We knew that these students had a basic understanding of copyright and wanted to build upon their existing knowledge. We therefore suggested a selection of recent news articles about *Prince* and *Koons*, as well as an article in *The New York Times*, about artists who are using other people's photography in their work.

In the classroom, first we contrasted Koons' and Prince's works with those of the plaintiff in each case in order to demonstrate how to conduct a fair use analysis using the four factors. Our work included a discussion of transformative use and the difficulty in quantifying it, particularly in cases that concern nonliteral material such as fine art and music. We wanted the students to understand that fair use analysis is subjective with no established or fixed limits and that well reasoned arguments often constitute the best defense.

For the second half of our workshop, we used a role-playing activity. We divided the students into four groups in order to consider the arguments of each side in the fair use analysis of two separate artworks. Two groups represented the artists' viewpoints, and the other two represented those whose work had been appropriated. Each group conducted a fair use analysis based on their assumed role. For this portion of the workshop, the authors walked around the room, answered questions, and helped get the conversations started. We asked the groups to record their findings on posters we have prepared in advance, listing the four factors. We closed with a full-class discussion. This session was effective because we were able to build on what we'd learned in our Engl 120 class, most significantly in transforming our exercise to one of active learning. As artists, our students more readily self-identified as creators, they had prepared with readings in advance, and we had great support from Professor Dudek. It was ultimately effective to have students work in teams, with each team formulating an argument.

In September of 2015, Professor Constance DeJong invited us to do a 1-hour presentation on fair use to the students in her Combined Media (ARTCR 290) course. This small class of undergraduates had already discussed the works by Omer Fast and Christian Marclay, two artists who make use of existing video material. Before our visit, DeJong had explained, "Almost every semester I am asked by students to explain the consequences/legalities of using found and/or appropriated materials" (DeJong, personal communication September 5, 2015). Encouraged by the students' already existing awareness and interest in the topic, we assigned them our reading list in preparation for our visit.

We knew that this small class was comprised of students who were already raising important questions about copyright in their own work, and we decided to experiment with a class discussion that was much less structured than our previous workshops. Our goal was to encourage the students to actively participate in a discussion about Marclay and Fast and to understand how skillfully these video artists utilize fair use in the making of their work. We began by asking the students to explain how they use other people's material in their own work. We wanted the students to think critically about how, why, and to whom their work may be transformative and to understand that this type of purposeful reasoning constitutes the very core of fair use. We let the students' questions guide the discussion, and, rather than provide simple yes-or-no answers to their questions about what may or may not be fair use, we made the class partake in our reasoning. The last few minutes of our presentation was spent on the so-called Dancing baby case (*Lenz v. Universal*), which had been settled a few days prior to our visit.

Lessons Learned

We were able to build upon our previous guided discussions with students and make what we felt was a strong lesson plan the second time around. The students in both art classes were engaged and inquisitive, and they had not only a firm grasp of the concept of fair use but also a vested interest in forming strong arguments for their opinions. According to Professor DeJong, the issue of fair use comes up in class:

> not so much because of the syllabus and/or specific assignments, but rather because appropriation has become such a common aspect of making art. And, the meaning of "appropriation" has changed from simply using found objects . . . to manipulating/transforming/metamorphosing existing material, particularly images but also sound/music.
> (DeJong, personal communication September 5, 2015)

DeJong also pointed to the persistent confusion that surrounds plagiarism and copyright and said:

> Nearly every college student is aware of plagiarism when it comes to fulfilling writing assignments in their classes. But the issue is more nuanced and confusing when it comes to using existing material in their art. On the one hand they see instances of appropriation all over the place—in art, on-line, in popular music, etc.—and on the other hand they hear of legal suits brought against artists like Richard Prince, Sherry Levine whose work entails appropriated material.
> (DeJong, personal communication September 5, 2015)

Referencing their own work during class discussions, these students naturally identified as content creators who wanted protection for their work but at the same time also understood the importance of being able to use and build upon other's works. They offered intuitive and well articulated responses and asked nuanced follow-up questions. Instructor Dudek thought his students had taken an active interest in the topic and said:

> I think because there were several prominent examples of artists having copyright issues (that we had previously discussed) helped the students engage. That, coupled with the texts you sent, and the Richard Prince exhibit which we saw . . . before you came, kept the students on point. Plus we have weekly dialogs/crits, so maybe verbal feedback . . . is more part of an art class (a requirement actually).
> (Dudek, personal communication May 20, 2015)

Asked what he thought the students had learned by our workshop, Dudek elaborated: "The students did think that copyright, in general, was historically more related to written material. And that artists are getting sued now simply because of the prices [that art] is selling for these days" (Dudek, personal communication May 20, 2015).

These workshops were one-offs in the sense that they included only a few preparatory readings and no assignment or other practical follow-up. However, we learned that the ability to identify as both consumer and creator of content is essential to the understanding of the transformative aspect of fair use. At first we thought that this "dual identity" may come more naturally to the creative art students—and perhaps even more so now than ever before as the definition of art continues to be stretched to include already existing content that has been made by people other than the artists themselves. As we prepared this chapter, however, we have come to realize that our skills and material improved over time as we became more comfortable in our roles as copyright educators and could engage the students more successfully by asking relevant and provoking questions.

Conclusion

Fair use and transformative use offer the potential to launch many interesting and worthwhile discussions with students and faculty. Returning to the questions that we asked ourselves in the introduction, we return as well to the authors' starting points. While we've outlined lessons learned from each of the four scenarios, we wonder what are the broader lessons learned over nearly two years of interacting with faculty and students on these issues?

The first time we took part in the hands-on faculty workshop, we had an interesting conversation about using work that wasn't one's own. In designing a hybrid course, one instructor wanted to show samples of past student work to assist her future students. When we changed the context and asked how she would feel if she learned that her own work could be included in a course without her permission, it was a great aha moment. From there, we were able to open the door to faculty's role as content creators, as well as consumers, and to help put a real purpose to the previously abstract notion of Creative Commons licenses. For faculty—and students too—illustrating their role as both creators and consumers has been a helpful model. In thinking about ourselves as producers and consumers, we can effectively start the conversation about copyright, fair use, and transformative use in a positive and creative place.

For students, it's time to be very clear about the differences between copyright and plagiarism, as well as the reasons for each. As Professor DeJong pointed out, most college students are highly aware of plagiarism being a problem but often confuse it with copyright when they want to incorporate existing material into their own work. While our workshops stress copyright over plagiarism, it's important for us, as teachers, to know and acknowledge where students are coming from in order to better understand their anxiety about this topic. Again, casting them as creators *can* help to change the conversation: we hypothesized that this *might* have been one reason that our workshops with art students were so successful. On the other hand, it might also be that our student-facing workshops became progressively less structured and instead focused more on being responsive. We started out with a structured three-part lesson plan (Program 3), and by the time we visited Professor DeJong's art students (Program 4), we relied entirely on specialized readings, tailored examples, and specific questions *directed to the students* about their work. Small-class discussions are also more effective than the larger-class lecture model that we used in the English classes (Program 4 versus Program 3). We are glad to see so many of our students working on academic and artistic projects that have a public face, and we believe with the increasingly public nature of student work—and of all of our lives—that a more sophisticated understanding of copyright, fair use, and transformative use is essential.

Finally, on some level, we believe it is our role to spread our enthusiasm for the *creativity* of fair use and transformative use. When we first began our outreach, we wanted to see if we could complicate the conversation around copyright and infuse it with a sense of possibility to counter the pervasive negativity. Faculty often find fair use analysis a tedious and time-consuming exercise that inevitably leads to unhelpful limitations. ("A clean-cut number or amount would be so much easier! Why not draw a line at 10%?") Many students, on the other hand, have strong ideas about the challenges of copyright and see no reason why or how it can benefit them as individuals.

Across the board, however, what seems to reach both students and faculty on a personal level are questions about authorship and other people's potential use of *their own work*. With good, real-life examples and relevant questions that are directly geared to a particular audience and/or use, students and faculty quickly understand that they are *both* consumers and creators with a stake in the ongoing conversation about copyright. From this perspective, the idea that recontextualization of copyrighted material may qualify as transformative fair use can take on a both personal and practical meaning, and the authors' enthusiasm about launching this copyright-related outreach project comes from this realization. Through our talks, workshops, and presentations, we have tried to bring these critical and pertinent questions directly to faculty and students. If we have accomplished nothing else through our work, we have at least approached the topic with a genuine interest and excitement.

References

King, M., King, R., & Schellhaas, L., (Writers) and Kennedy, B. (Director.) (2014, January 5). "Goliath and David." [Television series episode]. In "Scott Free Productions and King Size Productions." [Producers] *The Good Wife*. Los Angeles: CBS Television studios. Retrieved from www.amazon.com/gp/product/B00ESNE696/ref=dv_web_yvl_list_pr_0_ba

United States Court of Appeals for the 11th Circuit. (2014). *Cambridge University Press, Oxford University Press, Inc., Sage Publications, Inc. versus Carl V. Patton, et al.* D.C. Docket No. 1:08-cv-01425-ODE. Retrieved from http://media.ca11.uscourts.gov/opinions/pub/files/201214676.pdf

University of Minnesota Libraries. (n.d.). *Thinking Through Fair Use*. University of Minnesota Libraries. [Web page]. Retrieved from www.lib.umn.edu/copyright/fairthoughts

Further Reading

Adler, P. S., Aufderheide, P., Butler, B., & Jaszi, P. (2012, January). Code of Best Practices in Fair Use for Academic and Research Libraries. Retrieved from www.arl.org/storage/documents/publications/code-of-best-practices-fair-use.pdf

Aufderheide, P., & Jaszi, P. (2008). "Recut, Reframe, Recycle: Quoting Copyrighted Material in User-Generated Video." Center for Social Media, American University, 2008. Retrieved from http://archive.cmsimpact.org/sites/default/files/CSM_Recut_Reframe_Recycle_report.pdf

Fiesler, C., & Bruckman, A. S. (2014). "Remixers' Understandings of Fair Use Online." Retrieved from https://cfiesler.files.wordpress.com/2016/02/cscw2014_fiesler.pdf

Appendix

A Questionnaire to Assess Students' Copyright Knowledge

What kinds of materials can be copyrighted?

- Everything
- Nothing on the Internet
- Paintings, movies, books
- Commercially produced products like Disney and iPads

Where can you find copyrighted material?

- Everywhere
- Only in the library or on library websites
- Never on the Internet

Who benefits from copyright?

- Creative artists, musicians, and filmmakers
- College professors

- Big corporations, i.e., Apply and Disney
- Any individual

Who loses out with copyright?

- Creative artists, musicians, and filmmakers
- College professors
- Big corporations, i.e., Apply and Disney
- Any individual

Who can be a copyright owner?

- Creative artists, musicians, and filmmakers
- College professors
- Big corporations, i.e., Disney and Apple
- Any individual

What is the process of getting copyright?

- Add a © to your materials.
- Register with the U.S. Copyright Office.
- Do nothing. If your work is copyrightable, it's automatically under copyright.
- Big corporations hire expensive lawyers to do this.

What can happen if you violate copyright?

- You get lots of stuff (movies, books, etc.) without paying for it. No big deal.
- You may get sued.
- You may receive a request from the copyright owners' lawyers asking you to stop using the copyrighted material.
- Nothing

Why is copyright relevant to this class?

____

____

____

____

14

DIGITAL TRANSFORMATIONS IN THE ARTS AND HUMANITIES

Negotiating the Copyright Landscape in the United Kingdom

Smita Kheria, Charlotte Waelde, and Nadine Levin

The modern era—characterised by social media, Web 2.0 technologies, and the "Open Access" movement—is one of the most challenging legal, technological, political, economic, and social environments that the copyright framework has dealt with since it was formally recognised in the Statute of Anne in 1710. Copyright seems always to have raised challenges for arts and humanities researchers, for research processes and for the content that they develop, but these challenges have intensified in the digital era. Copyright was established with individual authorship, limited borrowings, and analogue copying in mind. While research content was once predominantly text based, it now takes many and varied forms, making the application of copyright increasingly convoluted. With digitisation and digital technologies—which embrace co-creation, unlimited reuse, and the absence of barriers to copying—the materials, processes, and outcomes of research have changed. Tensions arise at the interface of creating, managing, and exploiting copyright content and also of conducting innovative research, the outcomes of which are accessible, exchangeable, and engaging.

In this environment, an important question for arts and humanities research is how do the researchers themselves engage with copyright during the research process and in the production of creative works, and what copyright-related challenges emerge? In this chapter, we explore how researchers in the arts and humanities negotiate and navigate the legal landscape in the United Kingdom in order to obtain and use materials for creative and transformative use. We use findings from a pilot project, Copyright and Publicly-Funded Arts and Humanities Research, in which we examined six academic research projects as case studies in order to highlight two types of challenges: (1) the challenges faced by arts and humanities researchers in accessing material held in archives both in and out of copyright and (2) challenges posed by the exceptions to copyright as they carry out their research processes.

The Arts and Humanities Research Council (AHRC), which has more than fifty disciplines within its remit (AHRC 2013: 5), is a major funder of arts and humanities research in the UK. It has made a total of more than £700 million of funding available for arts and humanities research since it received its Royal Charter in 2005 (AHRC 2013: 6). In recent years, the AHRC has funded increasingly innovative research and has used increasingly innovative mechanisms to distribute funding to targeted projects. Recognising the growing importance of "digital," the AHRC established the Digital Transformations theme, which was designed to fund projects rooted in the expectation of transformation and experimentation. Conscious also of the opportunities for arts and humanities researchers to engage with the creative industries, the AHRC funded a series of Knowledge Exchange Hubs for the Creative Economy (KE Hubs), which in turn have funded partnerships between researchers and creative industry partners in relation to projects that straddle the academy and the creative economy.

We were commissioned by the AHRC to conduct a pilot project in which we examined the relationships between copyright, publicly funded arts and humanities research, and research processes in the digital era. Our research was based on case studies of six different AHRC-funded projects: three funded under the Digital Transformation theme[1] and three funded by one of the KE hubs, REACT. To study the cases, we conducted twelve semistructured interviews, lasting approximately 2 hours each, with selected participants from each of these funded projects, between May and July 2014. The Appendix provides a list of the six academic case studies.

In this chapter, we focus on two case studies: (1) Transforming Musicology, a three-year project to demonstrate how scholarly research into music can be transformed through digital culture and digital methods and whose main outputs are a searchable online database for analysing collections of music, and a collection of software tools for musicological analysis; and (2) JtR125, a three-month project, to develop a "playable documentary" about the Jack the Ripper murders, by combining historical photography and media with modern 3D game elements.

We highlight how researchers struggle to navigate the landscape of copyright exceptions and negotiate access to out-of-copyright materials and how they use creative workarounds to accomplish their research objectives. In each section, we first introduce the relevant legal framework in the UK and then discuss the challenges faced by the researchers by referring to previous research and drawing upon interview data from our two case studies. In doing so, we underline the tensions that arise for the researchers due to the nature and scope of copyright exceptions, the lack of ease in obtaining data and source material that is creatively satisfactory, and the need for commercialising outputs of funded projects, at the same time promoting the value of the research to the public and society. Ultimately, in the final section, we briefly comment on current policy developments to underline that arts and humanities researchers operate in a fluid and complex legal environment.

Navigating Copyright Exceptions in the UK

Although the copyright framework can pose a range of potential challenges for researchers, a key challenge lies around copyright exceptions. Copyright law in the United Kingdom provides for a number of exceptions that are designed to give to the user of a copyright-protected work a defence to an action of infringement of copyright if the use falls within the exception. The Copyright, Designs and Patents Act 1988 (CDPA 1988) sets out a range of "acts which may be done in relation to copyright works notwithstanding the subsistence of copyright," otherwise known as "permitted acts" (CDPA 1988: s28). These acts can be carried out by users without the copyright owner's permission or licence, subject to the terms and conditions specified by the statute. These exceptions to the rights of the copyright owner allow uses of copyright works for various purposes, such as private study, reporting current events, non-commercial research, criticism, review, quotation, parody, and also certain uses by various bodies such as educational establishments, libraries, and archives (CDPA 1988: ss 28–76).

The UK's copyright laws must also be in conformity with relevant European Union law, and the approximation and partial harmonisation of specific areas of copyright in the EU (Kur & Dreier 2013; Halpern & Johnson 2014). The Information Society Directive (InfoSoc Directive) (Directive 2001/29/EC 2001) introduced exceptions and limitations to copyright infringement in the EU by providing for a list of twenty-one exceptions. All but one of these exceptions are optional, in that member states may provide them in their national laws but are not required to (Article 5). The list is exhaustive in relation to digital uses of copyright and, as such, limits the ability of the United Kingdom to introduce new exceptions that fall outside the scope of this list (Bechtold 2006: 367).

The specific list of copyright exceptions and limitations in the UK (and EU) stands in contrast to U.S. law, where a general "fair use" defence covers a range of purposes for which copyright owner's permission is not required (U.S. Copyright Act 1976, § 107). The U.S. legislation only indicates the factors to be taken into account in the assessment of fair use, while the courts have developed purposes, such as criticism, research, and parody, to which the defence may apply. In the EU, a general copyright exception akin to the U.S. "fair use" defence was suggested during the negotiation of the InfoSoc Directive due to concerns that an exhaustive and predetermined list of exceptions would not allow quick adaptation to rapid technological changes (Mazziotti 2008: 79). However, the proposal for such a general fair use exception was rejected (Waelde et al. 2016). A recent review, aimed at copyright reform in the UK, also noted that the adoption of a fair use exception was unlikely to be legally feasible in European law (Hargreaves 2011).

The most important copyright exceptions in the UK for researchers have been (1) fair dealing with any kind of work for the purposes of criticism and review, if accompanied by sufficient acknowledgement (CDPA 1988 §.30(1)); and (2) fair dealing with any kind of work for the purpose of non-commercial research, if accompanied by sufficient acknowledgement (CDPA 1988 § 29(1)). However, these exceptions have posed problems for researchers, both in terms of how they are applied and interpreted in practice and also in terms of the scope and nature of copying and use that they permit.

For example, in 2006, a report from the British Academy considered the challenges posed by the restrictive interpretation of exceptions and limitations to copyright law for researchers in the humanities and social sciences (British Academy 2006). The report found that such researchers faced challenges due to copyright law and noted that "recent developments in technology, legislation, and practice have meant that the specific exemptions, which are provided by copyright to enable scholarly work to advance, are not in some cases achieving the intended purpose" (British Academy 2006: 3). While the exceptions for criticism and review and non-commercial research "[were] normally sufficient for academic and scholarly use," such use in practice was impeded by the narrow interpretation of these exceptions by rights owners and publishers (British Academy 2006: 8). A more recent collection of essays from The British Library also provided practical examples of how copyright affects the broader research community in the UK in relation to the restrictive interpretation and limited scope of existing fair dealing exceptions available to educators and researchers (British Library 2010).

In the last ten years, copyright exceptions have been a key issue in the discussions on copyright reform in the UK (Gowers Review 2006; Hargreaves Review 2011) with particular focus given to how they could be adapted suitably for the digital environment. For instance, an independent review of intellectual property (Hargreaves Review 2011) recommended the reform of copyright exceptions for researchers and scholars. It suggested that copyright was a barrier to text and data mining in the academic and scientific community and that the existing exception allowing non-commercial research was limited in scope (Hargreaves Review 2011: ch 5). Consequently, in 2014, major reforms to copyright exceptions were introduced in the UK.

A new exception allowing quotation from a work, whether for the purpose of criticism or review or *otherwise*, was introduced and came into force on October 1, 2014 (CDPA 1988, § 30(1ZA)). The existing fair dealing exception for criticism and review was considered to be too narrow, such that the new exception was expected to remove unnecessary restrictions to freedom of expression (Modernising Copyright 2012: 26). This new exception allows for quotations from any form of copyright work, such as films or photographs, and not just from literary works and for any purpose. However, a key requirement of the exception is that the extent of the quotation must be no more than is required by the specific purpose for which it is used. Although the exception gives the appearance of being quite broad, it is envisaged to permit only 'minor uses' such as quotations in academic papers, Internet blogs, and tweets and is not envisaged to be a substitute for obtaining commercially available content (Modernising Copyright 2012: 4, 27).

Another important reform that came into force on June 1, 2014, was the introduction of a new text and data mining exception. This exception permits copying of works by a person who has lawful access to the work for carrying out computational analysis of anything recorded in the work for the sole purpose of non-commercial research (CDPA 1988 s 29A). The review noted that valuable new technologies like text and data mining require the copying of large amount of data in order to computationally find patterns and associations that would assist researchers (e.g., research into the prevention of malaria can benefit from text analysis of a large quantity of research articles describing malaria in different communities in order to identify useful relationships and insights) and, as such, were prohibited by copyright. While such copyright reforms have direct relevance for researchers, our following case study will illustrate that the effect of these reforms in practice—and in particular for arts and humanities researchers—remains to be seen.

Transforming Musicology

Transforming Musicology, one of our six case studies, was a three-year research project—ongoing at the time of writing this chapter—which was funded from 2013 to 2016 as a Large Grant through the AHRC Digital Transformations Scheme. The goal of the project was to develop new computational tools and resources for the field of musicology and also to demonstrate how scholarly research into music could be transformed through digital culture and digital methods. The project was a collaboration between a number of UK and international institutions, including Goldsmiths, University of London; Queen Mary University of London; University of Oxford; Lancaster University; and Utrecht University. For our case study of this project, we spoke to Tim Crawford, a Professorial Research Fellow in Computational Musicology, who is the principal investigator (PI) on the grant. We also spoke to two people working in the Research Development Office, who handled the legal aspects of the grant's administration.

At the culmination of the project, the Transforming Musicology team aimed to produce a searchable online system/database, for developing music information retrieval (MIR) tools—pieces of software that use pattern recognition algorithms—and testing them on recordings and scores. MIR tools are commonly used by services such as Spotify and Pandora to deliver music streaming to customers. Transforming Musicology was interested in developing these tools to promote new musicological data analysis methods and to improve the quality and accessibility of musical data on the Internet, in particular to study 16th-century lute and vocal music, and to augment traditional study of Richard Wagner's leitmotif technique through audio pattern matching and supporting psychological testing.

To carry out MIR on musical recordings and scores, the project drew on a number of in-house, custom-made software tools—the majority open source and free—for analysing patterns in musical data. To test these MIR tools, they assembled a musical database that contained copies of musical recordings and musical scores, much of which was protected by copyright. Some of this music was contained within collections of commercial CDs and self-recorded audio that were purchased personally by members of the project or that had been legally obtained (purchased) through previous projects. Some of the previously obtained music had been acquired through the publicly funded Electronic Corpus of Lute Music (ECOLM) (Goldsmiths 2011) and Online Musical Recognition and Searching 2 (OMRAS2) (Queen Mary 2016) projects, in which the project PI, Tim Crawford, had previously been involved.

In addition, the project drew on several collections of musical scores, many of which were out of copyright because the author had died more than seventy years ago. The copyright period is usually tied to the lifetime of the author, and copyright in musical works lasts for the life of authors plus seventy years after their death (CDPA 1988 s 12(1)). Some of the scores were obtained from The British Library, from archives of photographed and digitised books containing the scores for 16th-century music, while others were obtained through online repositories such as Europeana (Europeana Foundation 2016) and the International Music Score Library Project (Project Petrucci 2016), which contained out-of-copyright scores that have been scanned and uploaded by the music community under a Creative Commons Attribution-ShareAlike 4.0 License. The project was also in the process of negotiating access to some copyright-protected scores from music publishers.

Ultimately, the project team wanted to make the MIR tools and database available beyond the academic community and the worldwide musical community as a whole: they wanted to make a resource in which people could see the results of the project's analysis and to use the project's MIR software tools to run their own analysis on musical collections. However, when we spoke to the project team in June 2014—which was in the first year of the project—they were unsure what the final form of such a system/database would be. Tim Crawford explained that it would appear like a website that would allow users to explore the patterns and links between musical sources (in what is known as linked data). In this system, users would likely not see original data and instead would search through the results of the MIR analysis of musical sources.

Overall, the main copyright-related challenges of the Transforming Musicology project were in both carrying out their planned research and in developing the final website in a way that did not infringe copyright for the rights holders of musical data. In other words, the copyright status of the project's research process itself and the main projected output were unclear, raising questions about (1) what rights-protected content could be used as part of the musical collections for analysis, (2) what rights-protected content, if any, could remain within the final online resource—and accessible to public users—at the end of the project, and (3) in what format public users would have access to rights-protected content—as metadata and links, or as full recordings and scores, or as snippets. Tim explained that the project had undergone significant discussion and planning as to how to manage and protect against the infringement of the copyright-protected works, upon which the project relied for research and results.

Due to the collaborative nature of the Transforming Musicology project, the Oxford e-Research Centre (University of Oxford 2016) was tasked with developing a storage system for the project data. When we spoke to the Transforming Musicology team, this phase of the project was still in progress but aimed to develop an infrastructure for enabling researchers to carry out data analysis on musical data and also for enabling end users to gain access to the results of the analysis and the musical collections via the final web-based resource.

For example, early in the project proposal stage, the project team had become aware of the potential copyright infringement that using personally purchased recordings for a public database might pose. They knew that they were working with copyright-protected recordings and scores, but because they were not planning to make any money from their work, they did not know if they were allowed to copy or reproduce parts of the works that were protected by copyright for research purposes. For example, it did not occur to Tim that copying music from a personal laptop onto a server in Oxford might be a copyright infringement. He noted:

> On my laptop, I've got copies of . . . I mean, I bought . . . actually before the project started, from money from a previous project . . . about eight recordings of Wagner's *Ring Cycle*. You know, that's quite a lot of stuff, and that's all on my laptop. I mean, I ripped them onto my laptop, and I'm doing this work on them. I think that would be acceptable. Now, sharing that with someone else gets a bit more problematic, and we have to make sure that we [aren't] treading on too many toes.

In the UK, private copying of copyright-protected works is an infringement unless an exception allowing the specific type or purpose of copying applies. Historically, there has been no general exception permitting private copying or place-shifting for private and domestic use, such as copying songs from a lawfully purchased CD on to a laptop. As a result of reforms in 2014, a new limited private use exception was introduced in the UK in October 2014 (CDPA s 28B). However, this exception was repealed in July 2015, with prospective effect, as a result of a court order (R (on the application of British Academy of Songwriters, Composers and Authors) v Secretary of State for Business, Innovation and Skills (2015) EWHC 2041(Admin).

Worried about the legality of this academic use and sharing—of personally purchased copies of copyright-protected music, which formed such a key component of the project's research—the staff overseeing the administration of the Transforming Musicology grant decided to formally address the issue of the copyright status of the musical material. According to Muriel, the project development officer involved in the project, an integrity committee was formed to draw up a data management plan (DMP), which was subsequently checked over by a solicitor. Muriel commented that the project "was a nice test case" for "thinking more carefully about discipline-specific needs when it comes to copyright and data management."

Anticipating the introduction of the UK Government's copyright exception for text and data mining for non-commercial research, the Transforming Musicology team decided to go ahead with the grant, albeit with relatively lax guidelines for how the storage of music in Oxford would proceed. With the introduction of these new laws into Parliament in 2014, the project members determined that the actual conduct of their research (copying and sharing music for academic purposes within the team and within the time bounds of the project) would not be an infringement of copyright. They determined that putting music onto a project serve, and limiting access to members of the project would be lawful under the new text and data mining exception.

The wording of the text and data mining exception (which had just come into force on 1 June 2014 when we spoke to the project team) suggests some key requirements for the exception to apply. Making a copy of a protected work does not infringe copyright if the copy of the work is made by a person who has *lawful access* to the work, the copy is made so that the person with lawful access may carry out computational analysis of anything recorded in the work for the *sole purpose of non-commercial research*, the copy of the work is accompanied by sufficient acknowledgement (CDPA 1988 § 29A(1)). However, the provision further indicates that the transfer to any other person of the copy made or the use of the copy for any other purpose is an infringement unless authorised by the copyright owner (CDPA 1988 § 29A(2)). Although lawful access to the work can be acquired through purchasing a copy or a licence for the work, there appears to be ambiguity as to whether copies of lawfully acquired works by a researcher, when shared with a research team, are permitted. In other words, if X owns a lawfully acquired copy of a CD of musical works, can he make copies of the musical works only for himself to carry out the computational analysis, or can he also allow access to such copies to other researchers (who don't themselves have lawful access to the work) for carrying out such analysis without permission from the copyright owner?

Although there is no "fairness" requirement for this exception, the requirement of "research for non-commercial purposes" also restricts the scope of this exception. The term "non-commercial"' raises the same uncertainties as applicable to the broader exception for non-commercial research previously noted. The British Academy report noted, a decade ago, that there was uncertainty around the meaning and scope of the broader exception and that it required clarification (British Academy 2006). The report recommended that the terms "research" and "non-commercial" should be broadly interpreted to give the text of the statute its full effect. However, somewhat in contrast, the limited case law on the subject suggests that, if at the time of the research, the "end use" is contemplated to be for a purpose with some commercial value, then this exception does not provide a defence (*Controller HMSO and Ordnance Survey v. Green Amps* [2007] EWHC 2755 [Ch]).

The project team were actively trying to adapt the way in which the project was designed—the way that data sources and outputs were designated for use in the conduct of the research—in order to anticipate and avoid any copyright-related problems. However, they also encountered further ambiguities and dilemmas surrounding the musical collection in Oxford in relation to the potential outputs of the project: (1) which, if any, collections would future users of this research be able to run software analysis on, and (2) to what extent—in links only or in small musical segments—could such users see the results of the software analysis?

Consequently, the project team wondered what would happen to the musical data—consisting of a mixture of in- and out-of-copyright recordings and scores—at the end of the project. During the project, the data would be acquired and used for academic purposes among the team members, but after the project the data would be stored indefinitely and potentially made available to users of the web-based resource. Tim questioned whether it would be necessary to delete the data after the end of the project, despite its potential use in future projects, or whether it would be necessary to negotiate for a particular licence with the various rights holders. He questioned what collections future users of a web-based resource would be able to access or run data analysis tools on. He said:

> It gets more complicated, doesn't it, when we start saying . . . What happens at the end of the project? Should we then delete all that stuff from the Oxford servers, or do we keep it there because we know how useful it'll be in future, you know, for a future project under the same terms? . . . Some of these are purely logistic issues, I mean . . . it's ridiculous to delete everything and then have to upload it all again. I mean . . . that would be logistically ridiculous, but I think technically speaking . . . we should negotiate with the rights holders before we do that uploading, [we should] take it down at the end of the project and redo it.

Such comments hint at issues of sustainability and at the ability of publicly funded projects to continue being of use and value to the researchers and public users. However, they also raise questions about how the text mining exception might play out in practice, when resources are developed in academic projects and for non-commercial purposes but when it is also difficult to ascertain whether the use of such resources is commercial or non-commercial.

Another main copyright challenge in the Transforming Musicology project concerned the format in which the users of the web-based resource would be able to see the results of the data analysis. To avoid infringing copyright, the project planned to give the public users access to the metadata—the relationships between scores and recordings—without giving them the ability to see the original scores or listen to recordings. This was an approach that had already been previously established by a project called the Million Song Dataset (Bertin-Mahieux et al. 2011), a freely available collection of audio features and metadata for a million contemporary popular music tracks. Importantly, the Million Song Dataset gave users access only to derived features and not directly to audio, making it impossible to reconstruct the original audio from the features and metadata. Echoing this approach, the Transforming Musicology project planned to give public users access to the intellectual property that it had generated rather than to the songs themselves, in an attempt to avoid infringing the rights of any of the copyright holders of the musical works. Tim commented, "It's the results of analysis that we want to share mostly, except where we can and we will share what we can or any of our own data." He said:

> It won't necessarily be either piece of data. You say you have to buy the score from Oxford University Press and you'll need to buy the CD from so-and-so. So there's one level of remove. . . . I don't think that's controversial from the point of view of copyright, because there we're saying. . . . "This is a copyrighted material at one end, and that's copyright material at the other." We're just saying "They link."

Tim also worried that providing access to metadata and links rather than to the original content itself would diminish the value of the web-based resource for public users. Although the Transforming Musicology project sought to use automated pattern recognition software and MIR tools to establish links within and between music, it still required human beings to validate the relevance or "correctness" of particular searches and results. The overall quality of the website would be better, he asserted, if it allowed human beings—perhaps in the form of public users—to test out musical links. But in order to do this, it would be necessary for public users to have access to the original musical data in its entirety, to the original scores and recordings. Tim commented:

> Once the analysis has been run . . . the only reason you need to have access to the data is when you want to audition something to make sure it's right. . . . So if you say "I found a

> quotation from . . . a guitar lick from Jimi Hendrix". . . . Suppose I think I've found that at a point 4.8 seconds into track x. If I want to tell my friends about it they'll say, "well, 4.8 seconds into track x, I don't have track x." What they want to do is press a button and listen to that little bit.

While Tim raised a number of questions about the legality of allowing public users to access copyright-protected musical data, he also questioned whether a lack of access to primary data would diminish the value of the resource as a tool for musical communities and also the academic "impact" of the project. He noted that sometimes it was necessary for musicians to play entire songs in order to analyse their content or appreciate their performance. One of the ways of measuring the "impact" of an online resource was to track the number of people who access and use it. If one of the main values of the Transforming Musicology project was in sharing the results of the musicological analysis, this could be achieved by giving public users the ability to listen to music in order to verify links and associations. Without this ability, Tim wondered whether users would see less value in the web-based resource, visit it less, and ultimately diminish the impact of the Transforming Musicology project. He said:

> There's a kind of circular problem here, because [there is] benefit to the project of being able to share everything. . . . Supposing it was a complete free-for-all [with copyright] . . . we could effectively get lots of hits on our websites by saying, "oh, listen to Wagner's *Das Rheingold* in eight different performances." You know, we could offer a special streaming service for people who are interested in that. Obviously we aren't going to do that, but . . . not having to think about these things would make those kinds of . . . impact related issues much easier to deal with.

Tim recognised that giving public users access to sections of copyright-protected works would be a copyright infringement. Yet, on the one hand, he raised the question of whether allowing a "snippet view" of music—a short section, of 5 or 30 seconds—could fall within the remit of the "fair dealing" copyright exception for non-commercial research or teaching. Not knowing the legality of such an approach, he also questioned whether giving access to a collection of snippets would be sufficient to allow people to piece together enough short sections to make a more holistic piece of music and in a way that subsequently infringed copyright. On the other hand, he raised the idea of negotiating a way to provide links to existing commercial content on websites like Spotify and Amazon. Making connections to content that public users could buy might "sweeten the deal for the rights holders" by encouraging public users to download and pay for licensed content and to generate royalties for rights holders. He commented:

> There's no reason why we shouldn't put Amazon links, for instance, to a particular track that we're playing. "If you want to buy this, you know, download this, you can do it from . . . Amazon, Spotify" . . . whatever pay site is involved, whereby a royalty or whatever would go back to the original. . . . I mean, that is a possibility. It's just an added layer of complication, but I think it's perfectly possible that we will do something like that.

Tim also discussed the possibility that the project's outputs could be developed into a tool for the music industry. Although still largely hypothetical, the software tools and annotated musical libraries could be commercialised and used by software developers in the music industry to better classify and understand music for clients, providing "added value" through links within and across music. This created tensions, however, between commercialising the project outputs and promoting their communal use. Because the project aimed to make many of its software tools open source and to develop resources and infrastructures for the musical community, Tim was concerned that commercialisation, which would create economic value for the researchers/university, could reduce the social and cultural value of the project for the public users.

Researchers have always faced difficulties in navigating copyright exceptions in the UK due to ambiguity around the scope of exceptions, narrow interpretation of exceptions in practice, and the risks involved in relying on an exception rather than obtaining a license. While the Transforming Musicology team "tempered the scope and scale of the project to the knowledge that there are copyright issues," they continued to face ambiguities and dilemmas in "operationalising" a type of research activity that the UK government explicitly wanted to promote through the new text and data mining exception. The case study demonstrates that both the benefit derived from the research itself and its outputs and future use are important considerations for researchers. However, the scope of the exception poses barriers: the exception doesn't provide any ability to allow some public access to the works that have been subjected to computational analysis, and the limitation of "non-commercial" to research related exceptions can limit the future benefits that can be derived from the research. These limitations pose dilemmas for researchers who may wish to use copyright-protected materials for transformative research but who may not be able to share the outputs of such research in the open, user-friendly way that is increasingly being expected by funders (and may be an important means for disseminating the research itself and achieving impact from it).

Negotiating and Obtaining Access to Copyright and Out-of-Copyright Materials

Arts and humanities scholars may wish to obtain licences for copyright protected materials, for instance, for research for a commercial use (or other similar uses where the framework of copyright exceptions doesn't apply). The British Library collection of essays (British Library 2010) flagged several practical challenges that researchers and scholars face in negotiating and obtaining access to copyright materials for use that does not fall within the scope of the available exceptions. While researchers may be willing to obtain a licence for rights-protected content, they often face challenges in accessing such materials. These challenges stem from limited time, limited project budgets and/or limited to no financial return on their outputs, lack of expertise or knowledge that may be required to secure a licence, refusal by the rights owners to license, or prohibitive cost of a licence for commercially owned content. In our research, several participants faced one or more of such challenges.

Arts and humanities scholars are also particularly interested in materials that are not themselves in copyright but that reside in the collections of libraries, archives, and other cultural and private institutions. Some of the practical challenges previously noted in the context of access to copyright materials can also arise when researchers wish to access and reproduce out-of-copyright materials. For example, the British Academy Report noted that copyright protection of photographs not only allowed museums and galleries "to claim fees for non-copyright works in their possession" but that "this has become more severe as museums and galleries all over the world, driven by the need to find additional sources of income, have demanded fees to use their photographs even in scholarly non-commercial publications" (British Academy 2006: 10).

The policy and law underpinning the controls on the copyright protection of, access to, and reuse of out-of-copyright materials found in public libraries and archives is complex and confusing. Government policy seeks to encourage the reuse of public sector content in the interests of regeneration of the economy. But in the face of shrinking public sector funding, the Government, as already noted, also encourages libraries and archives to contribute toward and support their costs.

Consequently, institutions seek to exploit digitised images and other information in several ways. They assert copyright in the newly digitised image, arguing that it is protected by a new copyright. Whether this is the case or not is a moot point. The emerging European standard for originality (required for copyright to subsist in many works) is that a work must be the authors' own intellectual creation, in that they must stamp their own personal touch on a work and in that it must not follow preset rules. In accordance with this, the UK Intellectual Property Office has produced guidance suggesting that a new copyright is unlikely to arise in the act of digitization (IPO 2015: 3).

Nevertheless, such institutions control access to and the reuse of content, some of which may be protected by copyright, some of which may not. For example, institutions may limit the time period for which access is given or the amount of and manner in which content may be displayed. This strategy rests on two legal foundations: the first, applicable within Member States of the EU, is the Database Directive, which protects copyright in the structure and arrangement of the content of the database and grants a sui generis database right to prevent use of the contents from a database where there has been substantial investment in the obtaining, verifying, or presentation of the contents. The latter right, which is intended to protect the investment in compiling the database, prevents the unauthorised extraction and/or reutilisation of the whole or part of the contents.

The second legal foundation is the Re-Use of Public Sector Information Directive as amended in 2013. The amended Directive extends the scope of the original directive to public sector museums, libraries, and archives where information is made available for reuse. The presumption in this amended Directive is that public sector information should be available for reuse. Institutions can charge, but this should in principle be limited to marginal cost. Where an institution needs the financial help of a third party for a digitisation programme, an exclusive arrangement can be entered into with that third party in relation to access but only for a period of up to ten years. These new rules came into force on 18 July 2015 (Re-use of Public Sector Information Regulations 2015).

Our following case study illustrates the continuing challenges in obtaining satisfactory access to out-of-copyright materials residing in the collections of libraries, archives, and other institutions, which is coupled with a general reluctance to negotiate licences for copyright-protected materials in case of commercial use of research-related outputs.

Case Study: Jack the Ripper 125

JtR125 was a three-month project, funded in 2013 through the Future Documentary Sandbox in the REACT Knowledge Exchange Hub for the Creative Economy. The goal was to develop a "playable documentary" about the Jack the Ripper murders, which combined historical photography and media with modern 3D game elements. The project was developed in commemoration of the 125th anniversary of the murder of Mary Jane Kelly, the Ripper's first victim, and was an attempt to develop the emerging genres of "playable documentaries" and "news games" (Werner 2013).

The project was a collaboration between academic partners Janet Jones, a professor of media at Middlesex University, and Patrick Crogan, a senior lecturer in film studies and a games theorist at the University of the West of England, as well as creative partner Tomas Rawlings, the design director of Auroch Digital, a games consultancy and independent development studio (Auroch Digital 2016). For our case study of the project, we spoke to both Tomas and Janet, who was the lead academic on the project and who had worked with Tomas for more than six years in a variety of journalism-related projects. With the JtR125 game, Tomas and the Auroch Digital team aimed to develop expertise and skills in the emerging genre of new gaming, positioning themselves in a competitive position to get future work and to elevate the profile of the studio. Janet, on the other hand, aimed to distribute news content to wider audiences with new technologies and channels, engaging younger publics in contemporary and historical issues.

The main output for the project was a prototype video game called JtR125 (Auroch Digital 2014), which was undergoing further development at the time of our research. Tomas and the Auroch Digital team planned to release the game on Steam, one of the main Internet-based distribution, digital rights management (DRM), and social networking platforms (Valve Corporation 2016). To do so, the project drew on historical materials in public archives, such as photos and illustrations, to create a gaming environment that had the look and feel of 19th-century London rather than a modern first-person shooter videogame. These historical materials were located in several public archives, including The British Library—which contained collections of *The Illustrated Police News*, one of the earliest British tabloid newspapers that featured sensationalised illustrations of murders and hangings—as well as the Wellcome Trust Library—which contained articles from *The Lancet*, a journal that was founded in 1823 and featured medical reports of the Jack the Ripper murders. The project also drew on large collections of material—thought to be out of copyright—that had been amassed into public websites (Jones 2016; Ryder 2016) devoted to the history and controversy surrounding the unsolved Jack the Ripper murders, which have achieved a cult following in contemporary society.

The main copyright-related challenge of the JtR125 project was in accessing out-of-copyright material in archives. We spoke to both Janet and Tomas about their experiences with this issue in The British Library and the Wellcome Trust Library. Access to out-of-copyright materials—such as the cartoon-style images contained within *The Illustrated Police News* and the original medical reports contained within *The Lancet*—was important because it enabled the team to create the JtR125 game in a historically accurate and ethically responsible way. Because the game was an attempt both to engage critically with the gruesome and sexual nature of the Ripper murders and also to provide an entertaining story for players, the team sought to design the game from the perspective of a journalist investigating the Jack the Ripper murders in 19th-century London. The team believed that using primary source materials would enable them to explore notions of crime, news reporting, and ethics, while also enabling players to discover clues and piece together the story.

The two main historical sources, *The Illustrated Police News* and *The Lancet*, had been produced more than one hundred years ago and were therefore out of copyright and in the public domain. Although both resources were housed in publicly accessible archives, our interviewees explained that their content was made available to the public through digitised copies only, as the archives had entered into agreements with commercial entities, which had carried out the digitisation and development of a digital infrastructure for historical records (JISC 2009; JISC 2011). This meant that the originally out-of-copyright content could be accessed only in the form of digitised copies, which were subject to copyright protection because users and institutions were given access only to digitised images through an online portal, and could not visit the original physical newspapers.

In order to access content and images from *The Illustrated Police News*, Janet visited The British Library News Archive in Colindale where she examined microfiche copies of the original *Illustrated Police News* documents. These copies, according to Janet, were only of "average quality" in comparison to the originals. Although the library charged her £100 to make A3 print copies of the microfiche, she explained that the JtR125 team was then able to use the printout images in the game development. She said:

> No, there aren't any limitations on what you can do with the images, because they [a]re in there for public domain, they're copyright free. So . . . what you're paying for is the labour of giving us a quality reproduction of it. So, in that particular instance, it's free.

In contrast, Tomas described the challenges of accessing *The Illustrated Police News* content at The British Library's main location in London. He was able to use The British Library computer systems to access on-screen digital versions of *The Illustrated Police News* but was able to get a copy of the content only as a physical printout and was unable to save a copy of the digital file. This was problematic because having access only to a physical printout made it difficult to use the content in the video game. To use a printout, the Auroch Digital team would have to scan it and digitally retouch it, which Tomas saw as "a whole load of resources to get a less than desirable outcome" and which he also attributed to "complicated copyright laws." Moreover, Tomas claimed that the printouts were of an "absolutely awful, unusable quality," as only sections of the digital scan could be printed, and the images could not be digitally manipulated before printing. Tomas described:

> The British Library [experience] was massively frustrating. To go down there to see these digital images on the screen, and I can't just right click "save as" and grab them. They are like, "No, you're not allowed to do that on our computers, you have to print them out."

Tomas's comment implied that the digitisation agreement prohibited the use of digitised images by the public and permitted access only via physical printouts.

Similarly, Tomas described the challenges of accessing content from *The Lancet* from the Wellcome Trust Library in London. Although he was able to view copies of old and out-of-copyright *Lancet* articles, as in The British Library, he was unable to make digital copies of the on-screen images. The staff at the library explained to him that because a particular company had been involved in the digitisation of *The Lancet* and subsequently had rights to the digital copies, he would need to speak to the company if he wanted to make a digital copy of a particular article or image. He explained: "The text is out of copyright, but the digitised version of that's not, because somebody's effectively taken a photograph of it . . . and they claim the copyright of the photograph they've taken." In order to use the material, he had to manually copy down the information and work with the Auroch Digital team to "recreate something that look[ed] like a page from *The Lancet*." Although he found the process frustrating, he noted that at least the Wellcome Trust Library, in contrast to The British Library, was explicit about its copyright agreements, with clear labels and indications as to what was and was not rights protected.

Although the JtR125 project encountered issues with accessing digital copies of out-of-copyright material, the Auroch Digital team was able to work creatively around this copyright challenge. In most instances and with a variety of games including but not limited to JtR125, the team was able to create their own creative content instead of paying to use or license rights-protected content. As Tomas explained, if it was expensive or difficult to procure a licence for content, his team would usually not pay for content and instead would look to other sources or other ways of achieving their goals. He said:

> Anything more complicated than "we can use it" we just don't use it. There's plenty of other stuff to draw from. . . . There's so much material we could cover, there's loads of stuff, even if we had the full development budget I'd like, we wouldn't be able to get to cover everything I'd like to cover. So as soon as something becomes complicated, it just gets dropped in favour of something else.

Similarly, Janet commented that in her experience, small creative companies made of only a handful of employees, like those involved in the indie games industry, looked to use and create content cheaply. They did not have the money "to invest in huge rights . . . to buy music . . . to buy copyright to images." Instead, smaller companies used digital means to access existing content for free—such as looking for open-source content on Google or Wikipedia—or creative means to make content that is similar to existing protected content—such as working with artists or designers to create visuals or sounds for virtual reality environments. Tomas commented:

> I've got a team of writers in there, and if we want something we can create it ourselves, and then we've got no copyright problems at all 'cos it's ours. So a lot of the time it's easier not to use copyrighted material and create your own thing, than use copyright material.

To illustrate this, Tomas described his previous work on another video game based on *The Great Escape*, a 1963 film about World War II, featuring Steve McQueen, James Garner, and Richard Attenborough—a game that because of its age still contained copyright-protected content. In trying to develop the dialogue for the game, the developers had to draw up licences with the film production company to use original parts of the film, which they felt was important for giving the video game an authentic feel. The developers were able to license use of the script but had trouble licensing any parts of the film in which the actors were speaking the script, as the rights of that type of content were partly owned by the actors. Consequently, the developers ran into significant problems licensing the opening dialogue of the actors Richard Attenborough and Steve McQueen because they wanted a sum of money that the publisher of the game was unable to afford.

According to Tomas, the video game team was able to creatively work around the copyright challenge of not being able—or wanting—to pay for copyright-protected film content. The developers attempted to recreate the scene, but using an actor who had the likeness of Richard Attenborough. However, to do so in a legal way they were unable to recruit actors by advertising for people who looked similar to Richard Attenborough, as that was thought to be a copyright infringement. To develop a creative way of working around this, the game developers launched a competition for people—for which they asked for photos—to see if anyone would like to be in the Great Escape Game. From the photos people sent in, the developers found a person who "coincidentally" looked similar to Richard Attenborough, and because copyright law in the UK does not protect lookalikes, they were able to come up with a solution whereby they avoided paying for licensed material.

Despite the benefits that the project team's ability to do creative copyright workarounds brought, the team questioned whether the quality and value of the end product, the JtR125 game, would be diminished if they used copyright workarounds instead of using original content. For example, Janet asserted that the accuracy of the sound effects and visual was important for conveying the historical and ethical nuances of the Jack the Ripper murders. Consequently, she felt it was important for the team to strike a balance between paying for historically accurate content and making the project economically viable. As Janet described:

> If you're going to create a London cityscape, the sound of that, it can't be too crude. So there'll be times when I'll want Tomas to pay for something, and there will be times when we'll say "just get it free." . . . That's what his creative team will be doing . . . and trying to make it as economically viable as I possibly can.

In some cases, the quality—and importance to the Jack the Ripper story—of original sound recordings or images were sufficiently high that it merited paying for rights-protected content. In fact, the Auroch Digital team emphasised that, in many cases, the value of rights-protected content was not sufficiently high to merit paying to license the content. According to Tomas, many people assumed that if something was protected by copyright it was automatically valuable and had "untapped" potential. This was, however, not the case: unless something was sufficiently valuable or central to a project, as perhaps the London cityscape was for the JtR125 game, the team would not pay for works protected by copyright. If they wanted to use or develop a particular idea, they had a variety of options available to produce new content. As Tomas commented:

> And as I say time and time again . . . we have a lot more options open to us, the biggest of which is, we simply just don't do it. But right through to us recreating things, us doing something different . . . as a developer, you're going to take not necessarily the path of least resistance, but you are going to use those options available to you. And if copyright becomes a problem, there's a solution to it, which is not necessarily paying the copyright dues.

Overall, the Auroch Digital team had an ambivalent attitude towards copyright, as project members articulated both its challenges and its benefits. Despite the team's frustration at times with the overzealous use of copyright, they still acknowledged that copyright was central to their video games business and allowed them to derive economic benefit from their work. Tomas said: "Copyright is the foundation of our business. . . . We sell games, and so people pay for a proprietary copy of what we sell. . . . You need copyright because that's what enables us to pay our staff." He emphasised that some aspects of copyright law were "archaic" and made it difficult to do creative work but also asserted that copyright was necessary "to be able to justify the costs and resources and investments we put into creating something." His comments articulated, in other words, the fact that copyright had to strike a balance between bringing benefits to individuals and society.

Conclusion

Previous literature interrogating the utility of the copyright exceptions for researchers in the UK has highlighted how difficult exceptions are to operate in practice. While the British Academy report in 2006 suggested that at least some of these challenges could be overcome by more expansive interpretation of the exceptions (British Academy 2006), The British Library essays in 2010 emphasised both the restrictive interpretation of the exceptions in practice and the difficulties for researchers in dealing with the limited scope of the exceptions (British Library 2010). Our research suggests that the scope and interpretation of copyright exceptions continue to be a persistent challenge for researchers. Exceptions are an important challenge to researchers working away from the market and with third=party works protected by copyright. Exceptions are also relevant, even if less important, for those working closer to the market with creative industry partners who tend to seek workarounds.

As noted in this chapter, the UK law on copyright exceptions underwent significant changes in 2014. At the same time, copyright exceptions have also been an important subject of discussions in the EU, and the text and data mining is a specific issue that the European Commission plans to tackle (Communication on a Digital Single Market Strategy for Europe COM (2015) 192 final). Earlier, in 2013–2014, the Commission undertook a major public consultation to review EU copyright rules (Public Consultation Report 2013). The consultation invited response on specific questions on text and data mining, with the aim to assess whether the practice is being hindered in the EU and, if so, how such problems should be addressed (Public Consultation Report 2103-2014). The report on the responses to the consultation noted that researchers and institutional users were "generally dissatisfied with the current situation" and that there was an EU-wide "legal uncertainty on whether and how copyright may apply to text and data mining and problems with existing licensing mechanisms, which were generally considered inadequate"(Public Consultation Report 2014: 63).

Two further points in the report are of note. First, some respondents considered that text and data mining was easier in countries with fair use provisions, such as the United States, which gave universities in those jurisdictions a competitive advantage over those in the EU (Public Consultation Report 2014: 64; Kretschmer et al. 2014). Second, researchers and institutional users did not want text and data mining to be subject to licences and considered the sharing of results of such mining with fellow researchers (without providing substitutes of original works that were mined) to be necessary (Public Consultation Report 2014: 64). At the time of writing, the EU-wide outcome on the issue remains to be seen, in particular, whether text and data mining will be accommodated within the framework of exceptions or whether an industry-led licensing solution will be favoured (Public Consultation Report 2014: 67).

In 2014, the UK took a bold step in implementing a specific copyright exception for text and data mining (Public Consultation Report 2014: 27; InfoSoc Directive Article 5(1)). Our findings from the Transforming Musicology project suggest that the exception appeared crucial to the methodology of the project and to realising some of its ambition. However, the case study also demonstrates that there remain significant operational challenges for researchers in the achieving the broader aim underlying the exception in the UK. Copyright exceptions can pose important challenges for those researchers who are working at the experimental end and away from the market. Our analysis indicates that researchers who may wish and also be encouraged to extend the boundaries of their disciplines by creating new data sets, analyses, and resources can find the landscape of copyright exceptions to be at odds with their goals and also difficult to navigate. To this end, the Transforming Musicology case study demonstrates how uncertainty over the scope and limitations of both existing and new copyright exceptions causes concerns not only over what research can be undertaken but also over how such research can be suitably disseminated and sustained. As such, the ability of the newly introduced and reformed exceptions to enable conduct of experimental research, which can also meet the dissemination and sustainability expectations of the funders, needs further investigation.

In addition, our findings from the JtR125 case study highlight the challenges posed in obtaining digitised records from archives, even where the originals of those records are in the public domain. The recently updated EU Re-Use of Public Sector Information Directive, the Database Directive, and the persistent lack of clarity over whether the act of digitisation results in a new copyright arising in the digitised work, combine to leave this area of law murky at best. This "murkiness" is exploited by archives and by those who digitise archival collections to claim control over the digitised content. While the Database Directive was enacted specifically to protect investment in the development of databases, and the Re-Use of Public Sector Information Directive allows for a limited period of exclusivity for those who invest in digitisation, for arts and humanities researchers, this could result in a worrying loss of authenticity when it is not financially viable to access and license the digitised record. While the challenges posed may be less acute for creative industry partners, the boundaries of the law are not clear. As alternative sources of information are often sought if obtaining the digitised original proves too expensive—in terms of both time and money—this is in itself a cost to the business.

These laws, however, have been developing and changing. As we have noted, such is the advance in the law at the European level on originality that it seems unlikely that a new copyright could be successfully claimed in a digitised record; the Database Directive has been under attack almost since it was enacted for its lack of proper economic justification, and the Re-Use of Public Sector Information Directive was remodelled in 2013 to expand the number of institutions to which it was relevant and to change the emphasis from one of permissive reuse of public sector information to that of expectation of reuse. All of this means that research projects at the intersection between academe and industry operate in a copyright environment that is in a constant state of flux. This is an environment that should be kept under review to ensure that the integrity of the research and the outputs are not compromised and that the expense of reusing digitised works does not become too costly within the legislative frameworks.

Our research, consistent with the existing albeit limited empirical research on copyright exceptions, has demonstrated that arts and humanities researchers find the copyright framework in the UK to be challenging in practice, especially in their pursuit to conduct innovative and transformative research. In addition, it has also illustrated how researchers face a variety of challenges in negotiating access to and the use of out-of-copyright materials in archives. In doing so, this chapter has outlined both topical and lesser known but pertinent legal challenges faced by arts and humanities researchers that can have a significant impact on the nature and type of research that is ultimately produced and disseminated.

Note

1 The Digital Transformations theme is one of four research themes within the AHRC and aims to encourage experimentation around the transformative potential for digital technologies in the arts and humanities. The theme has provided support under several different funding rounds, which include Exploratory Grants of several thousand pounds awarded in 2012, and Large Grants of over £1 million awarded in 2013, both of which make up our case studies in this theme. The theme is driven by research rather than infrastructures, standards, and tools, particularly with regard to issues like innovation, cultural memory and identity, and communication. Within the Digital Transformations themes, intellectual property is managed by each of the higher education institutions who are awarded grants. This provides opportunities to negotiate IP in a contextual way.

REACT is one of four KE Hubs, whose goals are to bring together academics and creative partners to stimulate knowledge exchange and process learning. It is a collaboration between the University of the West of England, Watershed—a cross-art form media centre—and the Universities of Bath, Bristol, Cardiff, and Exeter. REACT has provided support for sixty projects, which receive an average of £50,000 of funding, providing support for collaborative work over a three-month time span. Such collaborations provide tangible benefits to both academics and creative partners: for academics, they create opportunities for knowledge transfer, impact, and publications, as well as the time and space to create new methodologies and strands of research. For creative partners, they create opportunities to have a first-mover advantage, to develop new intellectual property, and to pursue financially infeasible, high-risk projects. Within REACT, intellectual property is managed through a fixed contract between the University of the West of England and iShed—a subsidiary of Watershed—as well as the other participating higher education institutions.

References

AHRC. (2013). "The Human World: The Arts and Humanities in Our Times." *AHRC Strategy 2013–2018*. Retrieved from www.ahrc.ac.uk/News-and-Events/News/Documents/AHRC-Strategy-2013-18.pdf at pg.5

Auroch Digital—GameTheNews. (2014, May 28). "JtR125—Jack the Ripper Playable Documentary—Prototype Test (v2)." [YouTube]. Retrieved from www.youtube.com/watch?v=2rKprmntnAE

Auroch Digital Ltd. (2016). "Auroch Digital." Retrieved from www.aurochdigital.com/#what-we-do

Bechtold, S. (2006). "Information Society Directive.art.5." In T. Dreier & P. B. Hugenholtz (Eds.), *Concise European Copyright Law*. Alphen aan den Rijn: Kluwer Law International.

Bertin-Mahieux, T., Ellis, D. P. W., Whitman, B., & Lamere, P. (2011). "The Million Song Dataset." Retrieved from http://labrosa.ee.columbia.edu/millionsong

British Academy. (2006). "Copyright and Research in the Humanities and Social Sciences: A British Academy Report." Retrieved from https://www.britac.ac.uk/sites/default/files/Copyright-report.pdf

British Library. (2010). "Driving UK Research: Is Copyright a Help or a Hindrance—A Perspective From the Research Community." Retrieved from http://bufvc.ac.uk/copyright-guidance/mlr/index.php/site/394

"Directive 2001/29/EC on the Harmonisation of Certain Aspects of Copyright and Related Rights in the Information Society." Retrieved from http://eur-lex.europa.eu/LexUriServ/LexUriServ.do?uri=OJ:L:2001:167:0010:0019:EN:PDF

Europeana Foundation. (2016). "Europeana Collections." Retrieved from www.europeana.eu/

Goldsmiths College. (2011). "ECOLM—An Electronic Corpus of Lute Music." Retrieved from www.ecolm.org

Gowers, A. (2006) Gowers Review of Intellectual Property London: HMSO.

Halpern, S. W., & Johnson, P. (2014). *Harmonising Copyright Law and Dealing With Dissonance: A Framework for Convergence of US and EU Law*. Cheltenham: Edward Elgar.

Hargreaves, I. (2011). *Digital Opportunity: A Review of Intellectual Property and Growth*. London: Intellectual Property Office.

HM Government. (2012). "Modernising Copyright: A Modern, Robust and Flexible Framework." http://webarchive.nationalarchives.gov.uk/20140603094128/http://www.ipo.gov.uk/response-2011-copyright-final.pdf

IPO (Intellectual Property Office). (2015). "Copyright Notice: Digital Images, Photographs and the Internet." London: IPO. https://www.gov.uk/government/publications/copyright-notice-digital-images-photographs-and-the-internet

Jisc. (2009). "Final Report: British Newspapers 1620–1900." Retrieved from http://webarchive.nationalarchives.gov.uk/20140702233839/www.jisc.ac.uk/media/documents/programmes/digitisation/blfinal.pdf

Jisc. (2011). "New British Library Newspaper Archive." Retrieved from http://digitisation.jiscinvolve.org/wp/2011/11/29/1966/

Jones, R. (2016). "Jack The Ripper 1888." Retrieved from www.jack-the-ripper.org/

Kretschmer, M. et al. (2014). "The European Commission's Public Consultation on the Review of EU Copyright Rules: A Response by the CREATe Centre." EIPR 547.

Kur, A., & Dreier, T. (Eds.) (2013). *European Intellectual Property Law*. Cheltenham: Edward Elgar.

Mazziotti, G. (2008). *EU Digital Copyright Law and the End-User*. New York: Springer.

Project Petrucci LLC. (2016). "IMSLP—International Music Score Library Project." Retrieved from http://imslp.org

"Public Consultation on the Review of the EU Copyright Rules." (2013-2014). Held between December 5, 2013 and March 5, 2014. Retrieved from http://ec.europa.eu/internal_market/consultations/2013/copyright-rules/index_en.htm

Queen Mary, University of London & Goldsmiths, University of London. (2016). *OMRAS2: A Distributed Research Environment for Music Informatics and Computational Musicology*. Retrieved from www.omras2.org

Report on the Responses to the Public Consultation on the Review of the EU Copyright Rules. (2014, July). http://ec.europa.eu/internal_market/consultations/2013/copyright-rules/docs/contributions/consultation-report_en.pdf

Ryder, S. P. (2016). "Casebook: Jack the Ripper." Retrieved from www.casebook.org

University of Oxford. (2016). *Oxford e-Research Centre*. Retrieved from www.oerc.ox.ac.uk

Valve Corporation. (2016). "Steam." Retrieved from http://store.steampowered.com/

Waelde, C., Brown, A., Kheria, S., & Cornwell, J. (2016). *Contemporary Intellectual Property: Law and Policy*. London: Oxford University Press.

Werner, J. (2013). "Gamezebo." *JtR125 Preview*. Retrieved from www.gamezebo.com/2013/11/26/jtr125-preview/

Appendix

Overview of Case Studies

	Case Study	*Funding Scheme*	*Interviewees*	*Position*
1.	**Digital Panopticon**	Digital Transformations	Robert Shoemaker	Professor of 18th-Century British History, University of Sheffield
			Michael Pidd	Digital Director of Humanities Research Institute, University of Sheffield
2.	**Transforming Musicology**	Digital Transformations	Tim Crawford	Professorial Research Fellow in Computational Musicology, Goldsmith's University
			Muriel Swijghuisen Reigersberg	Research Development Officer, Goldsmith's University
			David Kuper	Solicitor, Goldsmith's University
3.	**JtR125**	REACT	Janet Jones	Professor of Media, Middlesex University
			Tomas Rawlings	Design Director, Auroch Digital
4.	**Data Objects**	Digital Transformations	Ian Gwilt	Professor of Design and Visual Communication, Sheffield Hallam University
5.	**The Risk Taker's Survival Guide**	REACT	Matt Golding	Creative Director, Rubber Republic
			James Lyons	Senior Lecturer in Film, University of Exeter
6.	**Ghosts in the Garden**	REACT	Steve Poole	Professor of History and Heritage, University of West of England
			Rosie Poebright	Creative Director, Splash and Ripple

Part III

PEDAGOGY OF MEDIA EDUCATION, COPYRIGHT, AND FAIR USE

15

THE BENEFITS AND CHALLENGES OF YOUTUBE AS AN EDUCATIONAL RESOURCE

Chareen Snelson

Now more than a decade old, YouTube has become well-known as a place to find entertainment videos on topics related to music, sports, pets, television, movies, games, comedy, and celebrities. However, news, documentary, do-it-yourself (DIY), and instructional videos are also found in abundant supply on YouTube. This is beneficial for educators or anyone else who wishes to seek free educational media from the vast YouTube repository. YouTube also offers online hosting and a suite of browser-based tools for basic editing, captioning, and management of videos that anyone, including educators or students, can use after uploading videos. YouTube can be tremendously valuable as a tool for managing and organizing online educational video collections. However, formidable challenges associated with using YouTube as an educational resource include inappropriate content, advertisements, copyright issues, and filters that block access to YouTube at schools and libraries. Critical benefits and challenges of using YouTube as an educational resource are discussed in this chapter to illuminate these issues and offer practical strategies for handling some of the problems. Information is drawn from a variety of sources including scholarly literature, online sources, and the author's experience teaching a university-level YouTube course for educators since 2008. The information in this chapter is geared toward current or future educators but should also be informative for anyone who uses YouTube for either formal or informal educational purposes.

A Brief History of YouTube and Its Role in Education

A discussion of the history of YouTube and the emergence of academic interest in the site provides contextual background related to its current role as an educational media resource.

YouTube was not created for education, but it has been adopted by educators and academic institutions for a variety of reasons and purposes. When YouTube was initially invented in 2005, the process of uploading, viewing, or distributing video online was a challenging endeavor. The creation of YouTube was inspired by the necessity of a simpler approach to online video distribution that reduced the technological threshold to a level within reach of the general public (Burgess & Green 2009). The story behind the initial development of YouTube can be found on various websites, but the version told by one of its founders, Jawed Karim, during his University of Illinois Commencement Speech provides a revealing account of the genesis of YouTube (Karim 2007). Karim explained that he and his colleagues, Chad Hurley and Steve Chen, began working on the site on Valentine's Day, February 14, 2005. Two months later, on April 23, 2005, YouTube.com went live, and the first video called *Me at the Zoo* was uploaded (Karim 2005). YouTube was initially launched as a dating site under the slogan "Tune In, Hook Up." This idea was soon abandoned, and YouTube's slogan was changed to "Your Digital Video Repository," followed by "Broadcast Yourself," in alignment with the emerging purpose of the site as a place where everyday users could share videos of their pets, vacations, families, and life experiences online.

Now, YouTube has no slogan displayed under its online logo, and the present version has advanced considerably in terms of interface and content. It is possible to explore the evolution of YouTube via the Internet Archive's Wayback Machine at https://archive.org/web/, which contains thousands of cached pages of YouTube from its earliest days in 2005 to the present time. The oldest snapshot, dated April 28, 2005, reveals what YouTube looked like shortly after the site went live. It was primitive and unremarkable. Nevertheless, the site soon attracted the attention of the online public as well as serious investors. In November 2005, YouTube received $3.5 million in funding from Sequoia Capital (YouTube 2005). A year later, in November 2006, YouTube was acquired by Google for $1.65 billion (Sorkin & Peters 2006; YouTube Spotlight 2006). At that point it seemed evident that YouTube was on its way to becoming an important social media entity. This has proven to be the case. At the time of this writing, YouTube is ranked as the second most popular online destination (Alexa n.d.), is used by six out of ten Internet users (Anderson 2015), and has an overall user base of more than a billion people (YouTube n.d.).

It is apparent that YouTube was created as an entertainment-oriented technology. Nevertheless, it was quickly adopted for educational purposes. Harvard University joined YouTube September 25, 2005, making it an early adopter with an institutional presence on the social media site (see Harvard University n.d.). Harvard was soon followed by other universities, including Stanford, Rutgers, Purdue, and many others, who flocked to YouTube to establish institutional channels. In 2009, a post on the Official YouTube Blog (Greenberg 2009) revealed that YouTube EDU, which had been created as a directory of partnering colleges and universities, had grown to include more than 200 U.S. and Canadian institutions with additional partners from the UK, France, Spain, Italy, the Netherlands, Russia, and Israel coming on board. At that time, more than 40,000 videos of lectures, news, and campus life were available through YouTube EDU.

During the early years of institutional adoption, YouTube also began finding its way into the classroom. In the fall of 2007, Dr. Alexandra Juhasz, a professor of media studies at Pitzer College, taught a course called Learning from YouTube that was about and also on YouTube with class sessions and coursework posted on YouTube for public viewing (Pitzer College 2007; Juhasz 2009). This was the first YouTube course offered at a college, but it was not the last. In fall 2008, an online graduate-level course called YouTube for Educators was offered at Boise State University where it continues to be offered annually (Snelson 2013).

By far the most common use of YouTube occurs when educators draw from its archives to find video clips that they can use as instructional media. The use of YouTube videos for educational purposes builds on a long history of educational film and video in the classroom (Snelson & Perkins 2009). Video makes it possible to bring information into the classroom that might normally be out of reach, such as expert talks, historical events, remote places, dangerous experiments, performances, views of microscopic life, and slow-motion or time-lapse recordings that alter the speed of phenomena to a point within the range of human visual perception.

Some examples of how YouTube has been used for classroom instruction include augmenting tourism curriculum with videos of an expert in the field (Forristal 2012), problem-solving activities with engineering students (Liberatore, Vestal, & Herring 2012), teaching Ugandan traditional dances in K–12 schools (Mabingo 2015), promoting antiracism in social work education (Deepak & Biggs 2011), prevention of sexually transmitted diseases in health education (Prybutok 2013) and for teacher professional development (Copper & Semich 2014).

The widespread availability of video recording and editing technologies has extended the role of video beyond classroom viewing to also enable the creation of YouTube videos as classroom projects. Student video projects have been implemented for various types of courses and purposes, including business and marketing (Alon & Herath 2014; Orús et al. 2016), English language learning (Hafner 2014; Sun & Yang 2015), and classroom video documentary projects (Hofer & Swan 2006; Lin & Polaniecki 2009).

YouTube has also been the focus of academic research and scholarship. Within a year of its creation, YouTube attracted the attention of scholars from multiple disciplines who engaged in research and theoretical discussion regarding educational applications of YouTube (Snelson 2011). Over time, researchers have continued to explore YouTube as an educational resource. A scoping review of research related to YouTube in the classroom identified thirty-five studies published from 2008 through 2015 (Snelson 2016). Analysis of these studies indicated that YouTube is used for two general purposes in education: to curate existing videos or as a place to host video creations. These categories correspond to findings from survey research conducted through the Pew Research Center (Duggan 2013), which categorized online photo and video sharing among adult Internet users as falling within curator and creator groups. Similar categories have been proposed by the Partnership for 21st Century Learning (n.d.) with respect to media literacy practices of analyzing media messages or creating media products. Essentially, these categories comprise central concepts and processes involved in media consumption (using what exists) and production (creating something new). With respect to the discussion of YouTube as an educational resource, video curation involves the selection, analysis, use, organization, and sharing of existing online video for the purpose of teaching and learning. Video creation involves production of video for upload and online sharing through YouTube as an educational media project. Video creation on YouTube may also integrate tools built into the online platform for captioning, editing, sharing, interacting with viewers, and tracking viewership.

The benefits of YouTube as a source of free video content and hosting are alluring, which helps to explain the continued interest. However, a number of tenacious and often intertwined challenges must be grappled with when using YouTube as an educational resource. These issues are discussed next within the respective roles of using YouTube for curating or creating videos.

Curating YouTube Videos

There has never been such ubiquitous access to educational videos on YouTube. This is beneficial for educators and students since it offers a seemingly endless pool of media resources

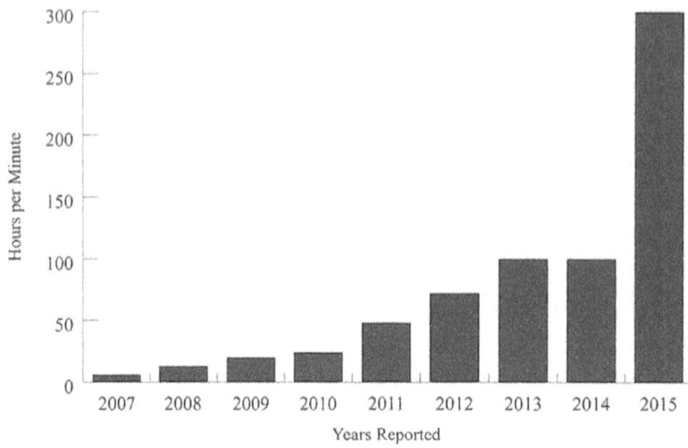

Figure 15.1 Hours of Video Uploaded per Minute to YouTube

from which to draw from. Yet this benefit is coupled with the challenge of sifting through irrelevant, inappropriate, or inaccurate content to find suitable videos for classroom use or curation into educational media collections. The problem is compounded by the apparent enormity of the YouTube video repository. It is impossible to calculate the overall amount of video on YouTube since it continually changes as video is uploaded or removed. However, it is possible to gain at least some perspective of the magnitude of YouTube through an examination of upload rates reported by YouTube. The graph in Figure 15.1 provides a visual depiction of the number of hours of video uploaded per minute to YouTube from 2007 through 2015. These numbers were drawn from posts published online in the Official YouTube Blog at http://youtube-global.blogspot.com. From this graph it can be observed that 6 hours of video was uploaded per minute in 2007 and the rate climbed over time until it reached 300 hours per minute in 2015. The amount of video uploaded to YouTube per day, based on the 2015 upload rate, is the equivalent of 3,600 two-hour feature films uploaded per day. Clearly, there is an enormous amount of video on YouTube. This is both a blessing and a challenge since there is an abundant supply of video to choose from but also a substantial time commitment when reviewing and selecting appropriate videos for educational purposes.

Unfortunately, there are multiple challenges to be aware of when using YouTube as an educational resource. Some of the challenges have been identified by the author of this chapter after years of working with educators in her YouTube course. These challenges include the need for knowledge and skills in using the technology; the challenge of finding, evaluating, and managing online video collections; dealing with inappropriate materials; ensuring accessibility; and working with the issues of blocked access to YouTube at schools, libraries, or other institutions. Some of these challenges can be addressed through development of skills in media and digital literacy. Others can be addressed by learning how to use tools available either through YouTube or externally in third-party applications. It is important to become aware of these challenges and some of the practical strategies available for addressing them so that YouTube can be used as an educational resource.

Media and Digital Literacy for YouTube Curation

Media and digital literacies are both relevant and important when using YouTube as an educational resource. This is because the competencies associated with media and digital literacy are so readily applicable when grappling with the enormity of YouTube, its technology, and the mixed collection of good, inappropriate, and inaccurate video content found there (Snelson 2015). Competencies discussed in various definitions of media literacy include accessing, analyzing, evaluating, using, and producing information in various forms (Aufderheide & Firestone 1993; Hobbs 2011; National Association for Media Literacy Education 2007; Potter 2014; Scheibe & Rogow 2012). These skills are essential when using YouTube as an educational resource. Furthermore, curation of content from social media sites has been associated with media and digital literacy competencies essential for the effective selection and use of existing information and media resources (Mihailidis 2016; Mihailidis & Cohen 2013). The application of media and digital literacy competencies on YouTube can be illustrated by considering them in three clusters that come into play during the process of curating YouTube videos: (1) accessing videos, (2) analyzing and evaluating content, and (3) designing educational activities that include the use of curated YouTube videos.

Access videos: YouTube videos can be accessed through the use of various strategies that include browsing known educational channels, such as the YouTube Education channel at www.youtube.com/edu, accepting video shares from peers, or finding videos through a serendipitous process via the related videos that populate the sidelines when watching a YouTube video. A more effective process is to use either basic or advanced search techniques (Google 2016b). The basic search is the foundational starting point that requires typing a relevant keyword or phrase into the search box on YouTube. This approach, although simple, can be effective depending on the topic and the educational needs. For example, a basic search for the "Tacoma Narrows Bridge disaster" should readily produce historical clips of the bridge collapse at or near the top of the search results. This is a very specific event that typically yields good results through a basic search. However, other search phrases may not yield desired results as readily. For example, a teacher might be interested in learning about how others are integrating videos in the classroom. One possible search phrase might be "educational uses for video," which yields a wide array of videos, some of which may be unsuitable for the teacher's needs or may be inappropriate for classroom viewing. A slight revision to the search phrase to "classroom uses for video" will yield somewhat different results. Appending the words "for children" to either search changes the results dramatically. It could take several tries to identify the best search phrase for accessing videos on this topic. Familiarity with how keywords and search phrases impact search results is a critical digital and media literacy skill for YouTube.

Advanced search techniques offer a way to refine a search through the use of filters or Boolean operators. When searching directly from within YouTube, a set of filtering options are revealed along with search results after entering a basic search word or phrase. At the time of this writing, it is possible to filter results by upload date (e.g., today, this month, this year), type (e.g., video, channel, playlist), duration (e.g., short, long), features (e.g., subtitles/captions, Creative Commons), and sorting by relevance, upload date, view count, and rating. These filtering options can be valuable when searching for video that meets specific needs such as closed captioned (CC) video for accessibility or channels that feature collections of video for a particular content area. In addition to filtering, simple Boolean operators commonly used with search engines (see Sullivan n.d.) can sometimes help to improve search results by specifying words to be included with a plus (+), by removing unwanted terms with a minus (−), or by searching for exact phrases with quotes ("). Potential candidate videos can be saved from the search results into a watch-later collection or a playlist until there is time to analyze and evaluate them.

Analyze and evaluate content: Once candidate videos have been located and accessed on YouTube, the next step is to analyze and evaluate them. These processes can run concurrently when assessing YouTube content for educational purposes. Caution is advised when selecting any YouTube video because what looks good at first glance may turn out to have problems on deeper inspection. YouTube videos should undergo an interrogation process where they are reviewed in their entirety for meaning, accuracy, age-appropriateness, relevance, and value for the instructional purpose at hand. A set of key questions, linked from the core principles page of the National Association for Media Literacy Education website at http://namle.net/publications/core-principles/, provides an excellent starting point for interrogating the YouTube videos during the analysis and evaluation process. These questions promote analysis of authorship, meaning, and credibility, which is of great importance when evaluating YouTube videos that could have been uploaded by anyone. This type of analysis can circumvent the challenges associated with inaccurate or inappropriate YouTube videos through a systematic process of evaluation and identification of problems that yield the videos unusable as educational media. An examination of the sideline content surrounding the videos, which includes comments, related videos, and advertising that might be distracting or inappropriate should also be conducted as part of the overall evaluation process.

Use and produce: Once videos have been accessed, analyzed, and evaluated, they may be used individually, or they may be curated into an educational media collection for use in educational activities produced for specific purposes. The YouTube website provides tools, such as channels and playlists, which make it easy to collect and organize videos into online collections. An online help center at https://support.google.com/youtube/ provides information about how to use the various tools available on the YouTube platform. This is a good starting point for anyone who uses YouTube to curate online video collections. Management of the collection, along with related benefits and challenges, is discussed next to delve more deeply into these issues.

Managing Curated Video Collections

A free YouTube account, available through Google, offers access to online tools that are valuable for managing curated educational videos. Three main areas become available after logging into YouTube and serve as a gateway to a different tool sets. The primary landing page for YouTube is its home page, which is customized based on user activity on the site. From the custom YouTube home page, users can access subscriptions, trending content, favorites, video playlists, and any videos that have been added to a watch-later collection. Only the account owner has access to the custom home page on YouTube. Another section is the YouTube channel, which is a public web page that can be customized to display sections of YouTube content such as playlists, favorites, activity feeds, and links to other channels. It can be used to organize curated video collections for any topic, including educational content. A teacher can set up a curated educational channel with sections devoted to classroom topics that students can access from any location with online access to YouTube. The third primary area of the YouTube site is called the Creator Studio. This is a dashboard that links to multiple tools and resources available to the owner of the YouTube account and its associated channel. It offers access to a video manager of videos and playlists, a live video streaming tool, a community area where messages can be accessed, default channel settings, analytics that show usage statistics for the channel, and an area for video creation that includes an online video editor where Creative Commons media found on YouTube can be curated and remixed into a new video. Overall, YouTube is a robust system containing numerous tools made available for free to anyone, including educators, for curation of existing videos and management of video creations.

The playlist tool on YouTube is useful for curating videos into a single page with lesson plan, instructions for students, and links to related resources typed in the description box of the YouTube playlist (Snelson 2010). This entire collection of videos with lesson plan can be shared with students directly from the channel or by providing a link. Privacy settings can be adjusted to allow the playlist to be visible to the public, unlisted so that only people with the link can view it, or private so that it can be viewed only by the person who created the playlist and any other YouTube user it has been shared with.

Hiding Sideline Content

The process of curating YouTube videos for instructional purposes may lead to the discovery of excellent educational video clips, but they may be surrounded by advertisements or inappropriate sideline content such as comments or related videos. Fortunately, tools are available for handling these types of challenges. One approach for removing sideline content is to use an online tool designed for distraction-free viewing of YouTube videos. This involves pasting the link to a YouTube video into a simple form. After pressing a button on the form, the video is displayed on a new web page with all of the sideline content stripped away. Examples of these types of online tools are Viewpure at http://viewpure.com/ and Watchkin at https://watchkin.com/. Another site called TubeChop, located at www.tubechop.com/, takes this process a step further by making it possible to share a section from a video so that only that part is viewed while also hiding all sideline content.

Another approach to hiding sideline content is to embed the YouTube video in a website, online discussion forum, or other online tool that permits video embedding. Each YouTube video comes with a piece of HTML embed code that can be customized for size, for removal of access to related videos, or to hide the video title, which prohibits easy access back to the source page on YouTube and all of its sideline content (YouTube Help 2015). Embed options can be tested and previewed directly in YouTube after clicking the share button below the video after choosing the embed option. Once the video is embedded by pasting the embed code into the HTML area of the online application, all content on the surrounding YouTube video watch page is hidden from view.

Captioning Curated Videos

Captioning is another issue to consider when using YouTube videos or producing educational activities with curated videos. Captions are displayed as on-screen text representing speech and sounds recorded in the video, thus making the video accessible for people with hearing impairments (National Institute on Deafness and Other Communication Disorders 2011). Videos that are uploaded to YouTube are often automatically captioned through a machine transcription process. However, autogenerated captions typically contain mistakes. The owner of the video can make corrections to the captions directly in YouTube through the caption and subtitle tool (Google 2016a). However, there is no guarantee that this will happen. Those who are simply using the video and do not own it cannot make corrections to captions since they are unable to log in to the account associated with the video. In situations like this, an external tool, such as Amara found at www.amara.org/en/, may be used to create captions for videos created by other people and to work around this challenge.

Addressing Issues With YouTube Blocking in Schools

A tenacious challenge faced by teachers and students, particularly in K–12 settings, is that access to YouTube may be blocked. A contributing factor to the situation is an interpretation of CIPA (Children's Internet Protection Act) requirements for the E-Rate program, which helps eligible schools and libraries receive discounts on telecommunications services and Internet access (Federal Communications Commission 2017). In order to receive support for services, "school and library authorities must certify that they are enforcing a policy of Internet safety that includes measures to block or filter Internet access for both minors and adults to certain visual depictions" (Universal Service Administrative Company 2015: para. 1). CIPA does not specifically require schools or libraries to block access to YouTube, Facebook, or other online social media sites. Yet the end result of efforts to comply with CIPA, as required for E-Rate support, has been to deny or restrict access to social media sites (American Library Association n.d.).

Obviously, when YouTube is blocked at school, the carefully curated educational video collection cannot be used within the classroom. It can only be used off campus for the benefit of those who have access to YouTube at external locations. This might be useful in some situations, such as when providing students who are absent with instructional materials or when adopting a flipped classroom model where video instruction is viewed in advance of classroom activities (Bergman & Sams 2012). It should be noted, however, that some students might not have access to the Internet or YouTube outside of school and will miss out on these types of opportunities.

One so-called solution to the problem has been to download YouTube videos that can be carried into the classroom on a portable device, like a flash drive. This strategy requires use of a software tool or online service to download YouTube videos. An online search for information about downloading YouTube videos will produce links to a variety of tools and informational tutorials. At first glance, this sounds like a good solution. However, the problem with this approach is that it violates YouTube's terms of service, which states, "You shall not download any Content unless you see a 'download' or similar link displayed by YouTube on the Service for that Content" (YouTube 2010: 5B).

Confusion about this issue is compounded by the easy access to YouTube downloader tools and information from credible sources that makes it seem like a legitimate option. For example, Jones and Cuthrell (2011) published a peer-reviewed journal article on the topic of YouTube in the classroom that included instructions for how to use a tool for downloading and saving YouTube videos. This strategy was promoted as a solution for the challenge of YouTube being blocked at school, yet the authors did not address YouTube's terms of service or copyright issues related to downloading videos created by someone else. Richard Byrne, who maintains the popular Free Technology for Teachers blog, responded to this issue in a post where he explained how he is frequently asked about tools for downloading YouTube videos but that he has removed all information about these tools in order to respect copyright and terms of service, as well as to serve as a role model for students (Byrne 2015).

Another option has become available that makes it possible for schools to selectively filter educational content from YouTube. In 2011, the YouTube for Schools project was announced (Truong 2011). Through this project, school administrators could turn on a special network setting that granted access to the educational content on YouTube EDU while still restricting access to the rest of YouTube. In 2016, information on the YouTube Help website revealed that the YouTube for Schools program was in the process of being phased out. A new method for selectively restricting YouTube content was recommended for nonprofit organizations that use Google Apps for Work, Education, and Government (Google 2016d). Configurable settings enable restricted access to YouTube EDU and any other videos approved for school access. This solution provides a method through which the benefits of educational content can be realized while simultaneously addressing the challenges associated with undesirable content on YouTube. Unfortunately, this solution does not address issues of broadband limitations that might prohibit video streaming in the classroom.

Creating YouTube Videos

There are times when, despite the extensive access to video on YouTube, it is not possible to locate video segments that meet a specific instructional need. It may be necessary to create a video that is customized for a particular age group, context, or content area. In other situations, video production may be a central element of a classroom project, such as when developing student-generated video presentations. Video production can be a valuable experience that promotes attainment of multiple skills including those involving digital technology, media design, integration of content-area content, and media literacy competencies (Hobbs et al. 2013). For example, a classroom video documentary project might involve researching a topic, scriptwriting, production or selection of media assets (e.g., video segments, images, music), and use of video recording and editing technologies (Hofer & Swan 2006; Lin & Polaniecki 2009). One of the more difficult challenges when creating videos for YouTube is that of copyright and fair use due to the complexities of automatic scanning after upload.

Copyright and Fair Use Challenges on YouTube

When creating videos, it is important to consider how copyright and fair use apply to the project. Copyright protection in the United States is provided for original works of authorship produced in a fixed and tangible form (United States Copyright Office 2012). Owners of the copyright generally possess rights to reproduce, create derivative works, distribute, display, or perform the work. Why this matters to those who create videos, even for educational purposes, is that media assets used in a video project, such as images, music, or video segments, might be protected by copyright, and reuse could be prohibited. The use of copyrighted works is possible under certain conditions, such as when permission is granted or when fair use is applied for transformative purposes involving commentary, criticism, or parody (Stanford University Libraries n.d.a). Fair use is guided by a set of four factors that include (1) the purpose and character of use, (2) the nature of the copyrighted work, (3) the amount used, and (4) the effect on the potential market. Unfortunately, the factors are broad and leave those who wish to apply fair use in a state of confusion, fear, and doubt (Aufderheide & Jaszi 2011; Hobbs 2010). Codes of best practice for fair use may help to clarify the types of situations where fair use might apply (Center for Media and Social Impact 2008). Yet the situation is complicated when videos containing copyrighted media are uploaded to YouTube where companies or people might claim ownership and request actions such as video removal. For example, in 2007 Stephanie Lenz uploaded a 29-second recording of a toddler dancing to the Prince song, "Let's Go Crazy," which was playing in the background. The video clip was removed by YouTube after a copyright infringement claim was submitted by the music company that owned rights to it. An ongoing legal battle ensued, lasting over a decade at the time of this writing, after a lawsuit was filed by Lenz and the Electronic Frontier Foundation (Electronic Frontier Foundation n.d.b). The case went under consideration by the U.S. Supreme Court in October 2016. The final outcome of this case has ramifications for fair use and free speech on the Internet.

Although fair use should protect video makers who integrate copyrighted materials during commentary, criticism, or parody, complications arise after they are put on YouTube. Videos uploaded to YouTube undergo automatic scanning through the Content ID system, which compares the video content to reference files of copyrighted works (Google 2016c). The reference files serve as a digital fingerprint of copyrighted media. If a match is found, certain actions are taken based on what the copyright owner has chosen. Options for copyright owners include muting the audio to block copyrighted music, blocking the entire video from being viewed at all, putting advertisements on the video, tracking viewership statistics on the video, or blocking viewability on certain devices, apps, or websites. In addition, different actions can be set for different countries. People who upload videos containing content that is matched to copyrighted content might receive notice of a Content ID claim. The person who uploaded the video might take several actions in response, such as to do nothing, remove or swap music, or dispute the claim. The YouTube Copyright Center, located at www.youtube.com/yt/copyright/, provides several pages of essential information to explain the processes involved with copyright and Content ID.

The Content ID system is designed to help police the problem of users uploading copyrighted materials such as music videos or entire television shows. The volume of videos uploaded to YouTube makes it necessary to have some sort of automated system. Yet it does have its problems. An example is the case of Lawrence Lessig, who is a Harvard Law School professor and cofounder of the Creative Commons. A copyright problem surfaced after Lessig uploaded a video of one of his talks, titled "Open, to YouTube" (Lessig 2010). The video contains short media excerpts used to illustrate the commentary and criticism expressed in the talk and falls within the realm of fair use. Nevertheless, a take-down notice was issued by Liberation Music that claimed copyright violation due to some of the music in clips Lessig included in the recorded talk. After Lessig responded with a claim of fair use, he received a threat of being sued in federal court (Electronic Frontier Foundation n.d.a). The situation was ultimately resolved after Lessig successfully settled a fair use lawsuit against the music company. The lawsuit revealed that a single employee without any legal background had initiated the take-down process and issued the threat of a lawsuit without viewing the video.

Unfortunately, the problems with Content ID and the policy for take-downs have been a source of frustration for many individuals who do not have law degrees and find themselves grappling with copyright claims. The problems caused by Content ID and the associated frustrations have been articulated in blog posts describing erroneous copyright notices for content not actually in the flagged video, claims made by companies or individuals who did not actually own the content, and disregard for fair use (see for example, Richwalsky 2015; Kalia 2015). YouTube has responded by having a member of the YouTube Policy Team initiate an online discussion forum on the topic of Content ID appeals (YTSpencer 2016). Hundreds of people have responded to the discussion forum, and thousands have viewed the running conversation about issues and ideas for correcting problems. It has also been reported, in *The New York Times* online, that YouTube has been paying fees to fight take-downs for some video creators (Kang 2015). What these situations help to illustrate is that anyone who uses YouTube as a place to upload videos, even for educational purposes, should be aware of the potential for Content ID to flag videos even when fair use is in play. An appeal system is available, which might alleviate situations where a copyright notice has been submitted on video where fair use applies, but there are no guarantees of a successful outcome.

The Content ID system and the problems associated with it could be perceived as a substantial challenge for certain types of educational video projects such as in media education courses where clips from popular media are essential. Progress has been made toward allowing educators to legally extract and use media clips for educational purposes (Hobbs 2016). Yet when these clips are uploaded to YouTube, the chances of Content ID hassles are strong despite fair use. It may be necessary to either avoid YouTube or prepare to deal with the likelihood of copyright claims and appeals.

Creative Commons Licensing

When creating videos for upload to YouTube, it may be less problematic to obtain media assets such as texts, music, sound effects, images, and video segments from the public domain or Creative Commons sources. Generally speaking, use of public domain or Creative Commons media assets should minimize or even eliminate most problems with Content ID and copyright violation notices on YouTube. Anything in the public domain can be freely used without permission since no copyright protection is associated with it (Stanford University Libraries n.d.b). Works enter the public domain for various reasons, including old age, when the works are created by U.S. government officers or employees, when an author dedicates works to the public domain, or in some cases due to copyright that expired and was not renewed. Sources of public domain media can be located online by searching for public domain images, music, texts, and so forth. Internet search tools (e.g., Google, Bing) offer filtering of results by license. Online media archives (e.g., Internet Archive, Wikimedia Commons) can also be searched for media in the public domain. Terms of use or license agreements should be read carefully before downloading media assets since restrictions are sometimes required or must be agreed to when using collections or services that deliver public domain content (Fishman 2014).

Another alternative for obtaining media assets for video projects is to download files that have been released under a Creative Commons license. The Creative Commons licenses provide a way for copyright owners to grant permissions to use their works under conditions specified by the type of license (Creative Commons n.d.). Essentially, the licenses define permissions for commercial use, the creation of derivative works, and distribution. The least restrictive license is the CC BY license, which allows users to distribute or remix the work, even commercially, provided credit is given for the original creation. This is the license used in the YouTube Creative Commons. The CC BY license is designated by users who upload videos and select the Creative Commons licensing option. A post written for the Official YouTube Blog by former Creative Common CEO Catherine Casserly (2012) promotes the use of Creative Commons videos on YouTube, which may be reused and remixed online in the YouTube video editor (Google 2016e). After opening the YouTube video editor, users can search for Creative Commons video segments. The video clips can be selected and remixed in a new video project, after which they can be published directly to YouTube. This provides a unique opportunity to legally build upon works created by others. However, the system depends on users to correctly designate the Creative Commons license when uploading videos. This opens the possibility of selecting a clip that was illegally uploaded or incorrectly designated as CC BY, which could lead to copyright issues for the remixed video. This is something to be aware of prior to remixing videos on YouTube. It is sometimes better to locate media assets from external sources, verify the license and terms of use, and use video-editing software to create a video that can be uploaded to YouTube.

It can be an informative and educational experience to review media licenses, develop media literacy competencies associated with creating video, and learn the technical skills needed to work with various types of media assets for video-editing projects. An example of this is a mini documentary project that students complete in the author's YouTube for Educators course. After identifying a topic and storyboarding an outline of the video content, students acquire or create media assets (e.g., images, music, video clips) to use in the video. They are required to demonstrate lawful use of media before creating their projects. Before downloading media assets from the Internet, they review license information to ensure that the media may be legally downloaded and used in their video projects. If they record media, they must ensure that they protect the rights of others. For example, in a classroom they would need to acquire permission to record students. This project compels students to actively pay attention to the legal and ethical uses of media for educational video projects. Only then can they proceed with the process of composing the video with video-editing software and then upload the video to YouTube. This project illustrates the integrated learning potential for classroom video production.

Conclusion

Since early in its history, YouTube has been adopted and used by educators and educational institutions. The information in this chapter illuminates some of the benefits and challenges of using YouTube as an educational resource. The benefits include ubiquitous online access to a diverse and growing body of free video content and an expanding educational video collection. The user-friendly online platform simplifies the process of hosting and distributing videos. Tools on the YouTube website make it easy to organize videos into an educational collection on YouTube channels and playlists. Video creators can take advantage of online editing tools and a simple yet robust captioning tool to make videos accessible for people with disabilities.

Yet challenges exist when using YouTube as an educational resource. Although there is good educational content on YouTube, it is often necessary to sift through inaccurate or inappropriate content to find it. Furthermore, the sideline content, such as comments or related videos, can be distracting or might render the video unusable in a classroom. There are strategies for working around this problem, such as embedding video, or using a third-party tool to hide sideline content. Unfortunately, the effort involved in screening and carefully selecting videos may be of little value if YouTube is blocked and cannot be accessed from the classroom. This challenge now has a potential solution through selective filtering of YouTube content, via Google Apps for Work, Education, and Government (Google 2016d), to allow schools to access the good content while screening out the problematic content.

Additional challenges exist for those who create educational video and particularly when media assets created by others are integrated into the video project. Uploading a video to YouTube subjects it to scanning by the automated Content ID system, which may result in copyright violation notices. Fair use is applicable but will require action on the part of the video creator to dispute copyright notices. The system and policies are still evolving. Nevertheless, those who create videos should pay close attention to terms of use and licensing requirements for any media assets created by others that they use in video projects.

YouTube can be a fabulous educational resource as long as there is awareness of the benefits and challenges associated with using the content and the video-sharing platform. There are opportunities to develop digital and media literacy skills while taking advantage of the wealth of knowledge and technologies available through YouTube.

References

Alexa. (n.d.). "YouTube.com." Retrieved from www.alexa.com/siteinfo/www.youtube.com

Alon, I., & Herath, R. K. (2014). "Teaching International Business via Social Media Projects." *Journal of Teaching in International Business*, 25(1), 44–59. doi:10.1080/08975930.2013.847814

American Library Association. (n.d.). "Libraries and the Internet Toolkit: Legal Issues: CIPA and Filtering." Retrieved from www.ala.org/advocacy/intfreedom/iftoolkits/litoolkit/legalissues_CIPA_filtering

Anderson, M. (2015, February 12). "5 Facts About Online Video, for YouTube's 10th Birthday." *Pew Research Center Fact Tank: News in the Numbers*. Retrieved from www.pewresearch.org/fact-tank/2015/02/12/5-facts-about-online-video-for-youtubes-10th-birthday

Aufderheide, P., & Firestone, C. M. (1993). *Media Literacy: A Report of the National Leadership Conference on Media Literacy*. Washington, DC: Aspen Institute. Retrieved from Educational Research Information Center (ERIC), http://eric.ed.gov/?id=ED365294

Aufderheide, P., & Jaszi, P. (2011). *Reclaiming Fair Use: How to Put Balance Back Into Copyright*. Chicago: University of Chicago Press.

Bergman, J., & Sams, A. (2012). *Flip Your Classroom: Reach Every Student in Every Class Every Day*. Washington, DC: International Society for Technology in Education.

Burgess, J., & Green, J. (2009). "How YouTube Matters." In *YouTube: Online Video and Participatory Culture* (pp. 1–14). Malden, MA: Polity Press.

Byrne, R. (2015, August 31). "About Downloading YouTube Videos . . ." [Weblog post]. Retrieved from www.freetech4teachers.com/2015/08/about-downloading-youtube-videos.html#.VvL49BIrLaY

Casserly, C. (2012, July 25). "Here's Your Invite to Reuse and Remix the 4 Million Creative Commons-Licensed Videos on YouTube." [Weblog post]. Retrieved from Official YouTube Blog website https://youtube.googleblog.com/2012/07/heres-your-invite-to-reuse-and-remix-4.html

Center for Media and Social Impact. (2008). "Code of Best Practices in Fair Use for Online Video." Retrieved from http://cmsimpact.org/code/code-best-practices-fair-use-online-video/

Copper, J., & Semich, G. (2014). "YouTube as a Teacher Training Tool: Information and Communication Technology as a Delivery Instrument for Professional Development." *International Journal of Information & Communication Technology Education*, 10(4), 30–40.

Creative Commons. (n.d.). "About the Licenses." Retrieved from https://creativecommons.org/licenses/

Deepak, A., & Biggs, M. J. G. (2011). "Intimate Technology: A Tool for Teaching Anti-Racism in Social Work Education." *Journal of Ethnic & Cultural Diversity in Social Work*, 20, 39–56. doi:10.1080/15313204.2011.545944

Duggan, M. (2013). "Photo and Video Sharing Grown Online." Retrieved from Pew Research Center website www.pewInternet.org/2013/10/28/photo-and-video-sharing-grow-online/

Electronic Frontier Foundation. (n.d.a). "*Lawrence Lessig v. Liberation Music*." Retrieved from www.eff.org/cases/lawrence-lessig-v-liberation-music

Electronic Frontier Foundation. (n.d.b). "Lenz v. Universal." Retrieved from www.eff.org/cases/lenz-v-universal

Federal Communications Commission. (2017). "FAQs on e-Rate Program for Schools and Libraries." Retrieved from www.fcc.gov/consumers/guides/universal-service-program-schools-and-libraries-e-rate

Fishman, S. (2014). *The Public Domain: How to Find & Use Copyright-Free Writings, Music, Art & More* (7th ed.). Berkeley, CA: NOLO.

Forristal, L. J. (2012). "Using YouTube Videos of Anthropology of Tourism Pioneer Valene Smith's Work and Philosophy to Balance the Tourism Curriculum." *Journal of Teaching in Travel & Tourism*, 12, 91–104.doi:10.1080/15313220.2012.650098

Google. (2016a). "Add Subtitles & Closed Captions." Retrieved from YouTube Help website https://support.google.com/youtube/answer/2734796

Google. (2016b). "Advanced Search (Filters)." Retrieved from YouTube Help website https://support.google.com/youtube/answer/111997

Google. (2016c). "How Content ID Works." Retrieved from YouTube Help website https://support.google.com/youtube/answer/2797370?hl=en&ref_topic=4515467

Google. (2016d). "How YouTube for Schools Works." Retrieved from YouTube Help website https://support.google.com/youtube/answer/2695317

Google. (2016e). "Use YouTube Video Editor." Retrieved from YouTube Help website https://support.google.com/youtube/answer/183851

Greenberg, O. (2009, October 1). "The Global Classroom on YouTube EDU." [Weblog post]. Retrieved from http://youtube-global.blogspot.com/2009/09/global-classroom-gets-bigger-with.html

Hafner, C. A. (2014). "Embedding Digital Literacies in English Language Teaching: Students' Digital Video projects as Multimodal Ensembles." *TESOL Quarterly*, 48, 655–685. doi:10.1002/tesq.138

Harvard University. (n.d.). "About Description." Retrieved from www.youtube.com/user/Harvard/about

Hobbs, R. (2010). *Copyright Clarity: How Fair Use Supports Digital Learning.* Thousand Oaks, CA: Corwin.

Hobbs, R. (2011). *Digital and Media Literacy: Connecting Culture and Classroom.* Thousand Oaks, CA: Sage.

Hobbs, R. (2016). "Lessons in Copyright Activism: K–12 Education and the DMCA 1201 Exemption Rulemaking Process." *International Journal of Information and Communication Technology Education*, 12, 50–63.

Hobbs, R., Donnelly, K., Friesem, J., & Moen, M. (2013). "Learning to Engage: How Positive Attitudes About the News, Media Literacy, and Video Production Contribute to Adolescent Civic Engagement." *Educational Media International*, 50, 231–246. doi:10.1080/09523987.2013.862364

Hofer, M., & Swan, K. O. (2006). "Technological Pedagogical Content Knowledge in Action: A Case Study of a Middle School Digital Documentary Project." *Journal of Research on Technology in Education*, 41, 179–200.

Jones, T., & Cuthrell, K. (2011). "YouTube: Educational Potentials and Pitfalls." *Computers in the Schools*, 28, 75–85. doi:10.1080/07380569.2011.553149

Juhasz, A. (2009). "Learning the Five Lessons of YouTube: After Trying to Teach There, I don't Believe the Hype." *Cinema Journal*, 48, 145–150. doi:10.1353/cj.0.0098

Kalia, A. (2015, May 1). "Congrats on the 10-Year Anniversary YouTube, Now Please Fix Content ID." [Weblog post]. Retrieved from Electronic Frontier Foundation website www.eff.org/deeplinks/2015/05/congrats-10-year-anniversary-youtube-now-please-fix-content-id

Kang, C. (2015, November 19). "YouTube to Pay Fees for Some Video Makers to Fight Takedowns." *New York Times*. Retrieved from www.nytimes.com/2015/11/20/technology/youtube-to-pay-fees-for-some-video-makers-to-fight-takedowns.html

Karim, J. [Computer Science at Illinois]. (2007, June 5). "Jawed Karim, Illinois Commencement 2007," pt2. [Video file]. Retrieved from https://youtu.be/24yglUYbKXE

Karim, J. (2005, April 23). "Me at the Zoo." [Video file]. Retrieved from https://youtu.be/jNQXAC9IVRw

Lessig, L. (2010, June 8). "Open." [Video file]. Retrieved from https://youtu.be/KBTWoCaNKn4

Liberatore, M. W., Vestal, C. R., & Herring, A. M. (2012). "Advances in Engineering Education YouTube Fridays: Student Led Development of Engineering Estimate Problems." *Advances in Engineering Education*, 3(1), 1–16.

Lin, C-C., & Polaniecki, S. (2009). "From Media Consumption to Media Production: Applications of YouTube in an Eighth-Grade Video Documentary Project." *Journal of Visual Literacy*, 28, 92–107.

Mabingo, A. (2015). "Integrating Emerging Technologies in Teaching Ugandan Traditional Dances in K–12 Schools in New York City." *The Curriculum Journal*, 26, 313–334. doi:10.1080/09585176.2015.1035734

Mihailidis, P. (2016). "Digital Curation and Digital Literacy: Evaluating the Role of Curation in Developing Critical Literacies for Participation in Digital Culture." *E-Learning and Digital Media*. Advance online publication. doi:10.1177/2042753016631868

Mihailidis, P., & Cohen, J. N. (2013). "Exploring Curation as a Core Competency in Digital and Media Literacy Education." *Journal of Interactive Media in Education*, 2013(1), 2. doi:10.5334/2013-02. Retrieved from http://jime.open.ac.uk/articles/10.5334/2013-02/

National Association for Media Literacy Education. (2007). "Core Principles of Media Literacy Education in the United States." Retrieved from http://namle.net/publications/core-principles/

National Institute on Deafness and Other Communication Disorders. (2011). "Captions for Deaf and Hard-of-Hearing Viewers." Retrieved from U.S. Department of Health and Human Services, National Institutes of Health website www.nidcd.nih.gov/health/captions-deaf-and-hard-hearing-viewers

Orús, C., Barlés, M. J., Belanche, D., Casaló, L., Fraj, E., & Gurrea, R. (2016). "The Use of YouTube as a Tool for Learner-Generated Content: Effects on Students' Learning Outcomes and Satisfaction." *Computers & Education*, 95, 254–269. doi:10.1016/j.compedu.2016.01.007

Partnership for 21st Century Learning. (n.d.). "Media Literacy." Retrieved from www.p21.org/about-us/p21-framework/349

Pitzer College. (2007). "Pitzer College professor invites the public to online class to learn about YouTube, the popular videosharing website." Retrieved from https://www.pitzer.edu/communications/2013/12/13/pitzer-college-professor-invites-the-public-to-online-class-to-learn-about-youtube-the-popular-videosharing-website/

Potter, J. W. (2014). *Media Literacy* (7th ed.). Los Angeles: Sage.

Prybutok, G. (2013). "YouTube: An Effective Web 2.0 Informing Channel for Health Education to Prevent STDs." *Informing Science: The International Journal of an Emerging Transdiscipline*, 16, 19–36.

Richwalsky, M. (2015, May 18). "YouTube's Content ID Matching System Is Broken—2015 Edition." [Weblog post]. Retrieved from https://highedwebtech.com/2015/05/18/youtubes-content-system/

Scheibe, C., & Rogow, F. (2012). *The Teacher's Guide to Media Literacy: Critical Thinking in a Multimedia World*. Thousand Oaks, CA: Sage.

Snelson, C. (2010). "Mapping YouTube 'Video Playlist Lessons' to the Learning Domains: Planning for Cognitive, Affective, and Psychomotor Learning." In C. Crawford, R. Carlsen, K. McFerrin, J. Price, R. Weber, & D. Willis (Eds.), *Proceedings of Society for Information Technology & Teacher Education International Conference 2010* (pp. 1193–1198). Chesapeake, VA: Association for the Advancement of Computing in Education.

Snelson, C. (2011). "YouTube Across the Disciplines: A Review of the Literature." *Journal of Online Learning and Teaching*, 7, 159–169. Retrieved from http://jolt.merlot.org/vol7no1/snelson_0311.pdf

Snelson, C. (2013). "Teaching a YouTube Course Online." In H. Yang & S. Wang (Eds.), *Cases on Online Learning Communities and Beyond: Investigations and Applications* (pp. 323–344). Hershey, PA: IGI Global.

Snelson, C. (2015). "Integrating Visual and Media Literacy in YouTube Video Projects." In D. M. Baylen & A. D'Alba (Eds.), *Visualizing Learning: Essentials of Teaching and Integrating Visual and Media Literacy*. New York: Springer.

Snelson, C. (2016). "YouTube in the Classroom: A Scoping Review of the Research Literature." Manuscript submitted for publication.

Snelson, C., & Perkins, R. A. (2009). "From Silent Film to YouTube™: Tracing the Historical Roots of Motion Picture Technologies in Education." *Journal of Visual Literacy*, 28(1), 1–27.

Sorkin, A. R., & Peters, J. W. (2006, October 9). "Google to Acquire YouTube for $1.65 Billion." *New York Times*. Retrieved from www.nytimes.com/2006/10/09/business/09cnd-deal.html

Stanford University Libraries. (n.d.a). "Fair Use." Retrieved from http://fairuse.stanford.edu/overview/fair-use/

Stanford University Libraries. (n.d.b). "The Public Domain." Retrieved from http://fairuse.stanford.edu/overview/public-domain/

Sullivan, D. (n.d.). "Search Engine Math." Retrieved from Search Engine Watch website https://searchenginewatch.com/sew/how-to/2065976/search-engine-math

Sun, Y-C., & Yang, F-Y. (2015). "I Help, Therefore, I Learn: Service Learning on Web 2.0 in an EFL Speaking Class." *Computer Assisted Language Learning*, 28, 202–219. doi:10.1080/09588221.2013.818555

Truong, B. (2011, December 11). "Opening Up a World of Educational Content With YouTube for Schools." [Weblog post]. Retrieved from https://youtube.googleblog.com/2011/12/opening-up-world-of-educational-content.html

United States Copyright Office. (2012). "Copyright Basics." Retrieved from www.copyright.gov/circs/circ01.pdf

Universal Service Administrative Company. (2015). "Schools and Libraries e-Rate: CIPA." Retrieved from www.universalservice.org/sl/applicants/step05/cipa.aspx

YouTube. (n.d.). "Statistics." Retrieved from www.youtube.com/yt/press/statistics.html

YouTube. (2005, November 7). "YouTube Receives 3.5M in Funding From Sequoia Capital." [Blog post]. Retrieved from http://youtube-global.blogspot.com/2005/11/youtube-receives-35m-in-funding-from.html

YouTube. (2010). "Terms of Service." Retrieved from www.youtube.com/static?template=terms

YouTube Help. (2015, January 6). "Embed Videos and Playlists." [Video file]. Retrieved from https://youtu.be/kfvxmEuC7bU

YouTube Spotlight. (2006, October 9). "A Message From Chad and Steve." [Video file]. Retrieved from https://youtu.be/QCVxQ_3Ejkg

YTSpencer. (2016, February 24). "Note From YouTube's Policy Team." [Forum Post]. Retrieved from https://productforums.google.com/forum/#!topic/youtube/x3aGmn_MsqI

Further Reading

Aufderheide, P., & Jaszi, P. (2011). *Reclaiming Fair Use: How to Put Balance Back into Copyright*. Chicago: University of Chicago Press.

Baker, F. (2012). *Media Literacy in the K–12 Classroom*. Washington, DC: International Society for Technology in Education.

Google. (2016). "YouTube Help Center." Retrieved from https://support.google.com/youtube/#topic=4355266

Hobbs, R. (2010). *Copyright Clarity: How Fair Use Supports Digital Learning*. Thousand Oaks, CA: Corwin.

YouTube. (n.d.). "Copyright Center." Retrieved from www.youtube.com/yt/copyright/

16

TEACHING HISTORY WITH FILM

Teaching About Film as History

Jeremy Stoddard

Birth of a Nation (2016), a film by Nate Parker[1] that retells the story of Nat Turner and the rebellion he led against slaveholders in 1831, is a noteworthy film for several reasons. First, it is Parker's attempt to shift the narrative of slavery and to challenge the representation of Turner as presented in history textbooks and as part of the common U.S. historical narrative. This narrative speaks of a crazy Nat Turner who led a murderous rampage, killing one innocent plantation family after another.

The film is also noteworthy for its title and timing—as it comes near the 100th anniversary of another film titled *Birth of a Nation* (1915), D. W. Griffith's landmark film that glorified the Ku Klux Klan and instilled many racial stereotypes of African Americans that persist today on screen—most prominently the hyper sexualized and violent "Black buck" characterization of African American males in film (Bogle 1992). Griffith's film was viewed as landmark beyond its racist narrative and representations: it was also viewed as the first feature-length narrative film that greatly influenced filmmaking and the role of cinema in society. The original *Birth of a Nation* was initially titled *The Clansman* and was viewed as so influential that it is often quoted that then–President Woodrow Wilson screened it at the White House (Lennig 2004).

Taking the same title for his film illustrates Parker's media literacy and epistemic understanding of the current new media environment. *Birth of a Nation* reflects a complex understanding of not only the medium of film but also of the role of the Internet, streaming media, and even social media and web search engine algorithms in how audiences today access and engage with media, or what Jenkins (2006) refers to as media convergence within a participatory culture. Parker uses this knowledge to attempt to replace Griffith's place on Web searches with his own *Birth of a Nation* and thus challenge Griffith's power and legacy over the representations of African Americans—and the ongoing legacy of the institution of slavery and enslavement in the United States.

Media Literacy, History Education, and Film

In this chapter, I explore the research and scholarship on what media literacy looks like when it comes to films that represent the past and the implications for practice from this work. More specifically, I examine how film represents the past and influences collective memory and national historical narrative, the role of film in history classrooms, and models for promoting media literacy through the use of film in teaching and learning history. This is a disciplinary approach to media literacy with direct implications for critical citizenship (e.g., Hoechsman & Poyntz 2012; Kellner & Share 2007). At its core, media literacy practices need to focus on the media form, the content it represents, and the context of production. Hoechsman and Poyntz define media literacy as "a set of competencies that enable us to interpret media texts and institutions, to make media of our own, and to recognize and engage with the social and political influence of media in everyday life" (2012: 1). When applied to a discipline like history, core concepts of media literacy are combined with epistemic understandings of the discipline and the practices of the profession—as well as the role of film in shaping society's understanding of the past and present—as the example of *Birth of a Nation* illustrates.

Through exploring media literacy applied to the history film, I also attempt to highlight pedagogical models to apply this scholarship to classroom practice and the resources available to help teachers to engage in this pedagogy. The case of *Birth of a Nation* illustrates the power that film has on shaping what many Americans (and those outside of the United States) know about the past and illustrates the role that Hollywood has had on shaping and being shaped by the dominant culture that perpetuates a narrative of a search for freedom and progress with White men leading the way (Barton & Levstik 2004; Foner 1999; Stoddard & Marcus 2006). The goal of this chapter is to help teachers, media specialists, teacher educators, and researchers better understand how to develop young people who are able to understand the nature of film and the history it portrays, as well as the power this medium can have as a form of public pedagogy through shaping how we view the world (Hoechsman & Poyntz 2012).

Film and the History Classroom

The use of film in history classrooms is far from a new or rare occurrence (Marcus & Stoddard 2007). Film has had a role as a pedagogical medium for over a century (e.g., Dale et al. 1938; Wise 1939), but the developments of the past few decades have seen a rapid expansion of access to history-related media (e.g., streaming) and the ability for students to access this media in and out of the classroom on all manner of screens (Stoddard & Marcus 2016). By film here, By film, I refer here to the moving image in various forms, from feature length Hollywood films to archival raw film footage streamed over the World Wide Web. I will focus here on how to think about and teach with all forms of moving images, including feature film, documentary film, short film and television, and archival or educational film that can now be accessed through numerous media channels (e.g., DVD, streaming). I do not focus as much on teacher- or student-made film but attempt to include this important topic for media literacy where appropriate as well. Over the past two decades, there have been a growing interest and body of research into how film acts as a source of history and how it may be used to engage students in historical thinking as part of media literacy or as a way to engage in difficult or controversial history topics.

This interest in the topic has emerged in part because studies have identified the frequency with which film is used as a prominent medium for teaching in the history classroom (Marcus & Stoddard 2007; Marcus, Paxton, & Meyerson 2006). It is often viewed as being a tool to motivate students, to bring "history to life" and to help develop student empathy for those in the past (Marcus & Stoddard 2007; Metzger 2005, 2007; Metzger & Suh 2008). However, there is also a body of evidence that suggests film is often not used in ways that would be considered "best practices" for history or media literacy (e.g., Hobbs 1999, 2006).

Perhaps more importantly, the role that film plays in society more broadly as a source of historical knowledge has also been recognized, even when viewed outside of the classroom (Briley 2002; Pultorak 1992; Wineburg, Mosborg, & Porat 2001). This makes the need for developing student media and historical literacy with film that much more important—to give them the ability to understand the nature of film and how it represents the past—and how to evaluate a film more critically as evidence of the past or time of its production. Ideally, students will begin to reflect on the role that film and other visual media play outside of the school to shape national collective memory, as well as to influence their own understanding of the past. It is also of prominence given the growing availability of streaming video databases that allow teachers to incorporate archival and produced film into their classes. These databases require additional consideration on the part of teachers and their goals in engaging students with them, as the origins, contexts, and quality of the film they select is less transparent.

History on Film: Film as History?

So what happens when film attempts to tell history? And what does this mean for how we should engage students in films as historical sources? How does a filmmaker and screenwriter make a 300-plus-page work of academic history into a 90-minute film? Stories are compressed, historical figures are combined into one composite film character, and aspects of the story and events are dramatized or created to make the story more understandable for the audience and to make it more entertaining in order to make money (Metzger 2005, 2007; Toplin 1996).

First and foremost, films need to be viewed as their own kind of unique historical text (Rosenstone 2002, 2004). As Rosenstone (1995: 20) notes, "The history that finally appears on the screen can never fully satisfy the historian as historian (although it may satisfy the historian as film-goer)." Even documentaries are the result of many choices made by a director who has a particular perspective on the past, although many view them as "a direct representation of what happened in the past" (Rosenstone 2006: 71).

It is important, then, to think about common film forms as they influence how film is constructed, the story it tells about the past, and how it is received by audiences. Akin to literature as well as history, films often utilize genre formulas to help make complex stories more readily available to audiences. This is particularly true for historical fiction films or films based on real stories—but more often even documentaries are adopting narrative-driven genre styles. This is why, for example, films made in the tradition of the Western genre tend to have similar types of narrative structures and archetype characters, stereotypes, and stock characters.

Understanding genre forms is important for understanding how the historical record is presented on the screen. It is also not that different from common narrative templates used to tell and remember historical narratives as part of collective memory and also align with the kinds of narratives in history textbooks that describe U.S. history as a story for freedom and progress (Barton & Levstik 2004; Foner 1999; Wertsch 2004). When translated to the big screen, genres are used to help audiences make sense of the main story and as a way to reduce that several-hundred-page book into a digestible-length film.

In addition to the use of genre to mold stories from the historical record, conventions such as archetypes, stereotypes, and stock characters are widely used to help to compress the story and number of characters to a number that audiences can easily follow. What this also means is that war films tend to have similar types of characters, such as the gruff sergeant. It can also, however, mean that whole groups of historical agents can be reduced into one stock character, and this stock character can lead to the perpetuation of stereotypes. In *Glory* (1989), a film widely used in classrooms, the core group of African American soldier characters represented groups of African Americans who fought throughout the Union Army, not those who fought in the Massachusetts 54th. These stock characters include an educated freedman (Searles) who represented the majority of the actual regiment, an angry escaped slave (Trip), a former "field hand" (Jupiter), and a wise, older character who was previously working as a gravedigger for the army (Rawlins). These latter characters, however, also veer closely to the types of African American stereotypes described by Bogle (1992), including the Buck, the Tom, and the Uncle, respectively.

Film and Historical Inquiry

Given the characteristics, affordances, and constraints of film as historical texts, how might they be used within a history classroom emphasizing inquiry pedagogy? Within the field of history, the notion that film should be considered as either historical evidence for inquiry or as a product of historical inquiry is relatively sparse and not well respected. However, largely beginning with O'Connor (1988, 1990) and a result of the emergence of cultural and areas studies programs where history became more interdisciplinary, a new focus on film as evidence and film as historical text emerged. O'Connor identified a typology of how film may be used in historical inquiry: (1) as a historical representation, (2) as evidence for social and cultural history, (3) actuality footage as evidence, and (4) the moving image as art form and industry. Rosenstone (1995, 2006) went further to argue that film may be a medium for reshaping how history is told and as a way to engage audiences in thinking about the nature of the past and to raise questions about how we view history or to challenge common historical narratives. These initial frameworks laid the groundwork for much of the work that emerged from history, as well as the body of historical thinking scholarship with film over the following two decades—and the groundwork for what might be considered media literacy for historical film. To illustrate O'Connor and Rosenstone's ideas about film and historical inquiry, consider the following examples of historical inquiry with film.

Film as Historical Representation

O'Connor focused here on examining how film represented history in comparison to the historical record, with the intent of understanding inaccuracies and representations. However, this has evolved into a more fine-tuned focus aligned with goals of what Seixas refers to as second-order concepts in historical thinking—examining film as historical narrative for significance, showing cause and effect, and for empathy. One example of this comes from a book I coauthored (Marcus et al. 2010). In our chapter focused on inquiry into how film represents historical narrative, we examine a teacher's use of Ang Lee's *Ride With the Devil* (1999), which was used both to show the violence and nature of warfare in the Kansas–Missouri border wars that occurred before and during the American Civil War and to challenge the commonly known narratives of the Civil War among her North Carolina high school students. The film presents the asymmetrical nature of this conflict and the perspectives of who was on each side—including former slaves fighting for the proslavery Confederate forces. She used selected clips of the film along with reflective questions and discussions to engage students in reflecting on the nature of the narrative of the film, how it compared and contrasted with their view of the Civil War, and how this conflict was still present today in the form of popular culture (e.g., the University of Kansas Jayhawk mascot).

Film as Evidence of Social and Cultural History

This use is one of the most powerful and yet one of the least utilized strategies in engaging students in historical inquiry with film. When studying history beginning in the 20th century, film can serve as powerful evidence for the social, political, and cultural issues and events of the time and place of a film's production—regardless of what event that particular film may portray. The Cold War period in particular is a great place for using film to examine social critique and social views on what was occurring. For example, one case is a teacher who used an episode of *The Twilight Zone* titled "The Monsters Are Due on Maple Street" (original air date, 1960). This episode, set in an idyllic American suburban neighborhood, reflects the fascination with space and space travel, the "red scare" of anti-Communism of the time, and a critique of what was viewed as the American Dream. The teacher in this case of film pedagogy had students examine the different events that happen in the film and record the reactions of the characters—which essentially asked them to record the levels of paranoia and how they turn on one another as the episode continues—leaving them with evidence to discuss the group mentality of the Cold War era (Stoddard 2014a). Though completely fictional, this television episode would tell you more about the social and political views of the time than any documentary.

Actuality Footage as Evidence

Akin to perhaps only photographic evidence, film can serve as evidence of what an event actually looked like or how something occurred. Although O'Connor (1988, 1990) does not provide enough emphasis on this, any filmic evidence of an event still needs to be examined as a social construction. The following questions need to be asked of any evidence. Why was the camera there at that time? What was the goal of the person filming the event? What was missed by the angle and frame of the filming? What happened before and after the film?

Another example of examining film as historical evidence is looking at archival video from interviews and stock footage of events. In an example of this, Gaudelli, Crocco, & Hawkins (2012) reflect on engaging teachers with a database of cut footage originally part of filming for WGBH's *Vietnam: A Television History* (1983). The teachers in this professional development course were engaged in considering how the footage not used in the final version served as evidence of how the war was viewed in 1983—and in particular how some of the people being interviewed attempted to tell their perspectives on the story. This footage was then compared to actuality footage during the war years (e.g., news footage) and stock footage of the war in particular and how it added to the collective memory and engagement with difficult aspects of the teachers' engagement with these events. Teachers then decided how they may use clips of this actuality footage as evidence to be critiqued and used in inquiry. The primary goal of this project was to help teachers recognize the constructed nature of history in documentary films and the need to help students break the notion of documentaries as objective and instead recognize the perspectives that documentaries present. This is also an example of utilizing actuality footage—not of an event per se but of how key historical figures viewed the Vietnam War during the 1980s and clips from the war period captured on film. With the advent of national archives streaming databases, we have greater access to both old films as well as actuality footage with some or very little production value applied.

Film as Industry and Art Form

Another important aspect of looking at the role of film in history is the role of Hollywood and other studios and modes of production in shaping and reflecting history. For example, as part of a unit on World War II, students could be engaged in learning about the Army Signal Corps and the role of film industry personnel in shaping the messages and news the American public saw—from propaganda to the newsreels informing the public on the war. Teachers could also examine the impact of politics on Hollywood, for example by reading about how Japanese characters during World War II were largely played by Chinese actors because of the internment and marginalization of the Japanese.

This trend, of course, shifted as Chinese actors were viewed in the context of the Cold War and themselves replaced by other Asian groups or by white actors in "yellow face" playing Asian characters. Post World War II, students could also examine Hollywood's role in exporting culture as part of reconstruction in Europe and the occupation of Japan and other parts of Asia. This export of American film and culture influenced how the world viewed the United States and how Americans viewed the world—and was done systematically by Hollywood and the U.S. government.

Film as Postmodern Text

Rosenstone (1995, 2006) expands and challenges O'Connor's typology for using film in historical inquiry to also examine how film can act as historical text to shape how history is told and to challenge common historical metanarratives and Western historical epistemologies. While he focuses on examples such as *Burn!* (1969), which focuses on a Caribbean slave revolt at a sugar plantation, the introductory example from this chapter of the new *Birth of a Nation* (2016) also serves in this form. The explicit use of the title to challenge the status of Griffith's film, along with the reimagining of the Turner insurrection, works as a use of film as history and historical text—to challenge audiences and the historical record.

To challenge common historical narratives or to use film to question how we understand the past means that a film may not have the broad appeal or large audience of films that more closely maintain national or international collective memory. However, with more opportunities for producing smaller films through crowdsourcing (e.g., Spike Lee's *Chi-raq*, 2015) and less traditional methods of distribution (e.g., Netflix), it is possible for filmmakers to use the medium as Rosenstone (1995, 2006) describes: to raise questions about the past, challenge narratives, or even ask us to question our abilities to really understand history. An example could be Ava DuVernay's *Selma* (2014), which strayed from the popularly accepted portrayal of President Lyndon B. Johnson and Dr. Martin Luther King, Jr. as allies in the Civil Rights Movement to Johnson as less than supportive at best. In Rosenstone's view, this film could be seen as an attempt to challenge audiences to go against the Civil Rights Movement narrative of a story of progress where whites "fixed" the problem and put agency more fully within the African American community—even if some of the specific facts of the film are altered from the historical record.

Film Pedagogy

What can teachers do to be more successful in selecting and teaching with and about different types of film (documentary, feature, archival, teacher- and student-produced) thoughtfully in the history classroom in order to engage students in historical inquiry and media literacy with film? First, teachers need to comply with the 2002 TEACH Act that requires any copyrighted media, taken from a legally obtained copy, that is used for an explicit educational purpose must align with the course curriculum and be shown in a face-to-face educational and not public setting (Copyright Law of the United States 2011).

Selecting and Teaching With Different Film Forms

Several factors impact teacher views of film in teaching history and their decision making related to pedagogy with film. First, their epistemic views of film and media as representations of the past and the nature of media forms are often lacking (Mangram 2008; Metzger & Suh 2008; Marcus, Paxton & Meyerson 2006; Stoddard 2010). A focus on the nature of film as a medium and how it represents the past, from context and production to issues of representation and audience reception, is key (Marcus et al. 2010; Stoddard & Marcus 2016). Teachers must also reflect on the objective they have for using any particular film and consider how the film may reflect their own ideological views—selecting a film for the perspective it portrays versus the topic of the film being key (Stoddard 2010, 2009). They should also consider the particular characteristics and differences between various forms of history films, including feature or historical fiction, documentary, and archival films.

Feature Film

No film should be assumed to be 100% historically accurate; nor should any film be viewed as a neutral or objective historical source. Feature films, whether from Hollywood or another country should be assumed to have both a strong perspective and the primary objective to appeal to a particular audience in the hopes of garnering a profit. However, this does not mean these films do not have educational value—quite the opposite. They can be used to help students visualize what an event or period may have looked like, such as using *Saving Private Ryan* (1998) to illustrate the chaos on D-Day; to introduce and motivate students to a particular topic, such as using a clip from *Iron Jawed Angels* (2004) or *Suffragette* (2015), to spark an inquiry into the suffrage movement; as a concept example, such as using a clip from *Gandhi* (1982) to serve as a case of nonviolent resistance or *satyagraha*. Or they can be used to help understand the social and political issues or perspectives of the period and place of production, which the classic example of *Dr. Strangelove or: How I Learned to Stop Worrying and Love the Bomb* (1964) does so well. All of these are examples of powerful uses of historical fiction film that emphasize what film can tell us—and not examples of what feature film cannot show—exactly what happened.

Documentary Film

Documentaries present a particular issue in teacher decision making and epistemic understanding of film. As Rosenstone (1995) notes, even historians trust documentary films as a more objective source of history because of their powerful use of visual evidence and because they are viewed more like written history than like a fiction film. Therefore, Rosenstone reminds us that we need to take extra effort to examine documentaries as constructed texts that include the perspectives of the people who made them.

> The claim is that we can see (and, presumably, feel) what people in the past saw and felt. But that is hardly the case. For we can always see and feel much that the people

> in the photos and newsreels could not see: that their clothing and automobiles were old-fashioned, that their landscape lacked skyscrapers and other contemporary buildings, that their world was black and white (and haunting) and gone.
>
> (Rosenstone 1995: 52)

Further, given the trust that many have in documentaries as sources, teachers also tend to select documentaries that reflect their own views or understandings of an event as objective and present them as such as part of their pedagogy (Stoddard 2010, 2013). They may also emphasize programs on the History Channel or Discovery family of channels (or Discovery Streaming) as being quality sources of education despite the fact that these programs may sensationalize events or do more to appeal to their young male audience than to provide a complex story (Stoddard 2013). It is important to recognize the wide range of styles and quality within films considered to be documentary, with some documentary-style film being quickly produced by large production houses such as the History Channel or other Discovery family of networks and other documentary outlets that may have higher standards for their documentaries, such as the series shown on PBS, such as *Frontline*. Regardless of source, however, all documentaries should be assumed to have a particular perspective on the event they portray and should not be viewed as *the* story but rather as one perspective on any event.

Archival Film Footage

A growing body of archival film is now available through national archives databases, library historic databases, and even in the public domain via YouTube (see the References section for database information). These films include newsreels from the United States and United Kingdom (and later news broadcasts), official government archival film from national archives and libraries, and special collections housed at universities. Although archival film could fit within the two previous categories of feature or documentary, most often these are short films with the explicit purpose of government propaganda or ephemeral films that have captured a particular site or event of interest enough to be preserved and digitized.

Analyzing archival film can be a powerful exercise and can provide students with an understanding of how people at different time periods would have engaged with different forms of media. They also provide insights into the social and political issues of a particular time period. News clips or newsreels from the Civil Rights era can help students understand the challenge African Americans had in their fight for desegregation and equality. Other activities could include reverse storyboarding a short film. Students sketch out storyboards based on a short clip or film and are then asked to think about the decisions made while producing the film and the intended message of the producer. For example, a teacher could use the World War II–era propaganda film *Spirit of '43*, a short animated film featuring Donald Duck that emphasizes saving money and buying war bonds as part of the war effort. Like many archival films, it is short, has a strong message, and is easy for students to analyze and begin to place into context. It could also be compared to similar types of films today available via social media or clips from television programs posted online.

Pedagogical Models for Teaching With Film

Numerous specific pedagogical models have been promoted for use with film in the history classroom. Cates (1990) and Considine (1989) both provide specific heuristics for applying film studies analysis techniques to the history film in middle and high school classrooms. They emphasize aspects of power in film representations related to the way lighting, film angles, and sound are used to create particular filmic messages. These models provide useful starting points for a teacher interested in helping students learn basics in analyzing the nature of film messages. However, they are not specific to historical narratives or other aspects of context or representation that would make the practice align with historical film literacy. Historical film literacy includes "empowering young people to recognize, describe, question, and analyze a film's purposes and themes" (Marcus et al. 2010: 7). Historical film literacy in this way makes an attempt at combining disciplinary notions of historical inquiry with media literacy and a recognition of film's role in society in shaping what we know about the past and present.

Other models focus specifically on aspects of film and representations specific to history and historical thinking or historical literacy. These publications often focus on specific historical or contemporary issues, perspectives, or periods, including: gender (e.g., Marcus & Monaghan 2009; Scheiner-Fisher & Russell 2012); race (e.g., Brown & Davis 2014; Hess 2007; Justice 2003; Stoddard 2014b; Stoddard & Marcus 2006); global perspectives (e.g., Lee 2010; Russell & Benedict 2012); genocide and human rights (e.g., Goldstein 1995; Manfra & Stoddard 2008); and war (e.g., Horton & Clausen 2015).

Several themes emerge from across these models that may be useful in establishing some best practices for teaching history through film and for promoting student media literacy with film. First, teachers need to select films for the perspectives they contain versus the topic of any film, even for educational or documentary film. The film should work toward an explicit educational objective for what the teacher wants to engage students in related to the portrayal in the film or what the film may help students understand about the time and place where it was produced (Marcus et al. 2010).

Second, most models for teaching with film suggest preparing students for the viewing by introducing the context of the film, the educational objective for the viewing, and giving students some kind of task for the viewing. This task could be asking students to "shadow" particular characters during the viewing in order to be able to identify their perspectives and actions (e.g., Marcus et al. 2010; Stoddard & Marcus 2010) or to have them track events in the film or their own affective responses to what occurs in order to consider the purpose of the director and what the film illustrates about the time and context of production (Stoddard 2014a). Finally, postviewing activities should include some time for students to reflect and analyze what they viewed and time to debrief and listen to others' reactions as well. This could include how the film made them feel or react, what questions it raised, or what it might have told them about the perspective of the director or the intended message for viewers.

Teaching With *and* About *Film*

Regardless of the particular academic objective, type of film, or specific pedagogical model used, one key to media literacy with the history or historical film is to teach both *with* and *about* film (Stoddard 2014a). Teaching with film is previously well described, so here I turn to teaching about film. Teaching about film can come in several forms and have different objectives. Generally speaking, it can include teaching about film forms or technical aspects of lighting, sound, and their intended effects (e.g., Cates 1990; Considine 1989). More important, teaching about film means to teach beyond the diegesis of the film—or the story of the film world—this means focusing students on the context of the film's production, the intent of the producer and director, how the film was received and by asking students to consider whom the film was made for and how it reflects the social and political landscape of the time and place of production.

Representation and the Problem of Historical Empathy

Several aspects of how young people and teachers view film representing the histories of marginalized groups complicate teaching and learning with film. In particular, historical consciousness and historical empathy with film can be challenging if not addressed explicitly. Seixas (1993, 1994) found that the young people he studied were able to easily recognize stereotypical representations of American Indians in John Ford's 1954 Western *The Searchers* but not the more contemporary *Dances with Wolves* (1990). This study examined the historical consciousness of young people, and the primary contribution is the recognition that students need to be actively engaged in examining the representations, stereotypes, and narratives of historical film. Seixas's study illustrates the need to examine cultural representations of the past explicitly with young people in the classroom—and in particular films that represent the perspectives of those who are historically marginalized and portrayed stereotypically, such as American Indians. It also illustrates the challenges to developing historically conscious students when it comes to examining contemporary representations versus those easily distinguishable as racist or dated.

In two articles that present a framework for teacher and student analysis that builds from Seixas's findings, especially for film representing historically marginalized perspectives and narratives, Alan Marcus, David Hicks, and I built from Shohatt and Stam's (1994) conceptualization of the burden of representation in films representing marginalized groups (Stoddard & Marcus 2006; Stoddard, Marcus, & Hicks 2014). We developed this framework through first looking at films representing African and African American history used frequently in schools (e.g., *Amistad* 1997; *Glory* 1989) and then at the potential for films made for and by Indigenous peoples to engage students in Indigenous histories, perspectives, and worldviews (e.g., *Smoke Signals* 1998*; Battle for Algiers* 1966). The burden of historical representation, we argue, is met in a film "through developing complex characters and rich personal stories that challenge traditional historical and film narratives, which have generally focused on Eurocentric history and appealed to white audiences" (Stoddard & Marcus 2006: 27). We also found that film may be a medium through which Indigenous epistemologies and worldviews may be engaged with as an additional layer to meeting this burden (Stoddard, Marcus, & Hicks 2014). This framework can be useful both as a tool for reviewing films for teaching and as a pedagogical framework for engaging students in films focused on marginalized perspectives.

One goal of reaching this burden of historical representation is to foster better perspective recognition or empathy with those from the past and those from other groups. Historical empathy as perspective recognition, according to Barton and Levstik, "involves imagining the thoughts and feelings of other people from their own perspectives" (2004: 206) and should not be confused with sympathy. Film, because of the medium's affordance to tell rich stories and place audiences in the perspectives of characters, is a powerful tool for fostering this perspective recognition. Because of the issues previously raised about how the past is often presented in film, however, this empathy could lead to a naïve understanding of the perspectives of other groups or could lead students to believe they understand the decisions and experiences of those in the past without their developing any complexity of these perspectives and contexts (Marcus et al. 2010; Metzger 2012; Stoddard 2007).

Given that teachers often also see films as being a key to developing empathy in students, it is very important that teachers engage students in these films while also explicitly helping them understand the limits to fully understanding the actions and experiences of those in the past. One of the most important aspects of developing students' media literacy with history films in particular is that they should learn both with and about film—as described—and understand how the medium itself affords engagement with the past and with those who produced the film.

Considering Context, Controversy, and Difficult History on Film

In addition to the challenges presented by film representing marginalized histories and perspectives, film is often also used to engage students in difficult histories. We found that films were often used in history classrooms to portray war, genocide, and racial conflicts. These are historical events or perspectives that may be viewed as difficult to portray, to discuss, to teach, and to understand and may be difficult for different groups of students for different reasons (Stoddard, Marcus, & Hicks 2017). They may be sensitive topics, topics that evoke emotional responses, or topics that include trauma or violence that are difficult to understand. This is not to say that film should not be used to engage in these difficult histories, but teachers must consider how and why they are using these films. Otherwise you risk the "Holocaust fatigue" that Schweber (2006) described and what I saw in my own research, where high school students had already viewed films such as *Schindler's List* three times by the time they reached their eleventh-grade U.S. history course, with some students viewing it first in class in the sixth grade (Stoddard 2007).

In order to be successful, teachers must first create an environment in their classrooms to be able to discuss these difficult topics. They also must take the time to prepare students for the potential emotional response to difficult history on film. Finally, they need to help students understand that they will always be limited in the ways in which they can understand these events or perspectives, similar to the issue of empathy previously discussed. Perhaps more importantly, they need to consider their students' own perspectives and any potential issues that may arise because of their own experiences as refugees or in witnessing trauma.

Several logistical and pedagogical precautions can be made in order to successfully implement the study of difficult history through film. First, it is important to know your students and how they may react to the film and content. Make sure they feel comfortable opting out by leaving the room, putting their head down during uncomfortable scenes, or having them do an alternative activity instead of viewing the film. Teachers can also warn students when particularly violent or powerful scenes may be coming up. Further, this safe environment is also important so that students can fully debrief and share their reactions to the film without worrying about the reactions of their classmates.

In addition to student and classroom-level considerations, it is important to include administrators and parents in the use of films that may be viewed as controversial or potentially traumatic (Marcus et al. 2010). Teachers should include their administrators early in their planning as to their rationale and plans for using film to engage students in these events and issues. They should also include a list of films being shown during a semester or yearlong course in a syllabus or as part of information handed out during a parent open house or as part of a newsletter or communication home. This communication could include the rationale for showing students these films, as well as a way to opt students out of the viewing and into an alternative activity, especially where a film may contain violent or R-rated content.

Student-Produced History Films

In their description of media literacy 2.0, Hoechsmann and Poyntz (2012) describe the potential of student-produced media as a path to a more sophisticated understanding of media and its role in society. Media 2.0 shifts the focus from mass media to the ways in which young people in particular engage with media, interact with others through media, develop their own identities in media landscapes, and produce media in new forms. Within history education, this model of student production of media and how new media is used in society to think and talk about the past—with the objective of both historical understanding and media literacy—is a relatively small yet emerging body of work in the research and practice literature.

The most substantial body of research in this area views basic forms of historical documentary style of films as historical texts. Often referred to as "desktop documentary" making within history education (e.g., Schul 2010; Swan & Hofer 2013), this work focuses primarily on students' use of primary sources and historical inquiry while creating simple Ken Burns–style films that include still images, text, and music. For example, Primary Access, a web-based video production suite, allows students to develop short documentary-style films using a selection of images, text, and voice-over audio to construct historical narratives in documentary form. The site provides this opportunity for students to construct a historical story even if they do not have access to video production software (Ferster, Hammond, & Bull 2006). Tools are built into the Primary Access web application to help students develop their script, select images, and organize their story using the timeline tool. This model allows teachers to have some control over the sources that students use in their films and provides ample scaffolding for students to construct basic film stories.

Similarly, Swan and Hofer's and Schul's research into classroom practices with desktop documentaries emphasize the process of constructing a historical narrative, selecting images and sound, and developing a script and constructing the desktop video. They present good models for how to structure desktop documentary filmmaking in a history classroom setting. These models fit the goals of examining evidence, constructing a narrative, and telling a visual story.

A somewhat more varied, complex, and authentic model is encouraged by National History Day competition guidelines, according to analysis by Fehn and Schul (2011). They identify particular themes in student-made films that won the documentary category at National History Day. Similar to the preceding desktop documentary examples, students relied on voice-over narrative, soundtracks, image panning (now called the Ken Burns effect), and expository storytelling using historical evidence. They also identify, however, qualities in student-made films such as the use of animations, stock video, and interviews with experts or eyewitnesses. For example, one of the History Day winners included video testimony from African American and white college football players from the University of Wyoming who were involved in a boycott of a game against Brigham Young University to protest the exclusion of blacks from the priesthood in order to engage audiences in different perspectives on the controversy (Fehn & Schul 2011). These latter additions provide a richer documentary production versus the standard image, text, sound, and voice-over desktop documentary focused on a coherent expository narrative.

The National History Day guidelines require students to reference all sources used in the film, but there is no explicit reference to making fair use of copyrighted materials. History teachers see such requirements as helping students to develop good habits for referencing visual and audio material in their multimedia work. The requirements state that any documentary entry may "use professional photographs, film, recorded music, etc. . . . [but] must give proper credit in the credits at the end of the presentation and in your annotated bibliography" (National History Day 2010–11: 29). The instructions for how these credits must be included in student projects are very explicit, instructing students:

1. To "provide a list of acknowledgements and credits for ALL sources" in brief (i.e., title) at the conclusion of the documentary.
2. To not include a credit for individual images or video during the documentary.
3. To cite all sources, including images, video, and audio in the production, as well as books and other evidence used in constructing the narrative, in the annotated bibliography.

The National History Day model for student historical documentaries provides the flexibility for student creativity in producing the film, as well as the explicit guidelines for evaluation of the film and for referencing sources used. However, none of these models explicitly ask students to reflect on their own decision making with the films in terms of their choices of copyrighted content, how they are replicating or adapting various historical genres or styles, how those choices may shape the history they tell, and so on.

In the area of student-produced film in history, there has been less of a focus on student production of film outside of structured school projects or the effects of media production on students' identity construction, their relationship with the past, and their epistemic understandings of history and how media constructs history. There is far less scholarly or professional work exploring how to engage students in film theory or in explicitly teaching students media literacy concepts or analysis strategies or measuring the impact of their production of media on their media literacy. In general, history teachers do not ask students to reflect on the production process and how their decisions shape the narrative they produce in their films. This may limit the impact on students' understanding of the medium and how it impacts the representation of the past (Stoddard 2014a). It may also reflect cultural norms regarding how film serves as a *use of history* toward particular political views or goals (Nordgren 2016). For students to develop their own historical consciousness, such exploration and reflection are critical.

The common desktop documentary approaches to student film production also do not explicitly address other goals for having students engage in filmmaking about historical events or issues. For example, youth filmmaking may be used to engage students in exploring the relationship between identity and history or for engaging in counter-narrative or counter-storytelling with histories that are often marginalized. Quiñones, Bailey, Ehman, and Delehanty (2017) describe their model of using student filmmaking to help them explore the history of their communities and its resulting implications for them as minority youth in urban areas. Their model emphasized counter-storytelling and the exploration of relationship between history and identity. Similarly, Stanton and colleagues (2017) describe a program that brings together film students from a local university and high-school-age American Indian youth to make films that tell the story of their culture and heritage and that challenge stereotypical representations of Native culture and history through community storytelling. The use of filmmaking to engage in historical inquiry, identity development, and social change (as well as media literacy) is an area with great potential for future projects in and out of the history classroom.

The potential for student production of history film is an area for further research and practice—especially as video production capabilities have increased greatly—even on smartphones or tablet computers. Engaging students in analyzing and critiquing history film forms through conducting inquiry and producing their own films may be the best route to increasing both students' epistemic understanding of the nature of history and their understanding of media forms (Buckingham 2007). This production also likely does not need to be a full creation of a new film but could be a reinterpretation or media critique of existing film using documentary footage or using tools and services such as those provided by The LAMP (http://thelamp.org/). LAMP provides curriculum and the MediaBreaker tools that allow students to edit existing video as a mash-up to raise questions about representations or to add graphics or text in order to critique representations. This epistemic understanding and identity development are key to the development of media literacy 2.0 and of a view of history as represented in media that is necessary to be a thoughtful and engaged global citizen.

Conclusion

In this chapter, I have attempted to present important concepts, practices, and challenges for teaching history through film. Given the influx of moving image databases, online learning, and informal learning outside the classroom through engaging with media via the Internet, the preparation of thoughtful young citizens who hold a complex understanding of how history is represented on film is crucial. However, while models from practice and scholarship related to teaching are plentiful, empirical study of how these practices impact students' media literacy with history film is still scant.

However, the consistent nature of the pedagogical models in the literature is a positive sign that the field is maturing and coalescing around important pedagogical practices. Much of this literature fits within Media Literacy 1.0—and there seems to be much work to still do within this area. These include a focus on the intellectual work of students during viewing and post-viewing analysis and discussion with regard to the different potential educational objectives for using film as part of the history curriculum.

There also seems to be great potential to begin to apply theories from this research to how young people may be engaging with and producing history and historical media as part of a focus on Media Literacy 2.0. For example, how are young people discussing historical film portrayals of difficult or controversial historical events through social media—how are they using aspects of media convergence to critique these representations? Further, how are students producing media about the past—and does the media mimic the generic narratives of feature film or challenge these narratives? Finally, what is the impact on young peoples' epistemic understandings of history and media as a result? These are important questions for understanding the role film plays in our understanding of the past and how young people will grow up to be thoughtful and humanistic citizens.

Note

1 Despite the early hype around *Birth of a Nation*, the film is also noteworthy as it was not widely released and struggled at the box office after reports surfaced of allegations against Parker of sexual assault when he was a college student (he was charged but not convicted).

References

Barton, K. C., & Levstik, L. S. (2004). *Teaching History for the Common Good*. Mahwah, NJ: Lawrence Erlbaum Associates.

Bogle, D. (1992). *Toms, Coons, Mulattoes, Mammies, and Bucks: An Interpretive History of Blacks in American Films*. New York: Bloomsbury Publishing.

Briley, R. (2002). "Teaching Film and History." *Organization of American Historians Magazine of History*, 16(4), 3–6.

Brown, A., & Davis, C. (2014). "Race and Historical Memory on the Silver Screen: A Movie Review of *12 Years a Slave*." *Theory and Research in Social Education*, 42(2), 275–279.

Buckingham, D. (2007). "Digital Media Literacies: Rethinking Media Education in the Age of the Internet." *Research in Comparative and International Education*, 2(1), 43–55.

Cates, W. M. (1990). "Helping Students Learn to Think Critically: Detecting and Analyzing Bias in Films." *The Social Studies*, 81(1), 15–18.

Considine, D. M. (1989). "The Video Boom's Impact on Social Studies: Implications, Applications, and Resources." *The Social Studies*, 80(6), 229–234.

Copyright Law of the United States of America, 17 U.S.C. §110 (2011).

Dale, E., Dunn, F., Hoban, C., & Schneider, E. (1938). *Motion Pictures in Education: A Summary of the Literature*. New York: H. W. Wilson Company.

Fehn, B. R., & Schul, J. E. (2011). "Teaching and Learning Competent Historical Documentary Making: Lessons From National History Day Winners." *The History Teacher*, 45(1), 25–43.

Ferster, B., Hammond, T., & Bull, G. (2006). "Primary Access: Creating Digital Documentaries in the Social Studies Classroom." *Social Education*, 70(3), 147.

Foner, E. (1999). *The Story of American Freedom*. New York: W. W. Norton & Company.

Gaudelli, W., Crocco, M., & Hawkins, A. (2012). "Documentaries, Outtakes, and Digital Archives in Teaching Difficult Knowledge and the Vietnam War." *Education and Society*, 30(2), 5–25.

Goldstein, P. (1995). "Teaching *Schindler's List*." *Social Education*, 59(6), 362–364.

Hess, D. (2007, May/June). "From 'Banished' to 'Brother Outsider,' 'Miss Navajo' to 'An Inconvenient Truth': Documentary Films as Perspective-Laden Narratives." *Social Education*, 71(4), 194–199.

Hobbs, R. (1999). "The Uses (and Misuses) of Mass Media Resources in Secondary Schools." *Secondary Schools*, January. Eric Document No. ED439452. Retrieved from https://www.researchgate.net/publication/234622631_The_Uses_and_Misuses_of_Mass_Media_Resources_in_Secondary_Schools

Hobbs, R. (2006). "Non-Optimal Use of Video in the Classroom." *Learning, Media and Technology*, 31(1), 35–50.

Hoechsmann, M., & Poyntz, S. (2012). *Media Literacies: A Critical Introduction*. London: Wiley-Blackwell.

Horton, T., & Clausen, K. (2015). "Extending the History Curriculum: Exploring World War II Victors, Vanquished, and Occupied Using European Film." *The History Teacher*, 48(2), 321–338.

Jenkins, H. (2006). *Convergence Culture: Where Old and New Media Collide*. New York: New York University Press.

Justice, B. (2003). "Historical Fiction to Historical Fact: Gangs of New York and the Whitewashing of History." *Social Education*, 67(4), 213–215.

Kellner, D., & Share, J. (2007). "Critical Media Literacy, Democracy, and the Reconstruction of Education." In D. Macedo & S. R. Steinberg (Eds.), *Media Literacy: A Reader* (pp. 3–23). New York: Peter Lang.

Lee, T. (2010). "Ten Top Films for Teaching About China Today." *Social Education*, 74(1), 49–51.

Lennig, A. (2004). "Myth and Fact: The Reception of *The Birth of a Nation*." *Film History*, 16(2), 117–141. Retrieved from www.jstor.org/stable/3815447

Manfra, M., & Stoddard, J. (2008). "Powerful and Authentic Digital Media and Strategies for Teaching Genocide and the Holocaust." *The Social Studies*, 99(6), 260–264.

Mangram, J. A. (2008). "Either/or Rules: Social Studies Teachers' Talk About Media and Popular Culture." *Theory & Research in Social Education*, 36(2), 32–60.

Marcus, A. S., Metzger, S., Paxton, R., & Stoddard, J. (2010). *Teaching History With Film: Strategies for Secondary Social Studies*. New York: Routledge.

Marcus, A. S., & Monaghan, M. (2009). "Tasting the Fluoride: The Potential of Feature Film to Enhance the Instruction of the Women's Movement." *Social Studies Research and Practice*, 4(1), 13–30.

Marcus, A. S., Paxton, R., & Meyerson, P. (2006). "'The Reality of It All': History Students Read the Movies." *Theory and Research in Social Education*, 34(3), 516–552.

Marcus, A. S., & Stoddard, J. (2007, May/June). "Tinsel Town as Teacher: Hollywood Film in the High School History Classroom." *The History Teacher*, 40(3), 303–330.

Metzger, S. A. (2005). "The *Kingdom of Heaven*: Teaching the Crusades." *Social Education*, 69(5), 256–262.

Metzger, S. A. (2007). "Evaluating the Educational Potential of Hollywood History Movies." In A. Marcus (Ed.), *Celluloid Blackboard: Teaching History With Film* (pp. 63–98). Charlotte, NC: Information Age.

Metzger, S. A. (2012). "The Borders of Historical Empathy: Students Encounter the Holocaust Through Film." *Journal of Social Studies Research*, 36(4), 387–410. Metzger, S., and Suh, Y. (2008). "Significant or Safe? Two Cases of Instructional Uses of History Feature Films." *Theory and Research in Social Education*, 36, 88–109.

National History Day. (2010–2011). *Contest Rule Book*. College Park, MD: National History Day.

Nordgren, K. (2016). "How to Do Things With History: Use of History as a Link Between Historical Consciousness and Historical Culture." *Theory & Research in Social Education*, 44(4), 479–504.

O'Connor, J. (1988). "History in Images/Images in History: Reflections on the Importance of Film and Television Study for an Understanding of the Past." *American Historical Review*, 93, 1200–1209.

O'Connor, J. (1990). *Image as Artifact: The Historical Analysis of Film and Television*. Malabar, FL: Robert E. Krieger.

Pultorak, D. (1992). "Problems of Perception of Audio-Visual Information in Studying History." *History Teacher*, 25(3), 313–319.

Quiñones, S., Bailey, B., Ehman, J., & Delehanty, D. (2017). "What *Does* History Have to Do With This? Youth Filmmaking for Social Change." In J. Stoddard, A. Marcus, & D. Hicks (Eds.), *Teaching Difficult History Through Film* (pp. 125–142). New York: Routledge.

Rosenstone, R. (1995). *Visions of the Past: The Challenge of Film to Our Idea of History*. Cambridge, MA: Harvard University Press.

Rosenstone, R. (2002). "The Visual Media and Historical Knowledge." In L. Kramer & S. Maza (Eds.), *A Companion to Western Historical Thought* (pp. 466–481). Malden, MA: Wiley-Blackwell.

Rosenstone, R. (2004). "Inventing Historical Truth on the Silver Screen." *Cineaste*, 29(2), 29–33.

Rosenstone, R. (2006). *History on Film/Film on History*. Harlow, UK: Pearson Education Limited.

Russell, III, W., & Benedict, W. (2012). "The Reel History of the World: Teaching World History With Major Motion Pictures." *Social Education*, 76(1), 22–28.

Scheiner-Fisher, C., & Russell, III, W. (2012). "Using Historical Films to Promote Gender Equity in the History Curriculum." *The Social Studies*, 103(6), 221–225.

Schul, J. E. (2010). "Necessity Is the Mother of Invention: An Experienced History Teacher's Integration of Desktop Documentary Making." *International Journal of Technology in Teaching & Learning*, 6(1), 14–32.

Schweber, S. (2006). "'Holocaust Fatigue' in Teaching Today." *Social Education*, 70(1), 44.

Seixas, P. (1993). "Popular Film and Young People's Understanding of the History of Native-American–White Relations." *History Teacher*, 26(3), 351–370.

Seixas, P. (1994). "Confronting the Moral Frames of Popular Film: Young People Respond to Historical Revisionism." *American Journal of Education*, 102(3), 261–285.

Shohat, E., & Stam, R. (1994). *Unthinking Eurocentrism: Multiculturalism and the Media*. New York: Routledge.

Stanton, C., LeClair-Diaz, A., Hall, B., & Ricciardelli, L. (2017). "'I Saw a REAL Indian on TV Last Night!' Engaging Students in Historical Thinking for Social Justice." In J. Stoddard, A. Marcus, & D. Hicks (Eds.), *Teaching Difficult History Through Film* (pp. 106–124). New York: Routledge.

Stoddard, J. (2007). "Attempting to Understand the Lives of Others: Film as a Tool for Developing Historical Empathy." In A. S. Marcus (Ed.), *Celluloid Blackboard: Teaching History With Film* (pp. 187–214). Charlotte, NC: Information Age Publishing.

Stoddard, J. (2009). "The Ideological Implications of Using 'Educational' Film to Teach Controversial Events." *Curriculum Inquiry*, 39(3), 407–433.

Stoddard, J. (2010). "The Competing Roles of Epistemology and Ideology in Teachers' Pedagogy With Historical Media." *Teachers and Teaching: Theory and Practice*, 16(1), 133–151.

Stoddard, J. (2013). "Hillary: The Movie, the History Channel, and the Challenge of the Documentary for Democratic Education." *Teachers College Record*, 115(3), 1–32.

Stoddard, J. (2014a). "Teaching Thoughtfully With and About Film." *Social Education*, 78(5), 220–224.

Stoddard, J. (2014b). "*12 Years a Slave*: Breaking Silences About Slavery." *Rethinking Schools*, 28(4), 26–31.

Stoddard, J., & Marcus, A. (2006). "The Burden of Historical Representation: Race, Freedom and 'Educational' Hollywood Film." *Film & History*, 36(1), 26–35.

Stoddard, J., & Marcus, A. (2010). "More Than 'Showing What Happened': Exploring the Potential for Teaching History With Film." *The High School Journal*, 93(2), 83–90.

Stoddard, J., & Marcus, A. (2016). "Media and Social Studies Education." In M. M. Manfra & C. M. Bolick (Eds.), *The Handbook of Social Studies Research*. Boston: Wiley-Blackwell.

Stoddard, J., Marcus, A., & Hicks, D. (2014). "The Burden of Historical Representation: The Case of/for Indigenous Film." *The History Teacher*, 48(1), 9–36.

Stoddard, J., Marcus, A., & Hicks, D. (Eds.) (2017). *Teaching Difficult History Through Film*. New York: Routledge.

Swan, K., & Hofer, M. (2013). "Examining Student-Created Documentaries as a Mechanism for Engaging Students in Authentic Intellectual Work." *Theory & Research in Social Education*, 41(1), 133–175.

Toplin, R. (1996). *History by Hollywood: The Use and Abuse of the American Past*. Urbana: University of Illinois Press.

Wertsch, J. (2004). "Specific Narratives and Schematic Narrative Templates." In P. Seixas (Ed.), *Theorizing Historical Consciousness* (pp. 49–62). Toronto: University of Toronto Press.

Wineburg, S., Mosborg, S., & Porat, D. (2001). "What Can *Forrest Gump* Tell Us About Students' Historical Understanding?" *Social Education*, 65(1), 55.

Wise, H. (1939). *Motion Pictures as an Aid in Teaching American History*. New Haven, CT: Yale University Press.

17

PERSPECTIVES ON THE ROLE OF INSTRUCTIONAL VIDEO IN HIGHER EDUCATION

Evolving Pedagogy, Copyright Challenges, and Support Models

Scott Spicer

Dramatic changes in higher education are being fueled by innovation in media and technology. Providing access to instructional media resources is a messy, expensive, complex business, so it is essential to understand why this effort is worth taking up in the first place. It should be acknowledged that there is a rich history of local institutional, instructor-, and student-generated video used for instructional purposes (e.g., interviews, performances, documenting behavior, lab experiments, simulations, surgical procedures, etc.). As I will describe in the final section, these two types of content are frequently interwoven into teaching and learning contexts and offer some exciting directions for the future of media support.

At the most basic level, instructional video communicates information through aural and moving image modes, often supported by storytelling narrative, which would be difficult to effectively express through text or speech alone. In general, the subject content of a video is of primary consideration to instructors when selecting material. Otto (2014) found in a survey of 250 Rutgers faculty members that title selection varies significantly according to discipline and topic. For example, cinema studies instructors, the most frequent users of video according to the survey, utilize feature films to illustrate various elements related to the historical and cultural significance of film and filmmaking. With the exception of communication studies (a discipline that makes greater use of news and television programming), Otto reported that humanities and social science instructors prefer "documentaries, fictional films, and "locally produced video from YouTube and similar sites," whereas sciences faculty members reported a preference for "research video and footage documenting a process or activity" (Otto 2014: 124).

These findings are not surprising. Many informative documentary programs can help students understand complex topics in ways that connect cognitive and affective learning. For example, *Race: The Power of an Illusion*, a popular documentary series by Herbes-Sommers, Strain, and Smith (2003), is a powerful program that makes use of archival media and interviews, blended with explanation of science in a storytelling narrative, to help students across multiple disciplines (e.g., from addiction studies to sociology on my campus) interrogate their deeply held assumptions on race in history and society by demonstrating the fallacy of biological human differences.

Instructional video use extends beyond documentary and feature film genres. For example, social work and psychology students explore various approaches to psychotherapy treatment through videos of clinical case studies (e.g., the groundbreaking *Three Approaches to Psychotherapy* series, aka "Gloria Films" by Everett Shostrom (1965)). Language students watch foreign films and educational language videos to improve their proficiency and gain a greater appreciation for the cultures native to their chosen language of study. In biology and other sciences, students watch streaming video abstract clips embedded in research articles from the *Journal of Visualized Experiments* database to learn about specific lab processes and experiment results.

As a hybrid media librarian and learning technologist, I am interested in better understanding not only the value of the specific titles we offer our instructors to help them illustrate key concepts but also how elements such as video format, clip length, technical quality, and streaming platform functionality impacts instruction and can be leveraged to encourage innovative pedagogical practices.

For example, it is understandable that a cinema studies instructor may prefer a 16mm film or DVD/VHS video due to the inherent higher resolution of some physical formats, differing film versions released on specific formats, and disciplinary appreciation for the physical media itself. Further, some instructors may prefer the relative ease at which a DVD/VHS/Blu-ray segment can be cued using a classroom VCR/DVD player, perhaps mixed in concert with digital video clips and lecture slides on their computer, in a lecture style akin to a DJ. Also, in some higher education contexts, instructors may battle with issues of poor-quality classroom bandwidth whereby a physical medium may be preferable. Nevertheless, instructors and students have increasingly expressed a preference for digital streaming access, evidenced on our campus by an increase in licensed streaming adoption and a decrease in the number of advanced booking requests for physical media, further supported by Otto's survey that found streaming to be the most preferred video delivery format (Otto 2014: 130).

The streaming video format can offer some unique affordances over physical media that include and go beyond convenience. For example, instructor Steve Cardamone teaches a Shakespeare theater course. In his course, students are required to view streaming video of BBC professional performances from a variety of Shakespeare plays outside of class to prepare for their in-class performances. The University of Minnesota Libraries (Libraries) licenses online access to this content through the Ambrose Digital Video Streaming database. In terms of subject content, Mr. Cardamone suggested that he considered these videos to be primary course materials, "You can't equate reading a Shakespeare play to seeing and hearing it: it aides in clarity, relationship understanding, and is simply more interesting" (Cardamone, personal communication July 19, 2012). Before they were aware of the streaming access, Cardamone's students would come to the library to check out legacy, often degraded-quality VHS versions. For the students, being able to access this online collection is not only more convenient but also affords an opportunity to more easily preview a wide range of performances. Also, by offering streaming access through the Alexander Street Press Theatre in Video database to another title used in the class, *Playing Shakespeare*, a documentary television series that teaches Shakespeare performance technique by Royal Shakespeare Company actors, by John Barton (1982), the Libraries have helped Cardamone facilitate a "flipped" classroom model, whereby students are able to view the material outside of class and instead utilize class time for discussion and performance.

Instructors recognize the important affordances of audiovisual instructional materials as they advance the learning process. University of Minnesota School of Nursing instructional designer Nima Salehi echoes Cardamone's sentiment on the value of instructional video, in terms of both subject content and audiovisual modality, in supporting the development of applied skill sets within the contexts of course instruction, practicums, and professional exam preparation. Salehi also notes the benefits that the streaming format affords her program given their significant online presence, suggesting that instructional video offers students understanding and reinforcement of concepts learned in text and graphic course materials; the ability to prepare for and study practicum procedures that are then reinforced by follow-up text self-assessments; and the opportunity to review and reinforce clinical practicum procedures visually. In an interview, Salehi continues:

> In particular access to digital video brings to life many of the professional and interpersonal interactions between nurses, colleagues and patients. This significantly enhances instruction provided through text and graphic materials. Digital video has enhanced Nursing instruction for online and in class courses and practicums immeasurably. Since many of the digital video materials are housed by the library, this provides students with an opportunity for ongoing review as they prepare for critical Nursing state exams and certification. The visual component is vital as it provides a much richer and in depth experience than simple text or graphic content.
>
> (Salehi, personal communication October 30, 2012)

The ability to offer campus-wide streaming access provides additional benefits that span disciplines, notably the ability for a large number of students to consume this material at the place and time of their choosing. This capacity is more than a matter of simple convenience. For example, our institution licenses the aforementioned *Race: The Power of an Illusion* through the Kanopy streaming service. It is not uncommon for this and other popular titles to surpass over 150 digital playbacks in a single evening! Even if the library wanted to provide access to this material through DVD course reserves for in-library viewing, we simply do not have enough copies or DVD players to cover this class size. As a result, in the past, instructors would have either been required to screen these titles in-class, reserve a space for out-of-class screening, or bypass the use of this material all together. In addition, through a pilot project using text analysis software to scan digitized syllabi for course use of media, I found that sometimes a required response paper accompanies these out-of-class screenings. For this type of assignment, streaming video provides an opportunity for students to have ready access and playback control of the material, which is useful for writing an effective response.

Another compelling rationale for streaming video is that, in addition to traditional face-to-face course use, streaming video also offers an opportunity for instructors to create a more engaging, multimodal learning experience for their students in hybrid and fully online learning environments. With effective online course design, many of the pedagogical teaching and learning affordances of streaming video that apply to the in-person classroom environment could be applied to these online courses. Though there is a tradition of libraries circulating physical media in support of distance learning courses, as a practical matter given the rapid growth of online classes and the development of robust learning management systems (LMS), it is becoming increasingly critical that media support services are positioned to provide streaming video access.

Finally, the media librarian profession has an ethos to be format agnostic to the extent possible, out of respect for the needs of our instructors, students, and researchers. To best meet these needs, as suggested by Otto (2014), it is important that the media professionals continue to investigate and capture the many rich ways our users are utilizing video in their teaching and research. Through this investigation utilizing methods such as cultivating individual relationships, surveys, syllabi reviews, and professional networking, academic librarians can continue to improve our understanding and perhaps be better positioned to advocate and inspire new possibilities for innovative teaching and research uses of video resources. I believe this rich tradition and the limitless potential for future media resource use are very exciting and most certainly worth fighting for!

Historical Perspectives on Video Access in Higher Education

Though video has become increasingly ubiquitous in our culture and offers teaching and learning opportunities within the academy, a trend that has been projected to continue (Kaufman & Mohan 2009), this digital environment has also created unprecedented challenges due in large part to copyright law and a number of other related concerns.

The complexity of dealing with commercial media collections in higher education is not new (media support is a specialization after all!). From the advent of academic lantern slide collections in the late 19th century to 16mm film, ¾-inch videotape (U-matic), Betamax, ½-inch videotape (VHS), Laserdiscs, DVD, Blu-ray (Widzinski 2010), and more recently streaming video, colleges and universities have been pressed to constantly adapt to changing visual formats and user expectations. The greatest growth of academic library–based media collections and services began in the 1960s continuing through the 1990s (Widzinski 2010: 359). Previously, the responsibility for the management of audiovisual instructional collections and support for class playback equipment was primarily handled by professional "audiovisualists" through film support units administered largely outside the academic library (Loucks-DiMatteo 1985: 81). Widzinski suggests that this growing adoption was spurred by an increase in public investment in higher education and the consumer electronics marketplace, such as the evolution of media formats and related playback technology (Widzinski 2010: 359). During this period, the acquisition of instructional video became so common that by 2002 Brancolini suggested that nearly 100% of academic libraries held video in their collections (Brancolini 2002: 48).

While copyright and fair use have long been important considerations for media support services and our users, the impact on practice has evolved over time, especially in the modern digital era. For example, according to Handman, prior to the mid-1980s with greater adoption of the videocassette format, copyright challenges with respect to media replacement were more limited since it was difficult for most institutions to reproduce 16mm film in-house—a process that was expensive, required specialized equipment, and called for technical expertise (2002: 294–295). Even with the transition to VHS and later DVD formats, it is not clear from the literature the extent to which copyright law was a major obstacle to providing material access. This is not to suggest that there have not been video-related service practices that have relied heavily on fair use or similar developed community practice guidelines. For instance, many higher education institutions offered (and some continue to offer) off-air recording services, for which non–legally binding limited time access and use Guidelines for Off-Air Recording of Broadcast Programming for Educational Purposes ("Kastenmeier guidelines") (Guidelines for Off-Air Recording 1981) were negotiated between industry rights holders and education representatives. Another common practice intersecting with fair use has been the circulation of instructor-owned VHS/DVD materials placed on course reserves in the library. Differences among academic libraries regarding instructional support for audiovisual materials reflected different interpretations of the guidelines. As an illustrative early example on the differences of institutional fair use risk assessment, some libraries have maintained strict policies of accepting only lawfully produced instructor-owned copies, whereas others will accept instructor-owned material regardless of origination (e.g., off-air recordings and video clip compilations). For example, a film studies instructor may record an off-air broadcast program of the Americanized version of the film *Godzilla* (1954), *Godzilla, King of the Monsters!* by Ishirō Honda and Terry Morse (1956) that perhaps includes some special commentary in support of an assignment whereby their students contrast this film with the original Japanese version. To facilitate a more ideal playback environment, the instructor may decide to place a homemade VHS or DVD copy of the program with the library reserves collection for students to watch outside of class in the library. Among several requirements, including whether the library limits circulation of this material to ten consecutive school days, the material is screened within forty-five days of the recording, and the material is no longer retained thereafter; this service could be in violation of the Kastenmeier guidelines, which, as noted, are not legally binding. Given the legal ambiguity, this practice has some level of associated institutional risk.

Further, libraries have long dealt with fair use issues relating to public performance rights (PPR), particularly within the context of screening films in noncurricular contexts such as campus groups or events (Handman 2002: 288–291). This is not necessarily an issue related to campus media services, since, as I will further discuss, many libraries do not actively purchase PPR, but an issue arises because they often hold the proposed event title within their collections and employ media professionals that provide users with fair use guidance.

Finally, another ongoing fair use concern relates to the library's role in video preservation. As Clark notes, given the fragility of VHS materials (an estimated ten to twenty-five years before the magnetic media begins to degrade) ("Special Problems for Video Tapes," n.d.), in addition to format obsolescence concerns as a result of playback equipment no longer being available, libraries are sometimes required to consider the possibility of format migration (Clark 2002: 225, 231, 236–237). This issue is particularly acute with respect to irreplaceable Video At Risk VHS materials.

The mid-1980s began what the media librarian community sometimes refers to as the Home Video Era. Spurred by the availability of the affordable videocassette format, in addition to playback and recording equipment technology, King posits that it was the landmark Supreme Court decision *Sony Corp. of America v. Universal City Studios, Inc.* (1984), which legally allowed for home recording of television programs for time-shifting purposes, that served as a catalyst for library-based video collections to flourish (King 2014). Per King, ironically, in the educational context it was not this newly recognized consumer right to record off-air programming (of which the noted Kastenmeier guidelines provided some negotiated limited use agreement for educational use) but the entertainment industry's response to begin distributing their films at a reasonable price and through commercial retail channels in order to capture some revenue out of fear that consumers would amass large home video libraries of television programs and feature films (King 2014: 297–298). Because libraries are able to loan materials without rights holder permission under the first sale doctrine 17 U.S.C. §109, this marketplace movement had the effect of significantly increasing the number of television and film programs available for purchase while also relaxing the tight control that at least the entertainment industry had previously held through distribution channels and use terms.

The distribution of video material is only one of several copyright considerations in higher education teaching, learning, and research contexts that sometimes serve as barriers to access and use. In this section, I will provide more detailed examples in a few additional notable areas where copyright and fair use considerations intersect with user needs. Specifically, I will cover face-to-face and online course contexts; preservation of at-risk physical media materials (e.g., VHS tapes); accessibility (e.g., captioning); and the emergence of born digital content (content distributed online only in digital format, such as from an independent film producer website or web television programs that are restricted to individual subscribers on consumer-based streaming services, such as Netflix). I should note that several additional potential instructional video use cases face copyright challenges, as the full range of fair use provisions may not be available or may be more limited in a given academic instance. Notable examples include video use in massive open online courses (MOOCs), participation in inter-library loan (ILL) programs (Bergman 2010), non-course-related campus screenings (PPR), video use in for-profit higher education institutions, fair use rights applied to materials that may not have been lawfully produced or acquired (e.g., ephemera works), and reuse of video in so-called multimodal scholarship (fair use applied to repurposing commercial video through traditional and alternative publication channels and formats). I will touch on some of these areas in the final section.

Fair Use Classroom Viewing

Distribution and reproduction are two of the five exclusive nonaudio material–related rights granted to copyright holders under 17 U.S.C. §106 of the Copyright Act of 1976 (1976), the others being the creation of derivative works, public performance, and display. As Handman notes, because 17 U.S.C. §106 provides an exclusive right for content producers to control the public performance of their works, 17 U.S.C. §110(1) is critically important because this provision provides for the use of copyrighted material in "face-to-face" teaching or "similar places devoted to instruction" without the requirement to gain rights holder permission or to purchase expensive PPR licenses (Handman 2002: 288).

Given that the law does not typically require licenses for in-class screenings of film or video, libraries will often forego this purchase if the same title can be purchased without PPR through a mass retail outlet such as Amazon.com. Moreover, few feature film releases offer PPR directly with DVD purchases, which typically require paying an additional fee through a licensing agent. However, a variety of independent film and educational video producers who specialize in content geared toward niche markets and who thus have much lower sales volumes to recoup their high production costs use a tiered pricing model for home-use, public library, K–12 and higher education, with the latter almost always requiring PPR purchase as a condition of material acquisition (often at a much higher institutional rate!). This requirement places considerable stress on the academic library as librarians strive to provide users with access to requested content, whenever reasonably possible. Though I appreciate the critical role and value that this content affords our users and recognize the need for film producers to recoup their costs while making a living, this business model has long been contentious and ultimately unsustainable, as a result of shrinking library collections' budgets.

Digitization and Streaming for Online Viewing

Since copyright law is designed to provide content creators with limited exclusive rights to control the distribution, access, use, and performance of their works, balanced against noninfringing fair use rights by individuals, it is not surprising that disagreements between rights holders and users have become more complicated with the emergence of a digital environment that makes the reproduction, distribution, display, public performance, and derivative creation easier. Moreover, since fair use is a legal defense against a copyright infringement lawsuit decided on a case-by-case basis, absent clearly defined legal exemptions such as 17 U.S.C. §110(1), fair use is purposefully (and thankfully!) ambiguous, providing much needed flexibility. Within the context of streaming instructional video under fair use in higher education, much of the debate essentially boils down to what amount of the material, under what circumstances, and with what access restrictions can a film or video be digitally captured, stored, streamed, and accessed without permission?

Disagreement on the application of fair use for educational multimedia has persisted since the 1990s with a number of reports, guidelines, codes of best practices, and legal remedies since created to address this gap—solutions that in some cases have led to greater confusion than clarity. Case in point: the *Fair Use Guidelines for Educational Multimedia*, a nonlegislative report negotiated between rights holders and educators as a result of the Conference on Fair Use (CONFU), detailed specific limitations on the use of commercial film and video content for teaching and research purposes (i.e., 3 minutes or 10% of the work, whichever is less) (Educational Multimedia Fair Use Guidelines 1996). These guidelines, which were led in development by the Consortium of Colleges and University Media Centers (CCUMC), were sunsetted in 2012, when the organization instead adopted the more broadly defined Association of Research Libraries (ARL) Code of Best Practices in Fair Use for Academic and Research Libraries (Adler et al. 2012). The adoption of the Code was an acknowledgment by CCUMC that strictly defined limitations on instructional video access and use run counter to the flexible spirit of fair use, rights that are necessary for meeting the diverse needs of our teaching, learning, and research communities.

Though rights holders and educators generally agree that at least some limited clip making digitization and streaming are permissible under fair use (provided the video was lawfully made and legally acquired by a nonprofit institution, limited to students enrolled in the course, and accessed through a secured website), the amount of the video digitized is often a point of contention. To illustrate, in contrast to the articulated limited portions in the Fair Use Guidelines, Band and colleagues (2010) and Russell (2010) have proposed fair use application arguments that they contend could be legally defensible for the digitization and streaming of up to an entire work in limited circumstances. In this section, I will describe two of their provisional arguments in more detail (the primary fair use exemption (17 U.S.C. §107) and the Technology, Education, and Copyright Harmonization (TEACH) Act (17 U.S.C. §110(2)) (2002) and briefly mention a third (U.S.C. §110(1)). I will also address some of the additional challenges created by the Digital Millennium Copyright Act (DMCA) of 1998 (17 U.S.C. §1201) (1998).

Fair Use Rationale for Digitization and Streaming

In their brief prepared for the Library Copyright Alliance, *Streaming of Films for Educational Purposes*, Band et al. (2010) propose that perhaps the strongest educational argument for digitizing and streaming up to an entire video lies in the primary fair use copyright provision 17 U.S.C. §107. They suggest that courts are likely to favor the copying, performance, and display of video in nonprofit educational contexts, especially where the purpose of the video use differs from the intended audience of its creation, such as feature films that were made for entertainment purposes. When making a fair use analysis, the authors note the importance of balancing the use purpose, with the three additional fair use factors: nature of the work, amount used, and effect of use on the market (Band et al. 2010: 2). In referencing case law where entire digitized works were ruled to be fair use, the authors propose that a fair use argument could be further strengthened not only by physically "transforming" the work through alteration, such as compressing the video to lower the quality or, even while maintaining the original high quality, by repurposing or recontextualizing the work in a meaningful way. For example, they submit that a repurposing argument could be made if an assignment required the viewing of the entire feature film for the purposes of close analysis (Band et al. 2010: 2). Close analysis is a common pedagogical use practice in several disciplines such as film, media, and gender studies where the work's format and structure are analyzed in addition to an examination of the work's content and presentation of ideas. The authors also argue that a fair use rationale for digitizing up to an entire work could be further strengthened if the use of the video is recontextualized, for example where a digitized film is embedded on a secured course website and accompanied with related study materials and interactive features (e.g., additional materials, study questions, annotations, commentary, student feedback, etc.) (Band et al. 2010: 3). Further, Russell notes that the 17 U.S.C. §107 fair use provision of copyright law is applicable in digital environments (Russell 2010: 354). In addition, Russell cites the congressional record (Report of the Senate Committee on the Judiciary on the Technology, Education, and Copyright Harmonization Act of 2001, S. Rep. No. 107–31 (2001)) during the development of TEACH, suggesting that lawmakers made clear that the "limited portions" language in TEACH should not limit the right of an individual to also assert a 17 U.S.C. §107 fair use claim in certain circumstances, for example in the case of a distance education course if a greater portion of a feature film were required (Russell 2010: 354).

The TEACH Act and 17 U.S.C. §110(1) Digitization and Streaming Rationale

In addition to the primary fair use provision 17 U.S.C. §107, Band et al. (2010) suggest that TEACH 17 U.S.C. §110(2) could be cited as rationale to potentially digitize and stream up to an entire work in limited cases. TEACH is a complex statute that was designed to extend the fair use rights articulated in 17 U.S.C. §110(1) to the online environment with certain limits. Per Band et al., these limitations include the following:

1. The transmission must be a lawfully made and acquired copy.
2. The performance must be of "reasonable and limited portions" of works such as films.
3. The performance is made by, at the direction of, or under the actual of supervision of an instructor as an "integral part of a class session."
4. The transmitting institution applies technological measures that reasonably prevent the retention of the work by recipients for longer than the class session and unauthorized dissemination by recipients to others (Band et al. 2010: 5).

In describing a scenario where TEACH may allow for the digitization and streaming of up to an entire work, they note the first requirement is likely to be filled as institutions typically use lawfully made and acquired content. In addition, per the fourth requirement, streaming software and campus LMS course sites typically have the ability to prevent retention and unauthorized distribution. To meet the second requirement, the authors note that even though the statute specifies that "limited portions" of a film can be created, since the purpose of TEACH was to provide an online learning experience that is "analogous to the type of performance or display that would take place in a live classroom setting" (S. Rep. No. 107–31 (2001)) and in some cases the screening of an entire film may be required, a court may rule that this use case fits the definition of "reasonable and limited portion." Finally, they submit that, for the third requirement, a court may rule that it is permissible to digitize up to an entire work if, for example, instead of requiring students to attend an out-of-class screening session in a scheduled classroom (covered under 17 U.S.C. §110(1)), they viewed the entirety of a film remotely instead. Further, the authors suggest that according to the *Report of the Senate Committee on the Judiciary on the Technology, Education, and Copyright Harmonization Act* (S. Rep. No. 107–31 (2001)), the intent of the language requiring an instructor to be "supervising" the performance of a work was not meant to be literal but rather to distinguish the use of materials that could be used in the classroom from course materials designed to be used individually, such as textbooks (Band et al. 2010: 6).

To date, there is limited case law that specifically addresses the practice of digitizing and streaming commercial copyrighted video under a fair use rationale for course use. The most applicable case is the *Association for Information Media and Equipment and Ambrose Video Publishing Inc. v. The Regents of the University of California et al.* (2011) (*AIME v UCLA).* While AIME brought the case on behalf of their membership, the co-plaintiff Ambrose Video Publishing specifically represented their own content (the aforementioned BBC Shakespeare series). This case focused on whether a UCLA instructional support service (Media Lab) infringed on the rights of copyright holders and were in breach of contract when, without rights holders' permission, they digitized DVDs from their collection and hosted up to full-length video content on a campus streaming server in order to provide more convenient course-based access to instructors and students. UCLA claimed this practice was permissible under principles of fair use and the TEACH Act, while AIME and Ambrose Video Publishing contended this service was a violation of copyright law and a breach of contract.

U.S. District Court Judge Consuelo Marshall twice dismissed the plaintiffs' complaints, ruling in favor of UCLA on non-copyright-related grounds. In her judgment, Judge Marshall ruled that since AIME did not own any copyrights of the material in question, the group was not legally positioned to assert sufficient "standing" to represent the copy rights on behalf of the rights holders. Further, the language in the contract UCLA signed with the co-plaintiff, Ambrose Video Publishing, allowed for the public display of the material in question and did not specifically prohibit the digitization and streaming practice of the Media Lab. Therefore, UCLA was not in breach of contract. Finally, Judge Marshall ruled that AIME could not sue UCLA because the institution was covered under the legal doctrine of sovereign immunity, which essentially means that the state (in this case UCLA and the individuals working on its behalf) cannot be sued in federal court without first waiving their right to immunity.

Though the dismissal of this case on non-copyright-related grounds meant that there were no decisive fair use rulings to serve as precedent for future litigation, as Smith notes, Judge Marshall did provide some thoughtful fair use analysis of the four factors in her decision (Smith 2012) that in my opinion supports many of the arguments posited by Band et al. (2010) and Russell (2010) for digitizing and streaming up to an entire work in limited circumstances. In looking at the four factors, per Smith, Judge Marshall's analysis suggested that the educational use purpose of this material favored UCLA; that the creative nature of the Shakespeare plays was offset by the educational context of their use, favoring neither side; that the full-length digitization and streaming of this material "slightly" favored Ambrose (though she found merit in UCLA's "time-shifting" argument that digitization and streaming practice is comparable to the video recording fair use supported by *Sony Corp. of America v. Universal City Studios, Inc.*); and, finally, that in terms of the fourth factor (impact on market), this use favors UCLA given that in her opinion, there is no more market harm for accessing a streaming title than if the students were all viewing the video together in a classroom, which is clearly permissible under the law. Indeed, as Judge Marshall wrote in her ruling, "the type of access that students and/or faculty may have, whether overseas or at a coffee shop, does not take the viewing of the DVD out of the educational context." That said, as Smith critically notes, absent the vaguely written contract language written from Ambrose, it is quite possible that the fair use and sovereign immunity arguments may not hold up in future cases (Smith 2012). Therefore, it is important that institutions be mindful of the contract terms they are signing.

Digital Millennium Copyright Act (DMCA)

Even where fair use exemptions provide a strong fair use defense for an institution to legally digitize and stream commercial film or video, the Digital Millennium Copyright Act (DMCA) of 1998 (17 U.S.C, §1201(1998)) can act as a potential barrier to content access. The DMCA was enacted to comply with the World Intellectual Property Organization (WIPO) Copyright Treaty. This amendment makes it illegal to circumvent technology protection measures (TPM) (e.g., the content scrambling system (CSS) often found on DVDs) in order to access the video content required for streaming. To balance these restrictions with noninfringing fair uses, the Librarian of Congress holds triennial rulemaking proceedings that have led to the expansion of some limited exemptions for circumventing TPM. Unfortunately, these exemptions are applicable for only three years and can be rescinded at the next proceeding, making this remedy less than ideal. As of the most recent 2015 DMCA rulemaking ("Section 1201 Exemptions" n.d.), the Librarian of Congress has again ruled that screen capture software is a noncircumventing tool and can be used to create "short portions" of video clips from lawfully produced and acquired DVDs, Blu-rays, and streaming video for the purposes of instruction in nonprofit educational environments (this exemption also now applies to nonprofit MOOC environments with additional limitations). Further, whereas a screen capture of video creates a video file of inferior technical quality, the current DMCA exemptions continue to allow for the use of "ripping" software in order to create short portions of higher-quality video files directly from physical and streaming media sources in higher education courses for use in commentary or criticism (e.g., the "close analysis" of a film, where reduced quality may not suffice). The "short portion" language of the DMCA exemptions is generally interpreted to exclude the digitization and streaming of an entire work. As in the case of the general fair use provision 17 U.S.C. §107 and TEACH, depending on how one interprets this limitation, it often serves as a significant obstacle to providing streaming access of up to an entire work even where the instructional use case may be warranted and possibly justified under other fair use exemptions.

As illustrated, there is a great amount of variance in fair use interpretation applied to instructional video between rights holders, librarians, legislators, copyright experts, and even jurists. Given this diversity of opinion, it is no surprise that faculty members often do not have a good understanding of fair use (Otto 2014: 133). As a result, it is important that these constituencies collaborate to help educate one another and develop flexible shared understandings at both the institutional and professional levels, aided perhaps, by documents such as Code of Best Practices for Fair Use developed by American University in collaboration with individuals and organizations representing various communities of practice.

Though fair use provisions offer some additional rights, as earlier noted per Smith (2012) and further suggested by Band et al. (2010) and Russell (2010), agreed-upon contract terms as a condition of instructional video purchase that restrict distribution and access supersede these rights. Therefore, it is important to carefully read vendor contracts and to negotiate more favorable terms or be prepared to decline purchase if necessary. In addition, it is important to understand that not all video genres necessarily are granted the same fair use protections. To illustrate, in contrast to the 17 U.S.C. §110(1) classroom use exemption, TEACH specifically exempts "a work produced or marketed primarily for performance or display as part of mediated instructional activities transmitted via digital networks." Though other fair use exemptions may be applicable (e.g., 17 U.S.C. §107), TEACH may not be a good rationale, for example, in the case of digitizing and streaming VHS or DVD content of the type of nursing educational video material earlier referenced, as this content is typically produced for and marketed primarily toward nursing education programs.

Video At Risk

Given the complexities of the entertainment and educational media industries and marketplace, there are times when a title may not be available for purchase in new condition, at a reasonable cost, and in a format that is not obsolete (unlike film and arguably VHS). For example, this situation may arise because:

- Some of the most popular television programs and film documentaries used for instructional purposes were not produced specifically for the education market (e.g., certain PBS programs) and may never have been made available for sale or released in DVD or streaming video formats.
- Given the limited marketplace for specialized independent film/educational media content, it may not make economic sense for the rights holder to pay the considerable expense to reformat VHS content to DVD or streaming video.
- Sometimes an initial royalty contract between a film producer and the rights holders of content used within a film (e.g., music, footage) is such that the terms of agreement failed to negotiate compensation for future formats (e.g., the DVD version of *Eyes on the Prize*, a documentary produced by Judith Vecchione and Jon Else (1987–1990) was delayed for several years for this reason).
- Sometimes foreign films do not have a North American distributor, and/or the film producer prohibits the resale of their work outside specified regions.
- Sometimes rights holders refuse to license their works in new formats, such as streaming video, due to concerns over piracy or the potential for lost sales.
- Sometimes the rights to a film are in limbo (e.g., the original rights holder dies), a film production company goes bankrupt, or their back catalog is sold to another production company, with the new rights holder deciding not to release a title in a newer format or deciding to take the title out of distribution.

In these events, sometimes a video will fall into an orphan-like work status commonly referred to as Video At Risk. Acknowledging the cultural stewardship role of libraries, the Copyright Act includes the 17 U.S.C. §108 provisions that provide libraries with the ability to make a limited number of duplicate copies of at-risk materials for the purpose of preserving access. It is important to note that 17 U.S.C. §108 sets the bar fairly high for a library to make this determination before copies can be made. For example, if an item is available for sale in the marketplace at a reasonable price and not in an obsolete format, then a library is obliged to purchase that copy instead of making a duplicate. It is not clear how 17 U.S.C. §108 defines the concept of format obsolescence, other than "if the machine or device necessary to render perceptible a work stored in that format is no longer manufactured or is no longer reasonably available in the commercial marketplace."

For VHS materials, this definition is particularly timely, given that the last manufacturer of VCRs ceased production at the end of July 2016 (Pressman 2016). Further, the law requires that libraries take steps and document their efforts in search of a replacement copy and the rights holder before making an at-risk determination. While it is generally agreed that making a duplicate of a video from one physical format to another physical format is legal under 17 U.S.C. §108 (e.g., VHS to DVD), it is less clear if this provision also extends to the conversion of a physical video to streaming, as 17 U.S.C. §108 narrowly limits the viewing of preservation made copies to the "the premises of the library or archives."

Though I have found that instructors generally prefer more recent content, several VHS titles in my library collections that are still circulated regularly could be classified as Video At Risk. Further, because academic libraries collectively hold tens of thousands of specialized independent film, educational videos, television programs, in some cases rare versions of feature films, and other types of commercial video that were often not originally widely distributed, librarians have a cultural stewardship responsibility to preserve access to this material. Therefore, depending on institutional 17 U.S.C. §108 exemption fair use interpretation and application, this statute may or may not go far enough in preserving access to this valuable VHS content for current and future generations of scholars.

Lastly, as a practical matter, it is becoming increasingly difficult to play back VHS materials in the classroom. According to a 2015 survey of forty-nine classroom A/V professionals from Association of Research Libraries (ARL) institutions responsible for managing classroom video playback equipment, the vast majority of respondents reported that they have either begun or plan to begin the process of phasing out support for VCRs in their campus classrooms within the next three years (Spicer & Horbal 2017). Though most respondents reported that they intend to continue support for classroom DVD playback capacity for the foreseeable future (typically via the installation of DVD-backward-compatible Blu-ray players), given that the top reason provided for the phased retirement of VCRs was lack of device availability in the marketplace, it is likely that a time will come in the not too distant future (perhaps, five to ten years) that playback support for DVD and Blu-ray media will likewise gradually cease to be a standard A/V classroom component. Just as VHS format degradation is a concern, the loss of classroom VHS playback capability has and will continue to be a challenge for campus media support and instructors who rely on these materials for their teaching, especially in the case of irreplaceable Video At Risk materials. As a result, institutions need to develop thoughtful VHS collection management strategies and perhaps consider the application of more progressive fair use interpretation in preserving this access or risk losing this valuable content. (See "Video At Risk: Strategies for Preserving Commercial Video Collections in Libraries" (Besser et al. 2012) for guidelines developed to help institutions make fair use preservation determinations of at risk VHS materials.)

Born Digital Content

An instructional video copyright concern that has emerged over recent years is access to born digital commercial video, which includes, for example, films that are exclusively distributed online and original web television programming produced and distributed through consumer digital delivery services such as Netflix and Amazon Prime (e.g., *House of Cards* and *Transparent*). Whereas the negotiated Kastenmeier guidelines provided some agreed-upon guidelines to capture off-air television programming for instructional purposes, currently no analogous guidelines offer similar policy direction for capturing born digital programming through consumer channels. Further, because these services do not typically offer an institutional streaming access license (though some libraries have experimented with Netflix subscriptions [Healy 2010]) or distribute this content via DVD where they could be purchased through a retail channel such as Amazon.com, it is not typically possible to fill instructor requests for this material.

As a result, instructors often need to resort to either screening a required born digital video in the physical classroom using their own service account (which may be a violation of contract terms), or they may require their students to set up an account with these services. In addition, because this content is wrapped in digital rights management (DRM) software, the DMCA offers protections that once again serve as obstacles to being able to capture and stream this content under fair use. In response, Cross suggests that libraries consider taking the progressive step to subscribe to these services, and then implement policies that are aligned with the spirit of fair use exemptions, "enabling personal use, avoiding commercial advantage, offering lawfully-made materials, and facilitating uses that are likely to be fair such as teaching, scholarship, research, and especially transformative uses" (Cross 2016: 13).

Specifically, Cross suggests that a library could take a very broad reading of the "personal use" language found in consumer streaming services, as several have in the case of lending iPads that come preloaded with software that often include similar limited individual use terms of service. As I will elaborate further, this movement toward a tightly controlled born digital distribution environment presents a potential considerable harm to instructors and students for the use of this media in scholarship and to some extent a potential long-term existential risk to the campus media services that help facilitate this access.

Video Accessibility (Captioning)

The final copyright challenge that I will discuss relates to instructional video accessibility, in particular captioning. First and foremost, to the utmost extent possible, providing access to course materials to those who are hearing impaired, deaf, visually impaired, and blind is the right and humane thing to do. It is also a legal responsibility of educational institutions required under the Americans with Disabilities Act (ADA) of 1990 42 U.S.C. §12101 (1990). This legal responsibility has taken on greater visibility in light of *National Association of the Deaf (NAD) et al. v. Harvard University, et al.* (2015) and *National Association of the Deaf (NAD) et al., v. Massachusetts Institute of Technology* (2015), a pair of discrimination lawsuits brought against Harvard University and MIT for failing to caption their public MOOC courses and other online video content. These are just two of a growing list of accessibility challenges brought by either lawsuit or the Department of Justice, the agency responsible for monitoring ADA compliance, alleging failure to provide reasonable access to course materials in higher education (Carlson 2016).

Unfortunately, a significant amount of the VHS/DVD video collections and even licensed streaming content in library instructional video collections are not captioned. Further, as Morris notes, the DMCA does not offer an exemption allowing for the circumvention of TPM-protected video for captioning purposes (Morris 2016). I have seen firsthand how this tension between the ADA and DMCA has impeded course use of instructional video. At my institution, copyright barriers have meant that, in several instances, the captioning service unit in our Disability Resources Center has asked for permission from the rights holder to be able to circumvent TPM to create a digital file in order to provide captioning for a DVD video from our collections. In some cases, where the Libraries did not originally pay for PPR (as noted, not a required purchase for classroom use), the captioning unit has been told that they need to purchase PPR in order to circumvent TPM.

Commercial video producers should not release uncaptioned video to the public. In my opinion, in the event that they do, upon request a rights holder should take responsibility and try to provide a captioned version if possible. Short of that, I believe it is morally questionable to require additional payment so that a hearing impaired or deaf student can access this content, regardless of whether the institution originally purchased the optional PPR.

It is important to understand that instructional video copyright challenges do not exist in a bubble. On the one hand, there are several instructor and institutional pressures pushing for improved instructional video access (in both physical and streaming formats), while simultaneously there are significant non-copyright-related challenges that can sometimes serve as obstacles to implementing the most ideal solutions. Some of this pressure stems from evolved user expectations for streaming access, driven in part by increased use of consumer streaming services and web content but also by the exponential growth of hybrid and fully online e-learning courses, digital environments that necessitate streaming delivery. Though there are many considerations, the primary non-copyright-related challenges to providing improved instructional video access include the costs and expertise required to develop and maintain local technical infrastructure for the digitization and management of local streaming collections, significant costs for licensing streaming video, and relatively limited options and some trepidation by librarians in purchasing expensive streaming licensing for feature films and television programs that are often available for DVD purchase or at a reasonable rental cost via consumer streaming services.

An Overview of Contemporary Digital Video Delivery Access Models in Higher Education

Thus far I have described some of the critical roles and pedagogical benefits that instructional video affords in support of teaching and learning, in addition to some of the copyright and other challenges that can act as barriers to meeting user needs. Of course, the emergence of the online digital environment has significantly altered instructors' reliance on libraries (and similar campus media services) as a primary service point for this content. To illustrate, Otto found that the Rutgers Library was the fourth place instructors reported seeking content, after use of their own personal collections, online sites such as YouTube, and personal/departmental video purchases (Otto 2014: 127–128).

This transition toward streaming access has changed the dynamic between the media librarian, libraries, and instructors (Vallier 2010; King 2014; Widzinski 2010). For example, we have seen an overall decrease in demand for circulating physical media and decreased usage of media centers for screening videos. That said, libraries still perform a critical function in providing access to specialized independent films and educational media, television programs, feature films, and other types of video that instructors and students utilize every day. This shift is a natural evolution in the spirit of historical academic media use and support. Like all such transitions, this period of change comes with its own unique concerns and opportunities. For example, as suggested, streaming video provides instructors with more options to deploy pedagogical approaches appropriate to their courses and preferred teaching styles. For students, streaming video offers greater convenience and in many cases a wider array of direct access to materials that may not have been previously available. So whereas a single title may have been screened in a class before, that same streaming version of the title today may have a high digital hit count indicative of an out-of-class required viewing. Depending on the pedagogical context, this may or may not provide a better learning experience, but I believe it is overly simplistic to suggest that this change is necessarily good or bad without better understanding the contexts in which they are used.

Acknowledging this evolution, I believe the extent to which libraries are able to balance the capacity to expand access to streaming video, while maintaining quality physical media collections and related media resource support services (e.g., media cataloging, guides, and systems for easily locating and accessing media in library collections, providing title recommendations, etc.), the more relevant and valuable the media service and media support professionals are likely to remain in the future. The development of this quality media programming could be enhanced through adoption of the principles articulated in the American Library Association (ALA) Association of College and Research Libraries (ACRL) Guidelines for Media Resources in Academic Libraries (2012).

To provide greater context for the current state of these practices, in this next section, I will provide some insight into current instructor media use preferences and approaches that libraries are taking to expand streaming access. Unfortunately, there is no easy, inexpensive, unquestionably 100% copyright-compliant silver bullet solution that meets all of our users' instructional video needs. Most institutions rely on some patchwork of streaming delivery approaches implemented to the best of their ability according to their institutional context. According to Farrelly and Hutchison Surdi (2016), who conducted a survey of 260 academic librarians responsible for media collections and representing multiple types of academic libraries, nearly 89% of respondents currently offer a subscription to at least one commercial streaming video database. This response is comparable to their earlier 2013 survey results (Farrelly & Hutchison 2014), suggesting that streaming is a topic that touches virtually every academic library.

Practice: Licensing Streaming Video Content Through Video Producers and Distributors

One of the most common approaches libraries adopt to provide instructional streaming video access is through licensing. Video licensing is available in multiple content selection and pricing configurations. Typically, with the database license model, a campus media support unit (most often the library) pays to license access to a bundle of independent film/educational media distributor–curated collections of videos related to a discipline or topic, for a defined term limit (i.e., one, three, or five years), that are stored and delivered from the distributor's server and accessed through a secure Internet protocol (IP) campus login similar to other library-purchased electronic resources. These products began to appear in the marketplace beginning in the early 2000s, notably from Alexander Street Press and Films for the Humanities, and have continued to experience rapid growth and popularity over the past decade, driven in part by new streaming distributors entering the marketplace, such as Kanopy, Docuseek2, and many others. As Handman notes, there are several benefits of subscribing to curated collections, particularly for institutions with limited staff and smaller collections. Among the disadvantages to subscribing to bundled streaming content is that often these collections are of uneven quality, this model fails to leverage the librarians' expertise in developing a diverse media collection appropriate to their campus needs, and often these collections omit exemplar titles as a result of the distributor being unable to obtain streaming rights from the film producer (Handman 2010: 331).

Per Farrelly and Hutchison Surdi (2016), though licensing of curated streaming video bundles continues to be the primary choice for streaming acquisition, there has also been a significant increase of libraries licensing individual streaming titles through vendor-hosted services (70% in 2015, up from 29% in 2013). This response is in line with our own experience. For example, at my own institution, a few years ago we conducted an audit of heavily circulated physical media titles and in response made some streaming investments to license the entire California Newsreel and Media Education Foundation video collections hosted on the Kanopy streaming platform. In addition, we have also licensed select individual titles from Kanopy and other vendors as requested on a case-by-case basis. As a result, we have witnessed a considerable decrease in advanced booking requests for the VHS and DVD versions of these titles, while the digital playback usage statistics for many of these titles has been strong.

An alternative to licensing streaming video on vendor-hosted platforms is purchasing the digital site license (DSL) rights to stream a video locally (or through a shared video digitization, hosting, and streaming service such as NJVid, which is sponsored by multiple institutions). For DSL videos, sometimes the distributor will send a video file, but more often the DSL simply provides the right for an institution to digitize, host, and stream a video file ripped from a previously purchased DVD. The advantage of instructional video DSLs is that often (though not always) these licenses grant perpetual rights to access streaming, whereas vendor-hosted licensed content is typically term limited. The DSL is also a good solution for obtaining streaming access to one-off videos that may not be distributed through vendor-hosted streaming channels and is therefore often purchased directly from the film producer. Perhaps, somewhat surprisingly, according to Farrelly and Hutchison's 2015 survey, the purchase of DSL collections (bundles of video stored on a local server) has barely changed since 2013 (43% in 2015 compared to 42% in 2013) and only slightly changed for DSL of single titles (47% in 2015 compared to 44% in 2013) (Farrelly & Hutchison Surdi 2016).

There are several disadvantages to purchasing DSL rights, notably the need to either pay into a shared streaming service or develop local digitization, hosting, and streaming infrastructure using digital media asset management and delivery software such as the open-source Avalon Media System. This solution also requires resident technical expertise for legacy media conversion, cataloging, ongoing media asset management due to changing digital formats, ongoing server maintenance, and on-demand technical support for when user playback issues inevitably arise. Further, this solution requires a significant investment for staffing, conversion equipment, servers, storage space, software licensing, and the cost of the DSL itself (which often ranges from the cost of an independent film/educational video DVD purchase to twice as much or more). Additional disadvantages with locally hosting DSL content includes the resources required to vet, negotiate, and manage streaming contracts from a number of different film distributors or producers that may come with differing terms; these videos often lack captioning (which is also a significant problem for content that has been digitized and streamed under fair use as few titles were reported captioned using local streaming services) (Farrelly & Hutchison Surdi 2016), a functionality that is much more common (though far from ubiquitous) for titles streamed from vendor-hosted platforms; and DSL videos often lack quality cataloging that aid in the discovery of this material through the library catalog. Furthermore, depending on the local streaming video platform software being used, DSL content may lack some of the LMS embed, clip making, and transcript functionality often found in vendor streaming databases. Finally, the licensing terms of the DSL perpetual access is often limited to the "life of the file," a product of the industry practice of negotiating distribution terms according to the format distribution type (i.e., DVD or streaming) by film producers, distributors, and sometimes individuals who have licensed reuse rights to music and visual images used within the video itself. In practice, given constantly changing digital formats, coupled with bandwidth and device-aware video delivery systems such as Kaltura, it is unrealistic to expect that the exact DSL video file created or received will be the same one that will forever be stored and delivered. This issue is a matter of contract law, not copyright, but demonstrates some of the peculiar challenges that campus media and electronic resources professionals face in trying to expand streaming access through licensing approaches alone.

It should also be noted that only a small percentage of all the commercial video content ever produced is available for institutional licensing on either vendor-hosted platforms or through a DSL. This issue is a challenge not only for procuring digital streaming access to independent films and educational media but for television programs and feature films as well. To date, the only streaming service I am aware of that offers institutional licensing and hosted streaming access is the SWANK Digital Campus database, which contains some of the feature film catalogs from five of the six major studios (excluding Fox). Though this product is a popular solution that has been adopted by several campuses, like most commercial streaming media products, the price for this product is relatively high and requires an ongoing "serial" investment in contrast to a one-time $20 feature film DVD purchase. Further, whereas specialized independent film and educational media are often sold through a single distribution channel, there is some trepidation on the part of many librarians to invest heavily in streaming versions of feature films that are often readily available for rent at a reasonable cost through consumer streaming services. Finally, as is the case with term-limited vendor-hosted licensed streaming content, once the buyer stops paying the serial fee, access to the streaming video content disappears. As Handman suggests, this licensing shift to a more temporal "just-in-time" collection development strategy undercuts the traditional role of the academic library in "fostering discovery and use of valuable new resources and providing and preserving a range of unique materials not widely available in the information marketplace" (Handman 2010: 325).

As in the case of born digital format type content such as independent films and web television programming distributed online only with restricted user access terms, some educational media products (such as the SAGE Video database) have begun to produce original in-house and/or licensed exclusive online content. In contrast to the born digital film and television web programming, these materials can be purchased only via institutional licensing. I believe that, over the next decade, we will continue to witness this continued shift toward born digital content in both the independent film and educational media industries with extreme divergent institutional licensing options (i.e., either an institutional license is completely unavailable, or institutional licensing is the only way to access this content). Further, as witnessed with academic journal publishers, I believe the educational media born digital marketplace will ultimately become a major impediment in our mission to provide access to the content our instructors and students require for teaching (and research), due in large part to budgetary concerns. Finally, barring some kind of agreement between video rights holders and educators to deposit these works into a "dark storage" repository such as CLOCKSS, a not-for-profit venture between academic publishers and research libraries designed to provide preserved access to web-based scholarly content, I believe there is a strong potential risk for loss of content access over time.

Practice: Digitizing and Streaming Video On-Demand Under a Fair Use Rationale

As noted, no topic is as controversial, with respect to instructional video, as the practice of digitization and streaming video on demand under a fair use rationale. Farrelly and Hutchison's 2013 survey found that 41% of respondents reported offering library-based on-demand digitization and streaming (Farrelly & Hutchison 2014). For the 2015 follow-up survey, the question was amended to include not only the library but other campus units as well. Perhaps, because of this addition and/or the growing popularity of this practice, the 2015 response had a significant resultant increase, with 53% reporting this practice (Farrelly & Hutchison Surdi 2016). Furthermore, for institutions that have their own local streaming infrastructure, 81% reported offering an on-demand digitization and streaming service! When limited to a comparison of library-based digitization and streaming services, there was also a significant increase from 2013 to 2015 (73% in 2015 compared to 41% in 2013) an increase of 32%! While libraries may purchase a lot of instructional video, Farrelly and Hutchison Surdi's survey found that the library was not the primary reported campus streaming service but rather a campus IT department, e-learning support unit, or other department (Farrelly & Hutchison Surdi 2016).

Where the division of labor is spread across campus support units, fair use interpretation can sometimes differ among those responsible for acquiring and maintaining instructional video collections and those responsible for digitizing, hosting, and delivering streaming video. Therefore, it is important to communicate across units and try to collaboratively develop a shared understanding of fair use, institutional application of fair use and the development of a seamless workflow for acquiring content and rights as needed in addition to streaming delivery and related support. (See Carlisle Fountain [2011] for an example of campus streaming collaborative workflow negotiated across the library and an IT unit at Washington State University [Vancouver].)

As noted, several exemptions are specifically carved out in copyright law for fair use of video in nonprofit educational classroom contexts (e.g., 17 U.S.C. §110(1), 17 U.S.C. §110(2), and 17 U.S.C. §1201 (DMCA anticircumvention exemptions), the libraries' role in preserving access to our cultural record (17 U.S.C. §108), and, of course, the general fair use provision 17 U.S.C. §107 that likely allow for some level of digitization, hosting, and streaming of commercial instructional video content without permission. A few of the critical questions each institution needs to consider when thinking about the possibility of developing a digitization service are:

1. To what extent does the institution believe these exemptions allow them to digitize a video (e.g., limited portions of a video or up to an entire work if necessary? Different fair use interpretation for dramatic and nonfiction works?)?
2. What policies and security mechanisms present the best fair use defense, while balancing streaming service workflow and user access needs (e.g., limit the video to a single class (e-reserves model) or providing access to the entire campus? For a single class, can the video be made accessible for the entire semester, or does it need to be removed after a brief period of time? When the class is no longer using the video, does the video file need to be deleted from the server, or can it be stored for future use while making it no longer accessible?)?
3. Does the institution have an obligation to always license access to the streaming video if available or only under certain circumstances, such as when an entire work is requested in streaming?
4. What is the institutional fair use assessment for determining Video At Risk (VHS) digitization for preservation and sustained access purposes? Is streaming access acceptable, or is the institution only comfortable with format transfer from VHS to DVD (perhaps with a digital file stored as backup)?
5. What about fair use applied to digitizing and streaming VHS materials that may not technically qualify as at risk (e.g., a DVD may be available for purchase), but in the instance where the campus is no longer supporting classroom VCRs?

Per Farrelly & Hutchison Surdi (2016), for the increasing number of institutions that have been developing some level of on-demand digitization and streaming support services, there is a wide range of fair use interpretations and attendant practices and policies. Given the purposeful ambiguity of copyright law and fair use, ultimately these decisions are guided by a certain degree of institutional, organizational, and sometimes even individual risk assessment.

Perspectives on the Future of Commercial Video Use and Media Services in Higher Education

The previous three sections of this chapter addressed copyright and fair use challenges in the context of access and traditional instructional uses of video in higher education. This perspective is focused primarily on video consumption. To be clear, it is critical that media services continue to procure and provide access to instructional video content going forward for these use cases. However, we are now at a point in time where anyone with access to the Internet and a device can act as a self-publisher; and many of us communicate multimodally through images, video, audio, and text on a daily basis with little effort, for example via smartphone messaging apps and social media networks such as Facebook. Therefore, I believe it is appropriate to consider the future of instructional video use, media services, media centers, and copyright/fair use through a media literacy lens that considers both video consumption ("reading") and potential for creative productive uses ("writing").

This is not an original idea. Vallier asks the provocative question, "Twenty-first century academic media center: killer app or chindogu?" In other words, will media centers be a critical component of the 21st-century research library by evolving to meet the emerging needs of our faculty and students, or are they more akin to a *chindogu*, an invention that is not as useful as it appears (Vallier 2010: 378)? Despite the challenges articulated, I concur with the optimistic tone of Vallier's response, notably that through experimentation, partnerships, and outreach efforts, academic media centers (and related services) can better position our programs to adapt to users' emerging needs, thereby making us more like a killer app. As Vallier proposed, this progress will require our programs to further explore development of new service areas such as archiving and curating online content, working with faculty and students to develop new modes of scholarly communication and refining strategies through partnerships for how we acquire, manage, and support use of our [multiformat] collections (Vallier 2010: 383).

Several media services programs, including my own, have already expanded their service model to move in this direction, for example by providing support for user-generated media content (i.e., our program also specializes in supporting student produced video projects, while others additionally support audio production and emerging areas such as 3D printing exemplified by the makerspace movement). I submit that an ideal "killer app" media services program would not only focus on continuing to provide access to valuable instructional video content but would also strive to align services with what we know about instructors' preferences for use of their own content, online sites such as YouTube, and personal/departmental-purchased collections (Otto 2014: 124), a finding further supported by my own analysis of course syllabi. This suite of services would provide instructors, students, and researchers with the tools and support they need to easily locate, reformat, store, catalog, deliver, and repurpose content through whatever traditional or emerging channel is most appropriate for their teaching, learning, and/or multimodal scholarship needs.

For example, imagine that, in the spirit of the digital arts, sciences, and humanities (DASH) and multimodal scholarship movements, an instructor and students in a class would like to collaboratively work together to create a multimedia online resource illustrating mass media and social media representation of the Black Lives Matter movement, perhaps accompanied by some digital storytelling narrative. A "killer app" media services program could help in a number of ways:

- It could help in coordinating a team of relevant media, subject, digital scholarship librarians (with other library-based and campus support partners) to work with the class in quickly spinning up an online platform that allows for multimedia publishing (e.g., Word Press, Omeka, or Scalar, using a cloud-based service like DASH Domains (DASH n.d.)).
- This team could also work with the class to provide guidance on content curation, description, storage, and delivery of digital media content captured from online media sources (e.g., YouTube, Facebook, Twitter, media outlets), in addition to providing digitization support for clip making from VHS/DVD documentaries (and other physical source material) located in instructor, departmental, and library collections covering the topics of race and media.
- The media librarian (with other library-based and campus partners) could then work with the class to help students and the instructor create brief digital story videos providing their own perspectives on the topic. These videos could then be uploaded to the website or simply shared within the class environment.
- Finally, this team could cosponsor with the class a public launch event of the website in the media center, perhaps by inviting speakers to share various perspectives on the topic.

In the preceding example, I believe that multiple fair use provisions of the copyright law would support many of the activities involved in this project, with perhaps some challenge to the storage and republishing of online content depending on whether it was originally legally posted. Indirectly related to copyright, complications could also arise over privacy complaints if there were social media snapshots from, say, a private Facebook account. In addition, there is always the potential of a copyright and/or contract challenge (e.g., resulting in a safe harbor take-down request) coming from one of the online sources or independent film/educational media vendors depending on the contract terms signed by the library.

This project illustrates the kind of innovative potential and some of the institutional risk assessments that our media service programs, teachers, students, and researchers make on a daily basis. I believe that, when weighing the risks and benefits of fair use practice in media service programs or even simply determining whether to apply fair use to a specific project, it is critical that they be considered in balance with the enormous potential for rich innovative pedagogical and scholarship practice. Finally, I believe that these media use practices should be supported by thoughtfully applied fair use rationale on a case-by-case basis, balanced with ensuring the rights of content creators. In doing so, we can continue to advocate for copyright policies that better align with the ever evolving instructional and scholarly needs of our users, while encouraging rights holders to consider sharing their works openly through mechanisms such as Creative Commons licensing or placed in the public domain where they are available for all. (See Code of Best Practices for Online Video for further information on fair use considerations for repurposing video content. See Spicer (2014) for more information on multimodal scholarship in the context of scientific scholarly communication.)

References

Adler, P. S., Aufderheide, P., Butler, B., Jaszi, P., & Andrew, W. (2012). "Code of Best Practices in Fair Use for Academic and Research Libraries." Retrieved from Association of Research Libraries website www.arl.org/focus-areas/copyright-ip/fair-use/code-of-best-practices#.V_2Hz7VUioc

American Library Association (ALA) Association of College and Research Libraries (ACRL) Audiovisual Review Committee. (2006). "Guidelines for Media Resources in Academic Libraries." Retrieved from www.ala.org/ala/mgrps/divs/acrl/standards/mediaresources.cfm

Americans with Disabilities Act of 1990, 42 U.S.C. §12101 *Association for Information Media and Equipment and Ambrose Video Publishing Inc. v. The Regents of the University of California et al.*, 2:10-cv-09378-CBM (C.D. Cal 2011)

Band, J., Butler, B., Crews, K., & Jaszi, P. (2010). "Issue brief: Streaming of films for educational purposes." Retrieved from http://www.librarycopyrightalliance.org/storage/documents/ibstreaming-films_021810.pdf

Barton, J. (1982). *Playing Shakespeare* [Television series]. London: ITV Network.

Bergman, B. J. (2010). "Making the Most of Your Video Collection: Trends in Patron Access and Resource Sharing." *Library Trends*, 58(3), 335–348. doi:10.1353/lib.0.0096

Brancolini, K. (2002). "Video Collections in Academic Libraries." In G. Handman (Ed.), *Video Collection Development in Multi-Type Libraries: A Handbook.* (pp. 47–75). Westport, CT: Greenwood Press.

Carlson, L. L. (2016). "Higher Ed Accessibility Lawsuits, Complaints, and Settlements." Retrieved from www.d.umn.edu/~lcarlson/atteam/lawsuits.html

Clark, J. (2002). "Preserving the Image: Video Preservation." In G. Handman (Ed.), *Video Collection Development in Multi-Type Libraries: A Handbook* (pp. 225, 231, 236–237). Westport: Greenwood Press.

Copyright Act of 1976, 17 USC §§106–110, §1201.

Cross, W. (2016). "More than a House of Cards: Developing a Firm Foundation for Streaming Media and Consumer-Licensed Content in the Library." *Journal of Copyright in Education and Librarianship*, 1(1), 1–24. doi:10.17161/jcel.v1i1.5919

DASH Domains. (n.d.). Dash Domains: Webspace & Applications. Retrieved from University of Minnesota website https://dash.umn.edu/domains/

Educational Multimedia Fair Use Guidelines Development Committee. (1996). "Fair Use Guidelines for Educational Multimedia." Retrieved from University of Washington Copyright Connection Website http://depts.washington.edu/uwcopy/Using_Copyright/Guidelines/Fair.php

Farrelly, D., & Huchison, J. (2014). "Streaming Video in Academic Libraries: Survey Results and Copyright Information." Retrieved from www.slideshare.net/proquest/streaming-video-in-academic-libraries-survey-results-and-copyright-information-by-deg-farrelly-and-jane-hutchison-proquest-day-at-ala-annual-2014

Farrelly, D., & Huchison Surdi, J. (2016). "Academic Library Streaming Video Revisited." Retrieved from https://repository.asu.edu/items/39058

Guidelines for Off-Air Recording of Broadcast Programming for Educational Purposes, HR Rep No 495, 97th Cong, 2d Sess 7 (June 11, 1981).

Handman, G. (2002). "Video Collections in Academic Libraries." In G. Handman (Ed.), *Video Collection Development in Multi-Type Libraries: A Handbook* (pp. 288–291). Westport, CT: Greenwood Press.

Handman, G. (2010). "License to Look: Evolving Models for Library Video Acquisition and Access." *Library Trends*, 58(3), 324–334. doi:10.1353/lib.0.0094

Healy, C. (2010). "Netflix in an Academic Library: A Personal Case Study." *Library Trends*, 58(3), 402–411. doi:10.1353/lib.0.0089

Herbes-Sommers, C., Strain, T. H., & Smith, L. (2003). *Race: The Power of an Illusion*. [Documentary]. San Francisco California Newsreel.

Honda, I., & Morse, T. (1956). *Godzilla, King of the Monsters!* [Motion picture]. Los Angeles: Jewell Enterprises Inc.

Kaufman, P. B., & Mohan, J. (2009). "Video Use in Higher Education: Options for the Future." *Intelligent Television*. Retrieved from http://intelligenttelevision.com/research/entry/video-use-in-higher-education

King, R. (2014). "House of Cards: The Academic Library Media Center in the Era of Streaming Video." *The Serials Librarian*, 67(3), 289–306. doi:10.1080/0361526X.2014.948699

Loucks-DiMatteo, A. R. (1985). "The History of Media Librarianship: A Chronology." In J. Ellison (Ed.), *Media Librarianship* (pp. 72–89). New York: Neal-Schuman Publishers.

Morris, C. (2016). "Captioning and Copyright Law—Tensions and Work-Arounds in the Current Legal Landscape." Retrieved from the Association of Research Libraries (ARL) Web Accessibility Toolkit webpage http://accessibility.arl.org/2016/04/captioning-and-copyright-law/

National Association of the Deaf (NAD) et al., v. Harvard University, et al., 3:15-cv-30023 (D. Mass. 2015).

National Association of the Deaf (NAD) et al., v. Massachusetts Institute of Technology., 3:15-cv-30024 (D. Mass. 2015).

Otto, J. J. (2014). "University Faculty Describe Their Use of Moving Images in Teaching and Learning and Their Perceptions of the Library's Role in That Use." *College & Research Libraries*, 75(2), 115-144. doi: 10.5860/crl12-399

Pressman, A. (2016, July 21). "End of an Era as Last VCR Maker Ends Production." Retrieved from http://fortune.com/2016/07/21/last-video-cassette-recorder-maker/

Report of the Senate Committee on the Judiciary on the Technology, Education, and Copyright Harmonization Act of 2001. (2001). S. Rep. No. 107–31.

Russell, C. (2010). "The Best of Copyright and VideoLib." *Library Trends*, 58(3), 349–357. doi:10.1353/lib.0.0095

Shostrom, E. (1965). "Three Approaches to Psychotherapy I." [Documentary]. Corona del Mar, CA: Psychological & Educational Films.

Smith, K. (2012, November 26). "Another Fair Use Victory for Libraries." Retrieved from http://blogs.library.duke.edu/scholcomm/2012/11/26/another-fair-use-victory-for-libraries/

Sony Corp. of America v. Universal City Studios, Inc., 464 U.S. 417 (1984) Section 1201 Exemptions to Prohibition Against Circumvention of Technological Measures Protecting Copyrighted Works (n.d.) Retrieved from www.copyright.gov/1201/

Special Problems for Video Tapes. (n.d.). Retrieved from www.scancafe.com/image-preservation/videotape-decay

Spicer, S., & Horbal, A. (2017). "The Future of Video Playback Capability in College and University Classrooms." *College & Research Libraries*, 78(5), 706-721. doi: https://doi.org/10.5860/crl.78.5.706

Vallier, J. (2010). "Twenty-first Century Academic Media Center: Killer App or Chindogu?" *Library Trends*, 58(3), 378–390. doi:10.1353/lib.0.0091

Vecchione, J., & Else, J. (1987–1990). *Eyes on the Prize*. [Documentary]. Boston: Blackside Inc.

Widzinski, L. (2010). "Step Away From the Machine: A Look at Our Collective Past." *Library Trends*, 58(3), 358–377. doi:10.1353/lib.0.0092

Further Reading

Besser, H., Brown, C., Clarida, R., Forsberg, W., Righter, M., & Stoller, M. (2012). "Video at Risk: Strategies for Preserving Commercial Video Collections in Libraries." Retrieved from New York University Libraries website http://tisch.nyu.edu/cinema-studies/miap/research-outreach/research/video-at-risk.html

Carlisle Fountain, K. (2011). "Managing Expectations and Obligations: The Librarian's Role in Streaming Media for Online Education." In Proceedings of the Charleston Library Conference, Purdue e-Pubs, West Lafayette, IN (pp. 497–505). Retrieved from http://dx.doi.org/10.5703/1288284314954

Farrelly, D., Hutchison Surdi, J., & Lewis, C. (2016). "Section 108 Due Diligence Project." Retrieved from http://section108video.com/

Jaszi, P. A., & Aufderheide, P. (2008). "Code of Best Practices in Fair Use for Online Video." Retrieved from American University website http://digitalcommons.wcl.american.edu/cgi/viewcontent.cgi?article=1000&context=pijip_copyright

Spicer, S. (2014). "Exploring Video Abstracts in Science Journals: An Overview and Case Study." *Journal of Librarianship and Scholarly Communication*, 2(2), p. eP1110. doi: 10.7710/2162-3309.1110

Spicer, S. (2016). "Digital Video Collections Guide." Retrieved from ALA website http://connect.ala.org/node/183711

18

"I GOT IT FROM GOOGLE"

Recontextualizing Authorship to Strengthen Fair Use Reasoning in the Elementary Grades

David Cooper Moore and John Landis

In 2008, media literacy educators joined documentary filmmakers in establishing a code of best practices for fair use of copyrighted materials in their work. Documentary filmmakers' adoption of the best practices model had a real impact on how films are made: now, documentaries routinely employ fair use to justify the use of copyrighted materials in films that play at film festivals, that appear on television, and that are released to millions in movie theaters (Aufderheide 2007; Aufderheide & Jaszi 2011). Media literacy educators' adoption of the best practices model has been more of a grassroots effort. Much of the change we have seen, with the exception of the adoption of the best practices by major professional organizations like the National Council of Teachers of English, occurs teacher by teacher and school by school (Hobbs 2010).

What makes our job as advocates for the best practices model in media literacy education feasible is that fair use best practices look a lot like foundational media literacy education principles. Teaching learners how to understand authorship, message purpose, and other contextual elements in their analysis and creation of media are practices that media literacy educators have championed for decades (NAMLE 2007; Hobbs & Jensen 2009). Fair use is a natural complement to media literacy education because it requires users of copyrighted material to ask questions about their use that could be taken straight out of a media literacy curriculum. Who was the author of an original work, and what was the author's purpose? How was your purpose different from the original? How did you change or transform the original work to make it into something new or otherwise benefit society in your use of it? These are questions that are not only asked by judges presiding over copyright infringement cases; media literacy educators ask them every day in their classrooms.

Even though we have seen success in spreading the word about best practices among media literacy educators, much of the focus has, understandably, been on teaching teachers about their rights to use copyrighted material and to encourage their students to do the same in their creative work. In some contexts, there is no real difference between the learning process of the teacher and the learning process of the student when it comes to understanding copyright and fair use. In David's high school and undergraduate classrooms, creating new work from copyrighted materials goes hand in hand with learning about the four factors of fair use and formally applying the concept to transformative works of art and criticism.

But what about John's students, the youngest of whom are in kindergarten? Should kindergartners creating a magazine collage, a "logo alphabet," or a puppet show with designs based on cartoons and comics be expected to know whether their use of copyrighted material satisfies thinking about the nature, purpose, amount, and effect of their use? On the face of it, this seems absurd—even if a 5-year-old could technically be taught all four of these words, direct instruction of copyright law to young children is neither age-appropriate nor conducive to meaningful learning. And yet the spirit of fair use is that using and creating media, much of which is copyrighted, in a variety of forms is a process that creates new knowledge and new forms of creativity in the world. These ideas are important for kindergartners who are already the authors of their own works and who are already steeped in popular culture that is a locus for use, sharing, and commenting.

Rather than dive too deeply into the issue of whether young children can be taught fair use, we believe it is more productive to ask what kinds of reasoning skills does fair use require and how teachers can best help students at all levels to understand and use these reasoning skills to empower them as authors of their own work. Our model, developed from the perspective of an elementary school media arts teacher (John) and a media literacy consultant and scholar (David), allows teachers to explore fair use with children as young as 5 years old and to prepare even younger children. In this chapter, we will outline what use of copyrighted material looks like in elementary classrooms and what it could and (we believe) should look like. We will describe how empowering young students as authors in creative communities where fair use reasoning is the norm, not the exception, in multimedia composition ultimately prepares them for public, artistic, and professional communities where they will need to demonstrate their rights and responsibilities as users and creators under copyright law.

Getting It From Google

John, a Philadelphia elementary school media educator, is used to managing student distractions, as students try to sneak in YouTube and online games during class. But sometimes John is surprised to find students sneaking in work from their other classes. As he leads an activity in the computer lab, a small group of students from Mr. Baxter's science class break away from the assignment and start to argue about and giggle at adorable pictures of meerkats that they want to incorporate into a presentation on our planet's biomes. The students are using Google Slides, Google's online alternative to Microsoft PowerPoint, and they are comparing different pictures of the types of animals they want to use. One student is picking out the perfect meerkat—should she use a fuzzy baby meerkat with enormous black eyes, which is included in the licensed material automatically generated by Google Slides? Should she switch over to Google Images, where she might find a copyrighted picture of Timon from *The Lion King*? Which meerkat will best grab the attention of her classmates? Before the meerkats derail the lesson, John intervenes and, sensing a learning opportunity, asks the student where she found the picture she is debating whether to use. She looks up and responds cheerfully: "I got it from Google!"

Figure 18.1 shows an example of students' routine use of stock imagery from Google Presentations and other free online programs. Although students use images in their work, they often do not know where their pictures come from. Clearly, students enjoy using images as part of their learning experience. Mr. Baxter's students were indeed engaged and excited about their project. On the other hand, that response, "I got it from Google," shows us that students may not fully understand where their information comes from. As media literacy educators, we actively encourage our students to copy images from diverse sources into their work, but we also want students to think about photographs as visual texts constructed by authors for a specific purpose.

It wasn't always so easy to copy images into schoolwork or artwork. In the postcomputer, pre-Internet era of the 1980s and 1990s, creating digital art meant drawing by hand or selecting elements from a limited library of clip art. Collage usually meant cutting out images from magazines and other print sources and gluing them together. Later, students might have had access to a scanner that would create a digital copy of those collages. It was not really until the turn of the 21st century that students could regularly and easily delve into the world of digital art making with more sophisticated photo editing programs like Photoshop and the slowly developing image repository of the Internet.

Thanks to Google's search tools and cloud-based multimedia production tools, just about any image, text, sound, or interactive element imaginable can be cut, copied, and distributed in seconds, and the interface is easy enough for elementary school students to use. This new age presents opportunities for creativity, but tools like Google's have made it easier for students and teachers to quickly find different types of media to create, illustrate, and add sound, music, and special effects to school assignments.

On the other hand, image search engines by their very nature remove images from their original context. Scrolling through endless pages of pictures in a plain white grid, it is no wonder that students think of these images as an intrinsic part of Google itself rather than seeing them as indexed from diverse sources from throughout the web. For students using Google's presentation software, image search is built directly into the interface, bringing access to images

Figure 18.1 Students Use Images from Google Presentations

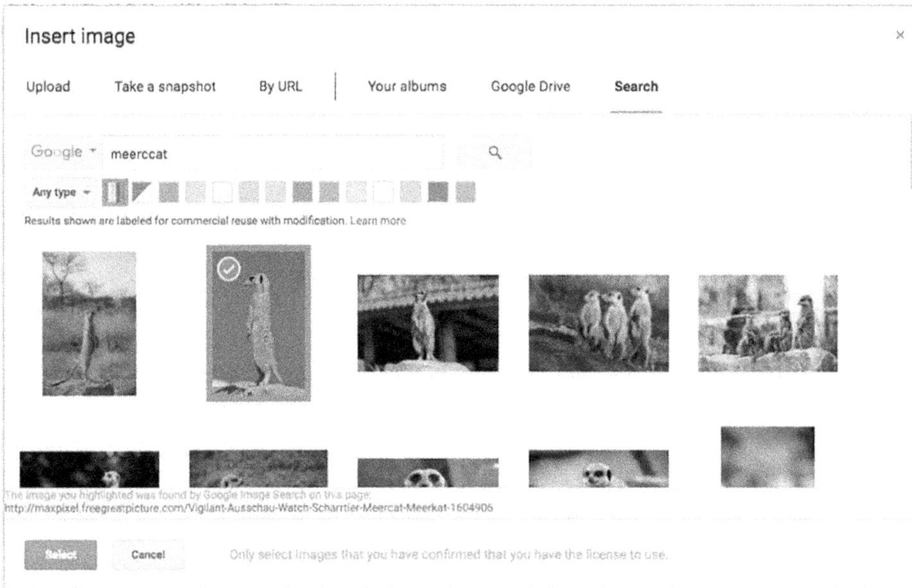

Figure 18.2 A Student Google Slides Image Search (with SafeSearch Enabled) for "Meerccat" [sic]

even closer to the fingertips and removing images even further from their context. When you search within the Google Slides app in Apps for Education—which is essentially a "safe search" with images licensed for reuse—the only hint of the image's origins in Google Slides is a note written in pale gray 8-point font. Figure 18.2 shows a Google Slides image search (with Safe-Search enabled) for "Meerccat [sic]."

In the creative communities of our classrooms, we can teach students to respect the rights of authors as a means to reinforce important literacy concepts such as authorship, purpose, and responsible media creation by adapting the principles of fair use to empower students as thoughtful creators of new media work. It's not just that "getting it from Google" is easy; it's that the interface actively discourages the critical thinking process behind the process of transformative use. Unfortunately, many of our most popular technologies are constructed to encourage accessibility at the expense of context.

Talking to Students About Copyright and Fair Use

Talking to students about fair use brings a potentially scary word into the classroom—and that word is "legal." One of the reasons that media literacy educators were brought together as a fair use community in the first place was because of the fear that many teachers felt that they were somehow breaking the law while using copyrighted materials in ways that seemed not only natural but necessary to their instruction (Hobbs, Jaszi, & Aufderheide, 2007). Getting teachers, administrators, and other educational professionals "on board" with fair use required the media literacy community to educate educators on their own rights and responsibilities around copyright law. Even among educators, building comprehension around legal issues was not easy—many of us tend to hear phrases like "the Copyright Act of 1976" or "DMCA take-down" or "cease and desist" and imagine that our normal and necessary teaching practices might land us in jail. Thanks to the best practices model, there is a growing fair use community among educators who no longer fear jail time for doing what they've always thought was right. However, even teachers knowledgeable about their rights and responsibilities under fair use still worry about setting a positive and morally upstanding model for their own students.

Teaching elementary school students about copyright law presents the added disadvantage that fears about legal implications are much harder to dispel in students who are still in the beginning stages of learning about how the world works. Formal civics education is rarely consistent prior to middle and high school, and even if we could assume that younger students had a working knowledge of documents like the Constitution, simply using the word "illegal" can immediately shut down any possibility of further conversation. In our experience with elementary school students, the word "illegal" connotes a grave crime deserving of harsh punishment. While directly discussing the legal dimensions of fair use may unleash a teacher's creativity, it may do just the opposite for a child.

David, who teaches older students in high school and undergraduate settings, has had some success teaching students about the legal dimensions of fair use and copyright as early as sixth grade. His work with the Media Education Lab at the University of Rhode Island as a filmmaker and educator gave him opportunities to adapt materials designed for high school and college students for younger students in an elementary-level media literacy summer enrichment program. In his summer course, David and a coteacher used the Transformers film series to explore fair use with sixth graders. His class took a silent "teaser trailer" for the Transformers blockbuster and created a new voice-over to imagine a film about Transformers-like characters who used the power of green energy to help stop global climate change (Hobbs & Moore 2013). After making their remix, students articulated exactly why their new work could be justified under fair use, noting that "we used the trailer; we didn't use it exactly what the movie was intended for," and "we changed the subject [of Transformers] to be about green and alternative energy" (Powerful Voices for Kids 2013).

However, we have questions about how applicable this model is to K–6 teaching as a whole. In the context of a media literacy enrichment classroom, David could devote a full week's instruction to fair use, including filling in gaps in students' background knowledge in civics, reviewing new terminology, and facilitating the production of a media project designed to demonstrate fair use reasoning. But few classroom teachers or technology specialists can devote this much time to the subject. Instead of thinking of ways to make fair use accessible to K–6 students as a legal concept, we instead focus on the potential to prepare students for legal reasoning by emphasizing the aspects of fair use that align with our broader goals as media literacy educators. We believe that children who use all media production opportunities as a chance to flex their "fair use muscles"—even if they do not call the process fair use themselves—will be better prepared for naming, understanding, and using fair use as creators when the time is right (perhaps as early as sixth grade) but probably not before the formal introduction of the U.S. Constitution.

Three Kid-Friendly "Big Ideas" for Developing Fair Use Reasoning Skills

As media literacy educators, we know that the reasoning process behind fair use, which itself is tied to the Constitutional spirit of copyright law (to promote creativity and the spread of knowledge), is good teaching practice. As we have demonstrated, we have had some limited success in teaching fair use directly to elementary age students. However, we have pared down the essential questions of fair use to three big ideas that are more applicable to a wide range of younger students, not for strictly legal reasons but rather for pedagogical ones. Figure 18.3

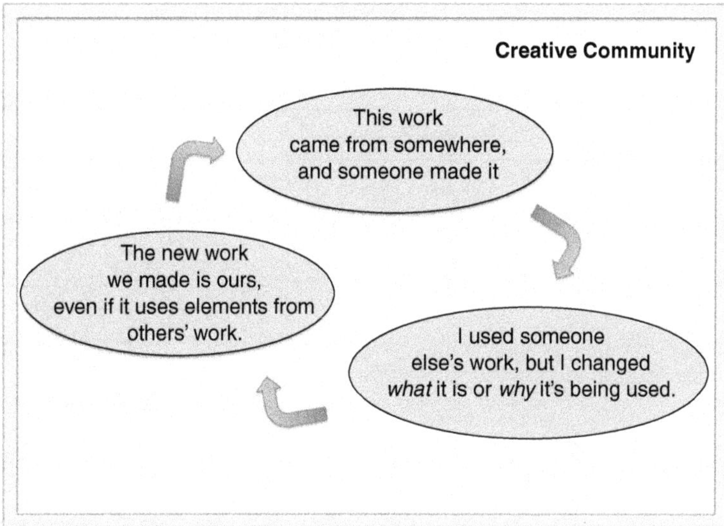

Figure 18.3 The Fair Use Reasoning Authorship Cycle

shows the fair use authorship cycle, a set of ideas that align with what we—and, we believe, other media literacy educators—already value in our classrooms: the thoughtful use, analysis, and creation of media. We have phrased these three big ideas in "kid-friendly" language to demonstrate that fair use reasoning isn't just a legal defense but also a way to promote critical thinking, empower students as responsible media creators, and engage students in conversations about and interactions with authentic audiences for their own work and the work of others.

"I Know Where This Media Came From and Who Made It"

In the context of developing information literacy and research skills, engaging students in understanding the who and where of online authorship is often presented as good in and of itself. School librarians and language arts teachers encourage students to determine online authorship to assess the credibility of a source—the idea being that ambiguous or unknown authorship necessarily undermines a source's credibility (Metzger et al. 2015). Unfortunately, systemic changes in how we retrieve information have undermined the relevance of this idea for many students who regularly engage in informal research such as population statistics or science facts without consciously engaging in the type of critical reading that their teachers might encourage. Instead, in our model, understanding authorship of all media in as much context as we can infer is one prong of a reasoning framework that includes students' own creative work. When students understand that their own work can be a part of this process, they will often want their audiences to understand their role as author in the same way that they sought to learn the authorship of the media they used.

Educators have developed simple strategies that help young children become more aware of where sources come from. Table 18.1 shows a worksheet that John uses with young children to help them document the visual sources they use in a collage project. When dealing with diverse Internet sources, it is inevitable that students at differing levels of digital and print literacy will sometimes misidentify a source or its purpose. A student may take an image or text from Wikipedia but incorrectly assume that Wikipedia is a news site because it features large

Table 18.1 Worksheet Helps Elementary School Students Document Their Sources When Creating a Digital Collage

Digital Collage Log		
I found a picture of. . .	*It is from the website. . .*	*I found it using. . .*
A meerkat	Geograph.org.uk	✓ Google Image Search ❑ Kiddle Image Search ❑ Open Clip Art ❑ ____________
		❑ Google Image Search ❑ Kiddle Image Search ❑ Open Clip Art ❑ ____________
		❑ Google Image Search ❑ Kiddle Image Search ❑ Open Clip Art ❑ ____________

blocks of text. However, the key here is not that students correctly identify the type of website they are sourcing images from every time but rather that they are making a meaningful attempt to understand the sources they employ. They are in effect operating in the good faith that they will come to expect within their own creative communities as authors.

"I Used This Media, but I Changed the What and/or the Why"

Our second idea speaks to what the media literacy education fair use community calls transformativeness. Beyond the distinctive legalese of this word, we prefer to break down as many fair use concepts as possible into intuitive and memorable concepts. So, instead, we phrase transformativeness as changing the what and the why of media. When students think about what media is, they notice its formal features and the ways in which it has been presented or distributed. To change the what of media is to alter in some meaningful way what a picture looks like, the length of a video, or the format of a media text, as, for instance, when an advertisement or logo is used in a magazine or digital photo collage. The why speaks more to the nature, context, and reasoning behind media.

Even young children can grasp the concept of changing what something is and why it might be used. In our media literacy education programs, rising second grade students used advertisements of Dawn soap featuring animals covered in oil, in the wake of the BP oil spill, to discuss their feelings about the disaster. What they used (the advertisement) was unchanged, but why they used it (to express their feelings) clearly was. Rising third graders used screenshots from popular films like Disney's *Aladdin* and the Will Smith vehicle *Pursuit of Happyness* to synthesize what they learned about homelessness in Philadelphia into a comic (Moore 2013). Students who are learning to use photo editing software to add splotches of color, text, and other elements to pictures of celebrities to change them—or deface them—understand that what they have created is not the same as the original picture. Figure 18.4 shows an example of students' use of copyrighted images and original drawings in a comic book created to explore the topic of homelessness. Students use examples as they critically examine the representation of the homeless in media and popular culture.

Figure 18.4 Children Use Copyrighted Images from Disney in Creating a Comic Book About Homelessness

Importantly, changing the what and why could be a gauge for the use of all media, regardless of its actual copyright status. We apply the what-and-why standard not only to copyrighted works but to public domain and Creative Commons works as well. In our view, one unfortunate side effect of the Creative Commons movement is the extent to which media arts professionals use media that does not fall under copyright as an excuse to create derivative work. We will see in our third big idea why a true appreciation of copyright law that balances owners' and users' rights—rather than making copyright a nonissue—is so important for how students think not only about the media they use but about the media they create.

"The Media We Make Is Ours"

The fair use reasoning process comes full circle when students understand that the new work they created from existing media—a new work that requires their understanding of where media they used came from and how it was changed (formally or contextually)—is now theirs and is therefore now part of the same process that they went through to make their work in the first place.

Students are taught to claim authorship in preschool, signing their names on crayon drawings even before they know all of the letters in the alphabet. By the time students are in elementary school, authorship takes on social dimensions as students compare their work to others', as when a student's art or design is copied by others when it is perceived as attractive or original. This is how many students are introduced to the idea of a creative community. In one class, copying another student's work might be a sign of great respect, as when an original cartoon or drawing is copied in appreciation; in another, copying might be seen as unethical or insulting, as when students take credit for someone else's work. Importantly, the classroom culture will determine what kind of copying is acceptable and what kind of copying is not—it is not the act of copying itself that determines whether a work is acceptable or unacceptable.

This sort of logic, which can be seen in classrooms of all kinds, from a science classroom where students might be encouraged to paraphrase nonfiction texts in a project to an art classroom where students make variations of a simple style or template, is not at a remove from fair use reasoning. Fair use depends on the communities in which copyrighted material is being used. Whether teachers and students realize it or not, their classrooms are already creative communities with established ways of understanding how different types of imitation are "OK" or "not OK" when it comes to student work. Once students reach later elementary grades, their conscious understanding of how they operate in creative communities in the classroom may translate to opportunities to produce and distribute work in public artistic communities. At this stage, the issue of fair use reasoning is not merely a question of understanding the cycle of authorship (from conscientious user to conscientious creator) but will also require them to exercise the reasoning they have developed in real-world situations. As we will see, even in these real-world situations, it is the knowledge of oneself as a member of a creative community, not specific legal knowledge about copyright and fair use, that both empower and protect students as creators who may use copyrighted materials themselves.

Fair use reasoning prepares students for civic competencies in seeing themselves as members of different kinds of communities, from their classrooms to their schools to their neighborhoods, cities, and the world. The classroom can be a safe space for students to try out new ways of thinking about authorship and to be authors whose work will be used and appreciated in creative communities. Since creative communities online frequently launch student work into a public space where issues of authorship and audiences are beyond any individual's control and require an understanding of complicated group norms, the classroom can be an important first step in practicing how to be a member of an artistic community.

Fair Use Reasoning in the Early Grades

To return to a question we posed at the beginning of our piece: can you teach a kindergartner about copyright and fair use? We admit that we are both still learning about the developmental characteristics of our youngest students and have followed with interest recent developments in the National Association for the Education of Young Children (NAEYC), the American Academy of Pediatrics, and scholars focusing on the effects of media and media literacy on young children (Christakis 2014; Guernsey 2012; NAEYC 2012). There is a lot that we don't know about how best to reach our youngest students with the principles of media literacy and how learning environments for young children might need to differ from those of their older peers.

However, when we think about what early childhood educators do well, we notice that something close to fair use reasoning is actually built into literacy and art activities with young children. If teaching about fair use reasoning asks students to imagine authorship as a two-way relationship between creators and users and if part of this relationship involves understanding oneself as a member of a community, these values are often already embedded in the earliest literacy activities. When students are asked to predict or provide their own ending for a children's story, they are becoming authors in their own right. When they use popular children's book characters to illustrate new ideas, like how they felt about a story or how a story relates to their own lives, they are transforming that text. And when our youngest students learn about collaboration, sharing in a group setting, and speaking at the front of the classroom, they are imagining themselves, often for the first time, as members of a creative community.

In Ms. Webster's first-grade class at John's elementary school in Philadelphia, students engage in a long term 'author study' of children's author and illustrator Mo Willems. In their author study, they learn about the job of an author and the characteristics that make Willems' work unique. In addition to reading several books by this author, the children explore Willems' style by imitating it. They write sentences that imitate his writing style, and they use paint and art materials to carefully recreate his pigeon illustrations. Figure 18.5 shows an example of work by students who, after studying the work of the children's author and illustrator, create their own version of Willems' iconic pigeon.

Although the act of copying the features of the Willems pigeon for the 6-year-olds is a more mechanical and manual process than it might be for older students creating work on a computer, these young students are still transforming the elements from Willems' work into new artworks that serve a new purpose. Students gain new understanding of Willems as an author and of themselves as authors. Similar author studies are conducted in elementary classrooms in schools throughout the country (Jenkins 1999; Snyders 2014). We believe that this awareness of authorship and the transformative nature of reuse can be continued as students mature and create more complex work using popular culture outside the limits of sanctioned children's literature in the elementary classroom.

Media literacy education adds on to a literacy paradigm that already introduces authorship and audience to young people by expanding teachers' and students' conceptualizations of literacy. When students learn about the authors of children's books, they might also think

Figure 18.5 Grade 1 Students Create Birds in the Style of Children's Author and Illustrator Mo Willems

of the people who film or animate their favorite TV shows or movies. They might expand their understanding of "who counts" as an author to media formats like music, comics, video games, or websites. Similarly, when students explore authorship on their own, they might expand their canvas beyond the development of print literacy and think about the visual language of film and video (how do framing or perspective change the way we notice things?) or the interconnectedness of online writing (how can we link one person's idea to another's?).

The work of young children frequently draws on copyrighted imagery, but often this imagery simply comes from copyrighted work that we don't think about as copyrighted—classic children's literature that is, nonetheless, still under copyright, or adaptations of fairy tales and other works that may or may not fall under copyright. In all cases, students rarely copy any of these works mechanically. Instead, they redraw, add ideas, and transform original works using their own imaginations. Even if kindergartners do not need to learn about section 107 of the Copyright Act of 1976, they can still begin to understand the relationship between an original author and a new work created by a user and to understand how they, too, are authors when they create these works.

Fair Use Reasoning in Later Grades

By the time children really start to bring pop culture media into the classroom directly, not just in conversation but through actual cut-and-paste from online and other sources, teachers may experience a shift in how they view the copying of media. All of a sudden, activities that were once limited to a teacher-curated set of texts open up into a media free-for-all, with major media companies, cable television, popular Internet sites, video games, and viral videos and memes all seeping into the classroom environment.

By the later elementary grades, students experience a graduation of sorts from highly protective and kid-centered environments, which are heavily curated by teachers, to a wide world of adult media texts and technologies, including massive databases owned and operated by companies like Google. This transition can be daunting for teachers who are accustomed to controlling which media is OK to use in the classroom and which is not. Employing our three-step authorship cycle, which is, we argue, essential to developing early fair use reasoning, can also help both students and teachers make sense of this newfound deluge of information and media from the Internet.

For instance, in John's fifth-grade media class, students study advertising by attempting to market a product to a specific target audience. In one version of this lesson, students invented an original brand of hand sanitizer. They researched the positive and negative impacts of the product and analyzed different advertising messages to learn how advertisers persuade audiences to purchase their products. One student decided that the best way to reach his target audience was through a celebrity endorsement. Since he had been assigned the task of marketing hand sanitizer to fans of the Pittsburgh Steelers, he chose the brand name "Germ Tacklers" and used an image of quarterback Ben Roethlisberger on the label. Figure 18.6 shows an example of work created by a fifth-grade student who created a promotional message about his new brand of hand sanitizer.

In John's classroom, students are free to use copyrighted pictures like this as part of his work, as long as they also document the images they use and the websites from which they get those images. This student's image was a still from a sports video blog, and he understood that his image differed from the original purpose. Educators and creative media professionals might debate whether this use is transformative enough, and (unlike the 10-year-old), we

Figure 18.6 Fifth-Grade Students Learn About Advertising by Creating Their Own Brands and Using Images to Simulate a Celebrity Endorsement

certainly know that fair use is not a valid defense for implying a celebrity's endorsement of a product without the celebrity's permission. However, the important element here is that the student has acknowledged the images' origins and his own role in recontextualizing the image. As educators, we are confident that such educational work among our students is legal, even though a similar use would likely not qualify as fair use in the context of an actual marketing campaign for hand sanitizer.

With the rise of social media, young students now participate in online communities and publish work to reach wider audiences. When students encounter real and sometimes quite large audiences for their work, grappling thoughtfully with the issues of fair use is not merely practice for adult interactions. For many children, the fair use reasoning they develop in classrooms can have an immediate bearing on their present lives. For example, Elena, one of John's former students, began publishing her work online at the age of 10 using Scratch, an online creative tool and community designed by the MIT Media Lab's Lifelong Kindergarten group to teach beginning programming skills through animation and game design. Elena's animations about cats have gained in popularity over the years. Figure 18.7 shows an example of her

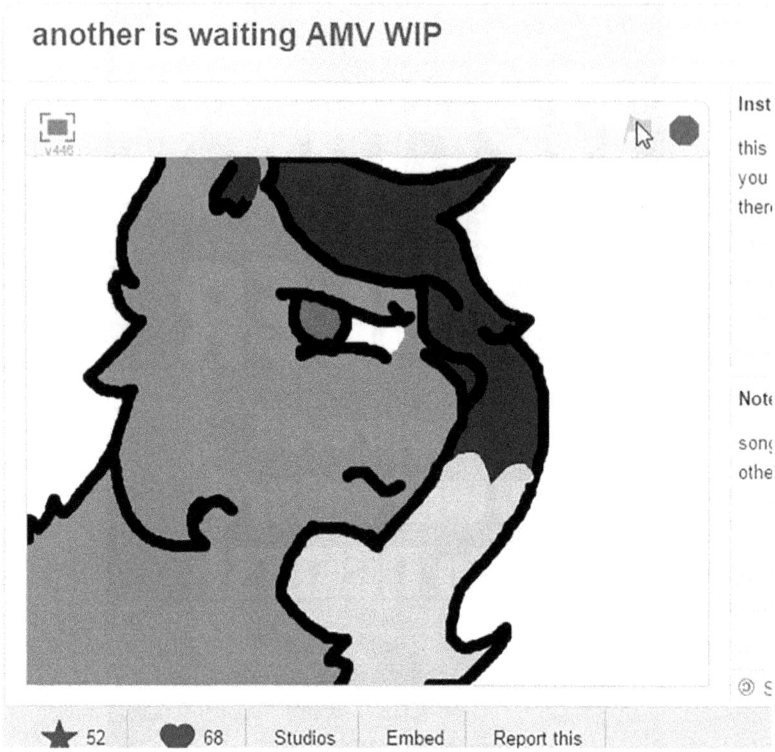

Figure 18.7 Elena's Work on Scratch Combines Her Original Drawings With Popular Music

creative work. Elena has been featured on the site's front page nine times (a real honor in the Scratch community), and her work is followed by over 1,400 other accounts on Scratch. Now a 15-year-old high school student, Elena returns to John's computer lab weekly to mentor younger students as a part of the school's coding club. Although Elena hasn't had any formal education in fair use, her experiences online as part of a creative community have given her an education in the complex ethics of remix and appropriation, in effect testing the skills she developed as an elementary student in John's classroom.

The design of the Scratch website encourages users to remix one another's work, and community guidelines are in place that emphasize the importance of giving credit to those whose work is remixed. Nevertheless, many students in coding club report that the Scratch community is rife with online "drama" when creators feel that their work has been copied inappropriately. One student, Alicia, felt particularly hurt when one of her followers reported her for having copied her work without giving credit. Elena consoled Alicia at coding club, telling her of her own experiences dealing with "recolorers"—Scratch users who remix other users' Scratch animations by simply recoloring them. When Elena first began using Scratch, she was upset when someone would repost her work having simply recolored it. Now that she has had more experience being recolored, she more or less accepts it but recognizes that different artists are likely to react differently. "Some people love it, they take it as a high compliment. Some people hate it. They think someone's not appreciating their work enough or something like that, it's disrespectful, it's stealing." She also makes a distinction between the recolorers and those who simply copy someone's project without transforming it. "That's not cool," she reflects. "It doesn't benefit them, and it doesn't benefit me."

As adults, we might rightly debate the extent to which recoloring an animation might be seen as a transformative fair use. Elena does not discuss her experiences in precisely these terms, but it is clear that navigating the creative and social space of Scratch has given her valuable insight into how to approach fair use issues as she grows as an artist. Now that she is moving on to more adult creative communities such as DeviantArt and SketchFu, both of which have their own cultures and customs surrounding the appropriate reuse of creative work, Elena feels that she is a more savvy and productive member of these communities because of her experience on Scratch. She has learned about "dealing with other artists." She reflects on the experience by noting that "it's different than my peer group at school. When so many people share your interests, you have to learn how to deal with it. Generally when you're copying someone else's work, you should do it with courtesy."

Conclusion

As we ask our students to use copyrighted materials in media literacy activities in our classrooms, we have some remaining questions about how we can best prepare students for the real artistic, academic, and professional communities we hope they will join. As educators and creative media professionals, we also reflect on our own experiences and acknowledge that we often just "play around" with a mix of original and copyrighted materials, as when John designs a T-shirt for a friend or David puts together a presentation for older students. In these more personal cases of media making, we often use copyrighted material in ways that are aligned with the so-called HOMAGO philosophy of "hanging out, messing around, and geeking out," popularized by Mizuko Ito and others (Ito et al. 2009). Though we might know the provenance of the images and texts we use, often this is a post hoc process of identifying materials after they have already been incorporated into our work. We notice that Google and other tools make it very easy to play with media, remixing and combining elements into new materials, but it can simultaneously make it difficult to identify exactly where these elements may have originated. How can we best give our students that creative space to try things out and play around when we also want them to exercise their fair use reasoning in the production of their work? Would Mr. Baxter's students think his assignment was as exciting if they needed to determine the authorship of every photo and document their transformative use, or would this extinguish the spark of curiosity that John observed in his own classrooms?

Ultimately, teachers serve as models of ethical behavior in their classrooms—we structure and scaffold lessons to meet their learning needs even while knowing that our students' understanding may be imperfect or incomplete despite our best intentions. The free-for-all nature of online search presents powerful opportunities to navigate millions of sources and images intuitively and easily, and incorporation of fair use reasoning into elementary school classrooms, for us, has required a balance between deliberate and intentional documentation with intuitive and spontaneous creativity. We see no real contradiction here with the spirit of fair use, which is flexible and dependent on the complete context and situation of an individual's use of copyrighted materials. Some fair use claims, like that of contemporary artist Richard Prince, rest on ambiguous—or even nonexistent—intentions of transformative use (Kennedy 2013). Similarly, as teachers, we find that we need to be sensitive to our own tolerance for questionable transformativeness based on our own standards. After all, it is our students who will ultimately be responsible for understanding their own rights as both users and creators of copyrighted material.

Successful teaching of fair use reasoning in elementary school leaves students equipped with the critical thinking, cognitive flexibility, and creative curiosity to use and create new works in real creative communities. To that end, we believe that it is a key responsibility as media educators for us to foster students' abilities to ask questions about authorship, to explain their own motivations and processes for transforming others' work, and to see themselves as authors within a creative community. These three components of fair use reasoning set the stage for more complex fair use reasoning among our students as they get older, encouraging them to confidently and thoughtfully claim their rights as both creators and users of copyrighted material.

References

Aufderheide, P. (2007). "How Documentary Filmmakers Overcame Their Fear of Quoting and Learned to Employ Fair Use: A Tale of Scholarship in Action." *International Journal of Communication*, 1(1), 11.

Aufderheide, P., & Jaszi, P. (2011). *Reclaiming Fair Use: How to Put Balance Back in Copyright*. Chicago: University of Chicago Press.

Christakis, D. A. (2014). "Interactive Media Use at Younger Than the Age of 2 Years: Time to Rethink the American Academy of Pediatrics Guideline?" *JAMA Pediatrics*, 168(5), 399–400.

Guernsey, L. (2012). *Screen Time: How Electronic Media—From Baby Videos to Educational Software—Affects Your Young Child*. New York: Basic Books.

Hobbs, R. (2010). *Copyright Clarity: How Fair Use Supports Digital Learning*. Thousand Oaks, CA: Corwin.

Hobbs, R., Jaszi, P., & Aufderheide, P. (2007). *The Cost of Copyright Confusion for Media Literacy Education*. Washington, DC: Center for Social Media.

Hobbs, R., & Jensen, A. (2009). "The Past, Present, and Future of Media Literacy Education." *The Journal of Media Literacy Education*, 1(1), 1–11.

Hobbs, R., & Moore, D. C. (2013). *Discovering Media Literacy: Teaching Digital Media and Popular Culture in Elementary School*. Thousand Oaks, CA: Corwin.

Ito, M., Antin, J., Finn, M., Law, A., Manion, A., Mitnick, S., Schlossberg, D., Yardi, S., & Horst, H. A. (2009). *Hanging Out, Messing Around, and Geeking Out: Kids Living and Learning With New Media*. Cambridge, MA: MIT Press.

Jenkins, C. B. (1999). *The Allure of Authors: Author Studies in the Elementary Classroom*. Portsmouth, NH: Heinemann.

Kennedy, R. (2013, April 25). "Court Rules in Artist's Favor." *New York Times*. Retrieved from www.nytimes.com/2013/04/26/arts/design/appeals-court-ruling-favors-richard-prince-in-copyright-case.html?_r=0

Metzger, M. J., Flanagin, A. J., Markov, A., Grossman, R., & Bulger, M. (2015). "Believing the Unbelievable: Understanding Young People's Information Literacy Beliefs and Practices in the United States." *Journal of Children and Media*, 9(3), 325–348.

Moore, D. C. (2013). "Bringing the World to School: Integrating News and Media Literacy in Elementary Classrooms." *Journal of Media Literacy Education*, 5(1), 5.

NAEYC. (2012). "Technology and Interactive Media as Tools in Early Childhood Programs Serving Children From Birth Through Age 8." NAEYC and the Fred Rogers Center for Early Learning and Children's Media at Saint Vincent College. Retrieved from http://www. naeyc.org/files/naeyc/PS_technology_WEB.pdf

National Association for Media Literacy Education. (2007). "Core Principles of Media Literacy Education in the United States." Retrieved from https://namle.net/publications/core-principles/

Powerful Voices for Kids. (2013). "City as Classroom." Retrieved from http://powerfulvoicesforkids.com/ideas/city-classroom

Schultz, J. (2007). "P10 v. Google: Public Interest Prevails in Digital Copyright Showdown." Electronic Frontier Foundation. Retrieved from www.eff.org/deeplinks/2007/05/p10-v-google-public-interest-prevails-digital-copyright-showdown

Snyders, C. S. B. (2014). "I Wish We Could Make Books All Day!: An Observational Study of Kindergarten Children During Writing Workshop." *Early Childhood Education Journal*, 42(6), 405–414.

Further Reading

Guernsey, L. (2014). "Envisioning a Digital Age Architecture for Early Childhood Education." New America Foundation. Retrieved from www.newamerica.org/downloads/DigitalArchitecture-20140326.pdf

Hobbs, R., & Moore, D. C. (2013). *Discovering Media Literacy: Teaching Digital Media and Popular Culture in Elementary School.* Thousand Oaks, CA: Corwin.

Scheibe, C., & Rogow, F. (2011). *The Teacher's Guide to Media Literacy: Critical Thinking in a Multimedia World.* Thousand Oaks, CA: Corwin.

19

RESOLVING COPYRIGHT CONCERNS IN THE DEVELOPMENT OF DIVERSE CURRICULUM MATERIALS FOR MEDIA ANALYSIS ACTIVITIES

Chris Sperry and Cyndy Scheibe

As educators, we have a fundamental responsibility to teach our students to think critically about the world in which they live and the messages they receive, including messages conveyed through popular and educational media. It is not possible for teachers to fulfill this responsibility without being able to view, discuss, and critique examples of these media materials—which are often copyrighted—in our classrooms. Fair use is therefore essential to one of the primary goals of education: teaching students the skills and habits they need to read their world.

Project Look Sharp is a not-for-profit grassroots initiative that was founded by Dr. Cyndy Scheibe at Ithaca College in 1996. Our mission is to give educators the training and support they need to integrate media literacy throughout the K–12 curriculum in ways that are literacy based, inquiry based, and curriculum driven. Over the past twenty years, we have reached more than 25,000 educators, librarians, and school administrators through our free online curriculum materials and professional development programs. When we first began working with teachers and librarians two decades ago, they quickly identified classroom media analysis as the key avenue for integrating media literacy into the curriculum, recognizing the need for diversifying the types of texts that were being discussed and analyzed by students (beyond traditional books and other print materials). Teachers understood the importance of developing critical reading skills through media analysis, particularly for students who were disenfranchised by strictly text-based analyses. Many of these early adopters were already using film clips, paintings, advertisements, magazine covers, excerpts from TV shows, and a host of other media forms to teach both content and critical literacy skills.

While these educators were excited about the possibilities that media literacy approaches could provide for their work with students, they also had a very consistent refrain: "Sounds great, but I do not have the time to find the right media examples to use with my students." They told us loud and clear that if Project Look Sharp wanted to support educators in integrating media literacy into their teaching, we needed to find ways to provide high-quality and diverse media materials they could use in the classroom. The content area educators teaching social studies, science, and health—particularly at the secondary level—said that they needed carefully chosen media documents with key questions and background information tied to their specific subject areas and grade levels. They told us that with the right materials that addressed their core content, they could consistently integrate media analysis across their curriculum.

Throughout the late 1990s, we began working with groups of educators and administrators in our local school district to develop these materials. At the elementary level, they were often used in interdisciplinary units that involved media production as well as analysis. One example was the development of *The Iroquois Kit* (Sperry 1999), produced by the Ithaca City School District in collaboration with Project Look Sharp and TST-BOCES (Anderson et al. 2001).

Working with fourth-grade teachers, librarians, the district social studies curriculum chair, and Haudenosaunee educator Freda Jacques, we created a series of slide shows that used diverse images of Native people to teach students about history, culture, and stereotyping through critical thinking and analysis of the media messages. Teachers throughout the district were then able to teach fourth-graders to analyze the historical representation of Native people while at the same time evaluating how paintings, advertisements, murals, money, cartoons, TV, film, and video games presented views of Native Americans from both historical and cultural perspectives. Figure 19.1 shows two different paintings representing first contact between Native Americans and European explorers. They are *Discovery of the Mississippi* by William H. Powell (1855) and *The Last Supper* by Jonathan Warm Day (1991). The Iroquois Kit involves teachers asking students questions about each of these paintings, such as:

- From whose perspective and point of view is this painting, and what makes you say that? What is the historical context for these events, and what is your evidence?
- What are the messages about Native people (and about Europeans) in this painting?
- Who created—and who commissioned—each of these paintings, and why?

In developing these materials, we also codified Project Look Sharp's constructivist approach to media decoding. The images depicted in Figure 19.1 were not accompanied by a script for teachers to provide the analysis for students; the students were to do the analysis themselves, with key questions and focused probing by the teacher. The teacher would not attempt to fill students up with the "correct" analysis of the messages found in the media example but rather unearth students' own meaning-making about the content and construction of each document by facilitating a developmentally appropriate dialogue with and among the students, enabling internalized understanding and analysis of content and building habits of asking key questions about all mediated messages. That philosophical approach to media literacy pedagogy is reflected in all of the free curriculum kits and lessons now available on the Project Look Sharp website (projectlooksharp.org), as well as in our professional development work with educators over the past two decades.

(a)

(b)

Figure 19.1 Sample Images for Decoding, The Iroquois Kit: (a) Discovery of the Mississippi; (b) The Last Supper

This work has been deeply informed by decades of international scholarship and practice in the growing field of media literacy education. In the United States, media literacy was initially defined as "the ability to access, analyze, evaluate, and create messages in a variety of forms" (Aufderheide & Firestone 1993, p. 7). Today, most media literacy educators emphasize analysis, evaluation, creation, reflection, and action as the main components of media literacy, all of which are featured in the graphic representation of the Process of Media Literacy created by

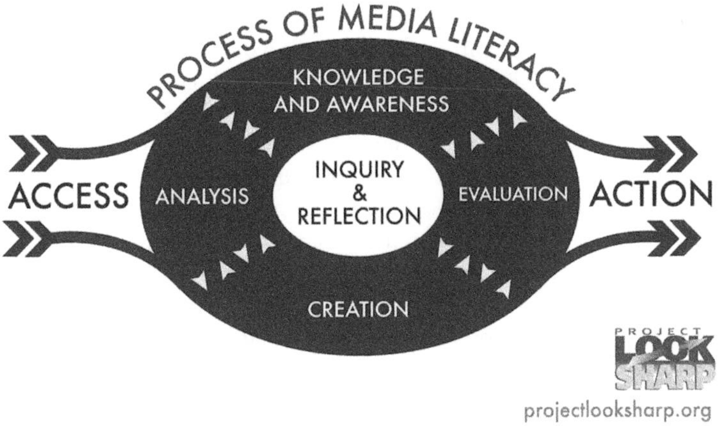

Figure 19.2 Project Look Sharp's Media Literacy Process

Project Look Sharp (see Figure 19.2), a process that is grounded in ongoing inquiry and reflection. Our work is also based on The Core Principles of Media Literacy Education developed and published by the National Association for Media Literacy Education (2007), as well as its rubric Key Questions to Ask When Analyzing Media Messages. Project Look Sharp uses these and other collaboratively developed frameworks for media analysis as the basis for our local, national, and international work with teachers, librarians, and other educators in shaping the critical thinking questions found in our curriculum materials.

The Importance of Professional Development for Media Literacy

Our early work with teachers also helped us to identify the critical connection between materials development and staff development. Our lessons were designed to be constructivist, with teacher's guides that feature suggested questions the teacher could ask in facilitating a group analysis of media documents. These were accompanied by "Possible Answers" to illustrate the types of evidence-based responses teachers should be probing to elicit. Sometimes we also include "Additional Information" that the teacher could provide as students explored the documents, but the pedagogy was designed to emphasize the process of questioning and probing.

When we observed teachers using our materials in the classroom, however, we sometimes witnessed the familiar (but disconcerting) practice where the teacher provides their own analysis of the media messages for the students. Rather than using the questions and discussion among the students as the core of the activity, teachers were telling students what to see. Rather than facilitating student deconstruction of media messages, students were falling back on their more traditional role of being passive observers, "learning" and adopting the interpretations of the media messages provided by the teacher. These teachers clearly needed training in the pedagogy of media analysis from an inquiry-based approach.

We also began to see patterns in how teachers—particularly secondary content area teachers—struggled with the constructivist approach to media analysis. These teachers were often experienced in using media examples in their curriculum but rarely for teaching critical thinking, analysis, and evaluation. In English language arts, some teachers were using film clips (and even whole films) as a "reward" for the rigorous analysis of traditional novels and plays.

For instance, once the class had read and discussed the print version of *Romeo and Juliet*, they would get to enjoy the film—but without any discussion or analysis of the differences between the two, or about the casting and production elements, or choices made by the film director in telling the story. This reinforced the view that the printed word was the "hard stuff," to be studied and discussed, while "media" like film was simply to be enjoyed. In social studies and science, media examples were typically used for providing information.

Science teachers regularly used educational videos, charts, and scientific reports to explore content, while social studies teachers often used historical writings, maps, and a library of documentary film and video clips to illustrate moments in history. But the integration of media literacy questions that taught students to critically analyze the construction of these media documents—as well as reflecting on the core content and information presented—was often new, even to experienced teachers. We needed to create staff development that would teach teachers (and teacher education students) to use media examples to teach literacy and critical thinking skills as well as to inform students about content. We needed to educate teachers and librarians about the ways in which a wide range of popular media examples (e.g., clips from TV shows, films, advertisements, comics, songs) could be used for analysis and discussion rather than simply viewing those media forms as purely for entertainment or information.

Classroom Media Use and Copyright Concerns

These distinctions would come to play an important role as we confronted copyright issues. We do not advocate for the use of examples from popular and educational media in the ways that they were originally designed to be used: to illustrate a concept, provide information about a topic, portray a compelling story, or persuade about a product. An inquiry-based media literacy approach may use media examples in service of the teacher's content goals, but it will also include some analysis and evaluation of how (and usually why) the media example was created and/or contrasting the same content presented in different media formats. Through a focus on critical analysis and constructivist decoding, transformative use occurs.

Technological changes in media access and availability have also played a critical role in our repurposing of copyrighted material for classroom use. We developed our first media literacy integration projects in the late 1990s when educational technology was evolving fast. The first draft of the *Iroquois Imaging Project* used 35mm color slides. Reproducing sixty slides for each of the eight elementary schools cost the Ithaca City School District over $500 and required teachers to find a slide projector and an almost totally dark room. Within 5 years, we would be able to make the same set of images available to all educators at no cost by creating digital files that could be downloaded free from our website and shown on LCD projectors, and by 2010 those projectors were in nearly every classroom in the district. At the same time, the rise of YouTube and similar online video providers has made it enormously easier to find and show short video clips in the classroom (replacing the old VCRs and DVD players). The increased ease of media access has not only made Project Look Sharp's media materials cheaper and easier to disseminate but has also fostered a new educational imperative to help students to think critically about their mediated environment—both inside and outside the classroom.

Media Construction of War

In 1999, we worked with Ithaca High School social studies teacher Andrea Kiely to develop a series of media literacy lessons for her ninth-grade global studies class. Her brother had fought in the Gulf War of 1991, and she had collected *Newsweek* covers and articles about the war during that time, using them to successfully teach a mixed-ability class both history content and media analysis. During her participation in a summer media literacy institute for educators led by Project Look Sharp, Andrea asked us if we could get her a similar set of *Newsweek* covers from the Vietnam War so that she could contrast both the events of each war and also the different ways in which *Newsweek* covered those events during each war. Working collaboratively with her, we were able to identify the core vocabulary and content about the Vietnam War covered in the state tests and chose engaging *Newsweek* covers and photo spreads that not only reflected that historical content but that would also lend themselves to rich media analysis in the classroom. Andrea began using those materials to teach the history of those two wars (and to develop media literacy skills) with her students.

Word of Andrea's success—especially in engaging her more academically challenged students—led to a slew of requests for copies of the materials. Then the events of September 11 led to a new war in Afghanistan in the fall of 2001, which was covered by *Newsweek* in an entirely different way than it had covered the previous two wars, and we decided to add materials for that new war to the existing set. With the growing request for those materials, we secured funding from Ithaca College and collaborated with the Center for Media Literacy to publish our first kit for a national audience of educators, *Media Construction of War* (Sperry 2003). Figure 19.3 shows the cover of the curriculum, which shows *Newsweek* covers featuring foreign political leaders Osama Bin Laden, Saddam Hussein, and Ho Chi Minh. That experience came to define Project Look Sharp's approach to constructivist media decoding and to the application of fair use for copyrighted materials.

Our first challenge involved what to do about copyright for the *Newsweek* materials we planned to use. Our interactions with lawyers taught us that copyright law is an extremely gray area. Since our initial plan was to use grant funds to create the media literacy curriculum kits and then sell those kits to raise money for future publications, one intellectual property attorney said that we could not publish without *Newsweek*'s permission (and likely royalty payments). Another said that the fair use doctrine clearly protected our right to publish these materials, even if we were selling the kits.

We decided to contact *Newsweek* to see how difficult and expensive it would be to get their permission, just to be on the safe side. They were very helpful in clarifying our perspective on fair use—although not in the way they intended. After multiple attempts, we were finally able to speak to a *Newsweek* representative to request permission to use images of the covers. He explained that we would need to pay a fee of $250 for each photo and cover image—so with nearly fifty *Newsweek* images in the kit, the total would be over $10,000. He also explained that *Newsweek* did not have permission to use the images for the purchase we intended, so we would need to contact each photographer to get their permission and likely pay them as well. Furthermore, we were told that we should also consider contacting each of the people featured in the photos (e.g., Saddam Hussein, Osama bin Laden) and get *their* permission to use their images in our kit. The implication was clear: *Newsweek* was telling us that it would be impossible for us to "legally" publish these materials for teachers to help students decode and evaluate *Newsweek*'s presentation of global events.

Around the same time, we came across a description for a workshop at the National Council for the Social Studies (NCSS) annual conference titled Media Construction of War, presented by *Newsweek* magazine. To our amazement, the presenter used some of the very same images Project Look Sharp had selected for use in the creation our kit. On the surface, the two curriculum approaches seemed very similar, but there was a key difference. The *Newsweek* approach used the magazine's coverage to analyze the war but not to analyze *media coverage* of the war. Any critical questions about the constructed nature of the magazine's covers, articles,

Figure 19.3 Media Construction of War

and photographs were missing. The presenter emphasized the "objective" nature of the coverage, rejecting any suggestion that *Newsweek*'s coverage may have been influenced by public opinion or corporate interests. In creating their curriculum, *Newsweek* was using the covers as illustration for a presentation of facts about the various wars.

At the end of the *Newsweek* presentation to social studies teachers, we had the opportunity to talk with the *Newsweek* coordinator who was attending the presentation. Without explaining our plans for the yet-to-be published kit, we asked her if she thought it was appropriate for educators to critique *Newsweek* content in the classroom without copyright permission. She agreed wholeheartedly that it was important for teachers to analyze and critique *Newsweek* coverage—*and* that they did not need the company's permission to do so. Furthermore, she agreed that media literacy organizations had the right—if not the responsibility—to support educators in that mission.

Her response helped to further clarify our approach to fair use. Project Look Sharp and the *Newsweek* educator shared a common understanding—that democracy is dependent upon having a thoughtful, media-literate, and independently thinking citizenry, and therefore it was essential that teachers and organizations supporting educators have the right to use all media documents in the classroom for teaching critical literacy. Fortunately, the members of Congress who constructed the Copyright Law of 1976 felt the same way when they codified the fair use exception. The provost of Ithaca College, Peter Bardaglio, agreed that we were on solid legal ground in publishing our new curriculum kit without getting licenses from *Newsweek* magazine. He informed us that the College would back us up in this endeavor—even if it meant going to the Supreme Court.

In 2004, we published *Media Construction of War: A Critical Reading of History*. The curriculum kit centered on classroom analysis of *Newsweek* magazine coverage of the Vietnam War from 1965 to 1975, the Persian Gulf War from December 1990 to March 1991, and the War in Afghanistan from October through December 2001. The kit included brief histories of each war, providing the background information needed to decode the slides of carefully chosen covers and photo spreads from *Newsweek*. Figure 19.4 shows an example of a slide used for an assessment activity, and Figure 19.5 shows a sample page from the teacher's guide. Notice that the teacher's guide presents an inquiry pedagogy based on the teacher asking questions about the interpretation of the covers with follow-up probing for both content knowledge and critical thinking on the part of students.

Figure 19.4 *Newsweek* Images Used in Lessons About the Vietnam War from *Media Construction of War*

THE VIETNAM WAR: 1965 - 1975 Slides 3-16 **MEDIA CONSTRUCTION OF WAR:** A Critical Reading of History

SLIDE #15

APRIL 12, 1971
"The Calley Verdict: Who Else is Guilty?"

QUESTION **What impression does this cover give you about the U.S. role in Vietnam?**

ANSWER That the U.S. military is tied to the killing of Vietnamese civilians.

EVIDENCE U.S. officer in clean dress uniform pasted over a photo of dead Vietnamese women and children

ANSWER That the officer shown was found guilty but that others are also guilty.

EVIDENCE text: "The Calley Verdict" and "Who Else Is Guilty?"

QUESTION **Is there a pro-war or anti-war bias to this cover? What is your evidence?**

ANSWER This is an anti-war cover.

EVIDENCE shows an American officer as a perpetrator of war-time atrocities

SEE INFO BOX →

QUESTION **How has this cover image been visually constructed or altered, and why?**

ANSWER This photo of Lt. William Calley was cut out and pasted over a photo of dead Vietnamese civilians to illustrate Calley's relationship to the My Lai Massacre.

Like all magazines, *Newsweek* frequently uses visual manipulation of photos on its covers in order to create dramatic and sensational visuals that will sell magazines. However, like other reputable periodicals, it does not alter photographs appearing within the magazine.

SEE FOCUS ON THE MEDIA BOX →

INFO

On March 16, 1968 **Lieutenant William Calley** led a group of American soldiers into the small South Vietnamese village of My Lai and proceeded to execute hundreds of unarmed villagers, mostly women, children and old men. The army tried to cover up the massacre but stories and photos made it into the press. Lieutenant Calley was tried and found guilty of war crimes in 1971 although he served only three years of a life sentence. The **My Lai Massacre** horrified many Americans who had perceived the U.S. role in Vietnam as just and honorable. It also further undermined the morale of U.S. troops who were increasingly turning against the war.

FOCUS ON THE MEDIA

News photos are always manipulated in some ways. For example, the photographer chooses the camera angle, source of lighting, and framing of the subject. Editors and art directors make other decisions such as cropping of the image, size, and placement on the page. These types of visual construction are considered within the accepted bounds of credible news photography. However, magazine covers are essentially considered to be advertisements, and photos shown on them are often altered in more sensational and manipulative ways in order to sell more magazines. Sometimes these kinds of manipulations have caused public criticism – like when *National Geographic* digitally moved two pyramids closer together, or when *Time* darkened O.J. Simpson's skin color after he was found guilty in a civil trial. But mostly the obvious and dramatic manipulation of photographs on magazine covers is considered to be within ethical bounds.

32

Figure 19.5 Sample Page from the Teacher's Guide for *Media Construction of War*

Both educators and reviewers found the kit's emphasis on analysis and evaluation of the events of each war and *Newsweek*'s coverage of them to reflect a powerful pedagogical approach to teaching history and current events. According to Howard Zinn, historian and author of *A People's History of the United States* (1980):

> [*Media Construction of War*] is an excellent teaching tool. It does an enormously important job in preparing students for a critical analysis of the media. In the course of that, it is

> an education in the history of three recent wars, and raises the moral issues that are very often lacking in traditional curricula. It does not preach, but by asking provocative questions it leads student to think carefully and re-examine traditional ideas. In short, it fosters independent thinking, which, after all, should be the chief objective of a good education.
> (Zinn, personal communication 2004)

With new grant funding from the Schumann Center for Media and Democracy, Project Look Sharp went on to develop and publish two more media literacy curriculum kits: *Media Construction of Presidential Campaigns: 1800–2004* (Sperry & Sperry 2005) and *Media Constructions of the Middle East* (Sperry & Sperry 2006). Each of these kits included many media documents from different sources and in different formats—all used within the fair use guidelines.

In 2006, we decided to provide all of those curriculum materials free online for educators, and that practice continues today. A decade later—thanks to the fair use clause and funding from the Park Foundation and others—we now have twenty-one full curriculum kits containing more than 800 lessons, using over 2,000 media documents with accompanying questions, all available on our website for educators across the world to integrate media analysis and content instruction, from kindergarten through college. To date, we have not been challenged in a court of law for the unauthorized use of any of these documents, including clips from Disney films, political cartoons, TV shows, journal articles, documentary films, websites, and many more. While we never had the opportunity to argue our case for democracy and fair use to the Supreme Court, we became part of a larger movement of media literacy educators for the repurposing of copyrighted documents for criticism and critique in an educational context. Somewhat surprisingly, our initial battle for the fair use of copyrighted material in media literacy education was hardest fought with the gatekeepers of copyright in K–12 education: librarians.

Misunderstanding 1: You Can Claim Fair Use Only If You Use Less Than 10%

The most consistent response we have gotten from librarians and other educators about the application of fair use has to do with the list of "guidelines" for copyright, most notably the so-called 10% rule (see, for example, Crews (2001) for discussion of the brevity component of Classroom Guidelines in Fair Use). While these guidelines were not created to limit the application of fair use, that has often been the impact. We needed to set aside significant time during our media literacy staff development presentations to discuss copyright issues if librarians were present. Only in recent years are we encountering a sizable number of librarians who understand that the educators need the confidence and support in applying fair use when appropriate, even if all aspects of "the list" do not apply.

The concepts articulated in the various fair use guidelines are confusing. When analyzing a painting, a TV commercial, or a magazine cover, clearly the 10% rule does not work. Teachers should be confident in their application of fair use as long as they are asking questions about the construction of the document. Should we need Don Black's permission when analyzing his white supremacist website, www.martinlutherking.org? Should Greenpeace be able to stop teachers from engaging students in an analysis of biases in its YouTube video, *Genetic Engineering: The World's Greatest Scam*? What would be the implications for our democracy if we needed Disney's permission to ask, "What are the messages about the Arab World?" when decoding the introduction to the film *Aladdin*? While Project Look Sharp has often needed to challenge this inaccurate and stifling application of fair use, we have also seen a tendency on the part of many teachers to apply the fair use clause overly broadly.

Misunderstanding 2: It Is Fair Use Because It Is for Educational Purposes

We hear this overly simplified statement about fair use quite a bit from teachers. While we understand the impulse to use whatever helps us to teach more effectively, copyright law appropriately protects legitimate intellectual rights, and not all educational uses of media content fall under the fair use exemption. Just showing a clip from *Aladdin* for classroom entertainment or distributing the Greenpeace video for teachers to use to teach about GMOs is not—by itself—a fair use. However, a teacher can repurpose the Disney clip or Greenpeace video by asking media analysis questions about the video itself and the way it was constructed, such as, "Who produced this?" "For what purpose?" "From whose perspective is this shown?" "What information seems to be left out, and why?" or "Who might benefit from—and who might be harmed by—this message?" These questions shift the use of the media document from solely entertainment or information to the use of the document for purposes of critique.

Misunderstanding 3: Distinguishing Between Fair Use and the Need for Licenses

Nearly all of the media documents on the Project Look Sharp website fall clearly under the doctrine of fair use because the media content there is repurposed to provide critique, evaluation, or criticism in an educational context. Only a handful of our media documents are used solely for illustrative or informational purposes in the way they were originally intended (including, for example, segments from the wonderful Consumer Reports TV programs *Buy Me That!* that appear in our *Critical Thinking and Health* kit for early elementary grades). In those cases, we do seek copyright permission and pay whatever license fees are required to use the materials.

For a small number of media documents, however, the distinction between using a document for its intended purpose and providing a critical analysis can be ambiguous. We have struggled with fair use application for political cartoons and documentary films. In both cases, the producers of the materials count on payments from schools or publishers for at least part of their income. Additionally, the purpose of these documents often overlaps with classroom goals—such as commentary on current events using political cartoons or teaching about social issues using documentary films. Our intent is not to undermine or otherwise steal from the value of the copyrighted material. However, if our purpose is legitimate critical analysis, we believe we should be able to apply fair use. In the case of using political cartoons, our lessons typically ask students to compare the political perspectives of different cartoonists or to analyze the editorial position of a particular cartoonist. Documentary films likewise rely on school-based markets for their products and are produced to teach their audience about a topic. However, we believe that fair use applies when a teacher shows a trailer for (or short excerpt from) the film and asks about the credibility of the source or the perspective of the filmmaker.

We have worked to respect the legitimate limits to fair use when publishing media literacy lessons online for educators, and we believe that teachers and librarians must be advocates for the liberal and appropriate application of fair use if we are going to do our job of educating a generation of literate citizens who think critically about the information, ideas, and images they receive through the media. This approach, as outlined in the *Code of Best Practices in Fair Use for Media Literacy Education* (2008), has become increasingly accepted and promoted with the advent of the new national standards that promote critical thinking skills (Hobbs 2010).

Media Literacy, Fair Use, and Educational Standards

The Common Core Standards for English Language Arts, the English Language Arts and Literacy standards for secondary social studies and science, the Next Generation Science Standards (NGSS) for science, and the C3 Framework for Social Studies all place a strong emphasis on teaching students to ask and answer critical questions about credibility, sourcing, accuracy, and meaning—the very questions codified by media literacy leaders decades ago. These standards promote inquiry-based methodologies that emphasize critical thinking skills over rote learning and memorization. They encourage close reading of diverse media documents, careful evaluation of sources, evidence-based analysis, and well reasoned thinking—core skills involved in media literacy. The Common Core ELA Standards make clear that views about "literacy" must be expanded to include "reading" and "writing" using the diverse media forms of the 21st century. For example, the ELA Common Core Standards: Reading for History (Grades 11–12) includes:

- Cite specific textual evidence to support analysis of primary and secondary sources. (CCSS.ELA.RH.11–12.1)
- Determine the central ideas or information of a primary or secondary source. (CCSS.ELA.RH.11–12.2)
- Evaluate authors' differing points of view on the same historical event or issue by assessing the authors' claims, reasoning, and evidence. (CCSS.ELA.RH.11–12.6)
- Integrate and evaluate multiple sources of information presented in diverse formats and media. (CCSS.ELA.RH.11–12.7)

The National Council for the Social Studies *College, Career, and Civic Life* (C3) *Framework for Social Studies State Standards* goes even further. C3 lays out four core dimensions that emphasize teaching students to ask and respond to questions, evaluate sources, provide evidence, communicate conclusions, and take action in addition to applying the skills and knowledge of various social science disciplines.

The National Council for the Social Studies "Position Paper on Media Literacy" lays out the case for integrating constructivist media decoding throughout the K–12 social studies curriculum (Sperry & Baker 2016). In social studies, ELA, science, and health, these new standards will push educators to repurpose media documents for critical analysis in their classrooms. And as the following example shows, classroom media analysis is dependent upon the application of fair use.

A High School Lesson on Hydrofracking

In 2014, Project Look Sharp published two curriculum kits that used media literacy approaches to study sustainability concepts and topics, one focused on food, water, and agriculture and the other focusing specifically on sustainability issues in the Finger Lakes Region of New York State that surrounds Ithaca. One lesson in *Media Constructions of Sustainability: Finger Lakes* uses three different media formats—scientific diagrams, documentary film and television videos, and Google search results—to examine the controversial natural gas extraction process known as hydrofracking. In this complex lesson, students are asked to use critical thinking skills to explore a compelling content question: what role should hydrofracking play in our national energy policy? In the process of media decoding, students are also asked to consider these key media literacy questions:

- Who paid for this message?
- What are the sources of the assertions about hydrofracking?
- Is this fact, opinion, or something else?

The lesson begins with some basic background information about aquifers and groundwater from an Idaho Museum of History webpage, accompanied by the listing of sources and references for the article. The accompanying questions probe both for content information ("What is an aquifer?") and for information about sourcing ("What organizations published the source information?"). Figure 19.6 shows an activity where students compare and contrast

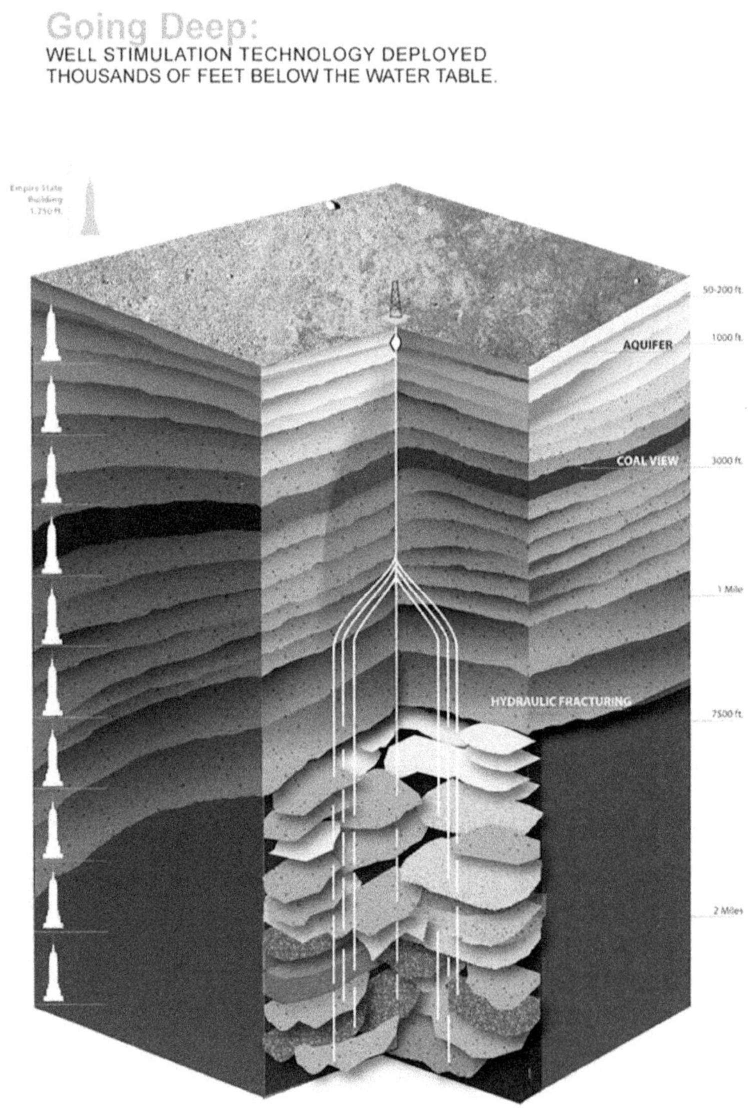

Figure 19.6 Compare and Contrast Activity: Diagrams About Hydrofracking From Two Different Sources

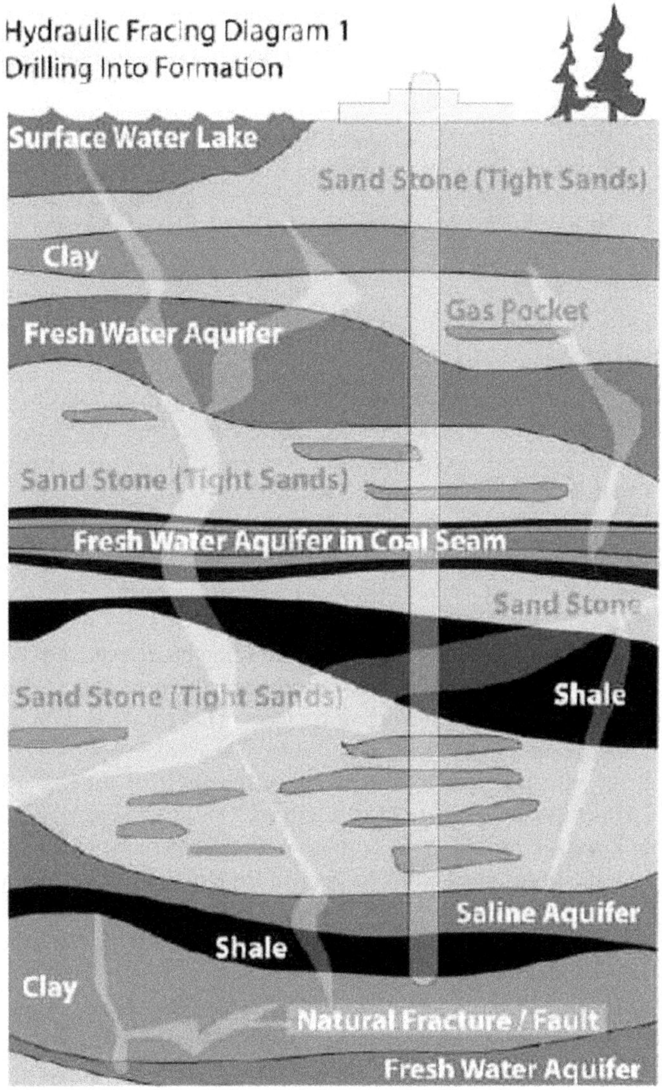

Figure 19.6 Continued

two scientific diagrams of the hydrofracking process. Each diagram leads to very different conclusions about the safety of the process. Students are invited to guess the likely source for each of the diagrams, giving evidence to support their conclusions.

As students reflect on the producers of these media documents, they are also asked to consider what questions *they* might ask about each of the diagrams in order to improve their understanding of the hydrofracking process and the credibility of the information being presented in each. This is an opportunity to extend the class discussion based on the students' own curiosities and observations. The lesson continues with three video clips reflecting very different perspectives on hydrofracking: a short clip from the Academy Award–nominated antifracking documentary *Gasland* by filmmaker Josh Fox; a clip from the film *The Truth About*

Figure 19.7 Three Video Clips for Critical Analysis From *Media Constructions of Sustainability: Finger Lakes*

Gasland sponsored by America's Natural Gas Alliance; and a clip from Josh Fox's appearance on *The Daily Show with Jon Stewart*. Figure 19.7 shows still images from the video clips.

After viewing each clip, students are asked:

- What are the messages about natural gas drilling?
- What techniques are used to convey the message?
- Do you consider this to be a credible source? Why or why not?

The goal of this questioning is not to lead students to some predetermined "correct answers" but rather to prompt them to analyze the content, construction, and credibility of media messages. In the process, students can develop deeper critical thinking skills, including being able to put their own assumptions to the test and to change their point of view as evidence warrants. The lesson concludes with students analyzing the first page of a Google search for the terms "Josh Fox" and "*Gasland*" (see Figure 19.8). The decoding question asks, "At first glance, which sources would you consider *more* credible and which *less* credible and why?" Once again, this is an opportunity to deepen students' understanding of the (perhaps unconscious) judgments they make about the credibility of different sources of information, helping them develop their own habits of inquiry whenever they encounter mediated information.

This complex activity addresses many of the Common Core ELA, C3 social studies, and NGSS standards. The lesson uses constructivist methodologies that ask students to apply knowledge while analyzing diverse media documents, and it would not be possible without the fair use ability to use these rich media documents in a classroom setting without worrying about copyright permissions. In essence, the rigorous critical thinking literacy standards promoted in Common Core and C3 are dependent upon the application of fair use to the critique and analysis of contemporary media documents in 21st-century classrooms.

Media Documents and Assessments

As Sperry (2015) noted in his article on constructivist media decoding in social studies classrooms, while media analysis can be an effective tool in addressing these standards, the structure of state tests will be the driving factor in shifting teachers' classroom methodology. As long as exams continue to test the memorization of facts, most teachers are likely to prioritize rote coverage of the content over deeper analysis and interactive discussion. In contrast, assessments that ask students to analyze diverse media documents can provide models for evaluating the critical thinking skills embedded in the standards.

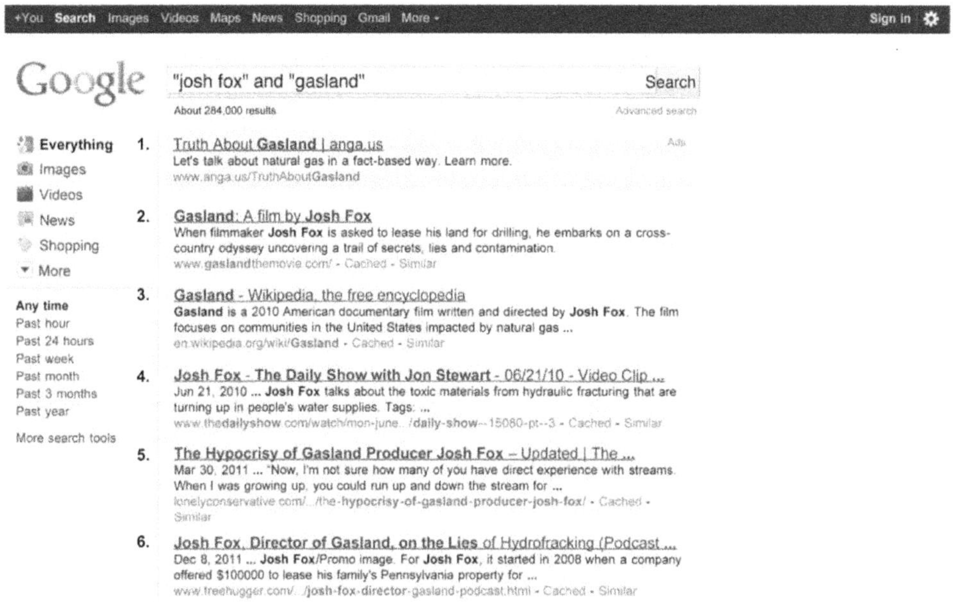

Figure 19.8 Spotting Point ofView in the First Page of Results from a Google Search

Perhaps in the future, students will be expected to demonstrate critical media analysis skills in order to graduate from high school. Project Look Sharp's model for media analysis was used at the Lehman Alternative Community School in Ithaca, New York, to develop a Common Core–aligned test for the school's teacher evaluation assessment. In 2015, all students in grades nine through twelve took part in that assessment of the school's progress in teaching the Common Core literacy standards in ELA, social studies, and science. The test was based on student analysis of three documents about genetically modified organisms (GMOs): a 3-minute video by *Greenpeace*, excerpts from a *New York Times* op ed piece "How I Got Converted to GMO Foods," and a website critical of GMOs.

The first set of questions assessed each student's ability to analyze and compare the three documents for messages and biases, with students identifying techniques used by the creators of the messages to communicate their perspective. Students were then given excerpts from the mission statements of Monsanto, Greenpeace, and the Cornell Alliance for Science and were asked to give evidence that linked the organizations to each of the three media documents. The next set of questions assessed students' understanding of the credibility of information (a core standard in ELA, social studies, and science) by asking them to write questions about each document that would help them assess its credibility. The ability for students to ask questions is a core component of the C3 standards for social studies, and it is rarely assessed in standardized tests. The final question asked students to "identify how your *own* views on the issue of GMOs might influence how you understand and interpret these documents." This question reflects one of the greatest contributions media literacy can play in educational reform—teaching students to reflect on *how* they think, their own biases in selecting and interpreting information from different sources, and the potential limitations of their own reasoning.

Nothing will have a greater impact on shifting teaching practice toward critical thinking standards than the design of these types of assessments of student learning and teacher performance. If media literacy skills and approaches can be built into state tests, then educators *will* integrate media literacy into their teaching. We in the field should be promoting media literacy practices and the inclusion of diverse media documents into these new assessments in order to support the shift to the Common Core and C3 standards. In the process, we will need to push those who will be revising the standards and creating new tests to incorporate progressively more complex metacognitive abilities taught through media analysis. Imagine a future where students are taught media literacy at every grade level and then assessed on their ability to make judgments about the credibility of information from different sources and to identify how their own biases influence those judgments.

The Future Is Global

The critical importance of fair use in media literacy education has become especially clear to us at Project Look Sharp as we have begun working in countries where copyright law includes no fair use clause. Media literacy organizations in some European countries have struggled with providing educators with the resources regularly available in the United States because of fears of litigation, while media literacy educators in countries like Iran struggle with much larger issues related to free access to media content and government restrictions on its use in education. While we have been able to do teacher training in media decoding in many of those countries (including Iran), their lack of fair use has hampered the creation and dissemination of curriculum materials relevant to their own histories and educational priorities. Because of fair use, in the United States we can legally disseminate media materials for use by educators around the world, supporting education much more broadly in an increasingly mediated world. It should come as no surprise, then, that Project Look Sharp's media decoding materials have been downloaded thousands of times by people from more than 150 nations worldwide. Documents from *Media Constructions of the Middle East* are being used in schools in the Middle East; documents from *Soviet History Through Posters* are being used in former Soviet Union countries. We can learn a lesson from these global experiences as we commit to defend, deepen, and disseminate the fair use of copyright law throughout educational systems in the United States and beyond.

References

Anderson, D., Hatcher, S., Horrocks, K., Salamon, B., Simons, D., Sperry, C., & Volckmar, A. (2001). *The Iroquois Kit: A Unit of the ICSD 4th Grade Social Studies Curriculum*. Ithaca, NY: Ithaca City School District.

Aufderheide, P., & Firestone, C. (1993). *National Leadership Conference on Media Literacy, Conference Report*. Washington, DC: Aspen Institute.

Crews, K. D. (2001). "The Laws of Fair Use and the Illusion of Fair-Use Guidelines." *Ohio State Law Journal*, 62(2), 599–702.

Hobbs, R. (2010). *Copyright Clarity: How Fair Use Supports Digital Learning*. Thousand Oaks, CA: Corwin/Sage.

National Association for Media Literacy Education. (2007, November). "Core Principles of Media Literacy Education in the United States." Retrieved April 15, 2016, from https://namle.net/publications/core-principles

Scheibe, C., & Rogow, F. (2012). *The Teacher's Guide to Media Literacy: Critical Thinking in a Multimedia World*. Thousand Oaks, CA: Corwin/Sage.

Sperry, C. (1999). *Iroquois Imaging Kit*. Ithaca, NY: Ithaca City School District.

Sperry, C. (2003). *Media Construction of War: A Critical Reading of History*. Ithaca, NY: Project Look Sharp/Ithaca College.

Sperry, C. (2015). "Constructivist Media Decoding in the Social Studies: Leveraging the New Standards for Educational Change." *Journal of Media Literacy*, 62(3–4), 46–54.

Sperry, C., & Baker, F. (2016). "NCSS Position Statement." *Social Education*, 80(3), 183–185.

Sperry, S., & Sperry, C. (2005). *Media Construction of Presidential Campaigns: 1800–2004*. Ithaca, NY: Project Look Sharp/Ithaca College.

Sperry, C., & Sperry, S. (2006). *Media Constructions of the Middle East*. Ithaca, NY: Project Look Sharp/Ithaca College.

Zinn, H. (1980). *A People's History of the United States*. New York: Harper Collins.

20

APPROACHES TO ACTIVE READING AND VISUAL LITERACY IN THE HIGH SCHOOL CLASSROOM

John S. O'Connor and Dan Lawler

A recent episode ofThe NewYorker Out Loud podcast (May 2016) featured editorial staffer Andrew Marantz contrasting the experience of virtual reality with mere movie watching. "I'm fine with passive experiences," Marantz said. "I don't mind sitting back and watching something like, you know, I think *Citizen Kane* is pretty good, and that's totally passive, but if we want interactivity, it's much easier with computer animation." Marantz was deliberately understating the greatness of *Citizen Kane*, of course, but he seemed sincere in his characterization of watching a movie—even a great movie, like *Citizen Kane*—as "passive," an experience that washes over viewers in waves of images.

This is exactly the sort of attitude we struggle with in our high school classes. We teach tenth-, eleventh-, and twelfth-grade students at a large suburban public school where students almost universally test "above average" in reading but who never (on beginning-of-the-year inventories) see visual images as texts that need to be "read." Instead, they, like Marantz, see visual images as something that audiences passively absorb rather than complicated texts that need to be interacted with in order to be fully understood. Mario VargasLlosa ends his brilliant defense of reading called *Why Literature?* by saying, "We must act. We must read." This same is true for visual literacy. In our classes—"regular" literature classes and a senior elective called Literature and Film—we want our students to become active readers and critical thinkers of not only print texts but visual texts as well.

This is one of our chief goals as teachers: to help students actively read visual texts. These days, the stakes have never been higher since students spend so much of their lives in front of screens. In fact, according to *Teen Health and the Media*, the average American teenager spends about 20 hours a week watching TV. The U.S. Bureau of Labor Statistics reports that teens spend an additional 1.2 hours a day playing video games on nonschool days. To watch visual images passively holds some troubling consequences, but to watch actively may safeguard against media bias, improve democratic citizenship, and make reading visual texts more enjoyable.

In this chapter, we hope to lay out some observations we've made of students in our fifty years of collective teaching and to share some strategies we have found effective in teaching students how to think critically about visual texts and how to make visual reading interactive. We focus on close reading, which is a practice that is especially dependent upon the active use of copyrighted materials. In doing so, we offer examples to help readers of this volume understand the particular ways in which close analysis depends on the fair use of copyrighted content. The specific visual texts we will consider are graphic novels, TV news, and both fiction and documentary films. We write from our distinctive points of view with John and Dan both employed as English teachers at New Trier High School in Winnetka, Illinois.

Graphic Novels as a Means to Build Fundamental Image Reading Competencies

Gene Yang's graphic novel *American Born Chinese*, like many graphic novels, doesn't initially present as "serious literature." Quickly flipping through the text presents hundreds of images that look cartoonish in nature: everything from a monkey looking like he could star in Saturday morning cartoons to fight scenes full of the "BONKS" and "THWACKS" that adult readers might recall from the Adam West *Batman* television series from the 1960s. A significant challenge to teaching this text—and any graphic novel, for that matter—is to encourage students to think deeply about the ways the images are constructed and to "read" them critically.

In this sense, graphic novels present a paradox for teaching visual literacy: how do we teach students to slow down in their reading of a text that by its very nature allows for a faster reading experience—if, that is, you are only reading words? (Many students have commented that they "read" graphic novels in less than an hour because they *only* attended the words.) Like many of the images that permeate our lives—billboards, advertisements, Instagram photos, and television—the graphic novel is a powerful tool for encouraging students to ponder how something seemingly simple and easy to gloss over (i.e., an image) is full of assumptions, meaning, and complexity.

Our approach to instruction is premised on the idea that "visual media is ubiquitous in contemporary society. . . . But visual literacy does not arise from sheer exposure to visual content" (Brown et al. 2015). So how do we guide our students' exposure to reading images in the graphic novel in a way that builds their visual literacy rather than merely passively allowing the images to wash over them? Dan's approach to teaching *American Born Chinese* consists of four parts: students learn explicit vocabulary for discussing images in the novel; they investigate visual elements and techniques that are present on each page; they annotate these elements in an ebook version of the book; and they write reflections explaining which elements of the book they annotated and why they annotated them. In the process of learning this critical reading process, students must handle, manipulate, and ultimately transform copyrighted images as study artifacts.

Explicit Terminology and *Understanding Comics: The Invisible Art*

Much of Dan's inspiration for teaching graphic novels was inspired, in part, by Scott McCloud's *Understanding Comics: The Invisible Art* (1993), a book that contains a treasure trove of images and text that are all about how images are constructed from the perspective of a graphic novelist. The value of the book is that McCloud takes nothing for granted: he doesn't assume that the reader is an experienced reader of graphic novels, nor does he assume that the reader who *thinks* he or she is an experienced reader of graphic novels deeply understands the art form.

But there's also a metacognitive element to the book: McCloud encourages his reader to pause and reflect on how images are working and to consider how these images impact the reader's thinking. For example, McCloud poses the question, "Can emotions be made visible?" and follows with a series of abstract images constructed to convey emotions, everything from anger, joy, and serenity to madness, pride, and anxiety. A powerful inclass activity is to have students take any of these examples and explain why the image he constructed does (or doesn't) accurately capture the emotion it intends to convey. Doing so forces students to think deeply about something as seemingly trivial as the length of a line in the image, the shapes of some parts of the images, or the degree to how shaded (or light) a particular part of the image seems to be. And this is without even looking at a single letter or word in the image. (In one of Dan's classes, students debated for 10 minutes whether or not McCloud's use of a jagged triangle accurately captured tension.)

Another example of McCloud encouraging his reader to think deeply rather than gloss over images is his section on transitions. He offers definitions and illustrated examples of different kinds of transitions, including paneltopanel, actiontoaction, and aspecttoaspect. Building on narratives that students wrote earlier in the academic year, Dan asks them to envision their stories as a visual text and have them indicate what kind of transition they would use in different parts of their essays. This activity helps students work from the written to the visual—and much like the activity of assigning abstract images to emotions—it helps them slow down and ponder not just the single image but the "invisible space" of the transition, the move of joining one image to another and how it creates its own meaning.

Dan doesn't use McCloud's book extensively as he builds to explore the graphic novel *American Born Chinese* (Yang 2006). He has found *Understanding Comics* to be too technical and written for an audience interested in an exhaustive reading of the graphic novel genre. For example, do students really need to know how Chester Gould's use of bold lines in *Dick Tracy* contrasts Jose Munoz's "puddles of ink and fraying linework"?

But the spirit of what McCloud is doing—namely, making the writer's moves more transparent to the reader—is crucial in helping students learn how to read Gene Yang's *American Born Chinese* at a deeper level. Building upon McCloud's second chapter, titled "The Vocabulary of Comics," as a first step, Dan has created his own version of a pared down vocabulary for discussing the parts of a graphic novel. In orienting students to visual literacy, Dan believes that if students can label an image with a word, then the odds are that they'll discuss it with greater clarity and think more deeply about it.

However, the challenge with terminology is to not let students get bogged down in jargon. What Scott McCloud calls a "panel" students call a "frame." (McCloud goes even deeper with terminology by calling the white space between panels the "gutter.") When students look at a page from the novel, they shouldn't be worrying about labeling things using the same terminology as that used by comic artists and professionals. The practice of naming is a means to a larger end: Dan is not quizzing students on using the *right* term; rather, he encourages them to use terms in order to slow them down, to stretch their minds, and to read visual texts critically. For example, when we start *American Born Chinese*, Dan explores four groupings of terms: "frames," "images," "words," and "film terms" (a series of terms describing different kinds of camera shots from our study of film earlier in the course). He defines "frames" as the lines surrounding images, just like the frame of a picture that they might see in their own homes. "Images" is the term used for any picture—not written text—drawn by the author on the page. "Words" are just that: written words usually but not always contained in speech bubbles. And finally, we use "film terms." Examples include "foreground," "background," "mis-eenscène" and a series of camera shot types: "closeup," "extreme closeup," "canted shot," "low angle shot," and others. These terms offer students a common vocabulary for analyzing images on the page. In addition, they allow students to express themselves with greater specificity and clarity. They just can't write that they see a character's face, for example. They need to ponder what kind of shot it is of the face. A close-up? An extreme close-up? A canted shot? In doing so, students dig deeper into the image and begin to see it as a "text" worthy of interpretation.

While Dan assigns the reading as homework, one of his instructional goals is to spend an entire class period discussing one single page of the text and to apply these terms. He accomplishes this by choosing a page rich with meaning and then assigning students to small groups where they label as many terms as possible. At first, the activity may seem mundane, even rote. For example, students usually have no trouble identifying a frame, a particular image, words, and finding film terminology to identify how an image is arranged. But once we've identified visual elements on the page, it's possible to transition to the ways that readers can pose questions about the labeled elements that then lead to deeper thinking.

For example, a student once identified one frame as containing a "long shot" of Jin Wang, the main character in *American Born Chinese*, sitting at a lunch table by himself. When we probed further by asking what is gained and lost with this kind of shot, the student mentioned that we see more of the surroundings and less of the facial expressions of the main character. Probing even further, Dan asked why it's important that the author decided to privilege the surrounding environment. One student mentioned that the "emptiness" of the surroundings made the narrator look even more isolated and alone. Another student chimed in and mentioned that the main character Jin Wang even looks "faceless" in the framed image. When Dan followed with the question, "Why might the author do this?" other students contributed answers that drove at larger thematic issues in the novel: they recognized that the boy's race in the predominantly white world of the book makes him feel like an outcast. They noticed that the faceless, mouthless character lacks a voice, and they were aware that the stereotyping the boy wrestles with in the novel suggests ways that he's typecast and not considered a unique individual. Clearly, the use of open-ended questions about the specific features of the text is designed to activate and externalize the complex dimensions of the reading and interpretation process.

Building on terminology, Dan then moves to investigate highly concrete elements on the page. Some of the prompts he uses to activate student engagement are as follows:

- Count the number of frames on a particular page. Does a page with more frames encourage you to read the page faster or slower? Why?
- Find a page with multiple frames that are different shapes and sizes. Why are some frames different sizes? What's happening with images within the frames that parallels the shape of the frame?
- Find three examples of words that are presented in different ways. How does the presentation of the words convey different meaning? Consider the size of letters, the shapes of letters, and the width of lines.

What makes these questioning activities rich with meaning for creating visual literacy is the first, crucial step of naming things on the page. Identifying parts of the text and giving them names grounds our discussion so that we can consider authorial intent and deeper issues within the work. And in doing so, students slow down as readers and ponder images more deliberately and intentionally.

Students Annotate an E-Text

After several class periods of large group discussion, students read sections of the book on their own and write about their observations so that they can bring them to class and share. A dilemma Dan originally faced in this process was deciding whether or not students should annotate a paper version of the novel. While annotation is a common practice in high school English classes, annotating graphic novels is an activity that raises some questions. Should the student write on a text that is by its very nature visual? Would writing on the text alter the meaning of the image? And what if they eventually pass on the book to a friend or family member? Would the annotated text (a new visual text, in a sense) alter the meaning of the novel in a profound way?

If students are fortunate enough to attend a school with ample resources, a solution is to have students read an electronic version of the book, thereby allowing them to easily take snapshots of pages, frames, and images on tablet computers and then import these pictures into a journaling app where they can annotate key elements and write a reflection on the images and their annotations. Like paper annotation, digital annotation is an instructional strategy that requires the transformative use of copyrighted materials. Dan has found this practice to be very productive as students deepen the quality of their thinking and writing. Following are two examples of ways that students have used digital annotation to create their own readings of *American Born Chinese.*

Sarah's Digital Annotation

Figure 20.1 shows Sarah's annotation, as she has drawn a rectangle around the two characters and has written "same size," indicating that each character is physically portrayed as equals. She also paid special attention to the detail of the Monkey King's "open" hand in a gesture of reconciliation with his mentor, someone he had previously rejected. What makes Sarah's reading of *American Born Chinese* compelling is the way she takes what seems to be a simple exchange consisting of three frames and explores the images in great depth and detail. In the portion of text she reflected on, one of the main characters (the Monkey King) is reconciled with Wong, his mentor. In her annotations of the frames, Sarah writes "no b.ground" ("no background").

In her reflective writing, Sarah focuses on the significance of the Monkey King's hand gesture: "The most foregrounded part of the image is his hand, which is offered to Wong. Monkey King's hands have been clenched into fists the entire storyline, and finally they are released." Note that Sarah's analysis features terminology: she uses the terms "foregrounded" and "shot." She also develops her thoughts in great detail on the significance of an open hand and how this image has connections to earlier images in the text, as well as larger themes the book explores. Just as an English teacher recognizes growing written word literacy in his/her students when they can ponder the complexities and meanings of a single word choice in a work of literature, Sarah shows her growing visual literacy by doing the same kind of indepth thinking with the single image of an open hand.

Cynthia's Annotation

In Figure 20.2, we see the work of another student, Cynthia, who offers her analysis of a single page of the same graphic novel. What's compelling about Cynthia's reflection is her concrete analysis of the page: she counts the page into six frames, notices that the hand in the

Figure 20.1 Sarah's Annotation of a Frame

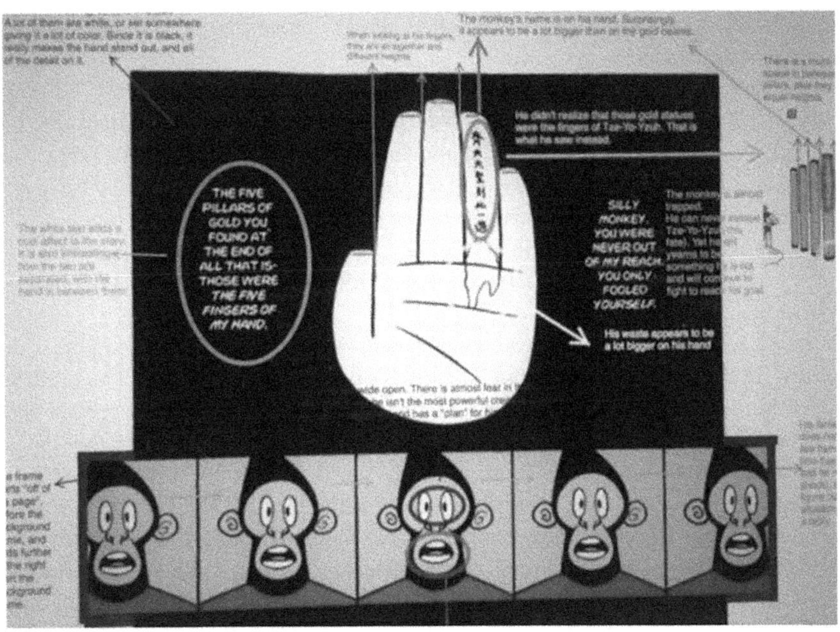

Figure 20.2 Cynthia's Digital Annotation

image is not "boxed in," and notices that the five frames at the bottom of the page "start a few centimeters before the background frame." Building upon these concrete observations, she considers authorial intent, noting that "the light hand in the middle stands out, focusing the reader's attention on the hand and what is on it. This is a larger frame because the author . . . must think that there is some sort of important message or clue that deserves its own page." Cynthia's work shows that she has, in a sense, created a new text with her reading of the book—her *own* version of *American Born Chinese*—and this is one of the highest marks of literacy: an ability to ponder the complexities in a text so deeply that the reader has a sense of ownership of the text.

Reading the World

Perhaps the real value of being visually literate is not only reading images with a more critical eye but being able to make connections between the images and the larger world of the reader. Specifically, the book explores ways Asian Americans (and all minority groups) can be subjected to sinister stereotypes. Much of the work's satire is in the section detailing the life of Danny and his embarrassing cousin visiting from China named ChinKee. It doesn't take a lot of work to help students recognize the way that this character is a work of satire criticizing Asian stereotypes: everything from his squinty eyes and buck teeth to the fact that he uses Chinese restaurant carryout boxes as his luggage. Students' reactions to the visual portrayal of this character run the gamut: some laugh, some are appalled, and many don't know how to react. The visual image carries much of the meaning here and important clues in reading tone. Danny has come to see his cousin through the cartoon lens of the "other": he sees only difference.

What all students agree upon, however, is that the portrayals of ChinKee are so over the top and cartoonish in nature that they clearly should be read as satire. However, when Dan explains that the author created ChinKee as an embodiment of stereotypical images that were applied to Asians decades ago (in some cases, by the U.S. government), their eyes are opened to a deeper layer of meaning in the text.

Images that are particularly useful for making this historical connection are U.S. propaganda posters from World War II. These are easy to find online, and they make evident that the way Gene Yang has drawn ChinKee is rooted as much in actual historical documents as they are in his own imagination. A powerful activity is to place images from *American Born Chinese* side by side with these propaganda posters and to ask students to find parallels between the two. In doing so, students take the skills they've developed in reading the graphic novel and apply them to historical artifacts. What starts as an exploration of images in fiction becomes an exercise in reading history.

The book even forces students to confront racial stereotyping in contemporary American culture. In one of the culminating scenes, ChinKee is embarrassing his cousin Danny (again) by dancing on a table in the school library singing Ricky Martin's 2000 hit, "She Bangs." These students are far too young to recognize lyrics from any pop hit songs from 2000, but when Dan tells them to research the lyrics, as well as the *American Idol* 2004 season, they quickly piece together a parallel that the author was making. Students reconstruct the meanings of this scene using intertextuality to understand the historical context of the time period. In 2004, one of the more popular *American Idol* episodes was when they aired the audition of William Hung, a Chinese American college student. For his audition, William sang Martin's song "She Bangs" off key. He became a national sensation for his poor audition or, more appropriately, a national joke, reinforcing ugly stereotypes about Asians.

It doesn't take high school students long to find a YouTube video of his audition. No one would mistake Mr. Hung for being a musical talent, and students laugh at the audition—as the producers of *American Idol* expected. But the deeper question students eventually explore is how this audition aired on national television and how it reinforces simplistic portrayals of Asian Americans.

As in many classroom debates, a variety of responses are expressed. Some students argue it's just harmless fun and that if he didn't want to be stereotyped then he shouldn't have gone on the show. Some students will even point out that Mr. Hung became a celebrity of sorts and may have even gained financially from his appearance on the show. Others, though, will argue that while Mr. Hung made the choice to go on the show, the real blame for stereotyping lies with the television network for airing his horrible audition to millions, thereby turning him into a caricature.

The goal of the debate is not to persuade students to believe that the stereotyping in this example is doing damage. Rather, the value of this classroom exercise is in the debate itself: that students are taking a dominant form of popular culture media that is usually consumed uncritically, transforming their relationship with the text by debating what the images mean and what potential implications these images have for audiences in the larger world.

Reading Graphic Nonfiction

John does similar activities with the graphic memoir *March* (2014), a nonfiction account of the life of John Lewis, one of the key figures of the Civil Rights Movement, whose commitment to justice and nonviolence has taken him to the halls of Congress. Written in collaboration with Andrew Aydin and Nate Powell, *March* is a vivid firsthand account of Lewis and his lifelong struggle for civil and human rights. In order to make sure students are actively reading the images as well as the printed words in the graphic novel, John keeps his questions concrete: why is the title *March* instead of, say, *The March*? Students readily see that the title is both a noun and a verb—a command, in fact, to become engaged, to *act*. Action is required of the reader of any visual text.

The search for parallels and contrasts helps students shift into an active reading stance. John asks students to find parallels and contrasts within any text. As a younger teacher, John usually asked questions and had students respond to what he himself found important. But he discovered that such a process breeds passivity. Students were eager to answer John's questions (in their quest to be "good" students) without asking any of their own. Students were interested in merely finishing the assignment rather than entering into a conversation with the text. Furthermore, John's own questions actually limited the scope of class inquiry without taking advantage of the myriad observations and insights his students discovered.

John asks students to find two parallels and two contrasts with each reading. By parallel, he means a repeated or related idea or image (the same word, the same object—think of Holden's hunting hat, Gatsby's green light), or *even the same kind of event* (an additional reference to weather or animals, for example). Contrasts are images or words that mean something opposite or encompass a different order or class: a convertible versus a sedan; flora versus fauna. To give equal weight to visual images and printed text, with graphic novels, John asks students to find two visual parallels and contrasts and two textual parallels and contrasts with each reading. With each parallel and contrast, students write a short explanation (usually one or two sentences) that explains their discovery. Students learn to accept that if a word or image comes up more than once, it *might* be significant. If it comes up three or more times, it is almost certainly important, and we, as careful readers, must attend to the pattern. This sort of technique requires students to read actively; they are making their own discoveries, finding their own patterns, and creating their own hypotheses. This is the essence of active close reading, and many students feel empowered when they discover the creativity of the reading process.

For example, one student, Callan, made this discovery with *March*: "[On] page 64, there is a contrast between the light and the darkness in bottom box. This image makes it appear as if the application for the American Baptist Theology Seminar was an enlightening thing for John Lewis." By attending to the pattern of light and dark imagery here, she has made a subtle observation about John Lewis's spirituality and his simultaneous inspiration as a Civil Rights activist.

Students learn to ask questions of the text with each reading. Their questions are shared at the start of class discussions. Why are the shapes of speech bubbles different? When are they the same? Where do you see similarly shaped frames? Frames of different shapes? *March* operates within a narrative frame as well. For example, the book opens with President Barack Obama's first inauguration and flashes back to Lewis's Civil Rights awakening, including the famous crossing of the Edmund Pettis Bridge. Generating questions automatically forces the reader to reread images—images that might otherwise be glossed over.

When students are asked to name the most interesting image within any particular section of the book, it might be considered an opportunity for them to simply choose the first image available. But John's students never seem to treat this activity so trivially. Instead, they sift through many competing possibilities and land on one that they are prepared to argue is pivotal to the text. When students share their responses, there is often a spontaneous debate, with students telling one another, "I almost picked that one," or "Oh, that goes with mine." Students discover that sharing interpretations makes literacy a social practice. Nabokov famously said, "There is no such thing as reading, only rereading." The same is surely true with visual texts as well. Dan and John both use instructional practices that urge students to engage in close reading, reexamining—to reread—visual texts as well.

Issues of Representation and Authenticity

To explore the concept of representation as a set of visual choices made by the author, John likes to pair competing texts that "cover" (or purport to cover) the same events. The events depicted in *March* are memorably depicted in the recent feature film *Selma* and also in the prizewinning documentary series *Eyes on the Prize*, episode 6, "Bridge to Freedom." Here, again, John starts with parallels and contrasts. Rather than telling his students how these media differ, he asks them to identify similarities and differences. John has used these three texts with a variety of different students: those enrolled in junior-level English classes, in senior-level literature and film electives, and even with his undergraduate education students at Northwestern University. He has never failed to learn new information from his students in any of these settings.

The graphic novel is in black and white, whereas the other two are in color. The graphic novel is told from Lewis's point of view, and readers benefit from the interior consciousness Lewis provides. On the other hand, *Eyes on the Prize* offers a more "objective" view—that of a bystander camera operator observing the chaos of the scene. One of the best features of that footage is the presence of other photographers. John often asks students how this footage might be different from other video footage. Why is this footage being taken? How was it received? Some of these questions are answered in subsequent interviews with participants, politicians, and other bystanders.

The film *Selma*, directed by Ava DuVernay and commercially released by Paramount Pictures in 2014, presents the most mobile camera—a camera that roams widely from broad aerial sweeps to intimate closeups of participants, including Lewis. The color of the movie footage is bold and vivid, a clear contrast with the other two. Perhaps the biggest difference of all, though, is the nondiegetic music (in other words, music the director has added to the scene). It guides the viewer's emotional responses. Some of John's students think this adds to the pathos of the scene; others think it takes away from the raw horror of the assault. Inevitably, class discussions explore the concept of authenticity: which is the truest portrait? John Lewis was there and claims firsthand knowledge. Does this trump all other accounts?

Students come to appreciate that all three versions are representations of a complex and multifaceted reality. The documentary offers a seemingly detached perspective of a journalist who is apparently turning on the camera and recording the scene as it's happening and as he or she witnesses it. There is a widespread conception that we "make art" but that we "take pictures" —as if the photographer is plucking objective reality from the world rather than constructing a version of reality from the choices he or she makes. *Selma* benefits from hindsight, from insights gained from other media representations of the march, and from the benefit of time. It is shot and scored with the idea of helping the viewer feel what it might have been like to be there. Students may recognize the celebrities featured in the film, such as the actor Wendell Pierce (who has had important roles in the HBO series *The Wire and Treme*). By exploring the question about his celebrity and wondering, "Does this disturb the authenticity or add to the pathos of the event?" students get to interrogate the political economy of Hollywood and the star system.

TV News: Constructing Narratives

In order to underscore the way in which television—like all visual media—is a construction, John shows a segment from a local CBS news broadcast on gun violence in Chicago. In the piece, a reporter has this discussion with a 4-year-old boy:

Reporter: What are you going to do when you're older?
Boy: I'm going to get me a gun.

At this point, the segment cuts back to news anchor Steve Bartlestein, who says, "That is very scary indeed." The news station created a narrative that suggests the cycle of violence will never end and that even very young children are eager to join in the gunplay that plagues their neighborhoods. The only problem with this narrative is that it is utterly false. According to video obtained by the Maynard Institute of Journalism Education, the "full" conversation proceeds thusly:

Reporter: Boy, you ain't scared of nothing! Damn! When you get older, are you going to stay away from all these guns?
Boy: No.
Reporter: No? What are you going to do when you get older?
Boy: I'm going to get me a gun.
Reporter: You are? Why would you want to do that?
Boy: I'm going to be the police.

Some, including the NAACP, questioned the ethics of interviewing a 4-year-old on TV without parental consent, but beyond the journalistic ethics—and more to the point of our classroom purposes—the edited version distorts the narrative completely. Rather than suggesting an interminable gun war with the "next generation" of gunslingers at the ready, the full footage shows a young boy who wants to stop the fighting. As one critic explained, "Airing a video of the boy saying he wanted a gun that edits out the context simply reinforces stereotypes that African American males are violent, even preschoolers" (Butler 2011: 1).

Reading Movies: Stranger Than Fiction

We both teach a yearlong senior English elective class called Literature and Film. The very name of this class is relevant to our argument here. When John first created the class (with our colleague Carlo Trovato), we pitched it using the name Film and Literature. The local school board wondered if such a class would be taken seriously by colleges, so they insisted we flip the title terms around. Turns out their fears may not have been entirely unfounded. In the first few years of the course, the National Collegiate Athletic Association (NCAA) questioned the validity of the course, wondering if it may, perhaps, be an easy pass credit for athletes, something on the scale of the infamous "basket weaving" courses in college. In order to satisfy this powerful association's concerns, we needed to demonstrate that we read canonical print texts in addition to film texts. Sadly, no one much seemed to care about our close reading of Chaplin or Coppola or Spielberg. The continued hierarchies in English education that privilege print over audiovisual media are still in place in 2017.

One of our challenges in this class is to get students to slow down and attend individual images rather than having the whole experience "wash over viewers." Here, too, we try to keep it concrete. Sometimes it is helpful to equip students with a particular hermeneutic. John landed on one at the start of his teaching career when teaching coming-of-age stories. A central motif in such stories concerns a move from dependent, linear lives to independent, complicated lives. Think of Little Red Riding Hood, whose fortunes change the minute she "leaves the path." Consider the consequences for Adam and Eve, who were expelled from Paradise (a word rooted in the Babylonian words for "walled garden") and forced to create their own order in the undefined expanse of the land east of Eden.

So, just as he has asked students to locate "lines and curves" in literary texts, John asks students to find lines and curves within the set designs of movies such as *Minority Report* and, for our purposes here, *Stranger Than Fiction*, directed by Marc Foster and featuring actor Will Ferrell as a mentally unstable IRS auditor, Harold Crick, whose life is utterly linear. At home he has a square mirror, he brushes his teeth up and down and side to side—never on an angle. In fact, his life is literally narrated by the author Karen Eiffel, who is writing the story of his life. The only round objects in his apartment are a wristwatch and a Granny Smith apple, both of which figure prominently in the narrative arc.

Students often enter our classes thinking that much of what shows up on film just happened to be there. They resist the idea of intentionality. This seems to result, in part, from the belief that a single director is responsible for making movies and not a team of specialists—sometimes dozens or even hundreds, whom the director orchestrates and manages. So, rather than tell students what we think is happening, we allow them to infer by analyzing two images from the film that depict Harold's workplace at the IRS and the bakery of a woman he is auditing, a woman who will end up changing Harold's life forever. At the IRS work space, students note the bland colors, the utter rectilinearity; the harsh lighting of fluorescent bulbs on hospital white tiles and folders; the sterile sonic environment, highlighted shortly after this shot by a woman walking by in echoey high heels; the slightly low camera angle suggests a stifling, claustrophobic work space; the deep focus, suggesting the relentless, undeviating linearity of his life.

When looking at the scene of the bakery, students immediately notice the bright colors, the people of color, the high-angle shot of Harold diminishing the rather tall and imposing Will Ferrell. On the table in front of him, we see his huge briefcase, a totem of personality from this workaholic, surrounded by a three-tier round cake platter, a small round pot of African violets, and an outsize jack (as in the children's game). In short, the bakery work space is the antithesis of his: it's vibrant, full of life and fun, nurturing and sustaining; his, in contrast, is a monochromatic world of bleakness and order.

In all of the instructional examples we have cited here, our goal is simple: to help students slow down and consider the wealth of information available from visual images. Visual texts need to be read too. They need to be seen as constructions, versions of the truth, some truer than others, but not The Truth. All this can happen only if students use a close reading practice to read visuals actively and with integrity.

References

Brown, N. E., Bussert, K., Hattwig, D., & Medaille, A. (2015). "Keeping Up With . . . Visual Literacy." Association of College & Research Libraries. Retrieved from www.ala.org/acrl/publications/keeping_up_with/visual_literacy

Butler, B. (2011, July 19). "Young Guns." Maynard Institute. Retrieved from http://mije.org/health/young-guns

Eyes on the Prize. Callie Crossley, James A. DeVinney, Steve Fayer. PBS. 1987.

Lewis, J. (2014). *March: Book One.* Top Shelf Books.

McCloud, S. (1993). *Understanding Comics: The Invisible Art.* New York: Harper Perennial.

Selma. (2014). Ava DuVernay [Director]. Paramount Pictures. [Film].

Stranger Than Fiction. (2006.) Marc Forster [Director]. Will Ferrell, Emma Thompson, Dustin Hoffman, Maggie Gyllenhaal. Columbia Pictures. [Film.]

VargasLlosa, Mario. (2001, May 13). "Why Literature?" *The New Republic.* Retrieved from https://newrepublic.com/article/78238/mario-vargas-llosa-literature

Yang, G. L. (2006). *American Born Chinese.* New York and London: First Second Books.

Further Reading

Bordwell, D., & Thompson, K. (2016). *Film Art: An Introduction.* New York: McGraw-Hill.

Golden, J. (2001). *Reading in the Dark: Using Film as a Tool in the English Classroom.* Urbana, IL: National Council of Teachers of English.

Villarejo, A. (2013). *Film Studies: The Basics.* New York: Routledge.

21

COPYRIGHT AND FAIR USE DILEMMAS IN A VIRTUAL EDUCATIONAL INSTITUTION IN MEXICO

David Ramírez Plascencia

The quick spread of online education around the world in the last decades has forced educational institutions to modify their administrative, academic, and technological procedures. The demand to increase educational opportunities has pushed institutions to look for alternative systems and strategies like the application of the massive open online courses (MOOC) model, as well as other novel forms, to extend learning to the masses. In this context, publishers, media enterprises, and universities are more cautious about how the Internet enables the circulation of online, free, open education. Although the Internet makes the circulation of academic materials possible across the web, many of the resources and materials are protected under local and international copyright laws.

As a professor with more than a decade of experience in virtual education, I have witnessed how educational media has evolved from physical books to online documents and into social media resources like videoconferences, animations, and podcasts. But, unfortunately, legal dispositions and educational institutional policies about fair use, copyright, and plagiarism have changed very little, leaving uncertainty and doubts about what kind of material can be used and under which circumstances. In Mexico, problems related with copyright and fair use are exacerbated due to the lack of legal certitude and the little institutional awareness about the importance of legal aspects when designing courses in virtual environments. This unfamiliarity with copyright laws and with a proper management of academic sources is very common between teachers and students too, who frequently fall into cases of plagiarism, incorrect quotation, and academic resource mistreatment.

The point of this chapter is to recount a decade of experiences related with copyright and fair use at The System ofVirtual University, a special education center that belongs to the

University of Guadalajara in Mexico (www.udgvirtual.udg.mx), dedicated to online education. This chapter will address some recurrent problems related with educational materials, fair use, and copyright law. I also want to show how this institution has worked over the years trying to reduce these glitches. The main legal and moral dilemmas during the years are linked with the improper use of copyrighted materials, cases of plagiarism, and how the staff has had to deal with the evolution of educational materials from printed books into more varied forms and supports. Although when dealing with legal and academic predicaments there are no easy solutions, experiences recollected over the years have proved that the best way to deal with these difficulties is to confront them as a whole. An integral solution that comprises the action not only to socialize copyright law amid faculty and students but also to educate both about the proper forms of using course resources in order to develop scholar competences. However, strong emphasis must be made in establishing clear institutional directives concerning the usage of copyrighted resources, about the correct management of bibliography, and about the protection of materials created by professors, like learning objects, rubrics, and educational resources generated cooperatively during online classes when working with Web 2.0 tools.

Virtual Higher Education: Context and History

With the arrival of the new millennium, universities around the world have become more conversant about encouraging their faculty and students to include information technology educational tools in class and to enable the opening up to a more global and interconnected society, where transnational exchange is fundamental (Houston 2006). As the use of technology has been established as mandatory in universities (Gosper 2013), there has been a huge increase of virtual platforms, open-source and proprietary, and virtual educational programs and courses, and also the inclusion of social media and online collaborative tools has become very usual not only for online education but in traditional "brick and mortar" teaching too, where it is not unusual to find programs that use online storage services, blogs, and social media profiles for sharing resources between students and educators, and keeping in communication after class.

Although efforts have been made to harmonize copyright law internationally, significant differences in national law make the application of copyright to issues of formal education distinctive to each country. Regarding Mexico's case, since the arrival of the Internet to public universities in the mid-nineties of the last century, the use of information technologies started expanding through academia over the years. Actually, many public and private universities offer several programs completely online; as important examples in the public sector, we could mention the University of Guadalajara (UdeG), the National Autonomous University of Mexico (UNAM), and the recent one created by the Federal Government Administration, the Open and Distance University of Mexico (UNADM). In the private sector are the Monterrey Institute of Technology and Higher Education (ITESM) and University of Mexican Valley (UVM). About the experience of the University of Guadalajara in virtual education, the first efforts for implementing it were assembled between 1989 and 1990 (Pérez 2004). But those energies endured unfinished until the creation of the System of Virtual University, or UDGVirtual, as this institution is advertised in 2005. During the last eleven years, UDGVirtual has produced numerous online academic programs. It now coordinates more than fifteen undergraduate and postgraduate programs and more than fifty continuing education courses. It has nearly 10,000 students in both modalities, regular and continuing education programs (Moreno 2015).

Currently, Mexican higher education is influenced by some global emergencies that have changed traditional learning procedures. On one hand is the increasing movement into the competency model in response to the global labor market requirements; in second place is the growing need to search for alternative means of financing; and last is the imperative of using information and communication technology courses in university curricula (The Economist 2014). In recent years, there have been local and international pressures for increasing the number of students and the scholarship level of the Mexican population. In this context, public universities are always under the social microscope, with a permanent demand for opening more programs and spaces; every semester, thousands of young prospects cannot enter into university due to the insufficiency of public universities' capacity. For example, in the 2016 Spring semester, in the University of Guadalajara, fewer than 50% of the 34,000 applications were accepted into the program, leaving more than 15,000 young people with no more choice than to enroll in a private school. For many students, alternative schools are not always a good option for getting suitable instruction. This lack of opportunity has generated an increasing necessity for generating more virtual programs to increase enrollment.

A Decade of Fair Use and Copyright Dilemmas

When dealing with copyright law and technology, no matter the country, it seems that the social use of a given technical device (not only information technologies like computers or the Internet but press and radio) comes into confrontation with the traditional legal framework. This is partly due to the fact that technology evolves more quickly than the legal codes and precedents. Here it is possible to quote some recent well-known cases that confirm this assertion: Napster's sharing of digital music starting in the early 2000s (Witt 2015) and the more recent issue about Google Books and the legal controversies concerning the act of digitalizing printed materials and publishing them freely online (Meyer 2015).

Nonetheless, these kinds of conflicts are not socially and economically isolated; they are not just problems related with legal inaccuracy and the social adoption of technological advances that noticeably exceed the traditional legal outline. Typically, these struggles between social use and law are surrounded by many private and public interests that fight side by side in order to tip the scales toward their side (Günnewig 2003). For that reason, regarding intellectual property subjects, finding the correct balance between public interest and private rights is not an easy task due to the fact that when one side is privileged, the other is undermined. This is even harder when considering digital goods. After all, the essential nature of digital goods challenges the implementation of mechanisms to assure not only the proper use of copyrighted material but their own integrity and authorship. In the case of digital goods for education, it is usual to think in terms of things like e-books and electronic articles, but there are new kinds of virtual assets, like learning objects and animations, that sometimes include several classes of multimedia objects from different authors, that come under diverse copyright licenses, and that defies traditional copyright policies.

Under these circumstances, international and local authorities must work fast and cooperatively in order to update the legal framework as much as the society needs it. This is especially important when dealing with some important and basic matters that affect many users, activities, private and public interests. The process of modernizing legal codes is particularly important in developing countries, like Mexico, where enforcing the law is a more complicated task than in the United States or Europe.

Legislative negligence inhibits the presence of robust and efficient regulations in Mexico and around the world. One of the biggest tribulations in Mexico is that sometimes there is not a deep and open discussion about the conveniences of modifying one law or creating a new one. This problem affects not only intellectual property regulation but all kind of legal codes. Many new legal considerations—copyright laws are no exception—are based on contemplating latest cases just as novel forms of the traditional legal institutions. So in the case of copyright in the digital era, it just follows on old-style legal criteria, formed to deal with tangible elements (Siriginidi 2003). But, of course, physical and digital educational materials are not really the same as printed texts. An e-book can be accessed simultaneously by several students and educators using different technical devices without losing its integrity, something completely different from accessing a printed book. Paradoxically, in spite of the fact that the Mexican intellectual property code has been reformatted recently (the last addenda was in March 17, 2015), it still embraces all digital applications as "personal computer software," thus barely mentioning cloud computing software or mobile devices. The new code also does not mention the existence of accurate legal mechanisms to protect collective creations produced in social media platforms (Congreso de la Unión 1996).

Copyright and Higher Education in Mexico

As in the case of Mexican educational institutions like the University of Guadalajara, the use of copyrighted materials in traditional and virtual academic programs generally occurs with no authorization and without paying any kind of royalties. This is a very common practice that has endured since the time of the first photocopy machines, and it continues until now with electronic books and mobile devices. For decades, the procedure used to access academic content in a higher education course has remained unaltered: students consult books from university libraries, or the material is borrowed from their teachers. The Mexican book market those days was very limited and without competent channels of distribution. So, in many cases, students made close summaries concerning important ideas, and these summaries circulated among learners. The cost of accessing textbooks was so high, and so few volumes were available at bookstores that purchasing secondhand books from other students was a common way of acquiring material. Reflecting on this old practice, at a distance, it is hard not to agree with the fact that sometimes unbending copyright protection did indeed discourage not only the action of producing the material but of gaining access to them (Einnhorn 2005).

Many scholarly volumes, just a few years before the appearance of photocopies, were simply inaccessible (Atkinson & Fitzgerald 2014). When copy machines became available for a wider public in Mexico, in the mid-eighties of the last century, educators and students began taking advantage of this new technology. Suddenly, a selection of chapters and articles prepared by the professor and used in class started circulating around university campuses, and a small-scale market of these kinds of educational materials was created in order to supply the demand. This type of distribution enabled many useful, expensive, and hard-to-find books to become available for students and professors. As part of this tradition, copying and distributing entire books and anthologies became a typical practice in private and public universities in Mexico. But now paper has been replaced by digital formats, like the Portable Document Format (PDF). Today, faculty and students have many options for accessing information, not only using personal computers but with mobile devices too.

I began working at UDGVirtual in 2006, about a year after its establishment. My first work here was as a professor of an online course on electronic government. After some months, I started coordinating all continuous education programs for public administration. My first challenge as an educator was centered on mastering the digital platform and creating an optimal instructional design for my future students. Of course, paying attention to the use of copyrighted material was not even important at that time. I simply assumed, as did many other professors, that any educational material in digital and paper format could be used for educational purposes by a public academic institution.

Having graduated from law school, I must confess that I was conscious of the legal implications of using unauthorized copyrighted materials, but since the usage of printed photocopies and digital documents was very common during my days as a student, I simply assumed that this practice, in my work as professor, was completely legal and protected by fair use legal clauses. Finding electronic resources in Spanish at that time was not an easy task, and most of the material hosted in virtual platforms came from printed books. Most of the material for my courses those days was uploaded directly to the virtual platform, sometimes in html or txt format, digital formats that do not preserve the integrity of the document. Occasionally works were preserved in PDF format. This practice, of course, does not represent a good example of how to properly use educational material, as the integrity of the work was compromised. Sometimes the absence of data made it difficult even to reference the work, and sometimes the institution added a legal disclaimer related to copyright law and fair use.

Today, the sort and number of digital articles and books published in Spanish are vast, and most of them are freely available for nonprofit use. In the case of Mexico, this change was inspired not only for economic reasons but due to the fact that publishing academic products in electronic format encouraged access and distribution. For researchers in a Mexican university, this is very crucial because the diffusion of academic production increases the possibilities that your production could be used by other colleagues, increasing its impact factor (IF), an aspect that is very significant for national and international scientific evaluation committees.

In Mexican regulation, the concept of fair use is established under Article 148 of the Federal Law of Authorship Rights. That article limits, in some specific cases, the right of copyright holders to ask for royalties when someone uses their work (Congreso de la Unión 1996: Art. 148). Most of those limits apply only when the action implies the reproduction for academic, critical, and research purposes. Under these premises, it is allowed that students make a copy of a book for private use or to utilize extracts of a work, like citing passages in an academic article. However, the code also mentions that fair use applies only for a "single reproduction of one work only once and without profit" (Congreso de la Unión 1996: Art.148). It is important to note that this, of course, never happens in daily life, as a huge number of books and articles are frequently copied and used in both tangible and virtual formats.

Besides the importance of giving proper information to faculty staff and students about how to manage digital resources in virtual education, institutions should work on establishing alternative mechanisms to collect digital material that is licensed under Creative Commons and available in educational repositories. However, establishing quality standards and digital infrastructure in order to guarantee the correct functioning of those spaces is not an easy task. In Mexico, it is possible to mention some virtual educational resources storehouses: UNID, Digital Resources Repository (http://brd.unid.edu.mx) and the RAD-UNAM, Institutional Repository of the National Autonomous University of Mexico (www.rad.unam.mx). These places are very good options when searching for open material when designing courses, like learning objects, rubrics, and multimedia presentations.

Another important action that has had a tremendous impact not only in disseminating scientific work but in increasing the amount of free access content online for education was undertaken in recent years, by the SNI (Sistema Nacional de Investigadores, National System of Researchers), a governmental agency that promotes the improvement of scientific research in Mexico by evaluating and awarding scientific research achievement. This institution has promoted some actions in order to accelerate the digitalization of paper-based academic journals, such as giving some resources to promote the use of open journal software in the process of editing academic journals in Mexican higher education institutions. Additionally, a new perspective concerning digital publications has established that paper-based and digital publications must be equally evaluated by the SNI when considering the entrance of new members or relocating associates to a higher ranking.

The massive spread of desktop computers, mobile devices, and Internet access has given new possibilities to educators not only to create virtual courses but to incorporate several digital tools for making and sharing content in the classroom and online in distance education. Those tools are not only associated with displaying and sharing presentation slides but also allow real collaborative interchange online. However, dealing with all these novel potentials of digital media and learning has forced professors to develop more complex and challenging digital competencies. It has also encouraged them to learn more about intellectual property rights issues in order to guarantee the appropriate use of educational material without exposing themselves and their institutions to charges of possible infringement (Ludlow & Duff 2007).

Think about copyright and fair use in education: they not only concern the use of protected documents and productive software like office suites, but, at organizational level, they affect the deliberation about choosing a learning management system (LMS), which is the term used for a virtual educational platform. Today these can be classified as proprietary or open-source. Over the years, UDGVirtual has worked with both kinds. In the beginning, some courses were published on LMSs like WebCT and Blackboard, but the high cost of licenses limited the number of users and courses. So, like many others, our higher education institution decided to avoid paying these fees and to expand the volume of students by creating its own learning management system. By the time I started working with online education in 2005, UDGVirtual had already developed its platform. It was named AVA (Ambiente Virtual de Aprendizaje, Virtual Learning Environment). AVA worked for many years and hosted several academic courses, but over time, it was not easy to get the human and economic resources to keep the platform, and the institutional requirements became more complex for the AVA platform. Actually, UDGVirtual operates almost all its academic programs in open-source digital learning platforms like Moodle and Sakai.

After ten years of experiences related to implementing diverse learning management systems, I have recognized the advantages and drawbacks of proprietary and open-source models. Educational institutions must pay attention not only to the licensing price in order to make a decision concerning which LMS should be preferred. If an open-source platform is chosen, the educational organization has to integrate an appropriate staffing model for operating and upgrading it: engineers, programmers, and information technology staff are needed. The cost of maintaining this group of specialists is not cheap at all. Sometimes acquiring licenses could be a better option especially for small institutions that do not have enough infrastructure and human resources for operating their own open-source platform. Such decisions, of course, depend much on the number of participants who will be using a learning management system for online learning.

Over the years, several copyright holders have established agreements with public universities in Mexico as a way of finding a middle point between asking for royalties and fair use limitations (Rory 2005). This has been especially notable concerning software applications like operative systems (OS) and office software. Companies like Microsoft have closed important deals with public institutions for authorizing the use of its products to students and educators under a special academic licensing program. However, the most perilous point concerning intellectual property rights policies in the context of Mexican universities is not to establish a general policy regarding the use of material or making agreements with software enterprise for obtaining institutional authorizations for the staff. Besides the fact that it is an organizational mandatory to fix the problems previously identified, there is an unsolved but crucial problem rooted in the lack of intellectual property legal awareness between educators and students.

In the Mexican higher education context, many copyright infringements are unintentional or grounded on a misunderstanding. Sometimes, professors are not even aware that they are committing a transgression. It is an institutional responsibility to adequately prepare the faculty for digital learning. Not only do they need instructional design courses on the use of collaborative online tools, but they also need a better understanding of copyright law and the proper use of educational resources, not only bibliographies but multimedia elements. This instruction, nonetheless, has to be extended to other people who work with this kind of learning material: librarians, graphic designers, and, of course, students. Throughout the years, many academic and legal problems could have been eluded in UDGVirtual if the institution had paid more attention in training their staff and students properly. Some situations were associated with simple plagiarism or copy-paste actions where students did not suitably cite their sources in essays or projects (Lipinski 2007). However, avoiding plagiarism cases is not merely related to the proper use of the APA citation style but also to giving students practical information for managing and using information when doing school assignments. Notably, the instructional design of online learning may encourage learners to copy-paste. When students have to work on monotonous and plain activities that just request them to look for some concepts in a text, to abridge information, and finally to upload a summary to the virtual platform, these assignments inhibit student inventiveness and creativity and favor apathy and indolence.

Since 2015, there have been many noteworthy cases of plagiarism in Mexico (Nexos 2015). One of the most famous situations was related to the Chilean academic researcher Rodrigo Núñez Arancibia, who worked at a public university in the Mexican state of Michoacán and who committed several acts of this nature many times. Arancibia lifted entire published works and presented them as his own work; his actions passed overlooked for years, unnoticed by the colleagues and the public institutions that evaluated his scholarly production. His work embraced unconnected and dissimilar topics from the colonial era of Latin America to modern Chilean history. This and other related situations, like the issue of Professor Juan Pascal Gay who was suspended from the National System of Researchers (Sistema Nacional de Investigadores, SNI), the highest academic consortium in Mexico, for plagiarism (Milenio 2015), are not, unfortunately, the exception that proves the rule. These highly visible examples represent very common and malicious academic conduct that splashes over into all spheres in Mexican academia. Practices such as these concerning students and researchers suggest that the misuse and malicious treat of digital information is a common issue in teaching and researching in Mexico. Fortunately, it appears that educational institutions, at least in recent years, are not willing to tolerate this conduct anymore, at least when they are uncovered in the news media and decried by public opinion.

But education is not the only sector that has these problems. The field of journalism suffers from these problems frequently. This is partially due to, as in the case of education, the lack of appropriate instructions concerning copyright issues but also because the industry deadline pressures to "get the story" are intense. In this context, another problem that exacerbates the situation is the absence of institutional strategies not only to make workers aware of these problems and the lack of information and education about how to avoid misconduct but also to help them find new ways for managing information and to innovate in the field (Ramírez Plascencia 2015).

Based on my experience teaching information technology law courses to journalists and information technology students, I find that one of the big problems to solve is increasing consciousness about the importance of intellectual property rights. This not only embraces the perils of using unauthorized protected assets (software, multimedia elements, and texts) but how to protect their own work from illegal reproduction or use (Soules & Ferullo 2008). As a professor, my first concern is about how to sensitize my students about the importance of knowing more about the value of digital assets and its protection. However, teaching this subject is not an easy task because many external factors influence students' and professional conduct regarding intellectual property rights, like the fact that many people still continue to conceive the Internet as a lawless and free environment.

From Lush to Teetotaler: The Evolution of Digital Resources Management

In the last ten years, UDGVirtual has developed some institutional policies concerning the use of educational material. Most of those guidelines are related to the establishment of limitations regarding the use of copyrighted resources in online courses. Nonetheless, over time, these limitations have become so rigid that, by now, it is practically more efficient to look for open access materials or to create your own educational resources than it is to optimistically wait for selected academic copyrighted literature to pass the institution's copyright filter.

In documenting the evolution of these restrictive institutional parameters concerning the use of educational materials, it is important to note that all forms of academic materials are involved, including documents, audio, video, and photographs as well. The university policy shifted from "all is allowed" to an approach that is highly restrictive. In its very beginnings in 2005, UDGVirtual, like many educational institutions in Mexico, used all kinds of material or multimedia resources. Sometimes professors even changed the original format of the resource, altering its properties and content. There were no minimum parameters for using the materials, so someone could scan a chapter of a book and upload it to the platform in plain text format (TXT) without pagination. Sometimes these practices even deprived the work of the most essential reference data, like the name of the author or the correct title of the publication.

But in 2007, institutional authorities attempted to place some kind of order to this situation. One of the first actions in UDGVirtual was achieved by the creation of a new department, the Coordination of Informative Resources. This department was dedicated to the management and use of institutional publications like magazines and books. The first guidelines created were designed to address the use of digital resources. New parameters established that it could be possible to scan only one or two chapters of a book, not the entire volume. A label with a phrase concerning legal fair use rights for educational institutions was added to every document uploaded to the virtual platforms.

Another important action was to set a narrower cooperation between two departments: the Coordination of Informative Resources and the Coordination of Educational Design, a department dedicated to instructional design. This close collaboration ensured the careful treatment of uploaded materials to ensure proper inclusion of bibliographic reference and in a digital format (PDF) that guarantees the integrity of the work. Since 2007, only a few UDGVirtual employees were authorized to post to virtual platforms. Educators lost their rights to modify the materials and were forbidden to independently add other resources to their own courses. The Educational Design staff became educational censors, in effect.

From 2007 to 2010, institutional authorities worked on developing more efficient copyright policies concerning the usage of academic resources. As an outcome of these efforts, some official documents were disseminated with the purpose of giving further certainty to students, educators, researchers, and general employees at UDGVirtual about what material is possible to use and how to use it correctly. Today the university publishes a guide for citing bibliography in essays and other scholarly assignments. Additionally, every student who enrolls in an academic program receives by e-mail basic recommendations about intellectual property rights.

But what I think was the most significant action is that UDGVirtual established a well-defined process by which all instructional designs must pass a filter where every multimedia element and document has to be reviewed. By establishing this control, this action has limited student access to available resources. This action of restricting academic bibliography has forced many professors to exclusively use free resources and, even in some cases, to create their own materials.

However, these actions are not completely negative. Based on my experience designing online courses and coordinating a postgraduate program, I would respectfully disagree with those statements that claim more academic freedom concerning the use of copyrighted materials (Moscon 2015). I clearly understand that sometimes the cost of academic databases subscriptions are prohibitive, especially for universities in emergent countries like Mexico (Scheufen 2015). But, at least regarding the design of online courses in higher education, something significant that I have noticed after the application of harder copyright policies at UDGVirtual is that there were more efforts than in the past to create and innovate instructional design or at least to work more on assignments, using further collaborative tools and working with open resources.

In previous years, having under your disposition thousands of copyrighted digitalized documents and multimedia resources not always represented the development of ideal online courses. On the contrary, in many occasions, the abundance of resources did not encourage educational innovation. In several courses, the instructional design was entirely lineal, just a loop of the same kinds of activities: to read a chapter or an article and to make a summary of the main ideas. The entire course was just a duplication of these kinds of scholarly duties. In these cases, having free access to all material only served for digitalizing an old and antiquate way of teaching, there was no real effort to innovate or to present, at least, an alternative model of instructional design.

Web 2.0 and Future Challenges of Virtual Education

Many debates about fair use and copyright laws are focused on how the legal framework tightened the possibilities of using copyrighted materials in education, especially in the Age of Information (Lee 2009). In recent years, the adoption of social media and collaborative digital tools, commonly named Web 2.0, has had a huge impact on the form of how people create and share information on the Internet (Hartshorne, Ajjan, & Ferdig 2010). Actually, it is easily possible to participate in online debates, surveys, and information exchanges. In the field of education, using digital platforms like Facebook, YouTube, or Google Docs offers countless opportunities for expanding virtual education experience into new spaces; this is especially important when stimulating innovation in traditional learning (Diaz & Christoph 2009). Many young Mexican students have at least one social media profile. More and more higher education scholars at UDGVirtual are familiar with blending Web 2.0 tools with learning management systems, so in many cases academic projects are completed through the online campus. This practice has given huge flexibility when working with mobile devices, for example, or when the assignments involve actions like making a video and sharing it on YouTube or Vimeo or like creating and displaying an online slide show or a text.

Certainly, the integration of multiple spaces and tools has some perils, especially when dealing with legal issues. Educational institutions have to face the circumstance that both educators and students will work outside the platform in an open environment. One important effort will be to define institutional recommendations that guide the incorporation and usage of Web 2.0 into university coursework, determining how this work should be best done and under which license it should be distributed (Fendler & Priem 2013). This is essential for online education, where publishing and sharing information result from a single instant action and where such activities are very hard to supervise or to control. In this context, institutions must assist educators and students when laboring in others' virtual spaces and counsel them about both the possible opportunities and the risks of using these kinds of spaces. In addition to copyright issues, other legal and ethics topics must be attended to, such as bullying and privacy issues.

In the last ten years, UDGVirtual, like many other educational institutions in the world, has survived through a variety of important transitions resulting from the huge increase in numbers of students and the changing demand for more diverse educational offerings. Besides the challenges originating from the new educational, economic, and social context, this paper has shown that institutional administrations recognize that information technology is always in transition, as are the educational technological tools themselves. The key matter in this context is to keep working on improving not only the informatics infrastructure but also the instructional design practices, organizational structures, and institutional policies.

References

Atkinson, B., & Fitzgerald, B. (2014). *A Short History of Copyright.* Cham: Springer International Publishing.

Congreso de la Unión. (1996). Ley Federal de Derecho de Autor.

Diaz, V., & Christoph, K. (2009). *Copyright, Fair Use, and Teaching and Learning Innovation in a Web 2.0 World* (Research Bulletin). Boulder, CO: Educause.

The Economist. (2014, June). "The Digital Degree." *The Economist.* Retrieved from www.economist.com/news/briefing/21605899-staid-higher-education-business-about-experience-welcome-earthquake-digital

Einnhorn, M.A. (2005). *Media, Technology and Copyright: Integrating Law and Economics.* Cheltenham, UK, and Northampton, MA: Edward Elgar.

Fendler, L., & Priem, K. (2013). "Material Contexts and Creation of Meaning in Virtual Places: Web 2.0 as a Space of Educational Research." In P. Smeyers, M. Depaepe, & E. Keiner (Eds.), *Educational Research: The Importance and Effects of Institutional Spaces* (pp. 177–191). The Netherlands: Springer.

Gosper, M. (2013). *Curriculum Models for the 21st Century: Using Learning Technologies in Higher Education.* New York: Springer.

Günnewig, D. (2003). "New Copyright for the Digital Age: Political Conflicts in Germany." In E. Becker, W. Buhse, D. Günnewig, & N. Rump (Eds.), *Digital Rights Management* (pp. 528–573). Berlin & Heidelberg: Springer.

Hartshorne, R., Ajjan, H., & Ferdig, R. E. (2010). "Faculty Use and Perceptions of Web 2.0 in Higher Education." In H. H. Yang & S. C-Y. Yuen (Eds.), *Handbook of Research on Practices and Outcomes in E-Learning: Issues and Trends* (pp. 241–259). Hershey, PA: Information Science Reference.

Houston, C. (2006). "Building Capacity for Global Education in a School Library Media Education Program Through International Exchange." *IFLA Journal,* 32(3), 209–213.

Lee, S. (2009). "Fair Use and the Vulnerability of Criticism on the Internet." In S. Westbrook (Ed.), *Composition & Copyright: Perspectives on Teaching, Text-Making, and Fair Use* (pp. 31–49). Albany: State University of New York.

Lipinski, T. A. (2007). "Legal Issues in the Development and Use of Copyrighted Material in Web-Based Distance Education." In M. G. Moore (Ed.), *Handbook of Distance Education* (2nd ed.) (pp. 481–507). Mahwah, NJ: Lawrence Erlbaum Associates.

Ludlow, B. L., & Duff, M. C. (2007). "Copyright Law and Content Protection Mechanisms: Digital Rights Management for Teacher Educators." *Teacher Education and Special Education*, 30(2), 37–46.

Meyer, R. (2015, October 20). "After 10 Years, Google Books Is Legal." *The Atlantic*.

Milenio. (2015, April 8). "Por plagio, Conacyt expulsa a dos investigadores." *Milenio*. México. Retrieved from www.milenio.com/cultura/expulsan-miembros-plagiar-investigaciones_0_566943309.html

Moreno Castañeda, R. M. M. (2015). *Informe de Actividades del Sistema de Universidad Virtual 2014–2015*. Guadalajara, JA: SUV-UdeG.

Moscon, V. (2015). "Academic Freedom, Copyright, and Access to Scholarly Works: A Comparative Perspective." In R. Caso & F. Giovanella (Eds.), *Balancing Copyright Law in the Digital Age* (pp. 100–135). Berlin & Heidelberg: Springer.

Nexos. (2015). "Sobre el plagio académico." Retrieved from www.nexos.com.mx/?p=25563

Pérez Alcalá, María del Socorro. (2004). *Historias de Innovación Educativa: Un Documento Conmemorativo*. Guadalajara, JA: University of Guadalajara.

Ramírez Plascencia, D. (2015). "El Periodismo Digital y las Políticas Editoriales en Materia de Plagio: Una Discusión Necesaria Pero Ausente." *Palabra Clave*, 18(1), 111–130.

Rory, M. (2005). "Copyright Wars and Learning Objects." *Interactive Technology and Smart Education*, 2(3), 141–153.

Scheufen, M. (2015). *Copyright Versus Open Access*. Cham: Springer.

Siriginidi, S. R. (2003). "Copyright: Its Implications for Electronic Information." *Online Information Review*, 27(4), 264–275.

Soules, A., & Ferullo, D. L. (2008). "Copyright Implications for Electronic Resources." In H. Yu (Ed.), *Electronic Resource Management in Libraries: Research and Practice* (1st ed.) (pp. 145–173). Hershey, PA: Information Science Reference.

Witt, S. (2015). *How Music Got Free: The End of an Industry, the Turn of the Century, and the Patient Zero of Piracy*. New York: Viking.

Further Reading

Cohen, J. E. (2015). *Copyright Global Information Economy Case and Statutory Supplement* (2015 edition). New York: Wolters Kluwer Law & Business.

Ferullo, D. L. (2014). *Managing Copyright in Higher Education: A Guidebook*. Lanham, MD: Rowman & Littlefield.

Frankel, S. (2015). *The Evolution and Equilibrium of Copyright in the Digital Age*. Cambridge: Cambridge University Press.

Hobbs, R. (2010). *Copyright Clarity: How Fair Use Supports Digital Learning*. Thousand Oaks, CA: Corwin.

Secker, J. (2016). *Copyright and E-Learning: A Guide for Practitioners* (2nd ed.). London: Facet Publishing.

Part IV

PAST IS PROLOGUE

22

COPYRIGHT, MONOPOLY GAMES, AND PIRATES

The Past, Present, and Future of Copyright

Thomas C. Leonard

Early in the 21st century, the novelist David Foster Wallace began a college commencement address with a joke:

> There are these two young fish swimming along and they happen to meet an older fish swimming the other way, who nods at them and says "Morning, boys. How's the water?" And the two young fish swim on for a bit, and then eventually one of them looks over at the other and goes "What the hell is water?"

Copyright in this century makes us all young fish. We may not be aware that the texts we read, the recorded music we hear, the videos we see are all wet with claims of copyright. Indeed, if these creative works were produced in our lifetimes, the claims that they are in copyright are likely valid. By the exception of fair use, copyright law allows us to borrow Wallace's words on fish and to do many other things with our cultural heritage. Fair use, however, is tricky for both newcomers and veterans in the field of intellectual property. How did we end up in the murky pool of copyright? This is most easily seen if we begin with printed books, the media that started the argument and gave us the law.

London Publishers and Pirates

Had you visited London taverns during the testing time for the first copyright law, the Statute of Anne (1710), you would have heard much talk about "piracy." This was not simply because convicted pirates from the high seas were being hanged along the Thames River nearby.

"Piracy" had somehow been stretched from its traditional use for murderous thieves to a popular epithet for people who borrowed words or illustrations. "Pirate" was the ready insult for rivals by people who held a monopoly. If you wish to be the one to hold tight to what you create with copyright, the term will come easily to your lips. What turned this sharing of texts into an overheated argument? Why couldn't people agree (as we often do today with fair use in American law) on what was fair?

Investigators are often told to "follow the money," and it is hard to picture pirates at work where there are no treasures. But in the formative years of copyright, fortunes from publishing books were not at stake. In all formats and subject areas, publishers used flatbed presses that required only modest investments and no upgrades. People who produced books did other types of printing as well and sold assorted goods in their small shops. Often, book publishers did not need authors as part of their diversified business. A newspaper or single sheet of paper (broadside) might simply contain government proclamations, shipping reports, or advertisements. Writers were not a drain on the publisher's bottom line. Terry Belanger, a librarian at Columbia University, concluded after long study that "the most common form of payment between publisher and writer in the eighteenth century was no payment at all" (Rivers 1982: 21). Money did matter in building a foundation for copyright but not as much as assertions of status and honor.

The seminal idea of intellectual property and the notion that it could be misused and branded as piracy took shape among people who witnessed the decline of royal authority and the growing role of the citizen. In his epic history of piracy in the realm of intellectual property, Adrian Johns, a historian at the University of Chicago, points out that while the root word for this thievery was ancient, the epithet for writings was new in literary circles. Neither Classical authors nor the Elizabethans used "piracy" to complain of the people who reprinted or otherwise misused what they created. "Piracy" was not a figure of speech that was applied to literature by William Shakespeare, John Milton, Sir Isaac Newton, or the other people we now associate with a century of genius. "Piracy" as a term for stealing words or pictures came when citizens themselves became more important in a public sphere shaped by authors. Johns finds that "precisely when authorship took on a mantle of public authority, through the crafts of the printed book, its violation came to be seen as a paramount transgression" (Johns 2009: 19).

Paramount and personal, for authors denouncing the use of their words by other people did not see this as a mere slight or a cost of doing business. Daniel Defoe (1704), the prolific author who gave us the novel *Robinson Crusoe*, denounced "Press-piracy" early in the 18th century, making even such acts as the abridgement of authors' writings "every jot as unjust as lying with their Wives, and breaking-up their Houses." Defoe's rage was not persuasive. The case of *Gyles v. Wilcox* (1740) would open the door to such abridgments in Anglo-American law.

Rights Talk Breaks Out

Defoe believed that he had a moral right to control his writings, a conviction that was to grow in the legal tradition of continental Europe but not in the Anglo-American world. Where books appeared in English, authors or artists who believed they had "rights" of any type to anything they created at the dawn of the 18th century were dreamers. Since the arrival of printing in Great Britain in Gutenberg's day, the Crown or Parliament had sought to license who could publish and what they could publish, often keeping "rights" out of the reach of creators. The state also acted to control publications coming into the kingdom, so the rights of foreign authors were beside the point. In some cases, "letters patent" and related grants were issued in Britain, giving an individual the exclusive right to print a work and to profit from it. But this cherished monopoly was losing favor by 1700.

Authors could not yet reasonably expect to earn a living by their pen, but their ideas of entitlement were growing. Less was now said about the humble role of writers in continuing a cultural tradition or being the simple agent to pass on truths of divine origins. Religious orders, the keepers of literacy for generations before the coming of copyright, had seen their role this way. In language that would have been presumptive earlier, authors of the 18th century spoke of their works as the spark of genius given to them by their creator, as a child that they begot and cherished and as real property, like an estate. Authors looked to the law to legitimize these deeply felt ideas. We should not look down on them for seeing things this way. With candor, writers or artists of the 21st century will feel the same attraction to what they create. But the compelling metaphors are blinding when used to make laws. If creative work marks you as a carrier of divine wisdom, how can it be right to keep this away from others? If a work you have produced is like your child, as Defoe swore it was, why do you think you should be able to sell it? If copyright represents real property, why is it wrong to tax it each year as your home is taxed? The emotionally rich arguments for copyright can as easily be used to make copyright seem odious.

Copyright in the Eyes of Publishers

It was not the authors who set up a working copyright order; it was their publishers. London's venerable Stationers' Company was, by habit, ready to suppress works assailing the government, but its passion was to see that its own members did not poach on the work of another bookseller. The core of this group was booksellers who fit the modern term, "publishers." Stationers' Hall, near St. Paul's Cathedral, kept a registry that became a foundation of Britain's new copyright regime. Turn a page of the Stationers' Company Register, showing who had published earlier and on what topic, and an argument about piracy could begin. Britain's first copyright law, the Statute of Anne (1710), supplemented the Register and set down the reference points for disputes about intellectual property that we have today.

The term "copyright" had grown out of the guild's authority over what could be in print, that is, *copied* legitimately. When the legislation that perpetuated this authority lapsed in 1695, the guild needed a new rationale to maintain its near monopoly. Booksellers devised the argument, rarely heard earlier, that it was the author who enjoyed copyright, knowing that members of the Stationers' Company, not scribblers, would have the power to exercise this enticing property right. The strong claimed to be pleading the cause of the weak. But the strong rather than the weak were the beneficiaries of the Statute of Anne, the world's first copyright law.

Few authors of this era ever got their hands on a copyright, their own or anyone else's. There was a robust market for such rights, but in practice it excluded nearly everyone in the kingdom, save London booksellers. They numbered fewer than a hundred and had agile, smaller groups to advance their control of the book trade. London booksellers used a term for their operations that suggested, today and at the time, a conspiracy: the "conger." The men (and a few women) in the various congers were obsessed with "pirates" as they understood this word: (a) someone inside their circle who, without clearance, issued a title that was owned by a fellow guild member; and (b) anyone outside London who printed a title without guild permission. The booksellers thought these rights should never lapse; they grumbled and took the 28 years of control of publications that was common for titles after the Statute of Anne.

With the assistance of "a Good dinner and a Glass of Wine," these entrepreneurs met often to reinforce their faith that, by the common law that was far older than the Statute of Anne, they controlled exclusive rights to their "stock" of Shakespeare, Milton, and other classic writers. Equally important, they traded shares in the copyrights they held of the new, as yet unproven authors. Booksellers claimed perpetual rights to these as well. Their business plan was what economists later called an oligopoly. Rights were distributed and passed on through families. Emerging from the tavern, a bookseller might be the owner of as little as 1/150th of a title and file this with paper that showed fractional ownership of dozens of titles that had been inherited or purchased. The enduring books of this era, from *Robinson Crusoe* to *Gulliver's Travels*, owed as much to deals in taverns as to any muse. And they were published at a time when it was certain that they would be pirated, as we shall soon see.

Though the Statute of Anne had seemed to settle the point that rights had time limits, booksellers worked the courts for six decades to create what scholars call an "impenetrable fog" (Spoo 2013: 93). Copyright holders harassed and bribed people who took them to court. They petitioned Parliament for exceptions and found sympathetic judges to conjure up a common law tradition making rights perpetual. The House of Lords finally threw out this specious feature of British law in *Donaldson v. Becket* (1774), but the underlying disagreements and opaque language in copyright battles persisted in Anglo-American law. U. S. Supreme Court Justice Joseph Story famously called intellectual property "nearer than any other class of cases belonging to forensic discussions to what may be called the metaphysics of the law where the distinctions are or at least may be very subtle and refined, and sometimes, almost evanescent" (Rose 1993: 141).

We should not assign selfish motives too readily to the bookseller-publishers who pushed for copyright protection. Cooperation and coordination were necessary to make a living in their trade. In their small shops, the printing of long works, even the storage of pages ready for binding, had to be distributed. Competition was not healthy for them. This was a devoted community; they married into one another's families and kept bloodlines running through elected positions in Stationers' Hall for two and a half centuries. Some kept an eye on eternity. One bookseller of the 1720s died with the wish that he be buried next to a fellow bookseller. For every day, the fractional transactions of rights were similar to what shippers did, dividing cargo and personalizing it in order to maximize recovery. Booksellers spread risk and reward by having an interest in many titles. Book pirates, they found, were best deterred by a swarm of interested parties who could blacken their name and harry them in court. For extra measure, Londoners who owned book copyrights frequently controlled newspapers.

Booksellers followed only the laws they found agreeable and gamed authorities and authors at every opportunity. For example, in order to protect their copyrights, booksellers were supposed to deposit copies in certain libraries. When this tradition was enshrined in the Statute of Anne, booksellers ignored it or cheated on deposits.

So-Called Pirates and Real Markets

Even if the Stationers' Company had been sincere in offering authors control over the books they wrote, their pious wish would have come to little. Salable titles that came from London presses were reproduced as it suited ink-stained pirates across the British Isles, in colonies, and in continental Europe. This was commonly done without permission or compensation, sometimes without any recognition for authors. Publishing in the English language was already "monopoly tempered by piracy" (Baldwin 2014: 131).

London printers strove to maintain their monopoly. But they were surrounded by publishers who did not follow their rules. Pirate publishing centers lay North, South, East, and West—from Glasgow, Edinburgh, and Dublin (unrivaled for English language books in the

18th century) to Amsterdam, as well as to German-speaking principalities. Switzerland was most honored (and denounced) for the way it sustained the "piratical Enlightenment," that is, printers willing to produce and circulate works banned by the state or titles asking for such trouble. (It was the circulation of the book across borders that triggered alarm, not the simple act of copying the work.) Foreign publishers could rush writing into print, sometimes with ideas that authors could not get printed under the Old Regime, with proceeds that the author or original publisher would normally not get. Pirates did not wait until a book was issued, bound or unbound. Journeymen printers were bribed so that the sheets meant for the press were in pirate hands before the entire work had been set in type. Books from this underground might not be of equal quality as the original. Sometimes they were better, incorporating elements that the original lacked. But they were always cheaper.

Printing pirates spread popular reading in the same way that seafaring pirates were good for local trade. (Getting goods from a pirate was the rough equivalent of getting goods "that fell off a truck" in modern times.) Economic historians have found that a great deal of the trade that enabled European empires to grow went on in such shadowy ways (Rediker 1987: 72). The glories of English literature, books destined to form a much honored canon, rest on the same raffish foundation.

Both in the United Kingdom and in the United States, setting limits on or even ignoring copyright put a vast new literature in the hands of ordinary people. This happened not simply because a cheaper edition of a work became available but also because what we today call a mashup became possible. London booksellers had feared abridgments and anthologies for they undercut revenue from the title they monopolized and forced them to share revenue because, by their lights, everything was owned by a fellow bookseller. This was true of works that we take for granted in the public domain (and so available for anyone to print): *Pilgrim's Progress*, *Romeo and Juliet*, and *Paradise Lost*. Opportunities for readers changed quickly at the end of the 18th century when, for example, booksellers who thought they had exclusive rights to *Aesop's Fables*, realized they did not. Like the printers or editors who threw works together, hawkers of these varied imprints were encouraging a mashup culture that took off as literacy rates rose. Readers were binding up shorter works for personal use, to be shared by family members. Crucially, women and men without property, some in the humblest stations of society, joined the circle of readers, making the culture more democratic.

American Copyright, American Piracy

Book pirates were fledglings in North America. Few titles that came from the colonial press were more than pamphlet size. But printers had dreams of matching the publishing pirate nests in the old world. Print piracy (or at least deception) was present at the creation of the American press. The weekly banner "Published by Authority" on a colonial newspaper was a false flag since such designations were informal at best; no colonial government vouched for a paper. Bibliophiles have long noticed that the first Bible published in the colonies falsely claimed to be published in London, a deceptive trade practice of Yankee printers in the 18th century. Printer Benjamin Franklin capitalized on the popular novel *Pamela* from London, whose copyright arrangements are hard to determine, and Franklin may have published a pirated New Testament, contrary to a royal patent on the holy book. Detective work is difficult because Franklin scholars believe that he may well have used a fictional London imprint (Green & Stallybrass 2006). James Rivington, a bookselling son of the man who held copyright, appropriately, for the first edition of the well received *General History of the Pyrates* (1724), became notorious by pirating works owned within his own family and by sneaking pirated imprints into New York. At this safe distance from the London trade, he stumbled into more trouble as a controversial newspaper publisher.

Journalism itself was antithetical to calls that the public sphere be organized around copyright. Authors could not hold copyright in the early republic when their works were first published in newspapers and journals. A writer's name could not be easily detected in the columns of a newspaper. Bylines were not used. Pseudonyms marked the most significant contributions, such as the widely reprinted Federalist Papers that came (without payment) from luminaries of the Revolutionary generation. What would be called plagiarism in later times was the mainstay of the early press. Columns and news articles were clipped by editors from the out-of-town papers they were first to see in the mails (many editors being postmasters). Then this text was reprinted in their paper. This borrowing was subsidized by the postal service, papers in "exchanges" requiring no postage as they circulated among editors who were hungry for copy. News was treated as a common good, the property of no one individual. Readers in the 19th century would have been astonished to see news spread any other way.

Printers who had trained as book pirates in Dublin before coming to America, such as Robert Bell and Mathew Carey, earned glory through the Revolution and beyond by publishing reprints. They were, proudly, pirates (as London colleagues defined that term). Bell, more the revolutionary in politics than Carey, looked the part, conducting business with a boisterous voice and with "a beer in one hand and a book in another" (Everton 2011: 57). Even prim and proper authors, who insisted that copyright be extended, had piratical habits. Noah Webster gave instruction on proper English spelling and writing while swiping what others had published on the subjects without acknowledgment.

This Yankee business model prompted London booksellers to develop trans-Atlantic trade practices that resembled those of storybook pirates: sail fast boats to capture a prize, in this case payments from American publishers for the earliest possible page proofs of the new works. The American crew would then pirate, or "reprint"—the courteous phrase. The payment to the fast shipper compensated somewhat for the royalties that would never arrive. In 1823, Carey's publishing house in Philadelphia bragged of having the "Game completely in our hands" to Sir Water Scott's publisher. The boat carrying the great writer's new book had won the race. "We shall have complete and entire possession of every market in the Country for a short time" (Spoo 2013: 50) the Yankees crowed. This was a victory over "pirates," Carey asked the Scot to believe.

The new nation had only the flimsiest of shields for an author's intellectual property, imaginary in the case of foreign authors and not as sturdy as it looked in the case of writers living in the new republic. The United States copyright law of 1790 (and its revisions in 1831 and in 1870) applied only to authors within the country. Charles Dickens, the most popular novelist of his day, declared himself to be "the greatest loser . . . alive." He was probably wrong: because his works were pirated so swiftly and cheaply, he was universally known in America, and his lecture fees earned him a fortune here.

Few Americans celebrated the copyright protection offered by the new nation, and remarkably few writers even used it. Not more than 5% of works by American authors were copyrighted in the first decade of the law, and less than 1% of these titles were renewed for another 14-year term (McGill 2010: 199, 590 n. 44). Measures beyond copyright law to aid the book culture fell into the category of gestures. Most were ineffective, some were menacing. There was much talk about proper publishing ethics. But meetings in the new republic to discourage reprinting books without compensation whet the appetites for such piracy.

Elaborate "courtesies of the trade" among publishers were crafted to tame the marketplace. These were partly a response to the wailing from authors, both foreign and domestic. Some writers believed that the office of a leading publisher in New York was graced by a picture of an author's skull and that the early death of scribblers was part of their business plan. The side payments to British authors were part of the effort to sweeten the air with a show of justice. The discouraging of new "pirates" who would legally print a cheap edition and hurt your publishing house's more expensive one was done this way: knock your price down to bring ruin to the newcomer. American publishers dreamed of tariffs on the import of any book already published in the new country, lest the American imprint be undersold. Emulating the Stationers' Company in the old country, American publishers vowed not to reprint what a domestic publisher had already issued. In practice, they often did.

The game plan that book publishers tried to follow included payoffs to foreigners, exploitation of first-mover advantage, predatory pricing against competition, no-bid pledges so that only one publisher would accept an author's book, and ongoing noncompete agreements that bound the author to that publisher for as long as possible. American book publishers skirted piracy (they insisted) and drew a sword when needed.

Looking back, as international copyright enforcement arrived in the United States at the end of the 19th century, publishers took credit for giving "our young literature a chance to grow without the blighting shadow of unnatural competition." Legal historians have put this in the best light possible: "American copyright law made pirates of honest men, so they banded together to act honorably according to voluntary norms of fairness that took the place of law" (Spoo 2013: 42, 46).

Self-Interest and Overreach

No copyright regimen, however clearly written, can still the impulse to seek monopoly rights without limits. The London booksellers exemplified this after the Statute of Anne, insisting that authors swear in a contract that they were surrendering the exclusive right to publish "for ever, notwithstanding any Act or Law to the Contrary" (Mason 2008: 94). In the 18th century, only revolutionaries and pirates spoke so defiantly about authority. In a Monopoly game, the equivalent action would be to throw the rules away and tell other players to leave. A culture of overreach runs deeply through our centuries of argument over intellectual property.

The United States in the 19th century, like China in the 21st century, became far more protective of the rights of creators when they had exhausted the benefits of piracy and needed to protect the economic interest of their own media. To the cheers of American authors and publishers who sought revenue from abroad, Mark Twain, for example, this country began to accept and enforce foreign copyright in the 1890s.

The game of Monopoly did not stop. In the hands of Congress, the duration of copyright protection went in only one direction: up. Fourteen years with a further extension of another 14 years for a living author was adopted in the first U.S. Copyright Law of 1790, the same standard set eighty years earlier in the Statute of Anne. Congress lengthened the protection to 28 years with a possible 14-year extension in 1831; it legislated a 28 plus 28–year standard in 1908. A revision of the law in 1976 extended the term of protection to the life of the author plus 50 years. The Sonny Bono Copyright Term Extension Act of 1998 gave the author another 70 years of protection beyond the grave. No book published after 1923 in the United States automatically enters the public domain until 2019.

Had copyright rules of today been in place a century ago, some of the most creative minds in American culture would have been stymied by lawsuits. The Walt Disney organization would not have been able to so easily tap the stories for children that had circulated in the Victorian world. As the *Economist* magazine observed about the business plan of this media giant, "Disney's enthusiasm for fierce enforcement of intellectual-property laws, and the seemingly perpetual extension of copyright laws, [is] somewhat ironic" (*"Star War, Disney and Myth-Making."* 2015). What was true for early media giants was true for singular artists exploring new ground early in the past century. Ernest Hemingway would have been wise to have a lawyer advise him about reading the manuscript of F. Scott Fitzgerald's *The Great Gatsby* in order to produce his own, *The Sun Also Rises*. Modernists such as T. S. Elliott and Marianne Moore, with their habits of appropriating many words, published and unpublished, from other writers, would have been told it was unwise to write poetry in this way.

The second half of the 20th century was a frolic for copyright maximalists. Congress in these decades freed all creators of original works fixed in a format from the requirements to register with the government or mark "copyright" on the work they produced. This forgiveness of formalities extends back to 1923. Reproducing major parts of any commercial book published since that time, without the permission of the holder of its copyright, can prompt calls of piracy.

The arrival of new platforms and formats for storytelling and education complicated this picture. The rise of corporate publications where an author's work was "for hire" also made copyright a tangle. But the outcome of all of the legislation and court actions was clear: works published before 1923 in the United States were public domain, open for anyone to use as they pleased. Works published through commercial channels after 1923 (or post 1923 and not published) had to be used with great caution by readers who wished to share substantial parts of them to enlighten their fellow citizens or to create new works.

The fair use of copyrighted materials without permission or payment in the United States is always limited and must be for the good of society as a whole. We see this right exercised every day in, for example, the quotations that ordinary citizens and news organizations make in order to comment on current events or in academic courses that show students how knowledge in a field has grown. The limited right requires a persuasive case that four factors have been weighed and that, on balance, the circumstances dictate the use.

Section 107 of the U. S. Copyright Act of 1976 bridged court decisions going back many decades. What emerged was not so much a picture of fair use as a guide on how to think about the concept. A successful claim of the fair use privilege will have carefully considered four factors:

- **Use**: An educational or nonprofit purpose is helpful but not determining. Similarly, the transformational nature of the text being appropriated is common for fair use but not essential. Use of works for criticism and commentary advance a key objective of fair use. But to supersede and to provide a substitute for the original has long been held not to be fair use; "such a use will be deemed in law a piracy." (*Folsom v. Marsh* 1841).
- **Nature**: Works of the imagination in the arts are less likely to pass muster for fair use than nonfiction. Works that are in print and available in the market are given more protection than works that have no commercial pulse.
- **Amount**: Short excerpts, such as a quotation, gain more protection than more extensive borrowings from a work in copyright.
- **Market effect:** If reproduction truly harms the author or publisher in revenue, courts have been sympathetic to these rights holders.

On purpose, this untidy way of reaching a decision avoids inflexible or even enumerated "rules." Courts, Congress, and many creators believe that this serves justice and social progress in the long run. In the case of authors whose works are used, the fair use of earlier work under copyright may be what they themselves will need to tell a story or to educate. In print especially, what comes around, goes around.

Google, Search Engines, and Fair Use

Search engines of the 21st century, especially Google, inherited the onus of being "pirates." The term was spoken as carelessly and with as much self-interest as the booksellers used the term in 18th-century taverns. Witness the top manager of the world's fourth largest media company letting loose in 2015. On the announcement that Google had a new corporate name, Alphabet Inc., Robert Thomson of News Corp said the rebranding was apt, as in the alphabet game, "P"—for pirate (Markson 2015). Thomson had run *The Wall Street Journal*, an impossible feat without the privilege of fair use in reporting, and the permission granted Google's search engine to crawl News Corp's websites in order to gain public attention.

One flash point in the copyright wars of the 21st century occurred in the quietest place that most people can imagine: the library stacks where old books collect dust. No individual institution had the resources to digitize these legacy collections. Search engines did, and Google took the lead.

A series of projects led by Google began in 2005 and, in a decade, transformed more than 25 million titles into digital texts. Nonprofits, such as the Internet Archive (IA), the Digital Public Library of America (DPLA) and HathiTrust (where most university and other research libraries have placed digital copies of their holdings) were important in this revolution, but it was a company capitalized at more than $400 billion (then called Google) that was key in transforming books into online treasures.

Some publishers (many of them European) and some authors (many of them American) were alarmed and brought repeated legal actions against Google and against the libraries that furnished these old books. Google and its academic partners set out to make digital copies of every book not too fragile to be scanned but to provide only "snippets" of books that might be in copyright so that people seeking information could find out if the volume interested them. Google said it expected these users to go to libraries to borrow the works or to purchase the volume when it could be found for sale. The Authors Guild filed a class action suit that went to the root of the enterprise: no mass digitization without permission and agreement first. An electronic corpus of books was a danger in itself, the Authors Guild argued, since content could fall into the hands of people who would commercially exploit it with the original publisher and the author receiving no fair payment. Indexing books (as Google described its activity) must stop until there was such an agreement.

Google reached an accommodation with the Authors Guild in 2011 by offering substantial compensation. This deal was rejected by federal Judge Denny Chin on the grounds that this one organization could not speak for all authors and that no private groups could usurp the role of Congress in setting copyright law. By this time, academic critics of the agreement had also made a powerful case that reader privacy was at great risk from such a search engine–publisher marriage. Fair use was at the center of further actions in federal courts from the Authors Guild concerning the corpus of digitized books. After a decade of this dustup, the Google project was held to be protected by fair use in a unanimous ruling of the U.S. Court of Appeals for the Second Circuit in *Author's Guild v. Google* (2015). A year later, the Supreme Court turned down a final appeal against this understanding of fair use.

Where has this left the reader? More than a hundred institutions in North America offer rich primary sources on 20th-century America, bound by U.S. copyright law that make these riches "orphaned." That is, the rights holders to these materials cannot be easily determined.

These libraries hold thousands of published books from the mid-20th century whose copyright status is uncertain. In primary source materials held in archives, orphans are the norm. At the Bancroft Library at the University of California, Berkeley, for example, the whereabouts and/or copyright ownership of more than half of the correspondents in its 6,000-manuscript collections is unknown.

Researchers often have their hands tied. For example, students of conservative movements behind the rise of California Governor Ronald Reagan or students writing about advocacy by Latino and African American groups at the same time find it very difficult to determine which words can be quoted at length and which pictures can be reproduced. Users cannot share discoveries of a picture or map or speech made in much of the 20th century without placing themselves at risk—a risk they would not face if they had stuck to the 19th-century materials. For most of the 20th century, copyright owners, as well as people who simply assert this right, can come forward and demand unknown and possibly exorbitant amounts of compensation. This is a problem that can be solved only by Congress.

Fresh Approaches to Copyright

While so-called copyright wars have no foreseeable end, accommodations on several fronts are in view in North America. Thoughtful and practical work has been done in recent years to see that authors and publishers who want to share work with a larger circle of readers can do this without copyright mishaps.

This has been the work of many hands. The Association of Research Libraries (ARL) and like-minded archival groups, authors, editors, and foundations have suggested ways to break free of seemingly perpetual copyright restrictions. New organizations of the 21st century, such as Creative Commons (2001–present) and the Authors Alliance (2014–present), have gained considerable support in empowering authors who recognized that some of their older work will find new audiences when placed in the public domain and that it can be in authors' intellectual and financial interest to have versions of new works exposed in this way. Subject to conditions the authors can set, new works can be sampled to provide essential feedback and to build a market for the work.

Some publishers have embraced this model for scholarly books. The University of California Press, for example has launched Luminos, an *open access* publishing platform for monographs. "Rights reversion" (from the publisher to the author) can benefit publishers as well, freeing them of bookkeeping and warehousing while strengthening their relationship with authors whose future work they want to publish. The Authors Alliance has taken the lead in working with publishers as partners rather than as antagonists. Oxford University Press, Random House, and Little Brown, for example, have helped their authors and Authors Alliance to usher books that once sat only in the stacks of elite libraries onto every interested reader's digital device.

There are, however, few signs of a general peace over access to our heritage of printed books. Changes in copyright can come only from Congress and the Copyright Office of the Library of Congress. Hearings in recent years on copyright, even on quite technical matters, have been marked by the gnashing of outlooks that are as hard as teeth. Both academic libraries and public libraries maintain lobbyists in Washington to see that readers and writers who write to be read are protected.

The great university and public libraries of the 21st century took legal risks to create the millions of digitized volumes that now serve the public. They stood up to pressure from the government and from search engines to compromise reader privacy. They will have to be just as vigilant to protect readers' civil liberties in the future. There will always be a government agency that wishes to know what citizens are reading and corporations with a business plan to profit from that knowledge. Setting limits is an unfinished task of our civil society.

Other challenges come from all of us who write and publish. We are not all good citizens of copyright, any more than government or information companies meet this standard. Daniel Defoe's conviction that authors have an inalienable and expansive moral right to control what they create lives on in the 21st century. European countries have a long tradition of valuing "authors' rights" above access and use by readers. Many contemporary authors in both North America and abroad believe that information companies prosper at their expense, Google's or Amazon's rise being the most galling. "If authors keep being expropriated by peer-to-peer file-sharing networks and seeing their works digitally mashed-up beyond recognition," the *Economist* observed, they will fight for their moral right once again (2014).

Monopoly (aka copyright) is an honorable game when it actually helps to sustain authors and publishers and takes media users fully into account; it is a waste of time and a disservice to everyone when it is a perpetual board game with each player unable to move. This is what framers of copyright in the Anglo-American 18th century knew and what their counterparts in the 21st century risk forgetting.

References

Baldwin, P. (2014). *The Copyright Wars: Three Centuries of Trans-Atlantic Battle.* Princeton, NJ: Princeton University Press.

Defoe, D. (1704). *An Essay on the Regulation of the Press.* [Electronic resource]. London: n.p.

Everton, M. J. (2011). *The Grand Chorus of Complaint: Authors and the Business Ethics of American Publishing.* Oxford and New York: Oxford University Press.

Folsom v. Marsh, 9. F.Cas. 342 (C.C.D. Mass. 1841) http://www.yalelawtech.org/wp-content/uploads/FolsomvMarsh1841.pdf

Green, J. N., & Stallybrass, P. N. (2006). "Benjamin Franklin: Writer and Printer." [Online exhibit at The Library Company of Philadelphia.] Retrieved from www.librarycompany.org/BFWriter/publisher.htm

"Intellectual Property: A Clash of Two Copyrights." (2014, December 13). *The Economist*, 416(8917), 83.

Johns, A. (2009). *Piracy: The Intellectual Property Wars From Gutenberg to Gates.* Chicago: University of Chicago Press.

Markson, S. (2015, August 14). "Google Is a Pirate, Says News Corp Chief Executive Robert Thomson." *The Australian.* Retrieved from http://www.theaustralian.com.au/business/media/google-a-pirate-says-news-corp-chief-executive-robert-thomson/news-story/7e7de735d5873cfaea9f8e278ebe40cc

Mason, N. (2008). "William St. Clair: The Reading Nation in the Romantic Period." *Studies in Romanticism*, 1, 111.

McGill, M. L. (2010). "Part 3. Copyright." In R. A. Gross & M. Kelley (Eds.), *A History of the Book in America* (vol. 2) (pp. 198–210). Chapel Hill: Published in association with the American Antiquarian Society by The University of North Carolina Press.

Rediker, M. (1987). *Between the Devil and the Deep Blue Sea: Merchant Seamen, Pirates, and the Anglo-American Maritime World, 1700–1750.* Cambridge: University of Cambridge Press.

Rivers, I. (1982). *Books and Their Readers in Eighteenth-Century England* [Leicester, Leicestershire]: Leicester University Press and New York: St. Martin's Press.

Rose, M. (1993). *Authors and Owner: The Invention of Copyright.* Cambridge, MA: Harvard University Press.

Spoo, R. E. (2013). *Without Copyrights: Piracy, Publishing, and the Public Domain.* New York: Oxford University Press.

"Star War, Disney and Myth-Making." (2015, December 19). *The Economist*, 417(8969), 13.

Further Reading

Association of Research Libraries. (2012). "Code of Best Practices in Fair Use for Academic and Research Libraries." Washington, DC. Retrieved from http://www.arl.org/focus-areas/copyright-ip/fair-use/code-of-best-practices#.WjFkzbQ-fX8

Cabrera, N., Ostroff, J., & Schofield, B. (2015). "Understanding Rights Reversion: When, Why, & How to Regain Copyright and Make Your Book More Available." Authors Alliance. Retrieved from bit.ly/1z5tn8Q

CONTRIBUTORS

Malin Abrahamsson is the Acquisitions Manager and Copyright Assistant at Hunter College, CUNY. She, along with coauthor Stephanie Margolin, is an active member and former cochair of CUNY's Copyright Committee. A visual artist with a public practice, Malin's interest in copyright education is predicated on her ability to see herself as both creator and consumer.

Timothy R. Amidon teaches courses in digital rhetorics and multimodal composing as an Assistant Professor in English at Colorado State University. His scholarship has appeared in *Hybrid Pedagogy: A Digital Journal of Learning, Teaching, and Pedagogy*, in *Kairos: A Journal of Rhetoric and Technology*, and in *Cultures of Copyright* (Peter Lang, 2014).

Patricia Aufderheide is University Professor in the School of Communication at American University in Washington, D.C. The founder of the Center for Media & Social Impact there, she is the coauthor with Peter Jaszi of *Reclaiming Fair Use: How to Put Balance Back in Copyright* (University of Chicago Press, 2011), and author of, among others, *Documentary: A Very Short Introduction* (Oxford, 2007), *The Daily Planet* (University of Minnesota Press, 2000), and *Communications Policy in the Public Interest* (Guilford Press, 1999).

Jonathan Band is a copyright lawyer in Washington, D.C. He represents library associations and technology companies on copyright policy matters. He also is Adjunct Professor at Georgetown University Law Center.

Catherine Burwell is an Assistant Professor at the Werklund School of Education, University of Calgary. Her research interests include digital and media literacy, youth media production, and copyright education. Before joining the University of Calgary, Catherine worked as a secondary school English and media studies teacher with the Toronto District School Board for more than a decade. Catherine's research has been published in communication, cultural studies, and education journals.

Brandon Butler is a copyright lawyer and the first Director of Information Policy at the University of Virginia Library. He provides guidance and education to the Library and its user community on intellectual property and related issues, and he advocates on the Library's behalf for provisions in law and policy at the federal, state, local, and campus levels. He has written book chapters, white papers, amicus briefs, and policy briefs on copyright and fair use in libraries, research, and other contexts.

Dànielle Nicole DeVoss is a Professor of Professional Writing at Michigan State University. Her research interests include intellectual property, multimodal composing, and social and cultural entrepreneurship. She is author of eight titles, including *Because Digital Writing Matters* (Jossey-Bass, 2010, with Elyse Eidman-Aadahl and Troy Hicks) and *Cultures of Copyright* (Peter Lang, 2014, with Courant Rife).

Bill D. Herman is an Assistant Professor at the Gabelli School of Business at Fordham University, where he teaches and does research on topics such as information policy, media and technology industries, and political communication. His (first) book is *The Fight Over Digital Rights: The Politics of Copyright and Technology* (Cambridge, 2013).

Renee Hobbs is a Professor at the Harrington School of Communication and Media at the University of Rhode Island, where she directs the Media Education Lab, which advances media literacy education through scholarship and community service. She is author of *Copyright Clarity: How Fair Use Supports Digital Learning* (Corwin, 2010) and six other books that examine media literacy and learning.

Smita Kheria is a Lecturer in intellectual property law at Edinburgh Law School, University of Edinburgh, UK. She combines legal expertise in copyright and related rights with socio-legal research on intellectual property law in the real world. She has undertaken several research projects that have examined the intersection of copyright with the everyday lives of a range of creative practitioners and communities.

John Landis teaches digital citizenship and media literacy at Russell Byers Charter School, serving grades pre-K to sixth in Philadelphia. John's focus is on the use of technology as a creative tool rather than as a channel for media consumption.

Dan Lawler has taught English for 19 years, the last 15 at New Trier High School in Winnetka, Illinois. He has taught a variety of courses, including American studies, creative nonfiction, and literature and film. He has worked extensively with service learning projects and has also served in a role where he helps teachers experiment with integrating technology into their instruction. Past work of his has been published in *English Journal.*

Thomas C. Leonard is a media historian who was the University Librarian at the University of California, Berkeley, until his retirement in 2015. He is Professor Emeritus in the Graduate School of Journalism at Berkeley. He is a past president of the Association of Research Libraries. Leonard supported the Google mass digitization program from research libraries. He was a founding member of the Authors Alliance. He has published three books with Oxford University Press on political change in the United States and is writing a book on real pirates and their metaphorical counterparts in media history.

Nadine Levin is an anthropologist who studies contemporary science and technology and who is currently working at Facebook as a user experience researcher. Her work focuses on how the rise of data (big and small) is affecting biomedical and academic research practices. She is currently finalizing her book titled *Metabolizing Data*, which explores how big data is affecting biomedical research on metabolism.

Ed Madison is an Assistant Professor at the University of Oregon School of Journalism and Communication, where his research focuses on the intersection of media, education, and technology. At age 22, Madison was recruited to become a founding producer for CNN. He is the author of *Newsworthy: Cultivating Critical Thinkers, Readers, and Writers in Language Arts Classrooms* (2015) from Teachers College Press–Columbia University.

Stephanie Margolin is an Assistant Professor and the Instructional Design Librarian at Hunter College, CUNY. She is a member and former cochair of CUNY's Copyright Committee. Nature and character of use are her favorites of the four factors!

Ewa McGrail is an Associate Professor of Language and Literacy at Georgia State University. In her research, Dr. McGrail examines digital writing and new media composition, copyright and media literacy, technology in teaching and learning, and multimodal assessment.

J. Patrick McGrail is an Associate Professor of Communication at Jacksonville State University. His research interests include media law and policy, copyright, media literacy, and communication concerning people with disabilities. Prior to his career in academia, Dr. McGrail worked in television as an actor, announcer, and anchor.

David Cooper Moore is a media literacy scholar-practitioner who leads the media arts department at YESPhilly, an alternative high school in Philadelphia, Pennsylvania. He is the coauthor, with Renee Hobbs, of *Discovering Media Literacy: Teaching Digital Media and Popular Culture in Elementary School* (Corwin, 2013).

Caile Morris is a Law and Policy Fellow with the Association of Research Libraries. Her interests lie in copyright and trademark law and policy. As part of her fellowship, she researched and wrote about originality in copyright law and about copyright law's intersection with accessibility laws and policies.

Chris Morrison is the Copyright and Licensing Compliance Officer at the University of Kent, responsible for copyright policy, education, and advice, and a member of the UUK/Guild HE Copyright Working Group. He was previously Copyright Assurance Manager at The British Library.

John S. O'Connor teaches at New Trier High School and lectures in the School of Education and Social Policy at Northwestern University. His education essays have appeared in places such as *Schools*, *English Journal*, and *Magazine of History*, and he is the author of two previous books on writing: *Wordplaygrounds* (NCTE, 2004) and *This Time It's Personal* (NCTE, 2011). His most recent book of poetry is *Rooting* (Finishing Line Press, 2015). He is also the creator and host of the education podcast *Schooled*.

David Ramírez Plascencia is a Professor at the University of Guadalajara–SUV. He received a bachelor of law and master in political science at the University of Guadalajara and a doctorate in social sciences at The College of Jalisco. He is an academic researcher at the University of Guadalajara and member of the National Research System (SNI) in Mexico.

Clancy Ratliff is an Associate Professor of English at the University of Louisiana at Lafayette. She is interested in feminist rhetorics, authorship and copyright, computers and writing, English education, and writing program administration. Her research has been published in *Cultures of Copyright* (Peter Lang, 2014), *Composition Forum*, *Women's Studies Quarterly*, *Computers and Composition Online*, and elsewhere. She is currently chair of the College Section of the National Council of Teachers of English. More of her work can be found at culturecat.net/portfolio.

Cyndy Scheibe is Executive Director of Project Look Sharp at Ithaca College, where she is also Professor of Psychology, teaching courses in developmental psychology and media literacy. She was a founding board member of the National Association for Media Literacy Education and is coauthor of *The Teacher's Guide to Media Literacy: Critical Thinking in a Multimedia Age* (Corwin, 2012).

Aaron Schwabach is a Professor at Thomas Jefferson School of Law in San Diego, California, and the author of numerous books and articles on intellectual property law and a few on the law of the wizarding world of Harry Potter.

Jane Secker is Senior Lecturer in Educational Development at City University London. Previously, she was the Copyright and Digital Literacy Advisor at London School of Economics and Political Science. She is chair of the CILIP Information Literacy Group and a member of the UUK/Guild HE Copyright Working Group.

Chareen Snelson is an Associate Professor in the Department of Educational Technology at Boise State University. She has extensive experience with YouTube in education through her research and development of a university course, YouTube for Educators, which she has taught since 2008.

Chris Sperry is Director of Curriculum and Staff Development for *Project Look Sharp*, a media literacy initiative at Ithaca College. He is also Instructional Coach at the Lehman Alternative Community School, where he has taught middle school and high school social studies, English, and media studies since 1979. He is the author or coauthor of a dozen media literacy curriculum kits and delivers professional development presentations internationally.

Scott Spicer is Associate Librarian serving as the Media Outreach and Learning Spaces Librarian for the University of Minnesota Libraries, where he heads the Media Services program. Spicer's primary responsibilities and scholarship include student-produced media, media resources, multimodal scholarship, and media literacy skill set development.

Kyle Stedman is an Assistant Professor of English at Rockford University, where he teaches courses on digital rhetoric, professional communication, first-year composition, and creative nonfiction. His work has been published in *Computers and Composition*, *Harlot*, and *Composition Forum*, and he is the coauthor of *Agency in the Age of Peer Production* (NCTE, 2012, with Quentin D. Vieregge, Taylor Joy Mitchell, and Joseph M. Moxley).

Jeremy Stoddard is an Associate Professor of Education and associated faculty in Film and Media Studies at William & Mary. He coedited *Teaching Difficult History Through Film*

(Routledge, 2017) and has authored two additional books on teaching history with film and on museums.

Rebecca Tushnet is the Frank Stanton Professor of First Amendment Law at Harvard Law School. She specializes in copyright, trademark, and advertising law.

Charlotte Waelde is Professor of Intellectual Property Law at the Centre for Dance Research, Coventry University, UK. Her work lies at the intersections between intellectual property, creative industries, intangible cultural heritage, and new technologies.

Esther Wojcicki has served as a journalism/English teacher at Palo Alto High School, Palo Alto, California, for the past 30 years. She has grown its award-winning media arts program from 20 to 500 participants, who presently produce six distinct student-run publications. The program was acknowledged by President Barack Obama for excellence.

INDEX

For Product Safety Concerns and Information please contact our EU
representative GPSR@taylorandfrancis.com
Taylor & Francis Verlag GmbH, Kaufingerstraße 24, 80331 München, Germany

www.ingramcontent.com/pod-product-compliance
Ingram Content Group UK Ltd.
Pitfield, Milton Keynes, MK11 3LW, UK
UKHW050051200926
475702UK00019B/2782
* 9 7 8 1 0 3 2 0 9 5 7 2 1 *